CW01496915

Gianni Cancellieri

# All the cars
# Maserati

*Illustrations*
Michele Leonello

GIORGIO NADA EDITORE

# Giorgio Nada Editore

*Editorial Coordination*
Leonardo Acerbi

*Text and technical specification*
Gianni Cancellieri

*Captions*
Leonardo Acerbi
Enrico Mapelli

*Appendix "Maserati Victories"*
Alessandro Silva

*Drawings*
Michele Leonello

*Layout*
Giorgio Nada Editore

*Cover design*
Sansai Zappini

*Pictures*
Archivio Maserati
Archivio Giorgio Nada Editore

*Aknowledgements*
The author would like to thank the following people for their contribution to the research, information and revision of this book:

*Donatella Biffignandi, Fabio Collina, Ermanno Cozza, Giuseppe Di Coste, Alessandro Grimaldi, Enrico Mapelli, Daniele Redeaelli, Alessandro Silva, Manuel Taboada, Sergio Troise, Napoleão Ribeiro, Johnny Rives*

© 2015 Giorgio Nada Editore, Vimodrone (Milano)

Giorgio Nada Editore s.r.l.
Via Claudio Treves, 15/17
I – 20090 VIMODRONE (Milano)
Tel. +39 02 27301126
Fax +39 02 27301454
E-mail: info@giorgionadaeditore.it
www.giorgionadaeditore.it

Allo stesso indirizzo può essere richiesto il catalogo di tutte le opere pubblicate dalla Casa Editrice

*The catalogue of Giorgio Nada Editore publications is available on request at the above address*

*Distribuzione:*
**Giunti Editore Spa**
via Bolognese 165
I – 50139 FIRENZE
www.giunti.it

**Maserati. All the cars** - ISBN: 978-88-7911-609-1

# Index

| | | | |
|---|---|---|---|
| Readers' note | | | 9 |
| A Trident is forever | | | 10-13 |

## THE CATALOGUE

| | | | |
|---|---|---|---|
| 26 | 1926 | Corsa | 16-17 |
| 26 B | 1927 | Corsa | 18-19 |
| 26 MM | 1928 | Sport | 20-21 |
| 26 B MM | 1928 | Sport | 22-23 |
| 26 R | 1928 | Sport | 24-25 |
| 26 C (8C 1100) | 1929 | Corsa | 26-27 |
| V4 | 1929 | Corsa | 28-29 |
| V4 Gran Sport Zagato | 1930 | Sport | 30-31 |
| 26 M – 26 M Sport | 1930 | Corsa/Sport | 32-33 |
| 8C 2800 | 1931 | Corsa | 34-35 |
| 4C TR | 1931 | Sport | 36-37 |
| V5 | 1932 | Corsa | 38-39 |
| 8C 2500 T.A. | 1932 | Corsa | 40-41 |
| 4C S 1100 | 1932 | Sport | 42-43 |
| 4C M 1100 | 1932 | Corsa | 44-45 |
| 8C 3000 | 1932 | Corsa | 46-47 |
| 4C M 2000 – 4C 2500 – 4C M 2500 | 1933 | Corsa | 48-49 |
| 4C S 1500 | 1933 | Sport | 50-51 |
| 8C M | 1933 | Corsa | 52-53 |
| 6C-34 | 1934 | Corsa | 54-55 |
| 4C M 1500 | 1934 | Corsa | 56-57 |
| V8 RI | 1935 | Corsa | 58-59 |
| 6C M | 1936 | Corsa | 60-61 |
| 8C TF | 1938 | Corsa | 62-63 |

| | | | |
|---|---|---|---|
| 4CL | 1939 | Corsa | 64-65 |
| 8CL | 1940 | Corsa | 66-67 |
| 6C S-41 | 1941 | Sport | 68-69 |
| EC10-EC15-EC20-EC35-BC20 | 1942 | Commercial vehicle | 70-71 |
| 6C S-46 | 1946 | Sport | 72-73 |
| A6 (1500 Gran Turismo) | 1946 | GT | 74-75 |
| 4CL T – 4CL T-48 – 4CL T-50 | 1946 | Corsa | 76-77 |
| A6 (1500 GT) | 1947 | GT | 78-79 |
| A6 GCS (2000 Sport) | 1947 | Sport | 80-81 |
| A6 GCS carenata | 1948 | Sport | 82-83 |
| 8CL T | 1950 | Corsa | 84-85 |
| A6G 2000 Spider Frua | 1950 | GT | 86-87 |
| A6G 2000 Coupé Vignale | 1950 | GT | 88-89 |
| A6G 2000 Coupé Pinin Farina | 1951 | GT | 90-91 |
| A6G 2000 Coupé Pinin Farina | 1951 | GT | 92-93 |
| TM15 Muletto | 1951 | Commercial vehicle | 94-95 |
| Tarf II Italcorsa | 1951 | Record-breaking vehicle | 96-97 |
| A6 GCM-51 | 1951 | Corsa | 98-99 |
| A6 GCM-53 | 1953 | Corsa | 100-101 |
| A6 GCS-53 | 1953 | Sport | 102-103 |
| A6 GCS-53 Spider Vignale | 1953 | GT/Sport | 104-105 |
| A6 GCS-53 Spider Frua | 1953 | GT | 106-107 |
| A6 GCS-53 Coupé Pinin Farina | 1954 | GT | 108-109 |
| A6G-54 Coupé Frua | 1954 | GT | 110-111 |
| 250 F | 1954 | Corsa | 112-113 |
| 250 S (2500 Sport) | 1954 | Sport | 114-115 |
| A6G-54 Spider Zagato | 1955 | GT | 116-117 |

# Index

| | | | |
|---|---|---|---|
| A6G-54 Coupé Zagato | 1955 | GT | 118-119 |
| A6G-54 Spider Frua | 1955 | GT | 120-121 |
| A6G-54 Coupé Allemano | 1955 | GT | 122-123 |
| 300 S | 1955 | Sport | 124-125 |
| 150 S | 1955 | Sport | 126-127 |
| 200 S – 200 SI | 1955 | Sport | 128-129 |
| 250 F carenata | 1955 | Corsa | 130-131 |
| 250 F | 1956 | Corsa | 132-133 |
| 350 S | 1956 | Sport | 134-135 |
| 450 S | 1956 | Sport | 136-137 |
| 450 S Coupé Zagato | 1957 | Sport | 138-139 |
| 250 F T2 – T3 | 1957 | Corsa | 140-141 |
| 250 S | 1957 | Sport | 142-143 |
| 3500 GT Coupé Touring «Dama bianca» | 1957 | GT | 144-145 |
| 3500 GT – GTI Coupé – Spider | 1957 | GT | 146-147 |
| 420 M-58 Eldorado – 420 M-59 | 1958 | Corsa | 148-149 |
| 3500 GT Coupé Bertone | 1959 | GT | 150-151 |
| 3500 GT Cabriolet 2+2 Frua | 1959 | GT | 152-153 |
| 3500 GT Spider Vignale | 1959 | GT | 154-155 |
| 5000 GT Coupé Touring 2+2 «Scià di Persia» | 1959 | GT | 156-157 |
| 60 | 1959 | Sport | 158-159 |
| 61 | 1959 | Sport | 160-161 |
| 5000 GT Coupé Frua – Coupé Monterosa | 1960 | GT | 162-163 |
| 61 coda lunga | 1960 | Sport | 164-165 |
| 5000 GT Coupé Pininfarina | 1961 | GT | 166-167 |
| 5000 GT Coupé Allemano | 1961 | GT | 168-169 |
| 5000 GT Coupé Ghia | 1961 | GT | 170-171 |

| | | | |
|---|---|---|---|
| 5000 GT Coupé Bertone | 1961 | GT | 172-173 |
| Sebring 3.5 – 3.7 – 4.0 | 1962 | GT | 174-175 |
| 63 | 1961 | Sport | 176-177 |
| 63 Serenissima | 1961 | Sport | 178-179 |
| 64 | 1961 | Sport | 180-181 |
| 5000 GT Coupé Vignale | 1962 | GT | 182-183 |
| 3500 GT Coupé Boneschi | 1962 | GT | 184-185 |
| 151 | 1962 | Sport-Prototipo | 186-187 |
| 3500 GT – GTI Coupé Touring | 1963 | GT | 188-189 |
| 3500 GTI Spider Vignale | 1963 | GT | 190-191 |
| Quattroporte 4.1 – 4.7 | 1963 | GT | 192-193 |
| Mistral 3.7 – 4.0 | 1963 | GT | 194-195 |
| Mistral Spider 3.5 – 3.7 – 4.0 | 1963 | GT | 196-197 |
| 65 | 1965 | Sport-Prototipo | 198-199 |
| Mexico 4.7 – 4.1 | 1966 | GT | 200-201 |
| Ghibli – Ghibli SS | 1967 | GT | 202-203 |
| Simùn Ghia | 1968 | GT | 204-205 |
| Ghibli Spider – Ghibli SS Spider | 1969 | GT | 206-207 |
| Indy 4.1 – 4.7 – 4.9 | 1969 | GT | 208-209 |
| Bora 4.7 – 4.9 | 1971 | GT | 210-211 |
| Boomerang Italdesign | 1972 | GT | 212-213 |
| Merak – Merak SS | 1972 | GT | 214-215 |
| Coupé 2+2 Italdesign | 1974 | GT | 216-217 |
| Medici I – Medici II Italdesign | 1974 | GT | 218-219 |
| Khamsin | 1974 | GT | 220-221 |
| Quattroporte II | 1976 | GT | 222-223 |
| Kyalami | 1976 | GT | 224-225 |

| | | | |
|---|---|---|---|
| Merak 2000 | 1977 | GT | 226-227 |
| Quattroporte III | 1979 | GT | 228-229 |
| Limousine Diomante | 1986 | GT | 230-231 |
| Royale | 1986 | GT | 232-233 |
| Biturbo | 1982 | GT | 234-235 |
| 425 | 1984 | GT | 236-237 |
| 420 – 422 – 4.24v. | 1985 | GT | 238-239 |
| Biturbo Spyder | 1985 | GT | 240-241 |
| 228 – 222 4v. – 222 SR | 1987 | GT | 242-243 |
| 430 – 430 4v. | 1987 | GT | 244-245 |
| 222 – 2.24v. | 1988 | GT | 246-247 |
| Karif | 1988 | GT | 248-249 |
| Chubasco Coupé Gandini | 1990 | GT | 250-251 |
| Racing | 1990 | GT | 252-253 |
| Shamal | 1990 | GT | 254-255 |
| Barchetta | 1992 | GT | 256-257 |
| Ghibli – Ghibli 2,8 – 2,0 Cup 2,0 GT – 2,0 Open Cup – 2,0 Primatist | 1992 | GT | 258-259 |
| Quattroporte IV 2,0i – 2,8i – 3,2i 2,0i – 2,8i – Evoluzione | 1994 | GT | 260-261 |
| 3200 GT | 1998 | GT | 262-263 |
| Buran Italdesign | 2000 | GT | 264-265 |
| Spyder | 2001 | GT | 266-267 |
| 4200 GT – Coupé GT | 2001 | GT | 268-269 |
| Kubang Italdesign | 2003 | GT | 270-271 |
| Quattroporte V | 2003 | GT | 272-273 |
| MC12 Stradale | 2004 | GT | 274-275 |

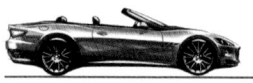
| Birdcage 75th Pininfarina | 2005 | GT | 276-277 |
| MC12 Corsa | 2006 | GT | 278-279 |
| GranTurismo – GT – S – Sport | 2007 | GT | 280-281 |
| GranCabrio | 2009 | GT | 282-283 |
| Kubang Centro Stile Maserati | 2011 | GT | 284-285 |
| Quattroporte VI | 2013 | GT | 286-287 |
| Ghibli | 2013 | GT | 288-289 |
| Alfieri Centro Stile Maserati | 2014 | GT | 290-291 |
| Levante | 2016 | GT | 292-293 |

## MASERATI ENGINES AND OTHER CHASSIS

| Motore 4CF2 | 1952 | | 296 |
| Motore 2500 Sport | 1954 e 1956 | | 297 |
| Motore 59 | 1959-1961 | | 298 |
| Motore 6 | 1960-1961 | | 299 |
| Motori 62 – 201 – 202 | 1962-1965 | | 300 |
| Motore 8 | 1962 | | 301 |
| Cooper T81-Maserati 9 | 1965-1966 | Corsa | 302-303 |
| Cooper T81-Maserati 10 | 1967 | Corsa | 304-305 |
| Citroen SM-Maserati C.114 | 1970 | GT | 306-307 |
| Ligier JS2-Maserati C.114 | 1972 | Sport | 308-309 |

## MASERATI VICTORIES

312-347

The technical and historical files relating to each Maserati car have been ordered chronologically from 1926 – when the first model appeared carrying the Trident badge (Tipo 26) – through to 2014, the year in which the Alfieri prototype was presented, with a few educated guesses about the Levante too, still shrouded in mystery and only due to see the light of day shortly after the publication of this book, early in 2016.

Each file is monographic, that is to say, dedicated to a single model, with a few exceptions where the model in question gave rise to one or more variants that it was felt merited only a mention: this occurs above all in the most recent years, with the numerous engine options in the same chassis and body type. The reverse is true with the design prototypes, concept cars and special versions where they proved significant in terms of their technical or aesthetic qualities, even when they remained as one-offs or were never produced in series. It should be emphasised that for many such creations it is rare to find any traces other than a few photos and scarce documentation.

Each historical presentation is preceded by a technical file detailing the principal characteristics of the model's engine, transmission, body, dimensions, weight, performance and the number of units produced. A serious problem was encountered when compiling the files in terms of the discrepancies frequently found in the data, figures and values supplied by the multiple sources consulted; a problem accentuated by the proliferation of Internet sites, with their undoubted utility in principle, polluted in practice by casual cut-and-pasting and the propagation of inaccuracies ad infinitum. The solution to such dilemmas is not however always found by making recourse to the "official" source, the constructor's archives, and when certain data could not be confirmed it was decided that no indication would be given.

The principle section of the book comprises the cars with Maserati chassis and engines and those constructed by the designer of the bodywork. There follow two less extensive sections, one dealing with the engines built by Maserati but not used if not for later developments and the other with the racing or road-going cars by other marques, equipped with the Trident's engines.

The work is completed with a compilation of all the Maserati victories by Alessandro Silva, pieced together for the first time in all its vastness and representing an exceptional added value for the book.

# A Trident is forever

It is wonderful to see that, as has been written, within the automotive world the name Maserati still identifies - today more than ever – a star of the greatest magnitude, a marque that has led the way in over a century of both racing and prestige car production. This is just one reason why it seems useful to repeat once again the epic story, through a model-by-model review of the cars that have carried the charismatic Trident symbol since 1926 and proudly continue to carry it on roads throughout the world.

It all began with the legendary Maserati brothers, with their adventurous, romantic story, their pioneering spirit and what we might define as their vocation and in any case, the passion that illuminated their days, from first to last: conceiving, designing, constructing and developing racing cars and engines, competing and by no means infrequently winning at the highest levels.

After having married Carolina Losi, Rodolfo Maserati, an employee of the Italian State Railways, moved from Piacenza to Voghera in the Province of Pavia, where the couple had seven sons. The first to arrive was Carlo (1881-1910) followed by Bindo (1883-1980) and Alfieri (1885). This last survived just a few months and his name, as was customary at the time, was given to the next son (1887-1932) who was in turn followed by Mario (1890-1981), Ettore (1894-1990) and Ernesto (1898-1975).

Mario was the only exception to the "rule": he devoted himself to the figurative arts, while the other five were confirmed mechanics. At the age of 17, Carlo built a single-cylinder engine, attached it to a bicycle and even won a few races. He enjoyed a sparkling career as an engineer but died in 1910 at just 29 years of age. His legacy was, however, taken up by Alfieri, Bindo and Ettore, whom he had had employed when very young at Isotta Fraschini. And it was there that Alfieri's talent soon revealed itself. The Milan-based company first sent him to Buenos Aires, then to London and finally, in 1912, to Bologna, charged with organizing the client service system.

His experience as an engineer and as a driver convinced him to set up on his own. On the 14TH of December 1914, at No. 1 Via de'Pepoli, he opened a small workshop specialising in the performance tuning of Isotta Fraschini engines. With him were his brothers Ettore (20 years old) and Ernesto (16) and five workers.

The First World War put an end to this kind of work, but Alfieri was not discouraged and opened a sparkplug factory in Milan, which in 1919 he moved to Bologna in new and larger premises at No. 179 Via Emilia Levante, Alemanni, in the Pontevecchio district. Alfieri tuned Isotta Fraschinis and Diattos, both for clients and to race them himself, on occasion with his brother Ernesto and frequently with success. The collaboration with Diatto ended in

1925, due in part to the Turin firm's economic difficulties. Alfieri, however, was already thinking about a car to which he could put his name. His brother Mario, the painter, was to design the badge, a trident, drawing inspiration from the famous Bolognese statue of Neptune.

The winter of 1925/26 saw the design and construction of the first car destined to be called a Maserati, a racing model identified as the Tipo 26 in a clear reference to the year of its birth. Alfieri drew inspiration from the eight-cylinder Diatto Grand Prix he had himself designed and on the 25TH of April 1926 drove the new car on its debut in the Targa Florio, finishing first among the 1500 cc cars and thus celebrating the new marque's arrival in the best possible way.

There followed years of vigorous growth under the tireless creative impulse of Alfieri and with the minuscule company's books being acrobatically balanced thanks to cars being purchased by client-drivers who at times were transformed into patrons. There were days of glory and front page headlines in the newspaper with the advent of the powerful 16-cylinder V4, at the wheel of which Borzacchini set a sensational world record: 246,069 kph over a flying 10 kilometres at Cremona. Further laurels were collected and the Maserati name acquired international fame, but tragically, Alfieri died on the 3RD of March 1932, ahead of his 45TH birthday, due to complications following surgery. His legacy was in turn taken up by his brothers Bindo, Ettore and in terms of design, above all Ernesto.

The 1930s saw the Trident's cars firstly winning major races with drivers of the calibre of Fagioli, Varzi and Nuovolari and then, from 1934, and the establishment of the Mercedes-Benz and Auto Union hegemony, production focussed on the smaller displacement categories, the *voiturettes*, thus satisfying the demands of the sporting clientele that kept the marque alive. Nonetheless, the company's financial position was always precarious, putting its very survival in question. In 1937, the Maserati brothers therefore sold the share package to Adolfo Orsi and his son Omer, Modenese industrialists and owners of steelworks, machine tool and agricultural machinery companies, haulage firms and more besides. This operation freed the Maseratis from concerns over economic affairs and for the next ten years they continued to work for the company, firstly as chief engineers and then as consultants.

Struggling in the European Grands Prix, like all the adversaries of the German marques, Maserati enjoyed an unexpected triumph in the Indianapolis 500 Miles in 1939, with Wilbur Shaw and his 8C TF, the first car to be built, engine and chassis, by an Italian company to win the famous race. Shaw drove the same magnificent car to victory again in 1940 and just missed out on an incredible triple in 1941.

With the outbreak of war racing was suspended, but Maserati was able convert its facilities to produce machine tools and electric vehicles that were particularly sought after in a period of rationing and a general scarcity of fuel. Ernesto continued to develop the project for a six-cylinder engine in two versions: one for racing and one with a lower power output that at the end of the war was to be fitted to the A6, Maserati's first road car. Pinin Farina created a thrilling coupé that was the star of the Geneva Motor Show in 1947 and inaugurated a new production path that was to change the destiny of the Trident marque.

Racing restarted and saw Maserati on top of the world. In 1954, with the brand-new 250 F, Fangio won the first two Formula 1 World Championship Grands Prix: the South American ace had already signed with Mercedes-Benz but as the German car was not yet ready, he was allowed to race with Maserati, which, thanks to those two wins appeared in the world championship standings along with the German marque. Three years later, again at the wheel of the magnificent Italian single-seater, Fangio conquered his fifth World Championship title. In that same 1957 season, the World Championship for Marques was also within Maserati's grasp until the last race of the season, the Venezuelan GP, concluded in a catastrophic series of accidents that eliminated all the cars entered by the company.

The competition record for the season was nonetheless flattering, but was closely followed by news that saddened many enthusiasts: the Trident marque was abandoning direct participation in racing, while continuing to service teams and privateers from whom further success would nonetheless arrive. However, the company's situation was still extremely difficult and was to lead to it going into administration, albeit only for a short period thanks to effective interventions by the owners, who among other actions had no hesitation in selling off the family heritage. The books were balanced and greater attention was directed towards the production of the GT cars that from 1954 the firm had begun to manufacture in small batches and with which it had carved out a significant market niche, progressing from a few dozen to a few hundred units a year. Motorsport continued to be a source of satisfaction, albeit on a smaller scale and with few resources, thanks to the Birdcage series and the 12-cylinder engines installed in Cooper chassis that won two F1 Grands Prix.

In the meantime, the 3500 and 5000 GTs, the Sebring, the Quattroporte, the Mistral and the fabulous Ghibli with their spectacular bodywork designed by the greatest stylists had pushed production towards even higher peaks, but at the end of 1968, the Orsi family sold the company to Citroën. It was a shared conviction – Ferrari was following the same path with Fiat - that a small car factory could not survive alone without a major industrial concern behind it capable of bearing the development as well as production costs. Key models continued to be introduced, including the Indy and the mid-engined Bora and Merak, the SM with its Citroën chassis and Maserati engine, but further upheaval was just around the corner. In 1975, ownership of Citroën passed from Michelin to Peugeot and Maserati was placed under liquidation.

Bankruptcy and closure were avoided by the intervention of GEPI (Società per le Gestioni e Partecipazioni Industriali) a publically owned financial holding company that acquired the Maserati shares – an operation permitted at the time – and appointed as the managing director Alejandro De Tomaso, then head of the group comprising the firm with his own name, Innocenti and Benelli. A controversial figure but one of undoubted competence and passion, the Argentine businessman to whom the survival of the Trident marque is tied, promoted the creation of new models including, above all, the Biturbo, an innovative car capable of excellent performance and sold at a competitive price, but unfortunately one that was developed hurriedly and was hardly reliable: a reputation with which it was labelled even when, with the successive series, the teething troubles had been resolved. In any case, with the Biturbo Maserati's output reached five figures for the first time: 11,919 units produced between 1983 and 1989.

The De Tomaso era also underwent a dramatically difficult that closed in 1992 with the sale of the company to the Fiat Group, which in its turn was shortly to be facing one of the most difficult chapters in its history. In 1997, Maserati was merged with Ferrari for a period of eight years, during which the synergy with Maranello (technology, know-how, mechanical components) and substantial investments set in motion a radical renewal of the range of which the models currently in production are the direct heirs. In 2005, the Trident marque regained its independence and proceeded to go from strength to strength. There was even a return to high level racing, albeit through independent teams and privateers, with the MC12 competing from 2005 to 2010 in the FIA GT championship and establishing a remarkable record: 22 victories, six team titles and five drivers' titles.

Innumerable articles in the mass media, mentions from international competition juries and above all a demanding clientele that has decreed and extended on a global scale the success of the marque, has certified Maserati's primacy in terms of the pursuit of quality, beauty and prestige, while the beginning of its second century of existence sees it a protagonist in a new and no less ambitious adventure: the expansion of annual production at a remarkable rate, from the 6,307 examples that left the factory in 2012 to the 15,400 of 2013, the 36,500 of 2014 and the similar figure predicted for 2015 for heading for 50,000 and 75,000 units in the years to come. (g.c.)

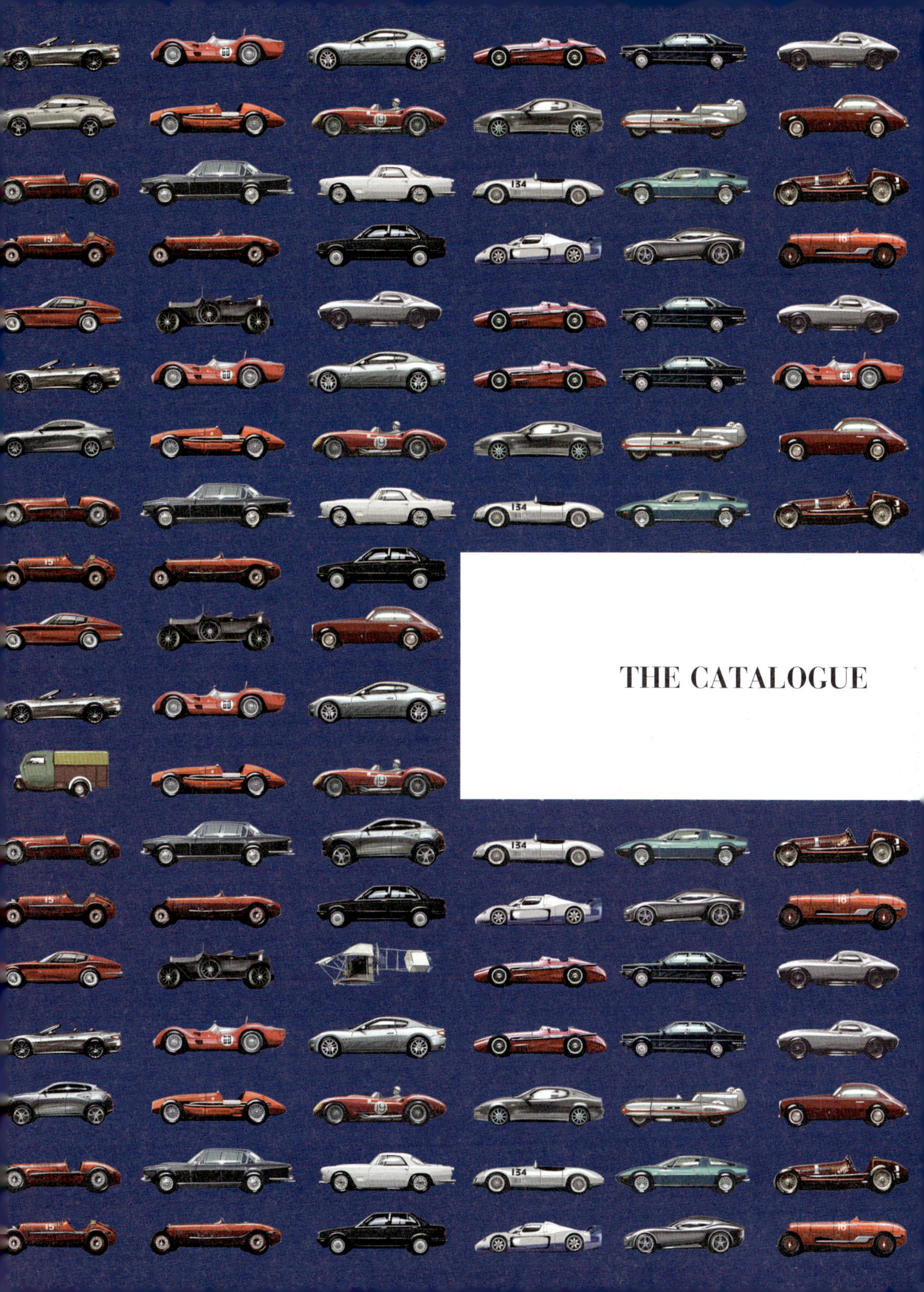

# THE CATALOGUE

The 25TH of April 1926 was the day the Maserati Tipo 26 made its debut in the 1500 cc of the Targa Florio. Driving it to 8TH place overall and first in class ahead of two Bugatti Type 37s was Alfieri Maserati himself. Seen aboard the sleek car in an "official" photo is instead Guarino (known to all as "Guerino") Bertocchi, the Trident marque's historic driver, tester and chief mechanic.

## TECHNICAL SPECIFICATION

### ENGINE
front, longitudinal, straight eight

| | |
|---|---|
| Bore and stroke | 60 x 66 mm |
| Unitary displacement | 186.61 cc |
| Total displacement | 1492.88 cc |
| Valvegear | twin overhead camshafts |
| Number of valves | two per cylinder |
| Compression ratio | 5.8/6:1 |
| Fuel system | Two Memini carburettors, Roots supercharger |
| Ignition | single, with Bosch or Scintilla magneto |
| Cooling | water, centrifugal pump and radiator |
| Lubrication | dry sump, pressurised, with delivery and scavenging pumps |
| Maximum power | 120 hp at 5300 rpm 1927: 128/6000 |
| Specific power output | 80 hp/litre 1927: 85,7 |

### TRANSMISSION
| | |
|---|---|
| Driven wheels | rear |
| Clutch | multiple dry-plate |
| Gearbox | 3 speeds (1927: 4) + reverse |

### BODYWORK
two-seater, racing

### ROLLING CHASSIS
| | |
|---|---|
| Chassis | longerons and cross members |
| Front suspension | rigid axle, leaf springs, friction dampers |
| Rear suspension | live axle, leaf springs, friction dampers |
| Brakes | mechanically actuated drums |
| Steering | worm and gear |
| Fuel tank | 80 litres |
| Tyres front/rear | 4.75-18 / 5.00-18 |

### DIMENSIONS AND WEIGHT
| | |
|---|---|
| Wheelbase | 2650 mm (1927 - 2580) |
| Tracks front/rear | 1340/1360 mm |
| Length | – |
| Width | – |
| Height | – |
| Dry weight | 720-780 kg |
| Weight to power ratio | 6 kg/CV (1927 – 6.09) |

### PERFORMANCE AND PRODUCTION
| | |
|---|---|
| Maximum speed | kph 180-200 kph |
| Units produced | 11 |

# 26                                          1926

The first car to be designed by Maserati and which also bore his name, dates from the winter of 1925-1926. The Tipo 26 racing car was inspired by the Diatto Grand Prix which Maserati designed in 1925. The number 26 was a clear reference to the year of its birth. Alfieri Maserati chose a supercharged engine with the same layout - a straight 8, with double overhead cam valve gear - but with a displacement reduced from two litres to one and a half litres, to bring it into line with the new limit established by the sporting authorities for the international racing formula. The chassis too shared the same length of wheelbase and track as the car from Turin, a choice probably dictated by the limited amount of time available to build and set up the car. In fact it was the 25TH April 1926 when Alfieri drove "his" car for the first time in the Targa Florio not only coming eighth in the general classification but also taking first place in the class for cars up to 1500 cc, thereby recording a victory on the first page of the new marque's golden book. The car underwent a wide range of improvements and modifications during production of the 11 cars which were made between 1926 and 1932. The most significant included the implementation of a four-speed gearbox in place of the three-speed one, a reduction in the number of carburettors from 2 to 1 - the carburettor was also moved from the outlet of the supercharger to the inlet. Development work on the Tipo 26 brought about an increase in the power output (from 120 to 128 hp) and performance improvements which attracted the first customer-drivers to the Trident marque, including Materassi, Tonini, Brunori, De Sterlich and the Spaniard Joaquín Palacio, who bought the first Maserati for export. During 1927 the Bolognese company's list of victories grew and grew, culminating at the end of the season in a noteworthy achievement when Emilio Materassi won the newly-established title of outright Italian Champion.

Among the cars kept in the National Motor Museum in Turin is this Tipo 26 B, the first "evolution" of the original Maserati, conceived and designed for use in road races. The straight eight engine enlarged to two litres (1980.590 cc) represented the car's most significant new feature and on paper provided a maximum power output of 155 hp at 5300 rpm and a top speed in the order of 210 kph.

## TECHNICAL SPECIFICATION

### ENGINE
front, longitudinal, straight eight

| | |
|---|---|
| Bore and stroke | 62 x 82 mm |
| Unitary displacement | 247.56 cc |
| Total displacement | 1980.50 cc |
| Valvegear | twin overhead camshafts |
| Number of valves | two per cylinder |
| Compression ratio | 5.6:1 |
| Fuel system | Two Memini carburettors (Weber from 1929) |
| | Roots supercharger |
| Ignition | single, with Bosch or Scintilla magneto |
| Cooling | water, centrifugal pump and radiator |
| Lubrication | dry sump, pressurised, with delivery and scavenging pumps |
| Maximum power | 155 hp at 5300 rpm |
| Specific power output | 78.2 hp/litre |

### TRANSMISSION
| | |
|---|---|
| Driven wheels | rear |
| Clutch | multiple dry-plate |
| Gearbox | four speeds + reverse |

### BODYWORK
two-seater racing

### ROLLING CHASSIS
| | |
|---|---|
| Chassis | longerons and cross members |
| Front suspension | rigid axle, leaf springs friction dampers |
| Front suspension | live axle, leaf springs friction dampers |
| Brakes | mechanically actuated drums |
| Steering | worm and gear |
| Fuel tank | 80 l |
| Tyres front/rear | 5.00-18 / 5.50-18 |

### DIMENSIONS AND WEIGHT
| | |
|---|---|
| Wheelbase | 2650 mm (1928: 2580) |
| Tracks front/rear | 1340/1360 mm |
| Length | – |
| Width | – |
| Height | – |
| Dry weight | 720-780 kg |
| Weight to power ratio | 4,64 kg/CV (1928 – 5.03) 5,03) |

### PERFORMANCE AND PRODUCTION
| | |
|---|---|
| Maximum speed | kph 180-210 kph |
| Units produced | 6 |

# 26 B 1927

The Tipo 26 cars took their name from the year of their birth, 1926. Three were built in that year, based on the specification of Grand Prix cars - one and a half litres with a supercharger. The fact that the car's appearance was almost identical to its predecessor dictated the use of the name 26B. What was new about the car was the engine, with the displacement being increased to 2 litres by increasing the size of the bore from 60 to 62 millimeters and the stroke from 66 to 82. The strong supercharged twin-cam eight-cylinder engine used a slightly reduced compression ratio - from 5.8/6.0:1 to 5.6:1, but at the same time, at the same number of revs, 5300 rpm, gave 29% more power, 155 hp against the 120 hp of the first series Tipo 26. As a result the top speed increased to 210 kph. Over the four years during which it was in production the 26B was of course modified and updated. In particular the engine benefitted from new casting technology with elektron taking the place of cast iron and aluminium for the crankcase, the sump, the steering box and other components. The chassis had the same set up as the 26 not just in terms of the use of stringers and cross-beams but also in terms of the dimensions of the track and the wheelbase (the latter was shortened in 1928 as it was on the 26 from 2650 to 2580 mm). The bodywork, from the second car to be built onwards, underwent a change which was then applied to the 26 as well - the radiator was no longer verti-cal but tilted backwards, and this became a classical feature of Maserati cars. The 26B had racing successes in 1927 with De Sterlich (Vittorio Veneto-Cansiglio, Tren-to-Bondone and Vermicino-Rocca di Papa) and with Maggi (Nave-Sant'Eusebio) and in 1928 with Borzacchini (Coppa Etna and Vermicino-Rocca di Papa).

The Tipo 26 evolved rapidly and this model introduced in 1928 was given the MM tag, standing for Mille Miglia. The first edition of the race had been dispute in 1927 and all the principal Italian car manufacturers realised that this endurance event was the ideal testing ground for men and machines. Maserati could hardly not be among them and lined up for the second Coppa delle Mille Miglia with a Tipo 26 MM that the Tonini-Parenti crew took to a modest 23RD place overall.

## TECHNICAL SPECIFICATION

### ENGINE
front, longitudinal, straight eight

| | |
|---|---|
| Bore and stroke | 60 x 66 mm |
| Unitary displacement | 186.61 cc |
| Total displacement | 1492.88 cc |
| Valvegear | twin overhead camshafts |
| Number of valves | two per cylinder |
| Compression ratio | 5.8:1 |
| Fuel system | One Memini Super carburettor Roots supercharger |
| Ignition | single, with Bosch or Scintilla magneto |
| Cooling | water, centrifugal pump and radiator |
| Lubrication | dry sump, pressurised, with delivery and scavenging pumps |
| Maximum power | 128 hp at 6000 rpm |
| Specific power output | 85.7 hp/litre |

### TRANSMISSION
| | |
|---|---|
| Driven wheels | rear |
| Clutch | multiple dry-plate |
| Gearbox | four speeds + reverse |

### BODYWORK
two-seater sport

### ROLLING CHASSIS
| | |
|---|---|
| Chassis | longerons and cross members |
| Front suspension | rigid axle, leaf springs friction dampers |
| Rear suspension | live axle, leaf springs friction dampers |
| Brakes | mechanically actuated drums |
| Steering | worm and gear |
| Fuel tank | 80 l |
| Tyres front/rear | 4.75-18 / 5.00-18 |

### DIMENSIONS AND WEIGHT
| | |
|---|---|
| Wheelbase | 2580 mm |
| Tracks front/rear | 1340/1360 mm |
| Length | – |
| Width | – |
| Height | – |
| Dry weight | 840 kg |
| Weight to power ratio | 6.56 kg/CV |

### PERFORMANCE AND PRODUCTION
| | |
|---|---|
| Maximum speed | 180 kph |
| Units produced | 2 |

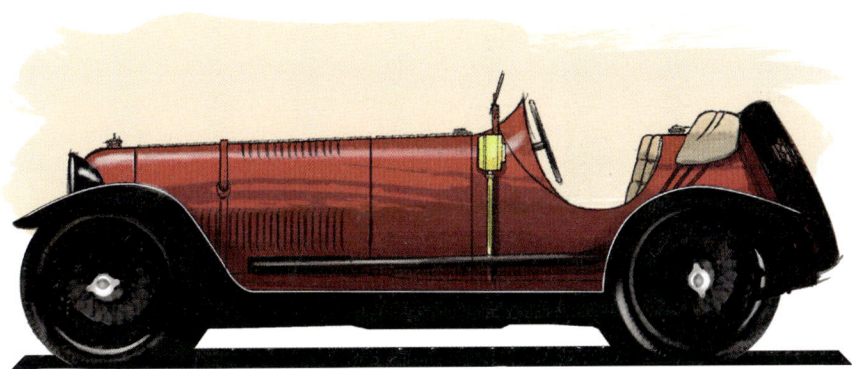

# 26 MM                    1928

Built for Grand Prix racing, the Tipo 26 could, with a few modifications, also be used for road racing in the Sport category, but Alfieri Maserati did not want to make compromises and at the beginning of 1928 this led to the birth of the 26 MM. The car was clearly based on the 26 but with modifications that bore in mind the very demanding conditions of competitions like the Mille Miglia which had been run for the first time in 1927 and which unsurprisingly inspired the initials MM. The chassis had been lengthened and reinforced and the bodywork was given a more roomy passenger compartment with two small windshields and a cloth hood which could be folded back above the fuel tank located in the tail which was now truncated and no longer protruding and where two spare wheels could be fixed. At the front of the car, which now had a vertical radiator as on the original version instead of the sloping one which had been introduced on the 26B, were mounted two or four headlights. The sides of the car were traversed by the lines of the slim mudguards that were connected to horizontal wooden running boards to which were fastened two toolboxes. The engine was practically the same eight-cylinder twin-cam supercharged 1.5 from the Tipo 26 in its most recent version and even though it was fitted with one carburettor rather than two it had the same power output of 128 hp at 6000 rpm. Of course the car's overall weight had increased from the 720-780 kg of the 26 to 840 kg, the top speed was around 180 rather than 200 kph and the acceleration was obviously less lively. Two 26 MM's were built and they were bought and raced by Carlo Tonini and Pietro Brunori but they were not very successful, finishing 23[RD] overall in the 1928 Mille Miglia. The inadequate performance was put down to carburation problems and the chassis's lack of rigidity. Brunori achieved the only outright win at the Circuito di Caserta the same year.

At the head of the group of competitors awaiting the opening of a level crossing during the second Coppa delle Mille Miglia (31 March-1April 1928), the photographer's lens has captured the Tipo 26B MM of Ernesto Maserati and Aymo Maggi. This last, as well as being a good driver, was also one of the organizers of the Mille Miglia, but in this his second participation in the event (after taking part in 1927 with an Isotta Fraschini) he failed to reach the finish in Brescia.

## TECHNICAL SPECIFICATION

### ENGINE

front, longitudinal, straight eight

| | |
|---|---|
| Bore and stroke | 62 x 82 mm |
| Unitary displacement | 247.56 cc |
| Total displacement | 1980.50 cc |
| Valvegear | twin overhead camshafts |
| Number of valves | two per cylinder |
| Compression ratio | 5.6:1 |
| Fuel system | One Memini Super carburettor (Weber from 1929) Roots supercharger |
| Ignition | single, with Bosch or Scintilla magneto |
| Cooling | water, centrifugal pump and radiator |
| Lubrication | dry sump, pressurised, with delivery and scavenging pumps |
| Maximum power | 155 hp at 5300 rpm |
| Specific power output | 78.26 hp/litre |

### TRANSMISSION

| | |
|---|---|
| Driven wheels | rear |
| Clutch | multiple dry-plate |
| Gearbox | four speeds + reverse |

### BODYWORK

two-seater sport

### ROLLING CHASSIS

| | |
|---|---|
| Chassis | longerons and cross members |
| Front suspension | rigid axle, leaf springs friction dampers |
| Rear suspension | live axle, leaf springs friction dampers |
| Brakes | mechanically actuated drums |
| Steering | worm and gear |
| Fuel tank | 80 l |
| Tyres front/rear | 5.00-18 / 5.50-18 |

### DIMENSIONS AND WEIGHT

| | |
|---|---|
| Wheelbase | 2580 mm |
| Tracks front/rear | 1340/1360 mm |
| Length | – |
| Width | – |
| Height | – |
| Dry weight | 840 kg |
| Weight to power ratio | 5.41 kg/CV |

### PERFORMANCE AND PRODUCTION

| | |
|---|---|
| Maximum speed | 200 kph |
| Units produced | 4 |

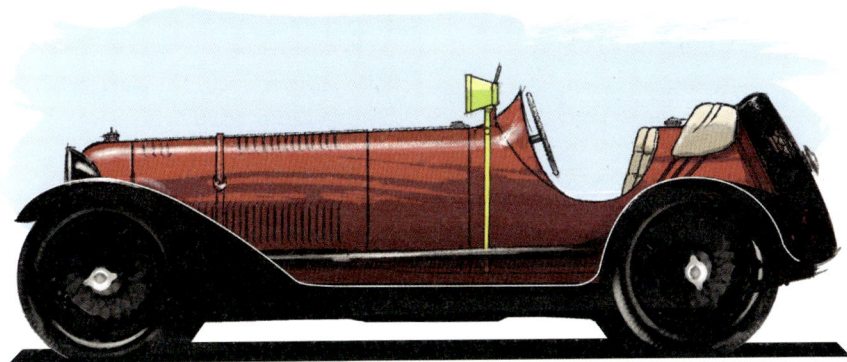

# 26 B MM                                    1928

Alfieri Maserati worked on the technical theme of the Tipo 26 and this resulted in the 26 MM and in the same way and at the same time he produced the 26B MM based on the 26B. It was built for the same races on closed roads, in the 2000 rather than the 1500 class for Sport category cars, which the great designers based on their production models although this was an unthinkable task for small workshops like the Trident at the beginning of their business life. In fact the two MM cars were developed from the Gran Prix cars which had come before them and this unorthodox line of development gave rise to complaints from the competition, who were certainly not pleased to see the growing competitivity of their new adversary. The new two-seater spider was powered by the twin-cam supercharged eight-cylinder engine from the 26B, with the same maximum power output (155 hp at 5300 rpm). The bodywork was the same as that of the 26 MM as was the stringers and cross-beam chassis but it had a shorter wheelbase than the 26B (2580 rather than 2650 mm). The increase in weight was the same too, from the 720-780 kg of the 26B to 840 kg. Between 1928 and 1930 four examples of the 26B MM were built and they benefitted from the modifications which were gradually made to the 26B too, especially regarding the engine and more specifically the use of elektron in place of aluminium for the crankcase, the sump, the steering box and other parts. The top speed was slightly lower than that of the 26B but was however, sensational for the time: 200 kph instead of 210 kph. However the car did not come up to the expectations of the Maserati brothers, as it had similar problems to those of the 26 MM which had not been solved, relating to the carburation and the flexibility of the chassis which limited its performance in races. And, unlike the 26 MM, the name 26B MM does not appear in the Maserati list of victories.

Ernesto Maserati and Umberto Borzacchini's Tipo 26 R is seen here in one of the most classic of Mille Miglia passages. The protagonists in a scintillating start to the race (they reached Bologna at the head of the overall standings after just an hour and a half at an average speed of 127 kph), the pair retained the lead through to Florence and then Rome which they reached in six hours and 23 minutes, but then shortly after passing through the capital they were forced to retire after the frenzied pace proved to much for the car.

## TECHNICAL SPECIFICATION

### ENGINE

front, longitudinal, straight eight

| | |
|---|---|
| Bore and stroke | 62 x 70 mm |
| Unitary displacement | 211.33 cc |
| Total displacement | 1690.67 cc |
| Valvegear | twin overhead camshafts camshafts |
| Number of valves | two per cylinder |
| Compression ratio | 6.5:1 |
| Fuel system | One Memini Super carburettor (Weber from 1929) Roots supercharger |
| Ignition | single, with Bosch or Scintilla Bosch |
| Cooling | water, centrifugal pump and radiator |
| Lubrication | dry sump, pressurised, with delivery and scavenging pumps |
| Maximum power | 140 hp at 6500 rpm |
| Specific power output | 82.80 hp/litre |

### TRANSMISSION

| | |
|---|---|
| Driven wheels | rear |
| Clutch | multiple dry-plate |
| Gearbox | three speeds + reverse |

### BODYWORK

two-seater racing

### ROLLING CHASSIS

| | |
|---|---|
| Chassis | longerons and cross members |
| Front suspension | rigid axle, leaf springs friction dampers |
| Rear suspension | live axle, leaf springs friction dampers |
| Brakes | mechanically actuated drums |
| Steering | worm and gear |
| Fuel tank | – |
| Tyres front/rear | 5.00-18 / 5.50-18 |

### DIMENSIONS AND WEIGHT

| | |
|---|---|
| Wheelbase | 2580 mm |
| Tracks front/rear | 1340/1360 mm |
| Length | – |
| Width | – |
| Height | – |
| Dry weight | 720 kg |
| Weight to power ratio | 5.14 kg/CV |

### PERFORMANCE AND PRODUCTION

| | |
|---|---|
| Maximum speed | 200 kph |
| Units produced | 2 |

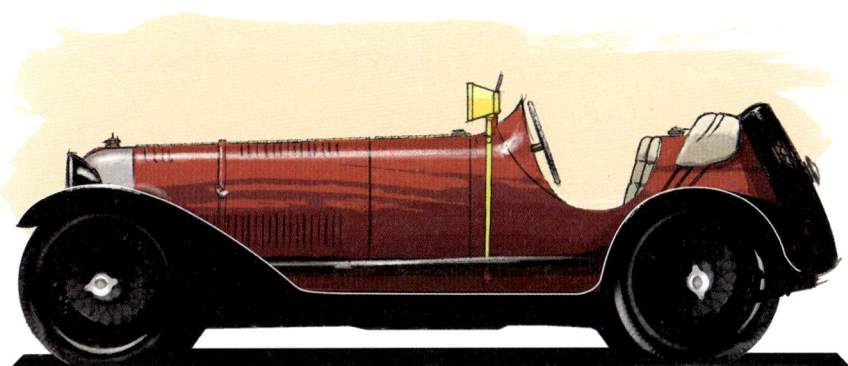

# 26 R                        1928

The Grand Prix formula for the 1928 season allowed cars of unlimited displacement weighing between 550 and 750 kg to take part. In order to build a car which matched the requirements of that rule, Alfieri Maserati used a chassis similar to the one made for the more recent versions of the 26B but made it narrower and lighter out of 4 mm thick steel, and designed it to house a completely new engine. It was still a twin-cam supercharged eight-cylinder with the same 62 mm bore size as the 26B, and a stroke shortened to 70 mm, meaning a displacement of 1690.67 cc which led to the unofficial but widespread name "Maserati 1700" for the new two-seater. The official name was, however, the 26R, combining a number which showed its link to the original car made by the Trident and the letter "R" which indicated the use of roller bearings at the top of the con rod in place of the traditional plain metal bearings. This mechanical refinement (which was already used for the crankshaft bearings of the Maserati engines) was, so to speak, "borrowed" from an 8 cylinder Bugatti, which was hurriedly dismantled and put back together one night, without the owner's knowledge. The owner was Bartolomeo Costantini, driver and sporting director of Bugatti, during a social call to Maserati. He had been invited by Alfieri and after leaving his car in the workshop the two men spent a number of hours together over dinner and in Bologna night-spots while Ernesto, the younger of the Maserati brothers and his mechanics carried out a careful inspection of the engine and gave it back to Costantini the next day in perfect condition. Although the 26R, of which two were made, had a very powerful output (140 hp at 6500 rpm) it was not very successful in racing and with the arrival of the new international formula, was not developed further. Fagioli had one victory in 1929 (Tolentino-Colle Paterno, 1929); and in 1931 Ruggeri (GP Monza) and Biondetti (Premio Reale Roma) had two further victories in the heats.

In 1929 Alfieri Maserati used the tried and trusted mechanical configuration of the Tipo 26 to produce a "Corsa" version. Even with the displacement reduced to 1100 cc (1078.60 cc), the new model boasted a power output of 105 hp at 6000 rpm. Among the Tipo 26 C's most important victories, mention has to be made of Alfieri Maserati's own win on the 25TH of May 1930 in the Voiturettes Category of the Rome Grand Prix, on the Circuito delle Tre Fontane.

## TECHNICAL SPECIFICATION

### ENGINE
front, longitudinal, straight eight

| | |
|---|---|
| Bore and stroke | 51 x 66 mm |
| Unitary displacement | 134.82 cc |
| Total displacement | 1078.60 cc |
| Valvegear | twin overhead camshafts |
| Number of valves | two per cylinder |
| Compression ratio | 5.5:1 |
| Fuel system | 1 Weber ASS carburettor Roots supercharger |
| Ignition | single, with Bosch or Scintilla magneto |
| Cooling | water, centrifugal pump and radiator |
| Lubrication | dry sump, pressurised, with delivery and scavenging pumps |
| Maximum power | 95-105 hp at 5500-6000 rpm |
| Specific power output | 88.07-97.34 hp/litre |

### TRANSMISSION

| | |
|---|---|
| Driven wheels | rear |
| Clutch | multiple dry-plate |
| Gearbox | four speeds + reverse |

### BODYWORK
two-seater racing or sport

### ROLLING CHASSIS

| | |
|---|---|
| Chassis | longerons and cross members |
| Front suspension | rigid axle, leaf springs friction dampers |
| Rear suspension | rigid axle, leaf springs friction dampers |
| Brakes | mechanically actuated drums |
| Steering | worm and gear |
| Fuel tank | – |
| Tyres front/rear | 4.75-18 / 5.00-18 |

### DIMENSIONS AND WEIGHT

| | |
|---|---|
| Wheelbase | 2580 mm |
| Tracks front/rear | 1340/1360 mm |
| Length | – |
| Width | – |
| Height | – |
| Dry weight | Corsa: 800 kg / Sport 880 kg |
| Weight to power ratio | 8.42 - 8,.8 kg/hp |

### PERFORMANCE AND PRODUCTION

| | |
|---|---|
| Maximum speed | 170-185 kph |
| Units produced | 4 |

# 26 C (8C 1100) 1929

With the aim of boosting sales of their cars, Maserati took on the flourishing voiturettes (light-weight racing car) sector of the market, which was contested by a dozen builders and a growing number of drivers, keen to make a name for themselves in the minor racing categories. To make an 1100 cc car, Alfieri Maserati converted a Tipo 26 8 cylinder engine by reducing the bore to 51 mm and the stroke to 66 mm. The rest of the components were now oversized and this meant that the engine could be pushed very hard with no threat to its reliability. With a rather high maximum rev limit of 6000 rpm the power output was 105 hp, with a supercharger pressure of 0.8 kgf/cm$^2$ (compared to 0.6 of the 26 MM and 0.7 of the V4) which meant a mean real pressure of 14.6 kgf/cm$^2$ compared to 13.28 in the 26 MM. The top speed was nearly 185 kph but the car was severely handicapped by its weight. Despite a reduction from 4 to 3 mm in the thickness of the sheet steel used for the chassis (otherwise identical to the one used on the 26R) the overall weight was 800 kg for the Corsa version and 880 kg for the Sport version. Comparisons with the most competitive rivals are unforgiving: the French Amilcar and Salmson cars were lighter by 150 and an amazing 250 kg respectively. This meant that production of the car was limited, with 4 being made between 1929 and the following year, before the 4-cylinder project started to take shape. There were however, two successes obtained by the 26C (the number shows the technical origin of the car and the letter C stands for "Corsa" version or third stage, stage C of the development cycle). The first success was obtained by Alfieri Maserati himself in the Premio Reale di Roma in 1930 (in the voiturettes category but in a separate race, therefore an overall victory) and the second victory was won by Beppe Tuffanelli and Guarino Bertocchi in the 1100 class of the 1931 Mille Miglia - a class victory but a very signficant one.

*Tipo V4 - 16 cilindri*

*Siluro*

La macchina detentrice del record mondiale dei 10 Km. lanciati su strada normale
Km. 246,500 all'ora (Cremona, Settembre 1929)

On this page, official advertising featuring the Tipo V4 16-cylinder in "Siluro" or Torpedo form; the slogan reads "The holder of the world record for the flying 10 km on open roads 246.500 km per hour (Cremona, September 1929)." The reference is to the record over a flying kilometres for the up to 5000 cc Class C, set by "Baconin" Borzacchini on the 28TH of September 1929.

## TECHNICAL SPECIFICATION

### ENGINE
front, longitudinal, 25° V16

| | |
|---|---|
| *Bore and stroke* | 62 x 82 mm |
| *Unitary displacement* | 247.56 cc |
| *Total displacement* | 3961.01 cc |
| *Valvegear* | twin overhead camshafts per bank |
| *Number of valves* | two per cylinder |
| *Compression ratio* | 5.5:1 |
| *Fuel system* | Two Weber DO carburettors 2 Roots superchargers |
| *Ignition* | single, with 2 Bosch or Scintilla magnetos |
| *Cooling* | water, centrifugal pump and radiator |
| *Lubrication* | dry sump, pressurised, with delivery and scavenging pumps |
| *Maximum power* | 280-305 hp at 5500 rpm |
| *Specific power output* | 70.68-77.00 hp/litre |

### TRANSMISSION
| | |
|---|---|
| *Driven wheels* | rear |
| *Clutch* | multiple dry-plate |
| *Gearbox* | four speeds + reverse |

### BODYWORK
*two-seater racing*

### ROLLING CHASSIS
| | |
|---|---|
| *Chassis* | longerons and cross members |
| *Front suspension* | rigid axle, leaf springs friction dampers |
| *Rear suspension* | rigid axle, leaf springs friction dampers |
| *Brakes* | mechanically actuated drums |
| *Steering* | worm and gear |
| *Fuel tank* | – |
| *Tyres front/rear* | 3.25-19 / 6.50-16 |
| | 5.35-29 / 5.50-31 |
| | 5.35-25 / 6.00-32 |

### DIMENSIONS AND WEIGHT
| | |
|---|---|
| *Wheelbase* | 2670-2750 mm |
| *Tracks front/rear* | 1350/1300 mm |
| *Length* | – |
| *Width* | – |
| *Height* | – |
| *Dry weight* | 1050 kg |
| *Weight to power ratio* | 3.75 – 3.44 kg/hp |

### PERFORMANCE AND PRODUCTION
| | |
|---|---|
| *Maximum speed* | 250-260 kph |
| *Units produced* | 2 |

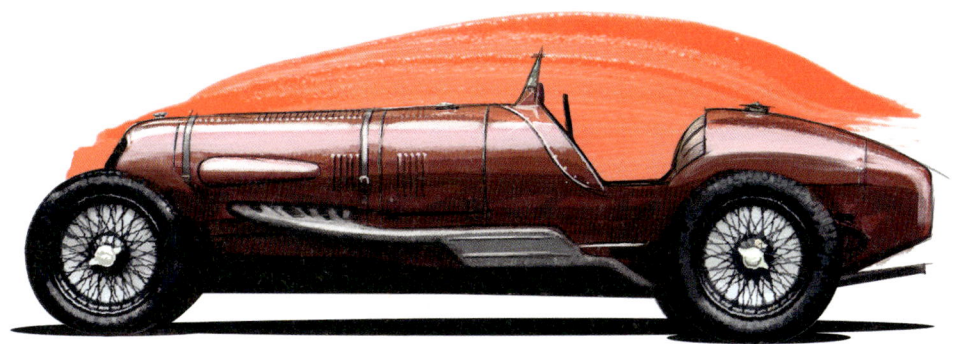

# V4 1929

In his attempt to create a racing car specifically designed to take part in Grand Prix races, with the V4, Alfieri Maserati reached one of the peaks of his designing career. He fitted a new engine made from two crankcases from the eight-cylinder 26B engine to a chassis which had its origins in the 26 series but which was bigger and stronger. This was not a completely new idea, as it had been tried by Fiat, Bugatti and later by Alfa Romeo but not with the same level of success which it gave Maserati. The V in the name indicates the layout of the engine with its 16 cylinders in (25°) V formation, and the number 4 indicates the number of litres of the displacement. Each of the two crankcases was fitted with a magneto, a carburettor, a supercharger and of course a crankshaft which was connected to the other engine - where it sat alongside it in a single casing - and power was taken centrally from a single, extremely sturdy gear. The power output - 208-305 bhp - was almost double that produced by the 26B and the top speed was close to 260 kph. The car's only weakness was its weight, at 1050 kg, which was well-distributed between the axles and did not affect how the car handled even on winding roads, but it was too much for the brakes and caused rapid tyre wear as well. Only one of these cars was made or perhaps two (the second one might have been converted into the following V5 model) but the weighty car had three significant successes. In 1929 Borzacchini won the flying 10 km race at Cremona, where it set a new world road record with an average of 246.069 kph. The same driver won the 1930 Tripoli GP and Ernesto Maserati won the Premio Reale in Rome the following year. In 1930 Borzacchini took the V4 to the starting grid of the Indianapolis 500 Miles but the car, without its superchargers according to the rules, retired after only 7 laps as a result of magneto failure.

In the 1930s, Carrozzeria Zagato was synonymous with Alfa Romeo thanks to the numerous cars built on the 6C 1750 rolling chassis. However, at the beginning of the decade, the Milanese firm also created a spider on the basis of the Maserati Tipo V4. The steeply sloping radiator grille is an unmistakeable Trident trademark, but the streamlined, aggressive shapes of the bodywork are in the best Zagato traditions.

## TECHNICAL SPECIFICATION

### ENGINE
front, longitudinal, 25° V16

| | |
|---|---|
| Bore and stroke | 62 x 82 mm |
| Unitary displacement | 247.56 cc |
| Total displacement | 3961.01 cc |
| Valvegear | twin overhead camshafts per bank |
| Number of valves | two per cylinder |
| Compression ratio | 5.5:1 |
| Fuel system | 2 Weber DO carburettors 2 Roots superchargers |
| Ignition | single, with 2 Bosch or Scintilla magnetos |
| Cooling | water, centrifugal pump and radiator |
| Lubrication | dry sump, pressurised, with delivery and scavenging pumps |
| Maximum power | 280-305 hp at 5500 rpm |
| Specific power output | 70.68-77.00 hp/litre |

### TRANSMISSION
| | |
|---|---|
| Driven wheels | rear |
| Clutch | multiple dry-plate |
| Gearbox | four speeds + reverse |

### BODYWORK
two-seater sport

### ROLLING CHASSIS
| | |
|---|---|
| Chassis | longerons and cross members |
| Front suspension | rigid axle, leaf springs friction dampers |
| Rear suspension | rigid axle, leaf springs friction dampers |
| Brakes | mechanically actuated drums |
| Steering | worm and gear |
| Fuel tank | – |
| Tyres front/rear | 3.25-19 / 6.50-16 |
| | 5.35-29 / 5.50-31 |
| | 5.35-25 / 6.00-32 |

### DIMENSIONS AND WEIGHT
| | |
|---|---|
| Wheelbase | 2670-2750 mm |
| Tracks front/rear | 1350/1300 mm |
| Length | – |
| Width | – |
| Height | – |
| Dry weight | – |
| Weight to power ratio | 3.75 – 3.44 kg/hp |

### PERFORMANCE AND PRODUCTION
| | |
|---|---|
| Maximum speed | 250-260 kph |
| Units produced | 1 |

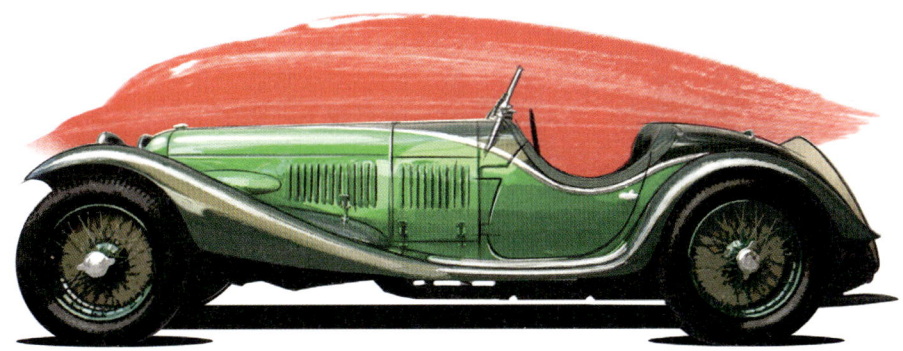

# V4 Gran Sport Zagato                1930

Of the two examples of the mighty V4, built in 1929, one was converted three years later into the V5, and was destroyed when it ran off the road during the 1934 Tripoli GP with Piero Taruffi at the wheel. The other one (which had been built first: the one with which Borzacchini established a world speed record) was "clothed" by Ugo Zagato with bodywork designed for sport-touring. This was an extremely elegant spider which took part in 1931 in the "Concorso delle carrozzerie" held at Pincio in Rome and won third prize. Reminiscent of the Alfa Romeo 8C 2300 of the same period, this car also appeared in the Maserati official catalogue, although it never went into production and after various adventures it ended up with us. The "road" set up did not stop the car being able to take part in races under the Formula libera banner as happened in the aformentioned Tripoli Gran Prix, where the customer who had bought it, Professor Riccardo Galeazzi of Rome, entered it for the driver Carlo Gazzabini, who did not get beyond the sixth lap when he was stopped by mechanical failure. We do not know anything about what happened to the V4 Zagato in the following years, until 1939, just before the outbreak of the Second World War when the car was found in a warehouse in Brussels by the Dutch driver Eric Werkade, who bought it for the price of scrap metal or little more. He managed to keep it hidden and prevent it being requisitioned by the Germans, dismantling the engine and restoring it - as the story goes - in his bedroom. At the end of the war Werkade started racing again at the wheel of his Maserati 4CL and used the V4 to get from one race to the next. Today the car is part of a collection in the USA and was put on show and admired in Modena at the Maserati 100 year anniversary celebrations. The splendid restoration which it has undergone allowed it to win the first prize in the Pebble Beach Concours d'Elegance in 2003.

The final representative of the versatile Tipo 26 series was the model distinguished by the letter M, available in "Corsa" and "Sport" versions. In this car, the displacement of the glorious straight eight, which up until this moment had equipped almost every car produced by the Trident marque, was 2.5 litres. On the same day that Alfieri Maserati was driving the Tipo 26 C to victory among the voiturettes in the 1930 edition of the Premio Reale di Roma, Luigi Arcangeli was winning the race outright with a 26 M.

## TECHNICAL SPECIFICATION

### ENGINE
front, longitudinal, straight eight

| | |
|---|---|
| *Bore and stroke* | 65 x 94 mm |
| *Unitary displacement* | 311.92 cc |
| *Total displacement* | 2495.36 cc |
| *Valvegear* | twin overhead camshafts |
| *Number of valves* | two per cylinder |
| *Compression ratio* | 5.5:1 |
| *Fuel system* | 1 Weber ASS carburettor Roots supercharger |
| *Ignition* | single, with Bosch or Scintilla magnetos |
| *Cooling* | water, centrifugal pump and radiator |
| *Lubrication* | dry sump, pressurised, with delivery and scavenging pumps |
| *Maximum power* | 185 hp at 5600 rpm |
| *Specific power output* | 74.13 hp/litre |

### TRANSMISSION
| | |
|---|---|
| *Driven wheels* | rear |
| *Clutch* | multiple dry-plate |
| *Gearbox* | four speeds + reverse |

### BODYWORK
| | |
|---|---|
| two-seater racing or sport | *(four-seater sport version with 2790 mm wheelbase)* |

### ROLLING CHASSIS
| | |
|---|---|
| *Chassis* | longerons and cross members |
| *Front suspension* | rigid axle, leaf springs friction dampers |
| *Rear suspension* | rigid axle, leaf springs friction dampers |
| *Brakes* | mechanically actuated drums |
| *Steering* | worm and gear |
| *Fuel tank* | 125 l |
| *Tyres front/rear* | 5.00-18 / 5.50-18 |

### DIMENSIONS AND WEIGHT
| | |
|---|---|
| *Wheelbase* | 2750 mm |
| *Tracks front/rear* | 1340/1360 mm |
| *Length* | – |
| *Width* | – |
| *Height* | – |
| *Dry weight* | Corsa: 820 kg Sport: 1000 kg |
| *Weight to power ratio* | Corsa: 4.43 kg Sport: 5.40 kg/CV |

### PERFORMANCE AND PRODUCTION
| | |
|---|---|
| *Maximum speed* | Corsa: 230 kph Sport: 180-200 kph |
| *Units produced* | 13 |

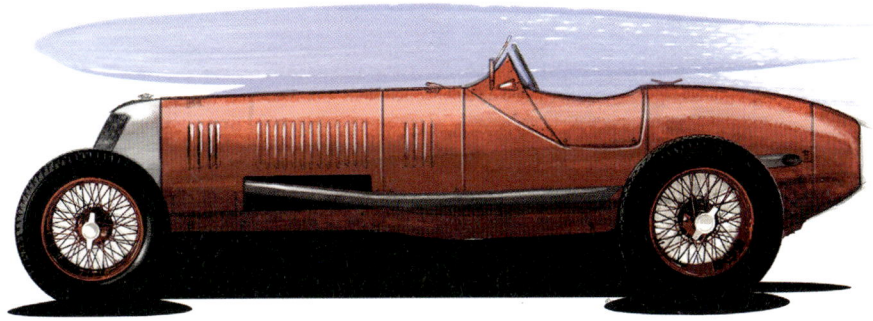

# 26 M – 26 M Sport                    1930

The development process of the Tipo 26, parent of the Maserati family tree, culminated in the 26M, both in its Corsa and Sport versions. The aim of this small but already successful factory was to complete a range of cars which went from the 1100 cc 26C to the 4 litre V4, and in between included the numerous 1.5 and 2.0 litre cars: 26-26B-26 MM-26B MM-26R. Alfieri Maserati decided on a 2.5 litre displacement and a thorough update of the straight eight which it was developed from. The displacement limit that had been chosen was obtained by a small increase in the bore (from 60-62 mm to 65) and a further increase in the stroke, which went from 66-70-82 to 95 mm. The fuel supply was as always supercharged but with the pressure increased to 0.75 kgf/cm$^2$ with a resulting improvement in volumetric efficiency. With its 185 bhp at 5600 rpm the 26M was more powerful than all previous Maserati cars, with the exception of the 16 cylinder V4. Extensive use of light alloy helped to keep the weight of the car down. By using the traditional chassis and the well-proven suspension set-up it meant that handling and roadholding were both excellent. The M in the car's name stood for Monoposto (single-seater). In fact for some time it had no longer been necessary to have a mechanic on board and the seat next to the driver, in Corsa trim cars, could be blanked off using a metal sheet fixed to the bodywork. The letter M was retained even for the 4-seater version, although it was accompanied by the explicit name, "Sport". In the hands of top-class drivers, the 26M won many prestigious victories. These were the most significant: 1930, Premio Reale Roma (Arcangeli), Circuito del Montenero (Fagioli), Coppa Acerbo, Monza GP and Spanish GP, the first international success (Varzi); 1931, Tunisia 6 Hours (Castelbarco/Dreyfus), Brooklands Mountain Championship (Birkin); 1933, Mont Ventoux (Straight); 1934, GP d'Albi (Featherstonhaugh) e and the Donington Trophy (Straight).

A modern photo of the 8C 2800, the model with which Alfieri Maserati attempted to fend off the increasingly fierce competition presented by Alfa Romeo. Taking his cue from the engine of the Tipo 26, the talented designer created a 2.8-litre engine (2811.93 c) that developed a maximum power output of 205 hp at 5500 rpm. The racing career of this car was however brief, with a sole victory in the hands of Luigi Fagioli in the Monza Grand Prix on the 6TH of September 1931.

## TECHNICAL SPECIFICATION

**ENGINE**
front, longitudinal, straight eight

| | |
|---|---|
| Bore and stroke | 69 x 94 mm |
| Unitary displacement | 351.49 cc |
| Total displacement | 2811.93 cc |
| Valvegear | twin overhead camshafts |
| Number of valves | two per cylinder |
| Compression ratio | 5,5:1 |
| Fuel system | 1 Weber ASS carburettor Roots supercharger |
| Ignition | single, Scintilla magneto |
| Cooling | water, centrifugal pump and radiator |
| Lubrication | dry sump, pressurised, with delivery and scavenging pumps |
| Maximum power | 205 hp at 5500 rpm |
| Specific power output | 72.90 hp/litre |

**TRANSMISSION**

| | |
|---|---|
| Driven wheels | rear |
| Clutch | multiple dry-plate |
| Gearbox | four speeds + reverse |

**BODYWORK**
two-seater racing

**ROLLING CHASSIS**

| | |
|---|---|
| Chassis | longerons and cross members |
| Front suspension | rigid axle, leaf springs friction dampers |
| Rear suspension | rigid axle, leaf springs friction dampers |
| Brakes | mechanically actuated drums |
| Steering | worm and gear |
| Fuel tank | – |
| Tyres front/rear | 5.50-19 / 5.50-19 |

**DIMENSIONS AND WEIGHT**

| | |
|---|---|
| Wheelbase | 2750 mm |
| Tracks front/rear | 1340/1360 mm |
| Length | – |
| Width | – |
| Height | – |
| Dry weight | 820 kg |
| Weight to power ratio | 4.00 kg/hp |

**PERFORMANCE AND PRODUCTION**

| | |
|---|---|
| Maximum speed | 210-230 kph |
| Units produced | 3 |

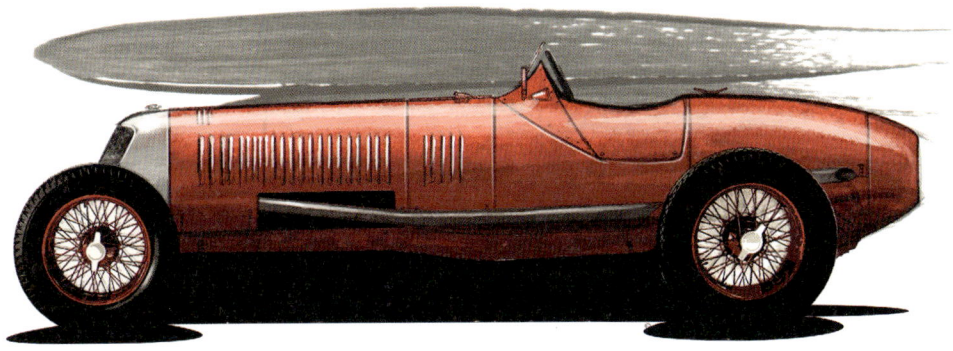

# 8C 2800                                    1931

Car manufacturers competing against Maserati and the company's ability to win as shown in the 1930 season did not waste time before fighting back and 1931 saw Alfa Romeo come to the fore with the new Tipo A and the 8C 2300 Monza and Bugatti with the twin-cam Type 51. Alfieri Maserati tried to batten down the hatches by modifying the 2.5 litre engine of the 26M: he left the stroke the same (94 mm) but increased the bore (from 65 to 69 mm) and achieved a displacement of 2811.93 cc. There was also substantial work on the lubrication system (greater rate of flow) and above all the carburation, with close cooperation with Weber. In its final version, the eight-cylinder 2800, with the same compression ratio (5.5:1) and a slightly lower maximum rev limit (5500 compared to 5600 rpm) developed considerably more power: 205 hp compared to 185, with much faster acceleration, also thanks to the unchanged weight (820 kg). The top speed increased from 180-200 to 210-230 kph. The need to build the car in a very short space of time led to the use of the excellent chassis from the 26M, while a few changes were made to the bodywork which was improved both from the aerodynamic and the aesthetic point of view. Its racing debut took place on the 21ST of June 1931 in the French A.C. Grand Prix at Montlhéry, where Fagioli (partnered by Ernesto Maserati) was among the leaders, retiring halfway through the race with braking problems after a sensational race in which he set the new lap record. He had his revenge the following September when he won the Monza GP, which was the only victory for the 2800. The factory's data does not allow us to establish which chassis the 2800 engines were fitted to. This is further evidence that Alfieri Maserati saw this as a temporary solution while he was waiting to give birth to a more radically innovative model which he was working on: the 2500 T.A. (front-wheel drive).

In what was sadly his last year, the inexhaustible Alfieri Maserati (who was to pass away on the 3RD of March 1932, at just 44 years of age) designed and built his latest engine: an 1100 cc straight four with bore and stroke dimensions of 65x82 mm, which was to power the Trident marque's new small car, the 4C TR. With only one example being produced, the car won the 1100 cc Sport class in the 1932 edition of the Mille Miglia in the hands of Tuffanelli and Bertocchi.

## TECHNICAL SPECIFICATION

### ENGINE
front, longitudinal, straight four

| | |
|---|---|
| Bore and stroke | 65 x 82 mm |
| Unitary displacement | 272.10 cc |
| Total displacement | 1088.40 cc |
| Valvegear | twin overhead camshafts |
| Number of valves | two per cylinder |
| Compression ratio | 5:1 |
| Fuel system | 1 Weber 48 ASS carburettor Roots supercharger |
| Ignition | single, with Bosch or Scintilla magneto |
| Cooling | water, centrifugal pump and radiator |
| Lubrication | dry sump, pressurised with delivery and scavenging pump |
| Maximum power | 90 hp at 5300 rpm |
| Specific power output | 82.69 hp/litre |

### TRANSMISSION
| | |
|---|---|
| Driven wheels | rear |
| Clutch | multiple dry-plate |
| Gearbox | four speeds + reverse |

### BODYWORK
two-seater racing or sport

### ROLLING CHASSIS
| | |
|---|---|
| Chassis | longerons and cross members |
| Front suspension | rigid axle, leaf springs friction dampers |
| Rear suspension | live axle, leaf springs friction dampers |
| Brakes | mechanically actuated drums (from 1935 hydraulically actuated) |
| Steering | worm and gear |
| Fuel tank | – |
| Tyres front/rear | 5.00-17 / 5.00-17 |

### DIMENSIONS AND WEIGHT
| | |
|---|---|
| Wheelbase | 2450 mm |
| Tracks front/rear | 1200/1200 mm |
| Length | – |
| Width | – |
| Height | – |
| Dry weight | 700 kg |
| Weight to power ratio | 7.7 kg/hp |

### PERFORMANCE AND PRODUCTION
| | |
|---|---|
| Maximum speed | 150 kph |
| Units produced | 1 |

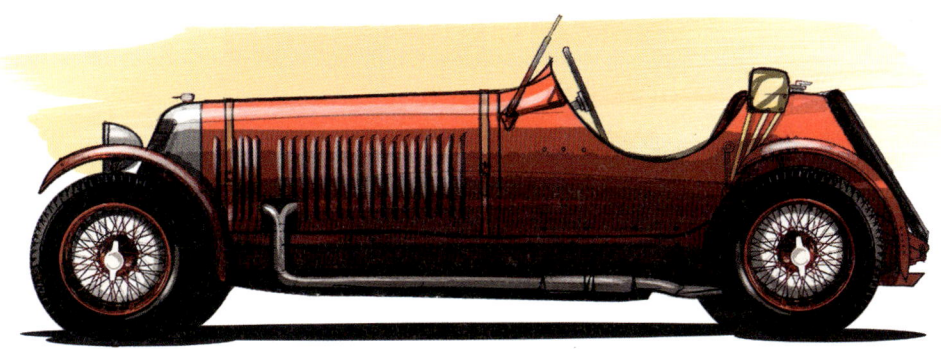

# 4C TR
# 1931

The diminutive 1100 cc 26C produced in 1929 had not come up to expectations: the 8-cylinder engine required complex and expensive maintenance and in any case the car, which was penalised by its excessive weight, always came off worse when racing against the French Amilcar and Salmson cars. Nevertheless, Alfieri Maserati rightly believed in the future of small displacement racing cars and in 1931 the final year of his career, he designed a new 1100 cc engine with half the number of cylinders and a displacement almost the same as that of the 26C: 1088.4 compared to 1078.6 cc. The chassis was also groundbreaking with its generous size and weight-saving holes drilled in the less-stressed parts which aimed to reduce the greatest handicap that the 26C had suffered from. This objective was realised as the overall weight was now 700 kg compared to the 800 kg of the 26C with the Corsa bodywork and the 880 kg of the Sport version. As regards performance figures, the 26C, with a power output of 95-105 hp, reached a top speed of 170-185 kph, while the 4C (90 hp) managed 150 but with much better acceleration figures. The name used for the new lightweight car was originally 4C, that is: "4 Cylinders". Subsequently the letters TR "Testa Riportata" were added (meaning that the head was fitted without a gasket, which meant that it had been made in an extraordinarily refined and precise way). Only one car was made and it debuted at Monza in the race preceding the 1931 GP d'Italia, coming fifth with Umberto Klinger at the wheel. The following year, driven by Giuseppe Tuffanelli, it won the 1100 class in the Corsa sulle Torricelle at Verona and again with Tuffanelli, partnered by Guarino Bertocchi, it was successful in the Mille Miglia (1ST place in its class and 20TH overall). In the meantime, from that prototype 4CTR the final versions were being developed, the two classic 4CM (Monoposto - single-seater) and 4CS (Sport) cars.

The Maserati V5 No. 28, photographed at a pit stop during the Coppa Acerbo at Pescara on the 14TH of August 1032. The car was driven to 5TH place overall by the crew of Ernesto Maserati, Luigi Fagioli and Arialdo Ruggeri. It was, however, Tazio Nuvolari who took outright victory with the Alfa Romeo P3 at an average speed of over 139 kph and set a fastest lap of 10 minutes and 25".

## TECHNICAL SPECIFICATION

### ENGINE
front, longitudinal, 25° V16

| | |
|---|---|
| Bore and stroke | 69 x 82 mm |
| Unitary displacement | 306.62 cc |
| Total displacement | 4905.93 cc |
| Valvegear | twin overhead camshafts per bank |
| Number of valves | two per cylinder |
| Compression ratio | 5:1 |
| Fuel system | 2 Weber DO carburettors 2 Roots superchargers |
| Ignition | single, with 2 Bosch or Scintilla magnetos |
| Cooling | water, centrifugal pump and radiator |
| Lubrication | dry sump, pressurised with delivery and scavenging pump |
| Maximum power | 330-360 hp at 5200 rpm |
| Specific power output | 67.26-73.38 hp/litre |

### TRANSMISSION
| | |
|---|---|
| Driven wheels | rear |
| Clutch | multiple dry-plate |
| Gearbox | four speeds + reverse |

### BODYWORK
two-seater, racing

### ROLLING CHASSIS
| | |
|---|---|
| Chassis | longerons and cross members |
| Front suspension | rigid axle, leaf springs friction dampers |
| Rear suspension | live axle, leaf springs friction dampers |
| Brakes | mechanically actuated drums (from 1934 hydraulically actuated) |
| Steering | worm and gear |
| Fuel tank | – |
| Tyres front/rear | 3.25-19 / 6.50-19 |

### DIMENSIONS AND WEIGHT
| | |
|---|---|
| Wheelbase | 2750 mm |
| Tracks front/rear | 1350/1300 mm |
| Length | – |
| Width | – |
| Height | – |
| Dry weight | 1050 kg |
| Weight to power ratio | 3.18 – 2.91 kg/hp |

### PERFORMANCE AND PRODUCTION
| | |
|---|---|
| Maximum speed | 260-270 kph |
| Units produced | 1 |

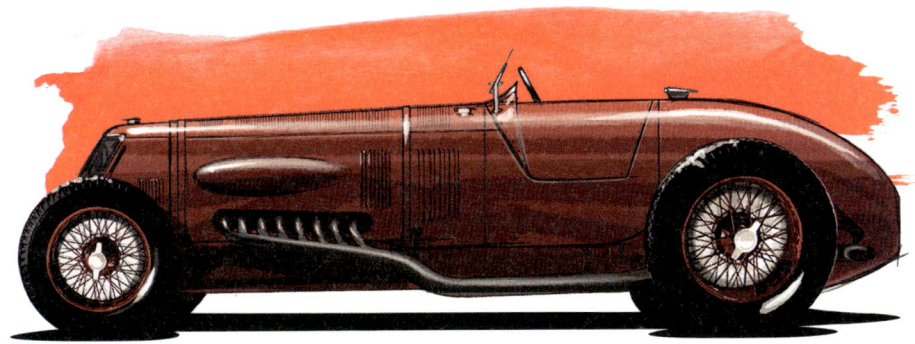

# V5 1932

While a growing domination in racing on the part of Alfa Romeo was gradually becoming apparent in the 1931 season, Alfieri Maserati, using the 8C 2800 as an emergency defence weapon, continued development of the V4 and made a bigger version of the 16 cylinder engine. The imposing power unit retained the same 82 mm stroke as the V4 but had an increase in the size of the bore from 62 to 69 mm, that is to say, the same size as the 2800, which was right on the limit of the cylinder block. The displacement increased from four to five litres and this gave rise to the new name. Even though the maxiumum rev limit was reduced from 5500 to 5200 rpm, power increased from 280-305 to 330-360 hp, figures which might have caused worries about possible problems in use, as had happened with the V4. Alfieri nevertheless fitted larger diameter wheels in order to limit tyre wear - the main weakness of the V4 - and beefed up the braking system. The weight of the car was still 1050 kg, the same as the V4 and thus, with the increase in bhp, the V5 benefitted from a very favourable weight to power ratio; 3.18-2.91 kg/hp (its greatest rival, the unprecedented Alfa Romeo B-P3, weighed 700 kg and produced 215 hp, with a ratio of 3.25: but its agility and easy handling made it impossible to keep up with on twisty roads). Regrettably, on the 3RD of March 1932 Alfieri Maserati died after an operation which he underwent as a result of injuries he had received in a crash during a race and with him the Bolognese factory lost its most brilliant technical talent. His place was taken by his brother Ernesto, who in time would show that he was not any less able. The V5 debuted on the 24TH of April, winning the Premio Reale di Roma with Fagioli, but this was to be its only victory. It missed out on a few victories because of silly breakdowns and inefficient work in the pits, after which the V5 was used in a record-breaking programme, which tragically came to an end on the 7TH of December 1932 after an accident on the Montlhéry track in which the driver Amedeo Ruggeri lost his life.

T.A. standing for Trazione Anteriore or Front-Wheel drive. This was the last project to be signed by Alfieri Maserati in 1931. The tireless designed created an avant-garde model that also boasted modern independent front suspension rather than the traditional rigid axle. The unexpected death of its creator who, moreover, had intended to extend the feature to almost all the models in the Maserati range, clipped the wings of a project that was never taken any further.

## TECHNICAL SPECIFICATION

### ENGINE
front, longitudinal, straight eight

| | |
|---|---|
| Bore and stroke | 65 x 94 mm |
| Unitary displacement | 311.92 cc |
| Total displacement | 2495.36 cc |
| Valvegear | twin overhead camshafts |
| Number of valves | two per cylinder |
| Compression ratio | 5.5:1 |
| Fuel system | 1 Weber ASS carburettor Roots supercharger |
| Ignition | single, Scintilla magneto |
| Cooling | water, centrifugal pump and radiator |
| Lubrication | dry sump, pressurised with delivery and scavenging pump |
| Maximum power | 185 hp at 5600 rpm |
| Specific power output | 74.13 hp/litre |

### TRANSMISSION
| | |
|---|---|
| Driven wheels | front |
| Clutch | multiple dry-plate |
| Gearbox | four speeds + reverse |

### BODYWORK
single-seater

### ROLLING CHASSIS
| | |
|---|---|
| Chassis | longerons and cross members |
| Front suspension | independent, leaf springs friction dampers |
| Rear suspension | rigid axle, leaf springs friction dampers |
| Brakes | hydraulically actuated drums |
| Steering | worm and gear |
| Fuel tank | – |
| Tyres front/rear | – |

### DIMENSIONS AND WEIGHT
| | |
|---|---|
| Wheelbase | 2580 / 2530 mm |
| Tracks front/rear | 1300 / 1300 mm |
| Length | – |
| Width | – |
| Height | – |
| Dry weight | 800 kg |
| Weight to power ratio | 4.00 kg/hp |

### PERFORMANCE AND PRODUCTION
| | |
|---|---|
| Maximum speed | – |
| Units produced | 1 |

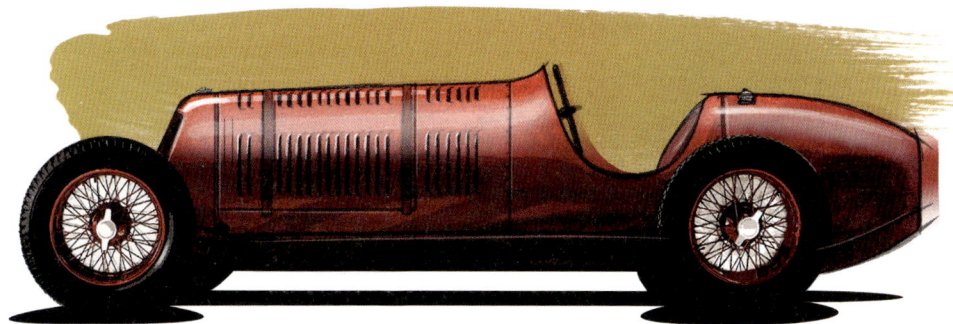

# 8C 2500 T.A. 1932

In the 1920s the Miller, a very successful American Grand Prix car, had not only won the Indianapolis 500 four times (1923, 1926, 1928 and 1929) but also shone in Europe as well, finishing in the top places at the Italian and Spanish GPs and establishing some world speed records at Montlhéry. The only car to use front-wheel drive, it had not escaped the attention of Alfieri Maserati, who, while looking for an innovative technical direction for the Trident's cars, considered following in its footsteps. He got the chance to have a closer look at the components of the mechanism on another American car, a Cord, which also had front-wheel drive and which belonged to a Maserati customer/driver, the Swiss Carlo Pedrazzini. Thus the 8C 2500 T.A. (eight cylinders, front-wheel drive) project took shape in 1931 and which by the end of the season had become an extremely interesting prototype which showed great promise. Of course the most significant feature was the front chassis which had wheels with independent suspension and, in place of the usual fixed axle, two conical load-bearing tubes which contained the half-shafts. The sprung element consisted of double semi-cantilever diagonal leaf-springs which were very short and robust. The engine was the 2.5 lire twin-cam eight-cylinder from the 26M which had been built the previous year, but Alfieri intended to gradually fit the new drive system to all Maserati cars, with the exception of the 16-cylinder V4-V5. The first road tests with Fagioli at the wheel on the Raticosa and Futa climbs consisted of comparisons with the 26M and had a satisfactory outcome. Unfortunately, Alfieri's death at the beginning of 1932 left the brothers in a state of technical disarray, to which they reacted by using the short-term solution of going back to producing traditional cars and deciding, after a few unsuccessful attempts, not to proceed with the complex development of the front-wheel drive 2500, which was not taken any further.

This photograph immortalises the brand-new 4CS 1100, fresh out of the factory. This was the logical evolution of the 4C TR as it too was equipped with a 1088.40 cc straight four. An agile, rapid car, it was at home in the great road races of the time, above all the Mille Miglia, in which it was victorious three years in a row, from 1934 to 1936, in the 1100 cc class of the Sport category.

## TECHNICAL SPECIFICATION

### ENGINE

front, longitudinal, straight four

| | |
|---|---|
| Bore and stroke | 65 x 82 mm |
| Unitary displacement | 272.10 cc |
| Total displacement | 1088.40 cc |
| Valvegear | twin overhead camshafts |
| Number of valves | two per cylinder |
| Compression ratio | 5,:1 / 5,5:1 |
| Fuel system | 1 Weber 48 ASS carburettor Roots supercharger |
| Ignition | single, with Bosch or Scintilla magneto |
| Cooling | water, centrifugal pump and radiator |
| Lubrication | dry sump, pressurised with delivery and scavenging pump |
| Maximum power | 90 hp at 5300 / 115 at 6000 rpm |
| Specific power output | 82.69 / 105.65 hp/litre |

### TRANSMISSION

| | |
|---|---|
| Driven wheels | rear |
| Clutch | multiple dry-plate |
| Gearbox | four speeds + reverse |

### BODYWORK

two-seater racing or sport

### ROLLING CHASSIS

| | |
|---|---|
| Chassis | longerons and cross members |
| Front suspension | rigid axle, leaf springs friction dampers |
| Rear suspension | live axle, leaf springs friction dampers |
| Brakes | mechanically actuated drums (from 1935 hydraulically actuated) |
| Steering | worm and gear |
| Fuel tank | – |
| Tyres front/rear | 5.00-17 / 5.00-17 |

### DIMENSIONS AND WEIGHT

| | |
|---|---|
| Wheelbase | 2450 mm |
| Tracks front/rear | 1200 / 1200 mm |
| Length | – |
| Width | – |
| Height | – |
| Dry weight | 700 kg |
| Weight to power ratio | 7.77 / 6.08 kg/hp |

### PERFORMANCE AND PRODUCTION

| | |
|---|---|
| Maximum speed | 150 kph |
| Units produced | 5 |

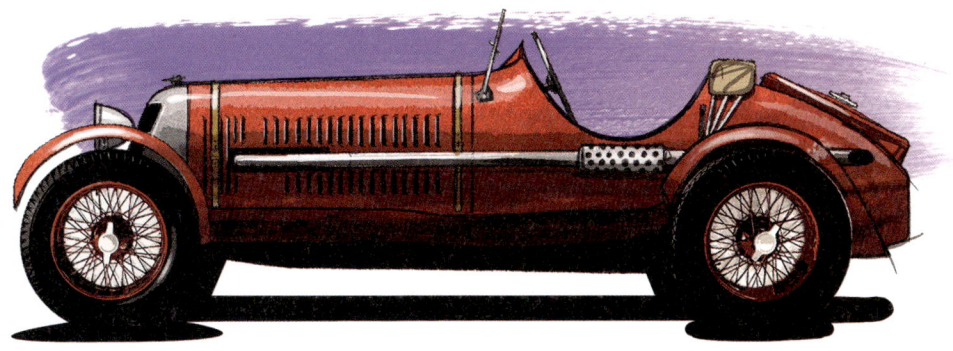

# 4C S 1100                                    1932

Two series of 4-cylinder 1100 cars were developed from the 4CTR of 1931: the 4CS (four-cylinder Sport) and the 4CM (four-cylinder single-seater). An elegant spider version of the Sport came out in 1932 presented by Carrozzeria Brianza of Milan. Another 4 cars in competition guise followed that prototype in 1935 and 1936. They were packed with innovations and significant updates. Gradually the engines benefitted from power increases that took them from the initial 90 hp to 115, with a corresponding increase in maximum revs from 5300 to 6000 rpm, which meant a top speed of 150 kph. A particularly significant modification that was adopted during the last round of updates to the car, was the use of hydraulics for the brakes, while other changes were made to the bodywork. The wrap-around mudguards were dropped in favour of motorcycle-type ones which were lighter and easier to remove if the car was to be used on the race track. The front end was redesigned with more compact lines and a new type of windscreen while the rear end housed a trapezoidal fuel tank and as usual the spare wheel. The exhaust, which previously ran along the lower edge of the side was mounted higher up almost touching the curve in the bodywork where the driver climbed into his seat. The large headlamps were attached to vertical supports which were anchored to the chassis rails and were linked by a horizontal bar on which the horn was mounted. The 4CS was successful both in various types of races which included 1100 cc cars and in races specifically for this displacement but the most brilliant wins were obtained in the Mille Miglia. In fact the 4CS won the 1100 class of the great Brescian event three times (in 1934, 1935 and 1936) as well as the win in 1932, with Tuffanelli at the wheel of the 4CTR, the car's direct predecessor. In 1934 Taruffi came into the limelight coming fifth overall. In 1935 and 1936 Ettore Bianco won.

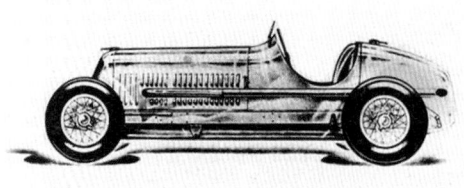

A drawing distributed at the time by the company shows the 4CM 1100, also derived from the 4C TR but conceived specifically for circuit races, as indicated by the absence of the cycle wings fitted to the Sport models, and the aero screen in front of the cockpit. As well as numerous track wins, the competition history of this model features the speed records set by Giuseppe Furmanik in 1934 and 1936.

## TECHNICAL SPECIFICATION

### ENGINE
front, longitudinal, straight four

| | |
|---|---|
| Bore and stroke | 65 x 82 mm |
| Unitary displacement | 272.10 cc |
| Total displacement | 1088.40 cc |
| Valvegear | twin overhead camshafts |
| Number of valves | two per cylinder |
| Compression ratio | 5:1 / 6,0:1 |
| Fuel system | 1 Weber 48 ASS carburettor Roots supercharger |
| Ignition | single, with Scintilla magneto |
| Cooling | water, centrifugal pump and radiator |
| Lubrication | dry sump, pressurised with delivery and scavenging pump |
| Maximum power | 90 hp at 5300 / 125 at 6000 rpm |
| Specific power output | 82.69 / 105.65 hp/litre |

### TRANSMISSION
| | |
|---|---|
| Driven wheels | rear |
| Clutch | single dry-plate |
| Gearbox | four speeds + reverse |

### BODYWORK
single-seater

### ROLLING CHASSIS
| | |
|---|---|
| Chassis | longerons and cross members |
| Front suspension | rigid axle, leaf springs friction dampers |
| Rear suspension | live axle, leaf springs friction dampers |
| Brakes | hydraulically actuated drums |
| Steering | worm and gear |
| Fuel tank | 90 l |
| Tyres front/rear | 5.50-16 - 5.00-17 / 5.50-16 - 5.00-17 |

### DIMENSIONS AND WEIGHT
| | |
|---|---|
| Wheelbase | 2400 mm |
| Tracks front/rear | 1200 / 1200 mm |
| Length | – |
| Width | – |
| Height | – |
| Dry weight | 580 kg |
| Weight to power ratio | 6.44 / 4.64 kg/hp |

### PERFORMANCE AND PRODUCTION
| | |
|---|---|
| Maximum speed | 185-210 kph |
| Units produced | 9 |

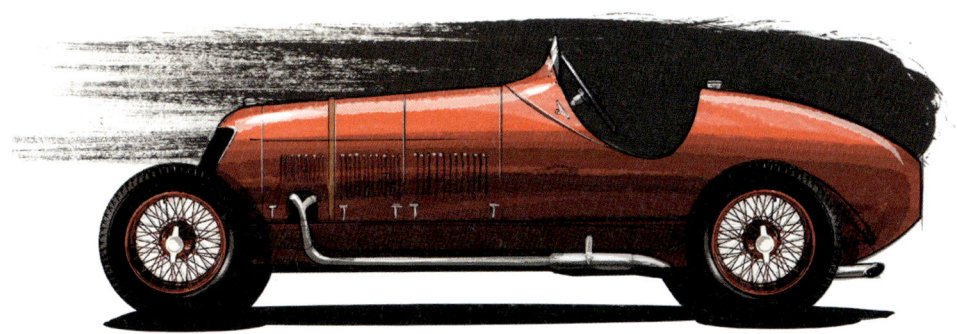

# 4C M 1100                    1932

While several features of the 4CS showed clearly that it had been developed from the 4CTR, the same could not be said of the 4CM, the "daughter" of the same basic mechanical design but inspired by a quite different design philosophy. If you removed the mudguards and headlamps, the 4CS lent itself to use on the race-track while the 4CM had been designed exclusively for that purpose making it impossible to convert it for use in road races. You could see this as soon as you looked at the car with its compact single-seater bodywork, naked wheels and minute windscreen. The weight had been cut down to 580 kg compared to the 700 of the CS and the CTR, something which caused problems for the chassis which in certain circumstances tended to flex. In order to keep costs down, Ernesto Maserati used parts from mass-produced Fiats such as the steering-wheel, the gearbox, the steering box, the steering column, but the build quality of these parts came up to Maserati standards. The first two examples of the 4CM (equipped from the start with hydraulic brakes) came out in 1932 alongside the 4CS. Similarly production began again after two years of inactivity when numerous improvements were made. The engine was uprated from 90 to 125 hp and the top speed rose from 185 to 210 kph. Alongside this car a more powerful (150 hp) and lighter (470 kg) version was prepared with aerodynamic bodywork designed by Giuseppe Furmanik and made by Viotti, in which Furmanik himself broke three international records in 1934 and 1935, recording average speeds of 131.43 kph and 146.415 (standing start kilometre and mile) and 222.634 (flying start kilometre).

Among the projects the Maseratis inherited from their brother Alfieri there was also that for a straight eight engine with a three-litre displacement (2991 cc) that, once realised, was to be installed in the 8C 3000 after being tested in two Tipo 26 M chassis. 220 hp developed at 5500 rpm and a top speed in the order of 220/240 kph enabled Luigi Fagioli to win, among other races, the Grand Prix de l'Automobile Club de France on the 11TH of June 1933.

## TECHNICAL SPECIFICATION

### ENGINE
front, longitudinal, straight eight

| | |
|---|---|
| Bore and stroke | 69 x 100 mm |
| Unitary displacement | 373.92 cc |
| Total displacement | 2991.42 cc |
| Valvegear | twin overhead camshafts |
| Number of valves | two per cylinder |
| Compression ratio | 5.26:1 |
| Fuel system | 1 Weber 55AS1 carburettor Roots supercharger |
| Ignition | single, Bosch or Scintilla magneto |
| Cooling | water, centrifugal pump and radiator |
| Lubrication | dry sump, pressurised with delivery and scavenging pump |
| Maximum power | 220 hp at 5500 rpm |
| Specific power output | 73.54 hp/litre |

### TRANSMISSION
| | |
|---|---|
| Driven wheels | rear |
| Clutch | multiple dry-plate |
| Gearbox | four speeds + reverse |

### BODYWORK
two-seater racing

### ROLLING CHASSIS
| | |
|---|---|
| Chassis | longerons and cross members |
| Front suspension | rigid axle, leaf springs friction dampers |
| Rear suspension | live axle, leaf springs friction dampers |
| Brakes | mechanically actuated drums |
| Steering | worm and gear |
| Fuel tank | 195 l |
| Tyres front/rear | 5.50-19 / 6.00-19 |
| Tyres front/rear | 5.50-19 / 6.00-19 |

### DIMENSIONS AND WEIGHT
| | |
|---|---|
| Wheelbase | 2750 mm |
| Tracks front/rear | 1340 / 1360 mm |
| Length | – |
| Width | – |
| Height | – |
| Dry weight | 850 kg |
| Weight to power ratio | 3.86 kg/hp |

### PERFORMANCE AND PRODUCTION
| | |
|---|---|
| Maximum speed | 220-240 kph |
| Units produced | 2 |

# 8C 3000                                1932

The development plan for the front-wheel drive 2500 foresaw the use of a new and more powerful eight-cylinder, three-litre engine, which Alfieri Maserati conceived and started to design but did not manage to complete. After his sudden death at the beginning of 1932, his brother Ernesto picked up the project and began to build the engine, which was reminiscent of engines used in the 26 series cars but was also similar to the 1.5-litre engine from the 4C that was being prepared at the same time with the same size bore and stroke of 69 mm x 100 mm. Other parts were also cast in elektron, from the fuel tank (which also served to stiffen the chassis), to the brake shoes, the brake drums and so forth, which led to a flattering initial weight of 725 kg, but which later increased to 850 as a result of other modifications which gradually became necessary. When the prototype of the 2500 T.A. was put to one side as a result of the complexity of the project, two examples of the new engine were installed in two-seater chassis's from the 26M series and after a few races in which they took part in 1932 but which it has proved difficult to find records of, given the car's resemblance to the 8C 2800, in 1933 the 8C 3000s were entrusted to Tim Birkin and Giuseppe Campari. And it was precisely the latter who was to add yet another win to the Maserati's list of victories when he won the French Grand Prix at Montlhéry. Another 8C 3000 engine was purchased by Count Luigi Premoli, who fitted it to a Bugatti tipo 35 chassis giving birth to a hybrid car known as the B.M.P. (Bugatti, Maserati, Premoli) with which he won the Colli Torinesi hillclimb in 1932 and again in 1934, together with the Varese-Campo dei Fiori, the Coppa Ascoli and the Lecco-Maggio.

Piero Taruffi, in the cockpit of his Maserati 4C 2500 about to get away from 8[TH] place on the grid for the 1934 Monaco Grand Prix (2 April). Problems with his engine prevented the Roman driver from finishing the race, won by Guy Moll in an Alfa Romeo Tipo B P3. To other Maseratis did, however, make it to the finish: Whitney Straight's 8CM, 7th, and the 8C 3000 of Eugenio Siena, 8th.

## TECHNICAL SPECIFICATION

### ENGINE
front, longitudinal, straight four

| | |
|---|---|
| Bore and stroke | 4C M 2000: 80 x 98 mm<br>4C-4CM 2500: 84 x 112 mm |
| Unitary displacement | 4CM 2000: 492.60 cc<br>4C-4CM 2500: 620.67 cc |
| Total displacement | 4CM 2000: 197040 cc<br>4C-4CM 2500: 2482.71 cc |
| Valvegear | double overhead camshafts |
| Number of valves | two per cylinder |
| Compression ratio | 5.8:1 |
| Fuel system | 4CM 2000: 1 Weber 55AS1 carburettor / 4C-4CM 2500: 55DCO carburettor Roots supercharger |
| Ignition | single, Scintilla magneto |
| Cooling | water, centrifugal pump and radiator |
| Lubrication | dry sump, pressurised with delivery and scavenging pump |
| Maximum power | 4CM 2000: 165 hp a 5500 rpm<br>4C-4CM 2500: 195 at 5300 |
| Specific power output | 4CM 2000: 83.73 hp/litre<br>4C-4CM 2500: 78.543 |

### TRANSMISSION
| | |
|---|---|
| Driven wheels | rear |
| Clutch | 4CM 2000: single dry-plate<br>4C-4CM 2500: multiple dry-plate |
| Gearbox | four speeds + reverse |

### BODYWORK
| | |
|---|---|
| | 4CM 2000: *single-seater*<br>*4C 2500: two-seater racing or sport*<br>*4CM 2500: single-seater* |

### ROLLING CHASSIS
| | |
|---|---|
| Chassis | longerons and cross members |
| Front suspension | rigid axle, leaf springs friction dampers |
| Rear suspension | live axle, leaf springs friction dampers |
| Brakes | drums |
| | 4CM 2000 and 4CM 2500: hydraulically actuated<br>4C 2500: mechanically actuated |
| Steering | worm and gear |
| Fuel tank | – |
| Front tyres | 4CM 2000: 5.25:17-6.00:16<br>4C-4CM 2500: 5.00-19 |
| Rear tyres | 4CM 2000: 5.25:17-6.00:16<br>4C-4CM 2500: 5.00-19 |

### DIMENSIONS AND WEIGHT
| | |
|---|---|
| Wheelbase | 4CM 2000: 2400 mm<br>4C-4CM 2500: 2450 mm |
| Tracks front/rear | 1200 / 1200 mm |
| Length | – |
| Width | – |
| Height | – |
| Dry weight | 4CM 2000: 580 kg<br>4C 2500: 700 / 4CM 2500: 600 |
| Weight to power ratio | 4CM 2000: 3.51 kg<br>4C 2500: 3.58 / 4CM 2500: 3.07 |

### PERFORMANCE AND PRODUCTION
| | |
|---|---|
| Maximum speed | 4CM 2000: 215 kph<br>4C 2500-4CM 2500: 220 |
| Units produced | 2 |

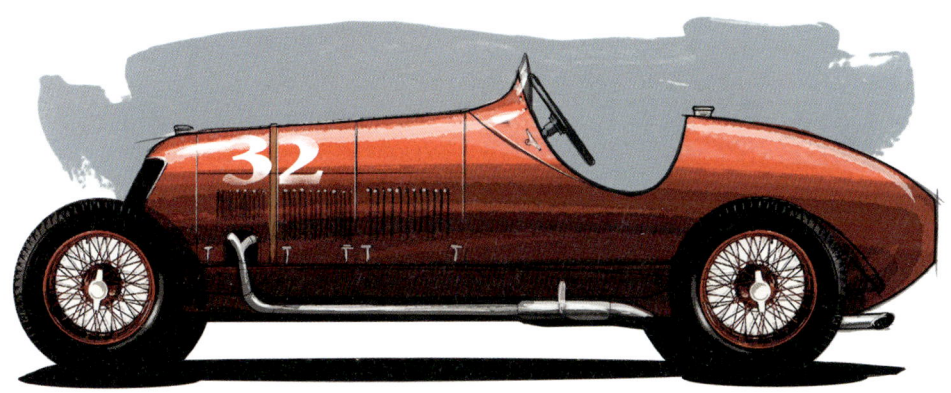

# 4C M 2000 - 4C 2500 - 4C M 2500     1933

In order to expand the range of four-cylinder models, which in 1932 had recorded their first victories and demonstrated their great potential, Ernesto Maserati designed two new engines, a 2.0-litre and 2.5-litre, with the bore and stroke increased respectively to 80x98 and 84x112 mm and the usual basic mechanical configuration: a supercharger and valvegear with two overhead camshafts. The first of the two engines was fitted to a car of which just a single example was built in 1933, in practice a 4CM with an increased displacement that was entrusted to Campari and immediately finished 3RD at Livorno in the Circuito del Montenero, but subsequently its race performance did not live up to expectations. Sold to Ippolito Berrone, over the following years it obtained a few results in minor races. The career of the car equipped with the 2500 cc engine was similarly chequered; it too was built in a single example but with two different bodies being used, firstly a two-seater Sport and then a single-seater Corsa (hence the two different names 4C 2500 and 4C M 2500). The wheel of this versatile machine was take by drivers of the calibre of Taruffi, Zehender, De Villapadierna, Farina, Trossi and Hartmann. Only Farina however drove to any great effect in the 1935 season, finishing 2ND in the Circuito di Bergamo and 3RD in the Circuito di Biella. Both the 2000 and the 2500 are to be considered as among the less successful cars in the history of Maserati. Leaving aside their indubitably valid technical specification, they paid the price for a error of judgement whereby they had very few commercial prospects. The two-litre displacement did not allow the 4CM 2000 to compete in the Voiturettes category while that of the 2500 was insufficient to allow it to be competitive in Grands Prix. In both sectors, in fact, Maserati was committed to racing with different and progressively more effective vehicles.

A crowd of bystanders and enthusiasts surround the Maserati 4C 1500 that Fernando Righetti has just driven to 3ᴿᴰ place in the Voiturettes Category (not the lack of mudguards) in the Circuito di Modena on the 20ᵀᴴ of September 1936. Apart from this fine result, there was plenty to celebrate that day as the winner of the race was the other Maserati 6 CM driven by Carlo Felice Trossi.

## TECHNICAL SPECIFICATION

### ENGINE

front, longitudinal, straight four

| | |
|---|---|
| Bore and stroke | 69 x 100 mm |
| Unitary displacement | 373.92 cc |
| Total displacement | 1495.71 cc |
| Valvegear | twin overhead camshafts |
| Number of valves | two per cylinder |
| Compression ratio | 6:1 |
| Fuel system | 1 Weber 48 ASS carburettor Roots supercharger |
| Ignition | single, with Scintilla or Bosch magneto |
| Cooling | water, centrifugal pump and radiator |
| Lubrication | dry sump, pressurised with delivery and scavenging pump |
| Maximum power | 115 hp at 5000 rpm |
| Specific power output | 76.88 hp/litre |

### TRANSMISSION

| | |
|---|---|
| Driven wheels | rear |
| Clutch | single dry-plate |
| Gearbox | four speeds + reverse |

### BODYWORK

two-seater sport

### ROLLING CHASSIS

| | |
|---|---|
| Chassis | longerons and cross members |
| Front suspension | rigid axle, leaf springs friction dampers |
| Rear suspension | live axle, leaf springs friction dampers |
| Brakes | mechanically actuated drums (from 1935 hydraulically actuated) |
| Steering | worm and gear |
| Fuel tank | 90 l |
| Front tyres | 5.25-17 (dal 1935 6.25-16) |
| Rear tyres | 5.25-17 (from 1935 6.25-16) |

### DIMENSIONS AND WEIGHT

| | |
|---|---|
| Wheelbase | 2700 mm |
| Tracks front/rear | 1200 / 1200 mm |
| Length | – |
| Width | – |
| Height | – |
| Dry weight | 630 kg |
| Weight to power ratio | 5.47 kg/hp |

### PERFORMANCE AND PRODUCTION

| | |
|---|---|
| Maximum speed | 170 kph |
| Units produced | 6 |

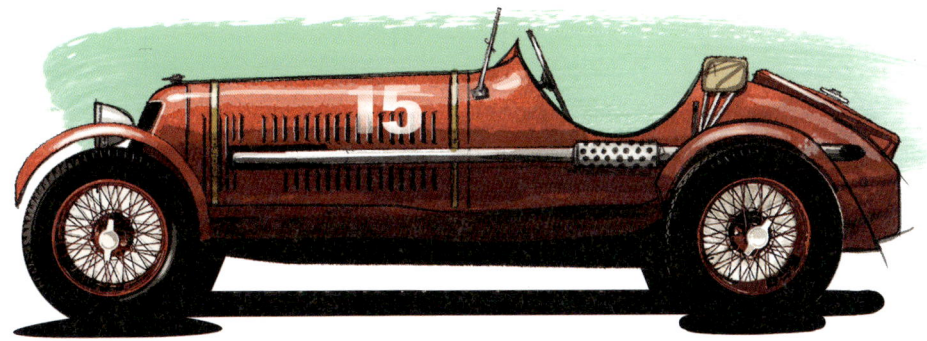

# 4C S 1500                                1933

Towards the end of 1932 a new 4-cylinder Maserati saw the light of day, thought to be the latest development in the 26 series, it was really a development of the 4CS-4CM car with an 1100 cc engine bored out to 1500. The increase in displacement was obtained by increasing the bore from 65 to 69 mm (a size difference which had already been tried out on the 8C 2800 of 1931) and the stroke was increased from 82 to 100 mm. As had been the case with the 1100, two versions of the 1500 were also planned - a two-seater for road racing (4CS) and a single-seater for circuit races (4CM) but with the possibility - which had already been done before, amid protests from purists that this was just paying lip-service to observance of the technical specification rules - of converting the cars from one version to the other. The engine of the 4CS 1500 which was first to leave the factory in March 1933, had a power output of 115 hp at 5000 rpm and, weighing 630 kg instead of the 700 of the 1100, the car was able to reach a top speed of 170 kph. Even though the basic technical features of the car stayed the same - supercharged twin overhead cam - the 4CS benefitted from several updates including, in 1935, the use of hydraulic brakes and a reduction in wheel size from 17 to 16 inches and tyres which went from 5.27-17 to 6.25-16. This Maserati was less successful in races than the 4CM which it stood alongside in 1934 but it recorded some successes in minor competitions, including - in the series reserved for 1.5-litre Voiturette cars - the Circuito di Varese with Giovannino Lurani (1935) and the Circuito della Superba with Marazza (1937). But the 4CS showed its enormous potential in the 1936 Mille Miglia when the motorcycle ace Omobono Tenni, partnered by Guarino Bertocchi, came fifth overall, behind four cars with engines larger than 2 litres.

The 15TH of August 1034, 10TH edition of the Coppa Acerbo, Circuito di Pescara. Tazio Nuvolari is about to conquer second place overall in his Maserati 8CM, a car which that season was a source of both joy and sorrow for the Flying Mantuan. On the 22ND of April, at the Circuito di Alessandria, he was at the wheel of one when he was involved in a bad crash that kept him away from the tracks for some time.

## TECHNICAL SPECIFICATION

### ENGINE
front, longitudinal, straight eight

| | |
|---|---|
| *Bore and stroke* | 69 x 100 mm |
| *Unitary displacement* | 373.92 cc |
| *Total displacement* | 2991.42 cc |
| *Valvegear* | twin overhead camshafts |
| *Number of valves* | two per cylinder |
| *Compression ratio* | 5.26:1 / 6.35:1 |
| *Fuel system* | 1 Weber 55AS1 carburettor Roots supercharger |
| *Ignition* | single, Bosch or Scintilla magneto |
| *Cooling* | water, centrifugal pump and radiator |
| *Lubrication* | dry sump, pressurised with delivery and scavenging pump |
| *Maximum power* | 220-240 hp at 5500-5800 rpm |
| *Specific power output* | 73.54 – 80.22 hp/litre |

### TRANSMISSION
| | |
|---|---|
| *Driven wheels* | rear |
| *Clutch* | multiple dry-plate |
| *Gearbox* | four speeds + reverse |

### BODYWORK
*single-seater*

### ROLLING CHASSIS
| | |
|---|---|
| *Chassis* | longerons and cross members |
| *Front suspension* | rigid axle, leaf springs friction dampers |
| *Rear suspension* | live axle, leaf springs friction dampers |
| *Brakes* | hydraulically actuated drums |
| *Steering* | worm and gear |
| *Fuel tank* | 195 l |
| *Front tyres* | 5.50-19 / 6.00-19 |
| *Rear tyres* | 6.00-19 |

### DIMENSIONS AND WEIGHT
| | |
|---|---|
| *Wheelbase* | 2560 mm |
| *Tracks front/rear* | 1300 / 1300 mm |
| *Length* | – |
| *Width* | – |
| *Height* | – |
| *Dry weight* | 785 kg (from 1934: 750) |
| *Weight to power ratio* | 3.56 – 3.12 kg/hp |

### PERFORMANCE AND PRODUCTION
| | |
|---|---|
| *Maximum speed* | 220-250 kph |
| *Units produced* | 19 |

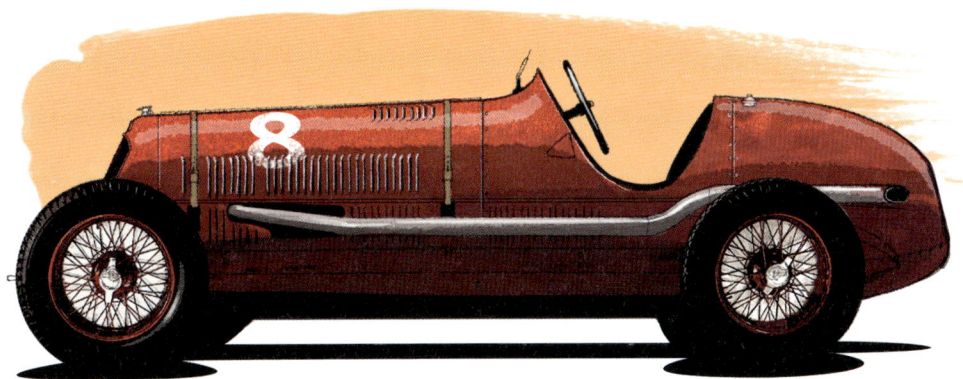

# 8C M 1933

The short but significant experience of the 8C 3000 encouraged Ernesto Maserati to give birth to another Grand Prix car, using the eight-cylinder, three-litre engine of the one that had preceded it (the bore and stroke were the same: 69 x 100 mm) but differing from it in the design of the bodywork and chassis. In fact, the two examples of the 8C 3000 which were built in 1932 used parts from the 26M in its two-seater guise which were available in the factory, while the new model called the 8CM, was inspired by the 4CM: the same chassis width, mm 620 and single-seater body. The way the car behaved on the road showed up the lack of stiffness in the chassis, a defect severely criticised by Campari, who refused to drive it in the Belgian GP in 1933. The chance was seized by Nuvolari whose "divorce" from Scuderia Ferrari was getting closer. He lined up for the start at Spa with the car after he had had the set up modified by his mechanic Decimo Compagnoni and the Maserati mechanic, Luigi Parenti. The stiffening of the chassis and a modification to the steering to make it less direct gave Nuvolari wings and he dominated the race, later also winning the Circuito del Montenero and the Nice GP. The car's success in races and the development work on the 8CM increased orders from racing customers to the extent that 19 cars were made. However in 1934 Mercedes and Auto Union came on the scene and the single-seater from Bologna, despite attempts to lighten it and keep it below the 750 kg maximum weight limit, began to lose ground on the international stage, even though it was still successful in less important races. Giuseppe Furminak successfully continued his hunt for speed records using not just the 4CM 1100 and 1500 but also the 8CM, with which he set new records in the D class (from 2000 to 3000 cc): standing start kilometre and mile, 150.846 and 165.532 kph; flying kilometre and mile, 249.653 and 248.546 kph.

Maserati mechanics and staff "escort" the Tazio Nuvolari's 6C-34 No. 8 (4TH place on the grid) to the start of the Italian Grand Prix at Monza on the 9TH of September 1934. The race was to bring the Mantuan yet another placing as he finished 5TH overall. At the wheel of the 6C-34, Nuvolari was to enjoy finish the season on a high: 3RD overall in Brno and two victories in the Circuito di Modena and the Coppa Principessa di Piemonte at Posillipo.

## TECHNICAL SPECIFICATION

### ENGINE
front, longitudinal, straight six

| | |
|---|---|
| Bore and stroke | 84 x 112 mm |
| Unitary displacement | 620.67 cc |
| Total displacement | 3724.06 cc |
| Valvegear | twin overhead camshafts |
| Number of valves | two per cylinder |
| Compression ratio | 6.4:1 |
| Fuel system | 1 Weber 55AS1 carburettor Roots supercharger |
| Ignition | single, Bosch or Scintilla magneto |
| Cooling | water, centrifugal pump and radiator |
| Lubrication | dry sump, pressurised with delivery and scavenging pump |
| Maximum power | 270 hp at 5300 rpm |
| Specific power output | 72.50 hp/litre |

### TRANSMISSION
| | |
|---|---|
| Driven wheels | rear |
| Clutch | multiple dry-plate |
| Gearbox | four speeds + reverse |

### BODYWORK
single-seater

### ROLLING CHASSIS
| | |
|---|---|
| Chassis | longerons and cross members |
| Front suspension | rigid axle, leaf springs friction dampers (in 1935 torsion bars) |
| Rear suspension | live axle, leaf springs friction dampers |
| Brakes | hydraulically actuated drums |
| Steering | worm and gear |
| Fuel tank | 170 l |
| Tyres front/rear | 5.50-18 / 6.50-18 |

### DIMENSIONS AND WEIGHT
| | |
|---|---|
| Wheelbase | 2650 mm |
| Tracks front/rear | 1300 / 1300 mm |
| Length | – |
| Width | – |
| Height | – |
| Dry weight | 750 kg |
| Weight to power ratio | 2.77 kg/hp |

### PERFORMANCE AND PRODUCTION
| | |
|---|---|
| Maximum speed | 250 kph |
| Units produced | 5 (+ 2 engines) |

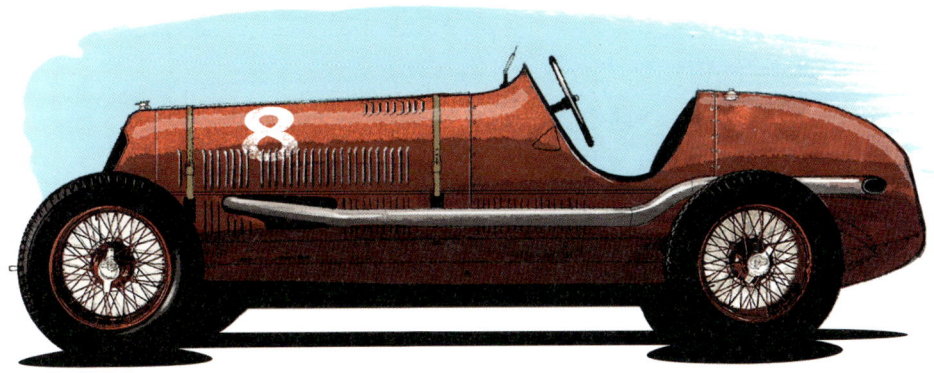

# 6C-34 1934

Ernesto Maserati was not convinced that he would be able to maintain the level of competitivity which he had achieved with the 8CM in the summer of 1933 so although he continued to do development work on it, he designed a completely new Grand Prix car to initially run alongside the 1934 car then gradually replace it, bearing in mind the new international formula based on a maximum weight limit of 750 kg. And, precisely because he was investigating every means of lightening the car, he abandoned the classic eight-cylinder layout and made the first six-cylinder engine in the history of the marque. The experience that he had gained from the 4CM and the genealogy of the fixed-head engines dictated the engine configuration, using a crankcase in elektron and the cylinder block cast in three groups of two. Using the same bore and stroke as that of the 4C and 4CM 2500 (84 x 112 mm) this gave the substantial displacement of 3724.06 cc and a power output of 270 hp, that is, 30 more than the eight-cylinder engine with a weight saving of 13 kg. Fitted to a traditional chassis with stiff suspension, the 6C-34 (6 cylinders, 1934) was born and it took part in the Italian GP just a few days after leaving the factory. Nuvolari, who was slowed by problems with the brakes, came fifth, then he was third at Brno, behind only two of the eight German cars from the dominant marques in the race, Auto Union (with Stuck) and Mercedes (Caracciola) but ended up winning the last two races of the year on the Modena and Naples race-tracks. Development of the 6C-34 continued in fits and starts: at the beginning of 1935 Nuvolari - about to return to the Scuderia Ferrari ranks - managed to test a version fitted with independent front suspension, which, however, did not live up to expectations. Then, as happened many times in Maserati's history, the concentrated effort on the production of a new eight-cylinder V-configured engine led to a reduction in the number of improvements and refinements made to the 6C-34. In 1935 a two-seater version was made which was given to Varzi to use in the Mille Miglia but ended in his retirement.

Circuit di Modena, 15 September 1935, the unmistakeable radiator grille of the Maserati 4 CM identifies the cars of Ippolito Berrone, with Ettore Bianco giving chase. It was to be Berrone who went on to win the race in the Voiturettes Category, demonstrating once again the competitiveness of the Trident's cars in the 1100 and 1500 cc classes. It was no coincidence that August Tuffanelli had won with the same car and in the same category in the Circuito del Montenero at Livorno.

## TECHNICAL SPECIFICATION

### ENGINE
front, longitudinal, straight four

| | |
|---|---|
| *Bore and stroke* | 69 x 100 mm |
| *Unitary displacement* | 373.92 cc |
| *Total displacement* | 1495.71 cc |
| *Valvegear* | double overhead camshafts |
| *Number of valves* | two per cylinder |
| *Compression ratio* | 6:1 |
| *Fuel system* | Weber 48 ASS or 55ASI carburettor, Roots supercharger |
| *Ignition* | single, with Scintilla magneto |
| *Cooling* | water, centrifugal pump and radiator |
| *Lubrication* | dry sump, pressurised, with delivery and scavenge pumps |
| *Maximum power* | 130-150 hp at 5600-6000 rpm |
| *Specific power output* | 86.91 hp/litre |

### TRANSMISSION
| | |
|---|---|
| *Driven wheels* | rear |
| *Clutch* | single dry-plate |
| *Gearbox* | 4 speeds + reverse |

### BODYWORK
single-seater

### ROLLING CHASSIS
| | |
|---|---|
| *Chassis* | longerons and cross members |
| *Front suspension* | rigid axle, leaf springs friction dampers (in 1937 independent torsion bar) |
| *Rear suspension* | live axle, leaf springs friction dampers |
| *Brakes* | hydraulically actuated drums |
| *Steering* | worm and gear |
| *Fuel tank* | 115 litres |
| *Tyres front/rear* | 5.25-17 / 6.00-16 |

### DIMENSIONS AND WEIGHT
| | |
|---|---|
| *Wheelbase* | 2400 mm (from 1937 - 2420) |
| *Tracks front/rear* | 1200 / 1200 mm |
| *Length* | – |
| *Width* | – |
| *Height* | – |
| *Dry weight* | 580 kg |
| *Weight to power ratio* | 4.46/3.86 kg/hp |

### PERFORMANCE AND PRODUCTION
| | |
|---|---|
| *Maximum speed* | kph 190-230 kph |
| *Units produced* | 12 |

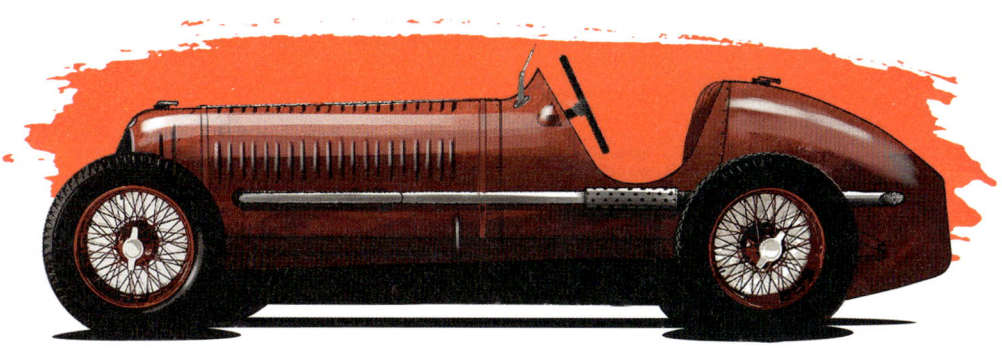

# 4C M 1500 1934

The first 4-cylinder 1500 built in the autumn of 1932 and intended as the power unit for the 4C M single-seater was sold to Count Theo Rossi di Montelera who fitted it to his Cinti speedboat, called Montelera XII. On the 26TH and 29TH of October he twice broke the speed record for the mile, raising it to 91.555 kph. In the meantime the factory in Bologna gave precedence to the Sport version of the 1500, equipped with a less powerful and lively engine, produced between 1933 and 1936. The 4C M first saw the light of day in August 1934 and was intended to be a star in races of its class. With a power output which grew from 130 hp to 150 hp and a weight of 580 kg, compared to the 630 kg of the 4C S, it had a top speed between 190 and 230 kph depending on the configuration of the car. It was produced until 1938 and benefitted from several updates (including independent torsion bar suspension) but it became less competitive compared to the English E.R.A., which had the advantage of a more constant and swifter development programme. In 1934 the 4C M won the Voiturettes' Eifelrennen at the Nürburgring with Castelbarco at the wheel and the Masaryk GP at Brno with Farina and those were its most significant successes. Over time the single-seater was used as a basis for specials by private drivers, including Castelbarco and Ruesch but above all by Furmanik, with a view to further record attempts, as he had already done with the 4C M 1100. Using his design which was developed by the Centro Sperimentale Aeronautico at Guidonia, Viotti "clothed" the chassis with an extremely streamlined enclosure-type body, with a large rear stabilizing fin that merged with the cockpit's windshield. The engine, which was specially tuned, developed 200 hp at 7000 rpm. On the 2ND of June 1937 on the Firenze-Mare autostrada, Furmanik broke the standing start kilometer and mile records for Class F cars (up to 1500 cc) with an average speed of 144.3 and 168.8 kph respectively and on the 3RD of June he broke the flying kilometer record with a speed of 238.568 kph.

The French driver of Argentine origins George Raphaël "Raph" seen at full speed in his Maserati V8 RI with which he competed in a number of races in the 1936b season, including the Vanderbilt Cup (12 October) as seen in this photo. It was, however, Nuvolari who in that edition of the race was to write one of the most stunning chapters in his incomparable career, winning the prestigious trophy today concerve4d in the Museo Nicoli at Villafranca di Verona.

## TECHNICAL SPECIFICATION

### ENGINE
front, longitudinal, V8 (90°)

| | |
|---|---|
| Bore and stroke | 84 x 108 mm |
| Unitary displacement | 598.51 cc |
| Total displacement | 4788.08 cc |
| Valvegear | single overhead camshaft per cylinder bank |
| Number of valves | two per cylinder |
| Compression ratio | 5:1 |
| Fuel system | two Weber 55 carburettors Roots supercharger |
| Ignition | single, with Bosch or Scintilla magneto |
| Cooling | water, centrifugal pump and radiator |
| Lubrication | dry sump, pressurised, with delivery and scavenge pumps |
| Maximum power | 320 hp at 5300 rpm |
| Specific power output | 66.83 hp/litre |

### TRANSMISSION
| | |
|---|---|
| Driven wheels | rear |
| Clutch | multiple dry-plate |
| Gearbox | 4 speeds + reverse |

### BODYWORK
single-seater

### ROLLING CHASSIS
| | |
|---|---|
| Chassis | longerons and cross members |
| Front suspension | independent suspension, torsion bars, |
| | friction dampers |
| Rear suspension | independent suspension, leaf springs friction dampers (from 1936 live axle on chassis no. 4501) |
| Brakes | hydraulically actuated drums |
| Steering | worm and gear |
| Fuel tank | 180 litres |
| Tyres front/rear | 5.50-18 / 6.00-18 |

### DIMENSIONS AND WEIGHT
| | |
|---|---|
| Wheelbase | 2560 mm |
| Tracks front/rear | 1350/1370 mm |
| Length | – |
| Width | – |
| Height | – |
| Dry weight | 750 kg |
| Weight to power ratio | 2.34 kg/hp |

### PERFORMANCE AND PRODUCTION
| | |
|---|---|
| Maximum speed | 270-280 kph |
| Units produced | 4 |

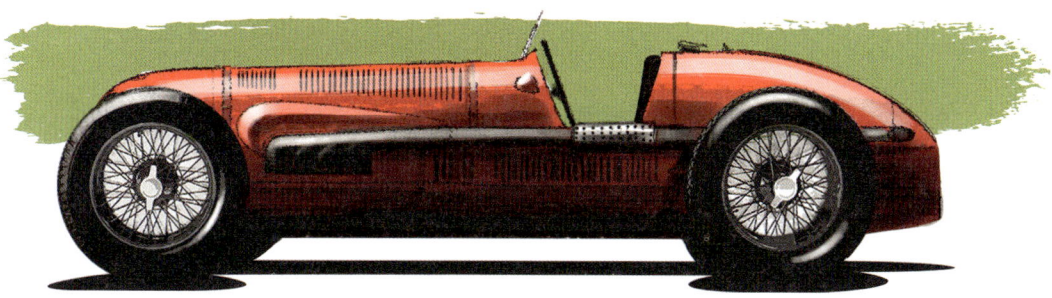

# V8 RI                                    1935

With Mercedes and Auto Union's dominance showing up the limitations of the 6C-34 and all the other "non-German" Grand Prix cars, Ernesto Maserati opted for a significant, not to say revolutionary technical change of direction with respect to the company's consolidated engineering traditions. Thus was born the V8 RI, a name that encapsulated the design characteristics of the innovative single-seater: a V8 engine and independent suspension. That engine, featuring extensive use of elektron and aluminium, was very light and compact, with integral heads and two banks of four cylinders, with a single overhead camshaft for each bank. The displacement was close to that of the V5 - 4788.08 cc against 4905.93 and the maximum power output was close to 330 hp. The chassis was also lighter compared with those that had been built hitherto in order to keep the car within the 750 kg weight limit imposed by the international sporting authorities from 1934 onwards. However, the most eye-catching innovation was the introduction of independent suspension rather than a rigid front axle and a rear live axle, characteristics that had been shared by all earlier Maseratis with the exception of the 2500 T.A. front-wheel drive prototype. The front suspension used torsion bars and the rear swing axles and semi-elliptic leaf-springs. Unfortunately it was precisely the rear suspension which was identified as the cause of serious roadholding problems that made the car uncompetitive. In 1936, a live axle was fitted to one of the Scuderia Torino's V8 RIs but failed to make a significant difference. The most significant result that this single-seater is remembered for was the Philippe Étancelin's win in the Pau Grand Prix in 1936. Two of the four V8 RI cars built ended up in the USA where they were raced for many years, enjoying some success.

In the spring of 1936, the time was ripe for the 4 Cm to be replaced and to this end Maserati was working on an agile, innovative single-seater equipped with a 1,5 litre (1493.23 cc) straight six engine. The 6C M as it was officially known (the photo shows an example still in the factory courtyard in the summer of that year), was to prove to be one of the most successful cars in the Trident marque's history, capable of racking up victories through almost to the Second World War.

## TECHNICAL SPECIFICATION

### ENGINE
front, longitudinal, straight six

| | |
|---|---|
| Bore and stroke | 65 x 75 mm |
| Unitary displacement | 248.87 cc |
| Total displacement | 1493.23 cc |
| Valvegear | twin overhead camshafts |
| Number of valves | two per cylinder |
| Compression ratio | 6:1 |
| Fuel system | Weber 55AS1 carburettor (from 1937 55-5-DCO) |
| | Roots supercharger |
| Ignition | single, with Scintilla magneto |
| Cooling | water, centrifugal pump and radiator |
| Lubrication | dry sump, pressurised, with delivery and scavenging pumps |
| Maximum power | 155-175 hp at 6200-6600 rpm |
| Specific power output | 103.8-117.19 hp/litre |

### TRANSMISSION
| | |
|---|---|
| Driven wheels | rear |
| Clutch | single dry-plate |
| Gearbox | 4 speeds + reverse |

### BODYWORK
single-seater

### ROLLING CHASSIS
| | |
|---|---|
| Chassis | longerons and cross members |
| Front suspension | independent with torsion bars, leaf springs friction dampers |
| Rear suspension | live axle, leaf springs friction dampers |
| Brakes | hydraulically actuated drums |
| Steering | worm and gear |
| Fuel tank | 122 litres |
| Tyres front/rear | 5.00-16/ 5.25-17 |

### DIMENSIONS AND WEIGHT
| | |
|---|---|
| Wheelbase | 2490 mm |
| Tracks front/rear | 1200/1200 mm |
| Length | – |
| Width | – |
| Height | – |
| Dry weight | 650 kg |
| Weight to power ratio | 4.19-3.71 kg/hp |

### PERFORMANCE AND PRODUCTION
| | |
|---|---|
| Maximum speed | kph 210-230 kph |
| Units produced | 27 |

# 6C M                    1936

The meagre success the V8 RI had achieved despite its excellent mechanical specification came under Ernesto Maserati's close scrutiny when he was preparing a new 1.5 litre racing car to replace of the 4C M, which was having increasing difficulty keeping pace with the British E.R.A in the Voiturettes category. The spring of 1936 thus saw the introduction of the 6C M single-seater powered, as the name suggests, by a straight six that was groundbreaking as even though it was under-square like all Maserati engines built until then, the stroke was considerably shorter than on the engines that had come before it, allowing it to achieve higher crankshaft speeds (maximum power output was 175 hp and 6600 rpm) with less wear on the pistons. The chassis was not dissimilar to the one used on the V8 RI but cautiously used independent suspension only at the front end, and a classic live axle at the rear. The bodywork had some unusual features, being more rounded and aerodynamically more efficient, a feature that was to become more marked when the second series was produced in 1938 and faired body parts were used that started at the front suspension and extended down the sides of the car. The 6C M enjoyed a long series of wins which continued unchallenged until the Alfa Romeo 158 came on the scene. This was the formidable "Alfetta" that prompted Ernesto Maserati to create the 4C L in order to compete with it on equal terms. In any case, of the victories obtained by the 6C M, the most significant were with Trossi in 1936 (Eifelrennen, Circuito di Milano and Circuito di Modena); in 1937 with Trossi again (Naples), Severi (Targa Florio), Dreyfus (Florence), Rocco (Coppa Acerbo and Campione d'Italia), Villoresi (Brno); in 1938, with Rocco (Targa Florio), Marazza (Naples), Villoresi (Albi, Coppa Acerbo and Lucca), Cortese (Varese); in 1939 with Villoresi (South African GP), Cortese (Grosvenor GP), Teagno (Circuito del Montenero) and De Teffé (Gávea).

One of the most celebrated photos in Maserati's sporting history: Wilbur Shaw smiles from the cockpit of the 8C TF (3-litre straight eight) he drove to victory in the Indianapolis 500 Miles in 1940, repeating the remarkable result he had achieved in 1939 at the wheel of the same car. Shaw came close to a third consecutive victory in the 1941 edition, but a sudden wheel failure put an end to his race.

## TECHNICAL SPECIFICATION

### ENGINE
front, longitudinal, straight eight

| | |
|---|---|
| *Bore and stroke* | 69 x 100 mm |
| *Unitary displacement* | 373.92 cc |
| *Total displacement* | 2991.42 cc |
| *Valvegear* | twin overhead camshafts |
| *Number of valves* | two per cylinder |
| *Compression ratio* | 5:1 |
| *Fuel system* | two Memini MA12 carburettors 2 Roots superchargers |
| *Ignition* | single, with Scintilla magneto |
| *Cooling* | water, centrifugal pump and radiator |
| *Lubrication* | dry sump, pressurised, with delivery and scavenge pumps |
| *Maximum power* | 350-366 hp at 6300 rpm |
| *Specific power output* | 117-122.34 hp/litre |

### TRANSMISSION
| | |
|---|---|
| *Driven wheels* | rear |
| *Clutch* | multiple dry-plate |
| *Gearbox* | 4 speeds + reverse |

### BODYWORK
single-seater

### ROLLING CHASSIS
| | |
|---|---|
| *Chassis* | longerons and cross members |
| *Front suspension* | independent wheels, torsion bars, friction dampers |
| *Rear suspension* | live axle, leaf springs hydraulic dampers |
| *Brakes* | hydraulically actuated drums |
| *Steering* | worm and gear |
| *Fuel tank* | 204 litres |
| *Tyres front* | 5.50-19 / 6.00-19 |
| *Tyres front* | 6.50-19 |

### DIMENSIONS AND WEIGHT
| | |
|---|---|
| *Wheelbase* | 2720 mm |
| *Tracks front/rear* | 1350/1380 mm |
| *Length* | – |
| *Width* | – |
| *Height* | – |
| *Dry weight* | 780 kg |
| *Weight to power ratio* | 2.22-2.13 kg/hp |

### PERFORMANCE AND PRODUCTION
| | |
|---|---|
| *Maximum speed* | 290 kph |
| *Units produced* | 3 |

# 8C TF 1938

At the beginning of 1938 a new international racing formula came into force that, as has often happened before and after in the history of motor racing, was dreamed up by the sport's governing body with the aim of limiting the power of the engines and the performance of the cars. There was transition from a formula that in practice restricted only the maximum weight to 750 kg to one that split up the cars into those without superchargers and a maximum displacement of 4500 cc and supercharged cars with a maximum displacement of 3000 cc. Ernesto Maserati, who was free of economic constraints after the company had been bought by the Orsi family of Modena, designed the 8C TF (eight cylinders, fixed head), still choosing to use a supercharger and arriving at the 3000 cc displacement limit by using a bore and stroke of 69x100, identical to the 4C M and the 8C M. However, the engine had a number of original features starting with the configuration of two groups of four cylinders, each of which had a separate fuelling system, but mounted on a single crankcase and cast in unit with the head. The chassis shared the same configuration as that of the 8C M, with independent suspension at the front and a live axle at the rear. The bodywork reprised the rounded shape of the 6C M, with faired sections along the sides that covered the steering gear and the suspension. The car's excellent roadholding, the power of the engine, eventually over 365 hp at 6300 rpm, promised a useful racing career, which in fact is what it enjoyed, although not in European Grands Prix. The 8C TF took America by storm as the first car to be wholly manufactured, including chassis and engine, by an Italian factory, to win the Indianapolis 500 miles. This happened in 1939, when a single-seater bought by Mike Boyle's racing team (and renamed according to the USA fashion as the "Boyle Special") finished first with Wilbur Shaw at the wheel, who won again in 1940 and nearly achieved a third win in 1941. This particular 8C TF is among the most valuable items in the Indianapolis Speedway Museum.

28 May 1939, Coppa Principessa di Piemonte, Posillipo Alto: the English driver Peter Wakefield takes the chequered flag in his Maserati 4CL 1500. The Trident's domination was overwhelming, with Piero Taruffi finishing 2ND and Franco Cortese 3rd, both in Maserati's. A few weeks earlier, Gigi Villoresi had won the Targa Florio in a similar car.

## TECHNICAL SPECIFICATION

### ENGINE
front, longitudinal, straight four

| | |
|---|---|
| Bore and stroke | 78 x 78 mm |
| Unitary displacement | 372.71 cc |
| Total displacement | 1490.84 cc |
| Valvegear | double overhead camshafts |
| Number of valves | four per cylinder |
| Compression ratio | 6.5:1 |
| Fuel system | Weber 45 DCO carburettor Roots supercharger (from 1947: two Roots superchargers) |
| Ignition | single, with Scintilla magneto (from 1947: Magneti Marelli ST24 DAS) |
| Cooling | water, centrifugal pump and radiator |
| Lubrication | dry sump, pressurised, with delivery and scavenge pumps |
| Maximum power | 220 hp at 8000 rpm |
| Specific power output | 147.56 hp/litre |

### TRANSMISSION
| | |
|---|---|
| Driven wheels | rear |
| Clutch | multiple dry-plate |
| Gearbox | four speeds + reverse |

### BODYWORK
single-seater

### ROLLING CHASSIS
| | |
|---|---|
| Chassis | longerons and cross members (from 1947: also a tubular chassis) |
| Front suspension | independent, torsion bars, friction dampers |
| Rear suspension | live axle, leaf springs, friction dampers |
| Brakes | hydraulically actuated drums |
| Steering | worm and gear |
| Fuel tank | 100 l |
| Tyres front/rear | 5.00-17 / 6.00-16 |

### DIMENSIONS AND WEIGHT
| | |
|---|---|
| Wheelbase | 2500 mm |
| Tracks front/rear | 1250-1272 mm |
| Length | – |
| Width | – |
| Height | – |
| Dry weight | 630 kg |
| Weight to power ratio | 2.86 kg/hp |

### PERFORMANCE AND PRODUCTION
| | |
|---|---|
| Maximum speed | 235-250 kph |
| Units produced | 15 |

# 4CL 1939

Firstly Alfa Romeo with the 158 and then Mercedes with the W165 gained strong footholds in the Voiturettes category at the expense of the Maserati 6C M, making its replacement indispensable. Ernesto Maserati took the company in a new direction in designing the 4CL (4 Cylinder in-Line) powered by 1.5-litre engine with perfectly square architecture (bore and stroke of 78 x 78 mm). This configuration, which permitted very high engine speeds (the maximum power output of 220 was produced at 8000 rpm), required new valvegear with the usual double overhead camshafts actuating four valves per cylinder. The chassis recalled that of the 6CM, with independent suspension at the front and a live axle at the rear. An example of the 4CL was fitted with fully faired aerodynamic bodywork, realised in collaboration with Stabilimenti Farina and entered for the 1939 Tripoli GP, in which Gigi Villoresi recorded the best qualifying time at an average speed of 212.623 kph. He started from pole position by immediately broke his gearbox and head to retire. The standard version, with bodywork inspired by the Trident's earlier single-seaters, but even sleeker and more elegant, benefitted from constant development and - produced in 15 examples - enjoyed great racing success, both in the year preceding Italy's joining the Second World War and in those immediately following the conflict. In 1939, Peter Wakefield won the Circuito di Napoli and the Picardy and Albi GPs, while Villoresi was first at Abbazia and in the Targa Florio, which he won again in 1940. 1946 saw victories for Villoresi (Nice), Nuvolari (Albi), Pelassa (Peña Rhin) and Sommer (Marseille, Saint-Etienne, Saint-Cloud, Roubaix and Paris). 1947 was similarly successful, above all with Villoresi (Nîmes, Nice, Strasbourg and Lausanne) but in the meantime, the 4CL had been flanked by a more evolved version destined to take its place, the 4CL T.

The natural heir to the 8C TF, the 8CL, again powered by the straight eight with a displacement that fell within the three-litre limit (2981.69 cc) capable of producing a maximum power output of 430 hp at 6800 rpm, was produced in just two examples. The photo shows the one built for an Argentinian team in view of it participation in the 1940 edition of the Indianapolis 500 Miles. Driven by Raúl Riganti, the car failed to qualify.

## TECHNICAL SPECIFICATION

### ENGINE
front, longitudinal, straight eight

| | |
|---|---|
| Bore and stroke | 78 x 78 mm |
| Unitary displacement | 372.71 cc |
| Total displacement | 2981.69 cc |
| Valvegear | twin overhead camshafts |
| Number of valves | four per cylinder |
| Compression ratio | 6.5:1 |
| Fuel system | Two Memini twin-choke car-burettors (from 1946 Memini MA12) |
| | 2 Roots superchargers |
| Ignition | single, with Scintilla magneto |
| Cooling | water, centrifugal pump and radiator |
| Lubrication | dry sump, pressurised, with delivery and scavenge pumps |
| Maximum power | 415-430 hp at 6400-6800 rpm |
| Specific power output | 139.18-144.21 hp/litre |

### TRANSMISSION
| | |
|---|---|
| Driven wheels | rear |
| Clutch | multiple dry-plate |
| Gearbox | 4 speeds + reverse |

### BODYWORK
single-seater

### ROLLING CHASSIS
| | |
|---|---|
| Chassis | longerons and cross members |
| Front suspension | independent, torsion bars friction dampers |
| Rear suspension | live axle, leaf springs friction dampers |
| Brakes | hydraulically actuated drums |
| Steering | worm and gear |
| Fuel tank | 180 litres |
| Tyres front/rear | 5.50-19 / 6.50-19 |

### DIMENSIONS AND WEIGHT
| | |
|---|---|
| Wheelbase | 2790 mm |
| Tracks front/rear | 1350/1380 mm |
| Length | – |
| Width | – |
| Height | – |
| Dry weight | 780 kg |
| Weight to power ratio | 1.87-1.81 kg/hp |

### PERFORMANCE AND PRODUCTION
| | |
|---|---|
| Maximum speed | 280-305 kph |
| Units produced | 2 |

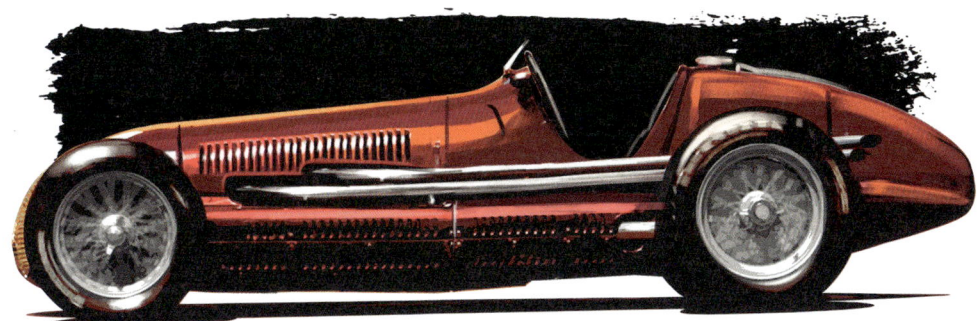

# 8CL
# 1940

Between 1939 and 1940 Maserati moved its headquarters from Bologna to Modena, where the Orsi family, who had bought the Trident company, lived. While production of the 4CL carried on normally, Ernesto Maserati designed a three-litre car which he thought would take the place of the 8C TF, which, although it had dominated racing at Indianapolis for a number of years at that time, had shown signs of mechanical fragility. The engine of the new single-seater, called the 8CL (straight eight), was very different from the one fitted to the 8C TF and other traditional Maserati long stroke engines, as it had exactly the same square measurements as the more advanced 4CL, with a bore and stroke of 78x78 mm. Similarities with the 1500 and 8C TF itself can be found in the conformation of the cylinders in two groups of four cast in-unit with the head, separate fuelling and twin cam valvegear with four valves per cylinder. The maximum power output reached at 6800 rpm was 430 hp, while the top speed was in excess of 300 kph. The chassis, with independent suspension at the front and live axle at the rear, differed mainly in the wheelbase which had been increased from 2720 to 2790 mm and in the lower height of the engine. The bodywork reprised the design of the 8C TF, with its large radiator grille and its substantial side fairings. Of the two cars that were made, one, which was commissioned by an Argentinian racing team for the driver Raúl Riganti, failed to qualify for Indianapolis in 1940 due to an accident, after which it was rebuilt before ending its days in South America without achieving any significant results. The other car, which was built shortly after the end of the war for the Scuderia Milan racing team, had its debut in 1946 at Indianapolis with Villoresi at the wheel, who, after starting in 28TH place after a poor qualifying session, managed to finish fourth and missed a place on the podium only because he had to stop three times to replace the magneto. The same single-seater had better luck in the hands of Farina, who won the 1948 Mar del Plata GP in Argentina.

The 11TH of May 1947, Circuit di Piacenza. An historical date as it was marked by the first race for a Ferrari-badged car, the 125 S, driven by Franco Cortese. However, among the entrants there was also Guido Barbieri with a Maserati 6C S-41 who in the photo can be seen the Maserati-powered Fiat of Giovanni Bracco on the street circuit's start line straight. It was to be Barbieri who won the race.

## TECHNICAL SPECIFICATION

### ENGINE
front, longitudinal, straight six

| | |
|---|---|
| Bore and stroke | 65 x 75 mm |
| Unitary displacement | 248.87 cc |
| Total displacement | 1493.23 cc |
| Valvegear | double overhead camshafts |
| Number of valves | two per cylinder |
| Compression ratio | 5:1 |
| Fuel system | three twin-choke Weber carburettors |
| Ignition | single |
| Cooling | water, centrifugal pump and radiator |
| Lubrication | pressurised, with delivery and scavenge pumps |
| Maximum power | 90 hp at 5300 rpm |
| Specific power output | 60.27 hp/litre |

### TRANSMISSION
| | |
|---|---|
| Driven wheels | rear |
| Clutch | single dry-plate |
| Gearbox | 4 speeds + reverse |

### BODYWORK
two-seater, sport

### ROLLING CHASSIS
| | |
|---|---|
| Chassis | steel beams |
| Front suspension | independent, torsion bars, friction dampers |
| Rear suspension | live axle, leaf springs friction dampers |
| Brakes | hydraulically actuated drums |
| Steering | worm and gear |
| Fuel tank | 100 litres |
| Tyres front/rear | - |

### DIMENSIONS AND WEIGHT
| | |
|---|---|
| Wheelbase | 2750 mm |
| Tracks front/rear | - |
| Length | – |
| Width | – |
| Height | – |
| Dry weight | 750 kg |
| Weight to power ratio | 8.33 kg/hp |

### PERFORMANCE AND PRODUCTION
| | |
|---|---|
| Maximum speed | 170 kph |
| Units produced | 1 |

# 6C S-41                                    1941

In the second half of the 1930s Ernesto Maserati was eager to introduce a new Sport model based on the rolling chassis of the 6C M, which was enjoying increasing success. He was inspired by what had been done with the 26, 26 B and 26 M cars. The idea, which was not pursued initially due to the enormous amount of work the small factory was undertaking, was taken up again during the war, when all racing was suspended but design work carried on, and this seed was to bear fruit years later. The design provided for use of the six-cylinder, 1.5-litre engine from the 6C M in two versions – neither fitted with superchargers. One was equipped with the Trident's classic double overhead camshaft valvegear, while the other had a single overhead camshaft and a reduced power output, perhaps in view of its use in a road-going car. Bearing in mind the understandable difficulties of wartime, only the twin-cam design was pursued. A prototype was made with the engine fitted to a chassis made of steel beams, the work of Cajani the chassis-maker. It was road-tested in 1941 and subsequently put to one side. After the war, development work began again with the contribution of the engineer Alberto Massimino alongside Ernesto Maserati. The only car made (known, unofficially as the 6C S, standing for 6-cylinder Sport) was powered by a one and a half litre engine based on the one used in the 6C M but without a supercharger and a maximum power output of 90 hp. The bodywork, with its all-embracing lines, indicated that special attention had been devoted to aerodynamics. The weight was limited to 750 kg and the top speed was nearly 170 kph. The car was sold to Guido Barbieri in co-ownership with Gigi Villoresi, to whom the engine belonged. Both men raced the car and both had a win – Barbieri in the Circuito di Mantova and Villoresi in the Circuito di Voghera. Barbieri continued to use it in races in 1947, winning in Piacenza, Novara and Voghera.

Like many other Italian firms, during the Second World War, Maserati had been obliged to convert its production facilities, but on the strength of its long experience in the production of sparkplugs, batteries and accumulators, it was also able to built a three-wheeled electric truck with a maximum carrying capacity of 1,000 kg known as the EC10. The Trident marque was to remain active in this sector through to beyond the mid-1950s.

## TECHNICAL SPECIFICATION

| ENGINE | | PERFORMANCE | |
|---|---|---|---|
| Front | | *Carrying capacity* | |
| | | EC10 | 1000 kg |
| *Fuel system* | batteries | EC15 | 1500 kg |
| *Potenza massima* | – | EC20 | 2000 kg |
| | | EC35 | 3500 kg |
| **TRANSMISSION** | | BC20 | 2000 kg |
| *Driven wheels* | rear | | |
| | | **PRODUCTION** | |
| **BODYWORK** | | EC10 | 321 |
| *3-wheeled delivery vehicle* | | EC15 – EC20 – EC35 | 120 |
| | | BC20 | 1 |
| **WHEELS** | | | |
| EC10 | 3 | | |
| EC15 – EC20 – EC35 | 4 | | |
| BC20 | 4 | | |

# EC10 – EC15 – EC20 – EC35 – BC20    1942

When Italy entered the Second World War on the 10TH of June 1940, and all car racing was suspended, Ernesto Maserati did not stop producing new designs or experimenting with and testing prototypes of sports and racing cars, that prefigured models destined to be revived life when hostilities came to an end. In the meantime the company had to suspend car production and start producing machine tools – lathes, milling machines and grinding machines – thus venturing into new branch of engineering. At the same time, they increased production of electrical equipment and started large-scale manufacturing of batteries alongside that of sparking plugs. This soon proved to be very useful – you only have to think how difficult it was to use any motorized vehicle when fuel was rationed and difficult to get hold of in general. So it was that in 1941 an extremely interesting prototype called the EC10 was built. The name was an acronym for Elettrocarro (electrically-powered three-wheeled delivery vehicle with a load capacity of 10 quintals – 1 quintal = 100 kg) that was to be used for commercial delivery work. It was, to be more precise, a three-wheeled vehicle driven by the two rear wheels with the front wheel equipped with motorcycle-style front forks. This vehicle, of which 321 were produced, had a metal chassis equipped with a customisable loading bed, and was manufactured from 1942 to 1950. Another prototype also saw the light of day – a four-wheeled conversion of the EC10 known as the EC15, the 15 referring to the loading capacity 1500 kg. The load carrying capacity was increased in the subsequent EC20 and EC35 models that were part of a small range produced in 120 examples between 1943 and 1949, including a BC20 variation of which only one was made in the final year. Maserati batteries were not just used for land-bound vehicles, but also to power boats used on rivers and lakes.

Among the entrants for the 1947 edition of the Circuito di Piacenza, alongside the Maserati 6C S-41 driven by the winner Guido Barbieri, there was also another original car carrying the Trident badge, the 6C S-46 driven by Mario Angiolini to 3RD place overall; second place between the two Maserati's was taken by Fernando Righetti in a Fiat 1100.

## TECHNICAL SPECIFICATION

### ENGINE

front, longitudinal, straight six

| | |
|---|---|
| *Bore and stroke* | 65 x 75 mm |
| *Unitary displacement* | 248.87 cc |
| *Total displacement* | 1493.23 cc |
| *Valvegear* | double overhead camshafts |
| *Number of valves* | two per cylinder |
| *Compression ratio* | 5:1 |
| *Fuel system* | Ttree Weber double-choke carburettors |
| *Ignition* | single, with a Marelli ST95DAS distributor |
| *Cooling* | water, centrifugal pump and radiator |
| *Lubrication* | pressurised, with delivery and scavenge pumps |
| *Maximum power* | 110 hp at 5300 rpm |
| *Specific power output* | 73.66 hp/litre |

### TRANSMISSION

| | |
|---|---|
| *Driven wheels* | rear |
| *Clutch* | single dry-plate |
| *Gearbox* | 4 speeds + reverse |

### BODYWORK

*two-seater, sport*

### ROLLING CHASSIS

| | |
|---|---|
| *Chassis* | tubular steel |
| *Front suspension* | independent, torsion bars, friction dampers |
| *Rear suspension* | live axle, leaf springs friction dampers |
| *Brakes* | hydraulically actuated drums |
| *Steering* | worm and gear |
| *Fuel tank* | - |
| *Tyres front/rear* | 5.25-17 / 5.25-17 |

### DIMENSIONS AND WEIGHT

| | |
|---|---|
| *Wheelbase* | - |
| *Tracks front/rear* | - |
| *Length* | – |
| *Width* | – |
| *Height* | – |
| *Dry weight* | 750 kg |
| *Weight to power ratio* | 6.81 kg/hp |

### PERFORMANCE AND PRODUCTION

| | |
|---|---|
| *Maximum speed* | - |
| *Units produced* | 1 |

# 6C S-46                                1946

The company's efforts to produce the single-seater 4C L and develop what would become the A6 and in more general the problems they encountered immediately after the war, prevented Maserati from satisfying Mario Angiolini, the Bologna driver's request for them to build a second example of the 6C S that had done so well in races. The company handed over the commission and the relevant financing to a team led by Guerino Bertocchi who, with Cajani the chassis builder, created a new Sport 1.5. The car, which was produced privately outside the company's factory, should not have had, strictly speaking, the right to use the Maserati badge. However, as it was produced by employees and associates of the company, used a Maserati engine and was inspired by the Trident's traditional technology, the prototype was considered to all intents and purposes to be a Maserati and unofficially it was known as the 6C S, meaning 6 Cylinder Sport, to be in line with the car that came before it (the 6C S-41). It used the same twin-cam naturally aspirated engine developed from the one fitted to the 6C M. The most original feature of the car was the chassis which no longer consisted of longerons and cross-members but used tubular elements welded together, an idea which Maserati themselves would later perfect and use in the more sophisticated versions of the 4C L and others. The bodywork too was unusual in that so-called "ala spessa" (thick wing) styling was used with the mudguards integrated with the flanks of the car. The radiator grille also had a new design, one which was to be adopted by the company for production cars. The engine, fuelled by three twin-choke carburettors, had a power output of 110 hp and good performance, which Mario Angiolini nevertheless only managed to enjoy for a short period of time - in fact on the 15TH of May 1947 he went off the road during the Sassi-Superga race and was seriously injured. The car was later restored but there were no more significant results in its racing "career".

A celebrated image marks an epochal turning point in the history of Maserati, which since 1926 had focussed its attention on racing cars; 20 years later the A6 1500 was born, the first road-going car to carry the trident badge: A for the initial of Alfieri, 6 the number of cylinders and 1500 the displacement of the engine. The spectacular and extremely modern body was designed by Pinin Farina. An authentic milestone in automotive design, not only in Italy.

## TECHNICAL SPECIFICATION

### ENGINE
front, longitudinal, straight six

| | |
|---|---|
| Bore and stroke | 66 x 72.5 mm |
| Unitary displacement | 248.36 cc |
| Total displacement | 1488.21 cc |
| Valvegear | single overhead camshaft |
| Number of valves | two per cylinder |
| Compression ratio | 7.25:1 |
| Fuel system | 1 Weber 36DCR carburettor |
| Ignition | single, with Marelli ST95DAS distributor |
| Cooling | water, centrifugal pump and radiator |
| Lubrication | pressurised, with delivery and scavenge pumps |
| Maximum power | 65 hp at 4700 rpm |
| Specific power output | 43.67 hp/litre |

### TRANSMISSION
| | |
|---|---|
| Driven wheels | rear |
| Clutch | single dry-plate |
| Gearbox | 4 speeds + reverse |

### BODYWORK
2 door/2 seats Pinin Farina

### ROLLING CHASSIS
| | |
|---|---|
| Chassis | tubular with longerons and cross members |
| Front suspension | independent, coil springs, hydraulic shock absorbers |
| Rear suspesnion | live axle, leaf springs, Houdaille hydraulic dampers |
| Brakes | hydraulically actuated drums |
| Steering | worm and gear |
| Fuel tank | 55 litres |
| Tyres front/rear | 5.50-16 / 5.50-16 |

### DIMENSIONS AND WEIGHT
| | |
|---|---|
| Wheelbase | 2550 mm |
| Tracks front/rear | 1274/1252 mm |
| Length | 4100 mm |
| Width | 1560 mm |
| Height | 1350 mm |
| Dry weight | coupé 780-950 kg spider 800 kg |
| Weight to power ratio | 12-14.6 / 12.3 kg/hp (1927 – 6.09) |

### PERFORMANCE AND PRODUCTION
| | |
|---|---|
| Maximum speed | kph 146-153.5 kph |
| Units produced | 2 |

# A6 (1500 Gran Turismo) 1946

Work on a design for the creation of a 1.5 litre Sport and Gran Turismo car, already started by Ernesto Maserati in 1936, continued at intervals until the war years, when the Sport project gained substance, culminating in the 6C S prototype. Plans for an engine which was not to be exclusively used for racing were, however, completed in June 1943 but not taken forward to the executive stage as a result of the turn of events. The first name given to the car was the A6 TR, where A was the initial of Alfieri, the founder of the company, to whose memory the car was dedicated, 6 was the number of cylinders and TR stood for Testa Riportata (detachable cylinder head), meaning that it was separate from the cylinder block and not fixed as had been the case with previous Maserati engines. The project, which was renamed A6, was resumed after the liberation of Italy and towards the end of 1945, the engine was run on the text-bench and subjected to the first road-tests. The original configuration was a 6-cylinder light alloy engine with a detachable head, a displacement of 1488.21 cc (only slightly smaller than the 1493.23 of the 6C M) and a single overhead cam. The power output was limited to 65 hp, which still allowed the car to reach a top speed of 150 kph. The engine was mounted on a new tubular steel chassis, which had a cross-shaped central reinforcement panel, it was "dressed" by Pinin Farina with extraordinary bodywork that made the car, called the 1500 Gran Turismo in the catalogue, the star of the 1947 Geneva Motor Show. Everyone admired the irresistible dynamism of the car's lines, with its windscreen mounted half-way down the car, the teardrop shaped upper body with its pop-up Plexiglas roof and its retractable headlights. A futuristic prototype, a concept car, as we would say today, which showed the world the first road-going Maserati in complete harmony with the Italian car styling revolution. The A6 was too far ahead of its time, so in order to satisfy market needs which could not be ignored, the design had to be "reworked".

Introduced in 1939 and already highly successful prior to the outbreak of the war, the 4 CL remained one of the Trident's key models in 1946. The adoption of a new tubular chassis carrying the 1.5-litre straight four engine explains the letter T 'n the official nomenclature. In the photo, the 4 CL of Luigi Fagioli at the Nice Grand Prix in 1946, a race won by Gigi Villoresi in another 4 CL.

## TECHNICAL SPECIFICATION

### ENGINE

front, longitudinal, straight four

| | |
|---|---|
| Bore and stroke | 78 x 78 mm (4CLT50: 78 x 90 mm) |
| Unitary displacement | 372.71 cc (4CLT50: 430.05 cc) |
| Total displacement | 1490.84 cc (4CLT50: 1720.20 cc) |
| Valvegear | double overhead camshafts |
| Number of valves | four per cylinder |
| Compression ratio | 6:1 |
| Fuel system | Weber 50 DCO / 52DCO carburettor two Roots superchargers |
| Ignition | single, with Marelli ST24DAS magneto |
| Cooling | water, centrifugal pump and radiator |
| Lubrication | pressurized, dry sump with delivery and scavenge pumps |
| Maximum power | 220 hp at 6600 rpm (4CLT50: 290 hp at 7000 rpm) |
| Specific power output | 147.56 hp/litre (4CLT50: 168.58 hp/litre) |

### TRANSMISSION

| | |
|---|---|
| Driven wheels | rear |
| Clutch | multiple dry-plate |
| Gearbox | 4 speeds + reverse |

### BODYWORK

single-seater

### ROLLING CHASSIS

| | |
|---|---|
| Chassis | tubular with longerons and cross members |
| Front suspension | independent, coil springs, Houdaille hydraulic shock absorbers |
| Rear suspension | live axle, leaf springs, Houdaille hydraulic shock absorbers |
| Brakes | hydraulically actuated drums |
| Steering | worm and gear |
| Fuel tank | 190 litres |
| Tyres front | 5.25-17 / 5.00-17 |
| rear | 6.00-16 / 6.50-16 |

### DIMENSIONS AND WEIGHT

| | |
|---|---|
| Wheelbase | 2500 mm |
| Tracks front/rear | 1250/1200 mm |
| Length | – |
| Width | – |
| Height | – |
| Dry weight | 630 kg |
| Weight to power ratio | 2.86 kg/hp (4CLT48: 2.25 kg/hp ) (4CLT50: 2.17 kg/hp ) |

### PERFORMANCE AND PRODUCTION

| | |
|---|---|
| Maximum speed | 260-270 kph |
| Units produced | 29 |

# 4CL T – 4CL T-48 – 4CL T-50      1946

The single-seater 4CL, which had already recorded several wins in 1939 and 1940, proved to be still competitive immediately after the war, but both Ernesto Maserati and Alberto Massimino were aware that it needed further development. At the end of 1946, a chassis made of circular section tubes was constructed and fitted with the engine from the 4CL, this new combination being named the 4CL T (T = tubular). The car competed in the Argentinian *Temporada* and won twice with Villoresi but for a some time afterwards a more powerful version of the 4CL was preferred. The turning point came in 1948 when a new car was produced, that while referencing the 4CL represented a clear break. The tubular chassis had been improved, acquiring greater torsional stiffness which made it possible to maintain higher speeds in bends, thanks also to the use of a suspension system that, while retaining the independent set up at the front and the live axle at the rear, had been redesigned and made more efficient. The engine, after a lot of experimental work, was fitted with a two-stage fuel supply, with twin superchargers fitted at the front, and it put out 280 hp with a specific power output of 187.81 hp/litre – the highest ever attained in the history of Maserati. The bodywork, made by Medardo Fantuzzi, had more compact lines, emphasised by a new radiator grille that was mounted horizontally rather than vertically. While the 4CL T won the Grand Prix of Nations in Geneva and the Monaco Grand Prix with Farina at the wheel, the new 4CL T-48, began to accumulate an impressive list of competition record with about 40 wins in Europe and America with Ascari, Villoresi, Fangio and Farina and many other private drivers who continued to be successful until 1952. At that time the 4CL T-48 made way for the 4CL T-50 a more sophisticated version with a larger 1720.20 cc engine and a maximum power output of 290 hp, while other new models gradually began to extend the Trident's range of cars.

While it is true that the Maserati A6 1500 was conceived as a road car, many gentleman drivers of the time chose to race it. This was the case with Filippo and Giuseppe Tassara who presented themselves at scrutineering for the 1948 Mille Miglia at the wheel of this Pinin Farina coupé; they drove it beyond Rome before being forced to retire.

## TECHNICAL SPECIFICATION

### ENGINE
front, longitudinal, straight six

| | |
|---|---|
| Bore and stroke | 66 x 72.5 mm |
| Unitary displacement | 243.36 cc |
| Total displacement | 1488.21 cc |
| Valvegear | single overhead camshaft |
| Number of valves | two per cylinder |
| Compression ratio | 7.25:1 |
| Fuel system | 1 Weber 36DCR carburettor |
| Ignition | single, with Marelli ST95DAS distributor |
| Cooling | water, centrifugal pump and radiator |
| Lubrication | pressurised, with delivery and scavenge pumps |
| Maximum power | 65 hp at 4700 rpm |
| Specific power output | 43.67 hp/litre |

### TRANSMISSION
| | |
|---|---|
| Driven wheels | rear |
| Clutch | single dry-plate |
| Gearbox | 4 speeds + reverse |

### BODYWORK
2 door/ 2+2 seats

### ROLLING CHASSIS
| | |
|---|---|
| Chassis | tubular with longerons and cross members |
| Front suspension | independent, coil springs, Houdaile hydraulic shock absorbers |
| Rear suspension | live axle, leaf springs, Houdaille hydraulic shock absorbers |
| Brakes | hydraulically actuated drums |
| Steering | worm and gear |
| Fuel tank | 55 litres |
| Tyres front/rear | 5.00-16 / 5.50-16 |

### DIMENSIONS AND WEIGHT
| | |
|---|---|
| Wheelbase | 2550 mm |
| Tracks front/rear | 1274/1252 mm |
| Length | 4100 mm |
| Width | 1560 mm |
| Height | 1350 mm |
| Dry weight | coupé 780-950 kg spider 800 kg |
| Weight to power ratio | 12-14.6 / 12.3 kg/hp |

### PERFORMANCE AND PRODUCTION
| | |
|---|---|
| Maximum speed | 146-153.5 kph |
| Units produced | 59 |

# A6 (1500 GT) 1947

The prototype of the A6, sold under the name of the 1500 Gran Turismo, which had been so admired at the Geneva Motor Show in March 1947, immediately showed that, even though it was not only extraordinarily elegant but also innovative, changes were necessary to lend the production model less extreme styling and make it more suitable for everyday use. At the Paris Motor Show, which was held the following October, alongside the original model, Pinin Farina showed a first version of a modified car identified as the "Extra lusso", which had a different front end with a wider and lower radiator grille, headlights which were no longer retractable, but mounted in the mudguards, with oval rims, side windows with a larger surface area and a few more chromium-plated parts. But the final version of the A6 was seen at the Turin Motor Show in May 1948. Pinin Farina had redesigned the upper body, which now flowed into the tail section with a line that was immortalised by the berlinetta Cisitalia 202 that had appeared the previous year. The flanks, where the trim and the horizontal air intakes had been removed, looked perfectly smooth - a styling feature which was a lesson for other designers of the era rather than a mere example of good design. The split windscreen made the passenger compartment brighter, while the more generous dimensions of the bodywork made the promise in the manufacturer's advertising that it was a 2-4 seater more credible. Sixty-one examples of the car including one or two spider versions were made up to 1950 without substantial modifications. Customers were offered one unusual option - a choice in the design of the front end with either a vertical or horizontal radiator grille. This was the last time the Maserati brothers were involved in the creation of car from beginning to end as they had come to the end of their ten-year consultancy period which had been stipulated when they sold the company to the Orsi family. They were about to give birth to Osca. Alberto Massimino and Vittorio Bellentani who had previously assisted them, took over as the new technical managers.

Before becoming Ferrari's lead driver and winning two F1 World Championship title with the 500 F2 in 1952 and '53, Alberto Ascari raced for Maserati for over two seasons. Here he is seen at the wheel of the A6 GCS Sport 2000 at the Circuito di Modena in 1947 (28TH of September) where he recorded his first victory.

## TECHNICAL SPECIFICATION

### ENGINE
front, longitudinal, straight eight

| | |
|---|---|
| Bore and stroke | 72 x 81 mm (from 1948: 75 x 75 mm) |
| Unitary displacement | 329.79 cc (from 1948: 331,33 cc) |
| Total displacement | 1978.74 cc (from 1948: 1988.03 cc) |
| Valvegear | single overhead camshaft |
| Number of valves | two per cylinder |
| Compression ratio | 11:1 |
| Fuel system | 3 Weber 36DO4 carburettors |
| Ignition | single, with Marelli ST95DAS distributor |
| Cooling | water, centrifugal pump and radiator |
| Lubrication | pressurised, with delivery pump (from 1949: dry sump with delivery and scavenge pumps) |
| Maximum power | 130 hp at 6000 rpm (from 1949: 140 hp) |
| Specific power output | 65.69 hp/litre (from 1949: 70.42 hp/litre) |

### TRANSMISSION
| | |
|---|---|
| Driven wheels | rear |
| Clutch | single dry-plate |
| Gearbox | 4 speeds + reverse |

### BODYWORK
two-seater, sport or racing

### ROLLING CHASSIS
| | |
|---|---|
| Chassis | tubular with coil springs, Houdaille hydraulic shock absorbers |
| Rear suspension | live axle, leaf springs, Houdaille hydraulic shock absorbers |
| Brakes | hydraulically actuated drums |
| Steering | worm and gear |
| Fuel tank | 100 litres |
| Tyres front/rear | 5.00-16 / 5.50-15 |

### DIMENSIONS AND WEIGHT
| | |
|---|---|
| Wheelbase | 2310 mm |
| Tracks front/rear | 1210/1150 mm |
| Length | – |
| Width | – |
| Height | – |
| Dry weight | 672 kg (Sport) 580 kg (Corsa) |
| Weight to power ratio | kg/hp 5.16 (Sport) 4.46 (Corsa) from 1949: kg/hp 4.8 (Sport) 4.14 (Corsa) |

### PERFORMANCE AND PRODUCTION
| | |
|---|---|
| Maximum speed | 190-205 kph |
| Units produced | 13 |

# A6 GCS (2000 Sport)    1947

The engine of the A6 was, of course, destined to be used for racing - compact, light, flexible and easy to maintain, above all thanks to the single overhead camshaft configuration. To enable it to compete with 2 litre cars the displacement was increased from 1488.21 to 1978.74 cc by increasing the dimensions of both the bore and stroke. A prototype was built using a tubular steel chassis with enclosed bodywork but this was set aside after a short period of testing. In the summer of 1947, after the Maserati brothers had left the company, the engineer Alberto Massimino had another look at the project and converted the car into a two-seater spider which was called 2000 Sport or A6 GCS - A for Alfieri Maserati, 6-cylinders, G crankcase made of ghisa (cast iron), CS Corsa (racing) and Sport, which were the two alternatives for competition use. In fact the "torpedo" body of the car designed by Medardo Fantuzzi the coachbuilder had motorcycle-type mudguards which were easy to remove, which meant that it was easy to go from road races to circuit races and vice versa, a practice that had already been followed by Maserati and others. The headlight assembly did not have to be removed as there was just one headlight embedded in the centre of the radiator grille - a feature which made the first version of the A6 GCS unmistakeable, giving rise to the name "monofaro" (single headlight). Another significant feature was the fact that the engine was mounted to the right of centre with the drive shaft running alongside the driver. This meant that the driver's seat could be lower, making the centre of gravity lower too. Compared to the A6 GT the engine's power output was doubled, from 65 to 130 hp with a top speed approaching 200 kph. The A6 GCS asserted itself immediately at its debut at the 1947 Circuito di Modena with Alberto Ascari, this being the driver's first win too. This was followed by Bracco's win at the Coppa delle Dolomiti and Bracco/Ascari at the Circuito di Pescara. The car subsequently won numerous hill-climbs and circuit races in Italy with Bracco, Musmeci and others and in the USA with the brothers Al, Fritz and Joe Koster to make a total of 30 overall victories by 1953.

2ND of May 1948, Piazza della Vittoria, Brescia. Alberto Ascari and Guarino Bertocchi immortalised by Alberto Sorlini, the official Mille Miglia photographer, aboard their covered-wheel Maserati A6 GCS. They were forced to retire in the section between Pisa and Florence with transmission problems.

## TECHNICAL SPECIFICATION

### ENGINE
front, longitudinal, straight eight

| | |
|---|---|
| Bore and stroke | 72 x 81 mm (from 1948: 75 x 75 mm) |
| Unitary displacement | 329.79 cc (from 1948: 331.33 cc) |
| Total displacement | 1978.74 cc (from 1948: 1988.03 cc) |
| Valvegear | single overhead camshaft |
| Number of valves | two per cylinder |
| Compression ratio | 11:1 |
| Fuel system | 3 Weber 36DO4 carburettors |
| Ignition | single, with Marelli ST95DAS distributor |
| Cooling | water, centrifugal pump and radiator |
| Lubrication | pressurised, with delivery pump (from 1949: dry sump with delivery and scavenge pumps) |
| Maximum power | 130 hp at 6000 rpm (from 1949: 140 hp) |
| Specific power output | 65.69 hp/litre (from 1949: 70.42 hp/litre) |

### TRANSMISSION
| | |
|---|---|
| Driven wheels | rear |
| Clutch | single dry-plate |
| Gearbox | 4 speeds + reverse |

### BODYWORK
two-seater, sport with faired mudguards

### ROLLING CHASSIS
| | |
|---|---|
| Chassis | tubular with longerons and cross members |
| Front suspension | independent, coil springs, Houdaille hydraulic shock absorbers |
| Rear suspension | live axle, leaf springs, Houdaille hydraulic shock absorbers |
| Brakes | hydraulically actuated drums |
| Steering | worm and gear |
| Fuel tank | 100 litres |
| Tyres front/rear | 5.00-16 / 5.50-15 |

### DIMENSIONS AND WEIGHT
| | |
|---|---|
| Wheelbase | 2310 mm |
| Tracks front/rear | 1210/1150 mm |
| Length | – |
| Width | – |
| Height | – |
| Dry weight | 672 kg (Sport) 580 kg (Corsa) |
| Weight to power ratio | kg/hp 5.16 (Sport) 4.46 (Corsa) from 1949: kg/hp 4.8 (Sport) 4.14 (Corsa) |

### PERFORMANCE AND PRODUCTION
| | |
|---|---|
| Maximum speed | 190-205 kph |
| Units produced | 4 |

# A6 GCS carenata 1948

The versatility of the A6 GCS could be put down to the ease with which the car could be converted to compete in the Sport category - all that was needed was to remove the spare wheel and the cycle wings and conceal the passenger seat beneath a piece of sheet metal. By doing this, the weight of the car was reduced from 672 kg to 580 kg. However, Alberto Massimino believed that for long distance road races the standard set up was inadequate and with the 1948 Mille Miglia in mind, he equipped the four cars with extra lights, mounting two new headlights on either side of the original central one. Moreover, he had Fantuzzi make mudguards that gave greater protection that were bolted to the flanks of the car, becoming an integral part of them. With this empirical solution the designer aimed at achieving improved aerodynamic efficiency while at the same time to shield the driver and mechanic from getting covered in mud when it rained seeing as the race was run on what were still mainly dirt roads. However, the outcome of the Mille Miglia was disappointing and the integral bodywork was eventually abandoned with a return to the previous version using cycle wings being rewarded with numerous victories. These were due to the noteworthy improvements the mechanical components benefitted from, with the engine displacement being increased from 1978.74 to 1988.03 cc thanks to the perfectly square 75x75 mm dimensions of the bore and stroke and the new cylinder block cast in light alloy, with dry sump lubrication and a power increase from 130 to 140 hp. A more sophisticated version of the A6 GCS (with double overhead camshafts and dual ignition) "clothed" in an all-enclosing body shell similar to the one which had been tried out in 1948, first saw the light of day in 1953 and was exported to the USA.

The Aerautodromo, Modena, 1950. The racing driver and tester Guarino Bertocchi "weaning" the new 8CL T single-seater. A maximum power output of 430 hp at 6500 rpm and a top speed in the order of 320 kph were among the credentials of this car, built in just two examples in view of its participation in the 1950 edition of the Indianapolis 500 Miles. This particularly ambitious project was never taken any further.

## TECHNICAL SPECIFICATION

### ENGINE

front, longitudinal, straight eight

| | |
|---|---|
| Bore and stroke | 78 x 78 mm |
| Unitary displacement | 372.71 cc |
| Total displacement | 2981.69 cc |
| Valvegear | double overhead camshafts |
| Number of valves | four per cylinder |
| Compression ratio | 6.5:1 |
| Fuel system | two Weber 52DCO carburettors two Roots superchargers |
| Ignition | single, with magneto |
| Cooling | water, centrifugal pump and radiator |
| Lubrication | pressurized, dry sump with delivery and scavenge pumps |
| Maximum power | 430 hp at 6500 rpm |
| Specific power output | 144.21 hp/litre |

### TRANSMISSION

| | |
|---|---|
| Driven wheels | rear |
| Clutch | multiple dry-plate |
| Gearbox | 4 speeds + reverse |

### BODYWORK

single-seater

### ROLLING CHASSIS

| | |
|---|---|
| Chassis | tubular with longerons and cross members |
| Front suspension | independent, coil springs, Houdaille hydraulic shock absorbers |
| Rear suspension | live axle, leaf springs, Houdaille hydraulic shock absorbers |
| Brakes | hydraulically actuated drums |
| Steering | worm and gear |
| Fuel tank | 190 litres |
| Tyres front/rear | 5.50-19 / 7.00-20 |

### DIMENSIONS AND WEIGHT

| | |
|---|---|
| Wheelbase | 2720 mm |
| Tracks front/rear | 1390/1355 mm |
| Length | – |
| Width | – |
| Height | – |
| Dry weight | 800 kg |
| Weight to power ratio | 1.86 kg/hp |

### PERFORMANCE AND PRODUCTION

| | |
|---|---|
| Maximum speed | 320 kph |
| Units produced | 2 |

# 8CL T                                                    1950

Two 8CL T cars were built with the ambitious aim of taking part in the 1950 Indianapolis 500, with the drivers Nino Farina and Franco Rol who had commissioned Maserati to produce the car, but it never went beyond the testing stage. The engine was an updated version of the 8CL, a three-litre straight eight, with the same square dimensions (78 x78 mm), supercharged using two compressors and with twin overhead camshafts and four valves per cylinder. The maximum power output was 430 hp at 6500 rpm and the top speed was about 320 kph. Recourse was made to the tubular chassis used on the 4CL T-48 but with different dimensions – the wheelbase was increased from 2500 to 2720 mm, given the longer 8-cylinder engine – and the chassis was also reinforced to take into account the higher stress it would undergo and also because it was a lot heavier (800 against 630 kg). The larger drums were fitted and the fuel and oil tanks were modified. The car was tested at the recently constructed Aerautodromo track in Modena and although it revealed certain position qualities it also needed complex fine-tuning, which quickly dispelled any chance of it competing in the 1950 edition of the American race. Work continued for a while with the prospect of taking part the following year but then things came to a halt. Farina was driving for Alfa Romeo in the first Formula 1 World Championship (which he would win) and the 8CL T, which had the right specification for the Formula Libre had no way of competing in Europe. One of the two cars was displayed at the Turin Motor Show in 1951, after which Maserati decided not to use them for racing under their direct or indirect control and both ended up in New Zealand, bought by the driver Fred Zambucka, who for years took part in local races in the colours of the team that bore his name.

The second road-going model to enter the Maserati catalogue was the 2000 GT from 1950. Its chassis with a 2550 mm wheelbase was bodied by some of the greatest Italian stylists of the era including Pinin Farina, Vignale and Frua who, at the 1950 Turin Motor Show, presented this sleek open-top version that featured lines which the designer would develop with alternating fortunes well into the second half of the 1950s.

## TECHNICAL SPECIFICATION

### ENGINE
front, longitudinal, straight six

| | |
|---|---|
| Bore and stroke | 72 x 80 mm |
| Unitary displacement | 325.72 cc |
| Total displacement | 1954.32 cc |
| Valvegear | single overhead camshaft |
| Number of valves | two per cylinder |
| Compression ratio | 7.8:1 |
| Fuel system | three Weber 36DO4 carburettors |
| Ignition | single, with Marelli ST95DAS distributor |
| Cooling | water, centrifugal pump and radiator |
| Lubrication | pressurised, with delivery pump |
| Maximum power | 100 hp at 5500 rpm |
| Specific power output | 51.16 hp/litre |

### TRANSMISSION
| | |
|---|---|
| Driven wheels | rear |
| Clutch | single dry-plate |
| Gearbox | 4 speeds + reverse |

### BODYWORK
| | |
|---|---|
| Frua: spider | 2 doors, 2 seats / 2 + 2 |
| Berlinetta | 2 doors, 2 + 2 |

### ROLLING CHASSIS
| | |
|---|---|
| Chassis | tubular with longerons and cross members |
| Front suspension | independent, coil springs, Houdaille hydraulic shock absorbers |
| Rear suspension | live axle, leaf springs, Houdaille hydraulic shock absorbers |
| Brakes | hydraulically actuated drums |
| Steering | worm and gear |
| Fuel tank | 55 litres |
| Tyres front/rear | 5.00-16 / 5.50-16 |

### DIMENSIONS AND WEIGHT
| | |
|---|---|
| Wheelbase | 2550 mm |
| Tracks front/rear | 1274/1252 mm |
| Length | 4080 mm |
| Width | 1560 mm |
| Height | 1350 mm |
| Dry weight | 1100 kg |
| Weight to power ratio | 11 kg/hp |

### PERFORMANCE AND PRODUCTION
| | |
|---|---|
| Maximum speed | 160 kph |
| Units produced | 3 2-seater spiders 2 2 + 2 spiders 1 berlinetta |

# A6G 2000 Spider Frua                    1950

In 1950, a year before the new Gran Turismo A6G with the two-litre engine went into production, Pietro Frua, one of the most active coachbuilders at the time, produced a simple, elegant spider as his first creation using a Maserati rolling chassis. In order to speed up the operation, he worked on a chassis from the A6 1500, fitting the 2000 cc engine and shortening its wheelbase from 2550 to 2450 mm, which meant that there was only room in the car for two seats. The version displayed at the Turin Motor Show and immediately afterwards at the Villa Borghese show in Rome in May 1950 had a very original front end - the radiator grille, with a fog-light fitted in the middle, reminded people of the front of the A6 GCS, which for this reason had been called "monofaro" (single headlight). In the following months Frua, on acquiring the new A6G 2000 chassis, took advantage of the longer wheelbase and increased the size of the passenger compartment, making it a 2 + 2. He redesigned the shape of the front grille, removing the central headlight and fitting two extra ones on either side, something many people did not approve of as it rather over-burdened the general appearance. Another feature which to a certain extent disturbed the overall harmony of the style was the air intake on the bonnet (which was actually similar to the one on Pinin Farina's coupé in 1951). However, at the behest of a local Maserati dealer Guglielmo "Mimmo" Dei, future founder of the Scuderia Centro-Sud racing team, Frua, who was have the opportunity to show his ability in the years to come when he created some of the most prestigious Maserati cars, built a berlinetta called the "Gransport", a show prototype that won a concours d'elegance in Rome in May 1951. The car, a 2 + 2 had an upper body that blended into the tail section with very balanced and pure lines: a unique car that still today is admirable and admired.

Vignale also tackled the 2000 GT theme and compared with the sharp, essential lines of the Pinin Farina version proposed a coupé laden with more chrome trim that was not entirely successful. In line with a trend seen in many of his designs, the Turin-based stylist opted for a two-tone livery that only in part alleviated the overall weight of the car.

## TECHNICAL SPECIFICATION

### ENGINE
front, longitudinal, straight six

| | |
|---|---|
| *Bore and stroke* | 72 x 80 mm |
| *Unitary displacement* | 325.72 cc |
| *Total displacement* | 1954.32 cc |
| *Valvegear* | overhead camshaft |
| *Number of valves* | two per cylinder |
| *Compression ratio* | 7.8:1 |
| *Fuel system* | three Weber 36DO4 carburettors or one Weber 40DCR |
| *Ignition* | single, with Marelli ST95DAS distributor |
| *Cooling* | water, centrifugal pump and radiator |
| *Lubrication* | pressurised with delivery pump |
| *Maximum power* | 100 hp at 5500 rpm |
| *Specific power output* | 51.16 hp/litre |

### TRANSMISSION
| | |
|---|---|
| *Driven wheels* | rear |
| *Clutch* | single dry-plate |
| *Gearbox* | four speeds + reverse |

### BODYWORK
| | |
|---|---|
| *Vignale coupé* | two doors, two seats |

### ROLLING CHASSIS
| | |
|---|---|
| *Chassis* | tubular with longerons and cross members |
| *Front suspension* | independent, coil springs Houdaille hydraulic dampers |
| *Rear suspension* | live axle, leaf springs, Houdaille hydraulic dampers |
| *Brakes* | hydraulically actuated drums |
| *Steering* | worm and gear |
| *Fuel tank* | 55 l |
| *Tyres front/rear* | 5.50-16 / 5.50-16 |

### DIMENSIONS AND WEIGHT
| | |
|---|---|
| *Wheelbase* | 2550 mm |
| *Tracks front/rear* | 1274-1252 mm |
| *Length* | 4080 mm |
| *Width* | 1560 mm |
| *Height* | 1350 mm |
| *Dry weight* | 1100 kg |
| *Weight to power ratio* | 2.86 kg/hp |

### PERFORMANCE AND PRODUCTION
| | |
|---|---|
| *Maximum speed* | 160 kph |
| *Units produced* | 1 |

# A6G 2000 Coupé Vignale                1950

In October 1950, one of the first of Alfredo Vignale's interpretations of the A6G 2000 GT theme, a 2+2 coupé was introduced at the Paris Motor Show. The car presented an elegant aerodynamic profile and displayed original features that would be repeated in the future and not only in cars produced by the Turin-based coachbuilder, for example the double front headlights and the two-tone paintwork. The latter, apart from its purely aesthetic function, had the aim of reducing a slight impression of heaviness caused by the rather substantial forms and the wealth of chromed parts and trim. Overall, the A6G 2000 was rather unsatisfactory: only 16 were sold over a period of a couple of years and there are a number of reasons for such a modest total. First and foremost, even though the rolling chassis was of a fairly recent design it retained the performance restrictions prudentially adopted by the manufacturer ever since the earlier 1500 version. Technological evolution was rapidly changing the nature of the market for high level sports if not racing cars and the A6G 2000, with its single overhead cam engine, maximum power output of 100 hp and 160 kph top speed was by now obsolete. Or rather, it did not meet the expectations of potential clients, who would like to have seen products that were exciting and "feisty" associated with the Maserati name and its glorious racing tradition. These were characteristics they did not see in cars like the A6G 2000, which was basically a car for touring. And the authentic luxury car bodywork crafted by designers with good taste, refinement and great attention to detail was not enough to make up for the gap in performance. Last but not least the price – about five and a half million lire, according to the level of trim – certainly did not help the car sell in large numbers.

Elegance and sobriety: the principal themes underpinning many of the designs by Pinin Farina from the early 1950s. This philosophy was also apparent in the Maserati 2000 GT coupé. A light chrome strip along the sill and another trim element on the front wing were the only concessions to decoration on the otherwise clean, essential flanks.

## TECHNICAL SPECIFICATION

### ENGINE
front, longitudinal, straight six

| | |
|---|---|
| Bore and stroke | 72 x 80 mm |
| Unitary displacement | 325.72 cc |
| Total displacement | 1954.32 cc |
| Valvegear | single overhead camshaft |
| Number of valves | two per cylinder |
| Compression ratio | 7.8:1 |
| Fuel system | three Weber 36DO4 carburettors or one Weber 4ODCR |
| Ignition | single, with Marelli ST95DAS distributor |
| Cooling | water, centrifugal pump and radiator |
| Lubrication | pressurised, with delivery pump |
| Maximum power | 100 hp at 5500 rpm |
| Specific power output | 51.16 hp/litre |

### TRANSMISSION
| | |
|---|---|
| Driven wheels | rear |
| Clutch | single dry-plate |
| Gearbox | 4 speeds + reverse |

### BODYWORK
| | |
|---|---|
| Coupé Pinin Farina | 2 doors, 2 seats |

### ROLLING CHASSIS
| | |
|---|---|
| Chassis | tubular with longerons and cross members |
| Front suspension | independent, coil springs, Houdaille hydraulic shock absorbers |
| Rear suspension | live axle, leaf springs, Houdaille hydraulic shock absorbers |
| Brakes | hydraulically actuated drums |
| Steering | worm and gear |
| Fuel tank | 55 litres |
| Tyres front/rear | 5.00-16 / 5.50-16 |

### DIMENSIONS AND WEIGHT
| | |
|---|---|
| Wheelbase | 2550 mm |
| Tracks front/rear | 1274/1252 mm |
| Length | 4080 mm |
| Width | 1560 mm |
| Height | 1350 mm |
| Dry weight | 1100 kg |
| Weight to power ratio | 11 kg/hp |

### PERFORMANCE AND PRODUCTION
| | |
|---|---|
| Maximum speed | 160 kph |
| Units produced | 1 |

# A6G 2000 Coupé Pinin Farina 1951

The market for Gran Turismo cars, which Maserati had entered in 1947 with the A6 1500, was gradually expanding as the economy that had been devastated by the war began to pick up in the face of rapidly growing demand. As early as 1949, two prototypes were already being prepared in Modena, prefiguring the heir to the A6 with a 2000 engine. By 1950, the mechanical specification of the car had been decided - the 6-cylinder single overhead cam engine from the A6 GCS was to be used with a displacement of 1978.74 rather than 1954.32 cc achieved by reducing the bore and increasing the stroke (from 75 x 75 mm to 72 x 80 mm). In order to make the car easier for less expert drivers, the power output was restricted: it was now 100 hp instead of 130 hp, a figure obtained by lowering the compression ratio from 11 to 7.8:1. The tubular frame using longerons and cross members and the configuration of the suspension was the same as on the A6 1500 but with one exception: at the rear Fiat semi-elliptical leaf springs were used instead of the coil springs. The top speed was about 180 kph but drivers were advised not to exceed 5500 rpm which was equivalent to a speed of 170 kph. The car was named as the A6G, with the A standing for Alfieri Maserati, 6 for the number of cylinders and G (ghisa) for the cast-iron crankcase, this initial remaining even when the engines' crankcase was no longer made of cast iron but of aluminium. Several coachbuilders worked to "dress" the car, starting with Pinin Farina, who had already produced the very first Gran Turismo car for the Trident. The 2 + 2 berlinetta presented at the Turin Motor Show in 1951 had sleek lines, harmonious proportions and an austere level of trim. It was reminiscent of the racing Maseratis with red paintwork and a vertical radiator grille unlike the horizontal ones that had been fitted to more recent models. It was not a masterpiece, and remained at the intermediate prototype stage, never going into production.

The Lancia Aurelia B20 which appeared in 1951 is considered to be the grandfather of the "Italian GT": a prominent grille, a windscreen with a modest inclination, ample glazing to lighten the upper body, a compact rear and a rather high belt-line. Features that were to set a trend and which Pinin Farina was himself to use on other designs including his Maserati A6G 2000.

## TECHNICAL SPECIFICATION

### ENGINE
front, longitudinal, straight six

| | |
|---|---|
| *Bore and stroke* | 72 x 80 mm |
| *Unitary displacement* | 325.72 cc |
| *Total displacement* | 1954.32 cc |
| *Valvegear* | single overhead camshaft |
| *Number of valves* | two per cylinder |
| *Compression ratio* | 7.8:1 |
| *Fuel system* | three Weber 36DO4 carburettors or one Weber 4ODCR |
| *Ignition* | single, with Marelli ST95DAS distributor |
| *Cooling* | water, centrifugal pump and radiator |
| *Lubrication* | pressurised, with delivery pump |
| *Maximum power* | 100 hp at 5500 rpm |
| *Specific power output* | 51.16 hp/litre |

### TRANSMISSION
| | |
|---|---|
| *Driven wheels* | rear |
| *Clutch* | single dry-plate |
| *Gearbox* | 4 speeds + reverse |

### BODYWORK
| | |
|---|---|
| *Coupé Pinin Farina* | 2 doors, 2 seats |

### ROLLING CHASSIS
| | |
|---|---|
| *Chassis* | tubular with longerons and cross members |
| *Front suspension* | independent, coil springs, Houdaille hydraulic shock absorbers |
| *Rear suspension* | live axle, leaf springs, Houdaille hydraulic shock absorbers |
| *Brakes* | hydraulically actuated drums |
| *Steering* | worm and gear |
| *Fuel tank* | 55 litres |
| *Tyres front/rear* | 5.00-16 / 5.50-16 |

### DIMENSIONS AND WEIGHT
| | |
|---|---|
| *Wheelbase* | 2550 mm |
| *Tracks front/rear* | 1274/1252 mm |
| *Length* | 4080 mm |
| *Width* | 1560 mm |
| *Height* | 1350 mm |
| *Dry weight* | 1100 kg |
| *Weight to power ratio* | 11 kg/hp |

### PERFORMANCE AND PRODUCTION
| | |
|---|---|
| *Maximum speed* | 160 kph |
| *Units produced* | 8 |

# A6G 2000 Coupé Pinin Farina    1951

The berlinetta 2 + 2 prototype presented by Pinin Farina at the Turin Motor Show in April 1951 was never put into production, moreover Pinin Farina himself was not satisfied with the car, to the extent that he was already working on a new version which was destined to see the light of day at the Paris Motor Show the following October. The rolling chassis was the same – a tubular spaceframe and a six-cylinder, two-litre, single camshaft engine – but the design of the bodywork had been completely revised. People were struck by the number of decorative features on the car compared with the formal austerity of the previous prototype. This gave a sense of luxury if not ostentation: - the large front grille, the conspicuous chrome bumpers, the trim along the flanks of the car and the rear lighting clusters brought to mind more of a luxury model than a sports car. However, the most significant aesthetic touch of originality was to be seen in the sharp profile, the harmony of the proportions and in the balance of the whole, which had already been seen in the previous prototype and which recalled another Pinin Farina coupé that was to become very famous, the Lancia Aurelia B 20, launched in the spring of the same year, 1951, when the first models started appearing on the roads. Incidentally, there has been some disagreement yet not been resolved over whether Felice Mario Boano actually designed the prototype of the B20 for Ghia. Leaving this aside, the Pinin Farina Maserati coupé proved not to be as successful as had been hoped for a variety of reasons, both mechanical and financial as well as aesthetic. There was also the fact that in June 1952, Pinin Farina built a cabriolet version of the Ferrari 212 Inter, which was the first step towards working with Maranello. His relationship with Ferrari soon became a lot closer making it impossible to carry on working with Maserati given the fierce rivalry that separated the two companies from Modena.

Produced from 1951 to 1956, the TM15 "Muletto" or Mule, was a continuation of and the final chapter in Maserati's production of electric vehicles. This model was also available with a twin-cylinder, two-stroke internal combustion engine with a displacement of 547 cc, but it proved to be under-powered for the vehicle, penalising it in terms of performance and therefore sales.

## TECHNICAL SPECIFICATION

| **ENGINE** | | **PERFORMANCE** | |
|---|---|---|---|
| Front | electric / two-stroke | *Carrying capacity* | 1500 kg |
| | | | |
| *Displacement* | 547 cc | **PRODUCTION** | |
| *Fuel system* | batteries and accumulators oil and petrol mix | 1951-56 | 51 |
| *Potenza massima* | 15.5 hp | | |

**TRANSMISSION**
*Driven wheels*     rear

**BODYWORK**
*Metal structure – delivery vehicle*

**DIMENSIONS AND WEIGHT**
*Wheebase*     2500 mm

# TM15 Muletto                            1951

Between 1942 and 1950, including the years of the Second World War, Maserati produced 441 electric vehicles starting with the EC10 (three-wheeled electric delivery vehicles) followed by a series of four-wheeled vehicles with their load-bearing capacity measured in quintals and gradually increasing as reflected in the initials of their names: EC15, EC20 and EC35 as well as the BC20 of which one experimental model was built in 1949. You have to bear in mind that at the end of the war the Trident, as was the case with a lot of other firms, went through a period fraught with economic, technical and sociopolitical problems which were all connected to getting back to normal productive activity. Maserati was committed to producing both sports and racing cars, with the continuous updates that these needed as well as designing and building the first gran turismo cars which were literally destined to change the history of the firm. However, using electricity as a power source, which had apparently only been a question of temporary necessity, was never abbandoned, when the EC series of vehicles ceased production. In fact in 1951, a three-wheeled vehicle called the TM15 Muletto (where the letters TM stood for commercial transport) was put on sale. There were two versions, one powered by batteries and accumulators like the models which had come before it and the other used a light alloy 2-cylinder 547cc engine which made 15.5 hp and ran on a mixture of petrol and oil like the scooters which crowded the Italian roads at the time. As a result of the modest power output of the tiny engine, the vehicle could not go up slopes steeper than 16% when fully loaded and this fact, as well as creating homologation problems, had a negative influence on potential sales of both this and the electric version, so neither of them were made for very long. The sum total of production between 1951 and 1956 was 51 vehicles.

The Roman engineer-driver Piero Taruffi is helped into his Tarf II-Bisiluro Italcorsa with which on the 20TH of March 1951, on the "Fettuccia" at Terracina, he set the records for the flying kilometre and mile with averages speeds of 298.507 and 290.552 kph respectively. This original vehicle was fitted with the 1720 cc engine from the Maserati 4CL T-50.

## TECHNICAL SPECIFICATION

### ENGINE
Maserati 4CLT-50, straight four

| | |
|---|---|
| *Position* | in the left-hand pontoon |
| *Bore and stroke* | 78 x 90mm |
| *Unitary displacement* | 430.05 cc |
| *Total displacement* | 1720.20 cc |
| *Valvegear* | double overhead camshafts |
| *Number of valves* | four per cylinder |
| *Compression ratio* | 7:1 |
| *Fuel system* | Weber 52DCO carburettor two Roots superchargers |
| *Ignition* | single, with Marelli ST24DAS magneto |
| *Cooling* | water, centrifugal pump and radiator |
| *Lubrication* | pressurized, dry sump with delivery and scavenge pumps |
| *Maximum power* | 290 hp at 7000 rpm |
| *Specific power output* | 168.58 hp/litre |

### TRANSMISSION
| | |
|---|---|
| *Driven wheels* | rear |
| *Gearbox* | 4 speeds |

### BODYWORK
*double torpedo for record-breaking*

### PERFORMANCE AND PRODUCTION
| | |
|---|---|
| *Maximum speed* | over 310 kph |
| *Units produced* | 2 |

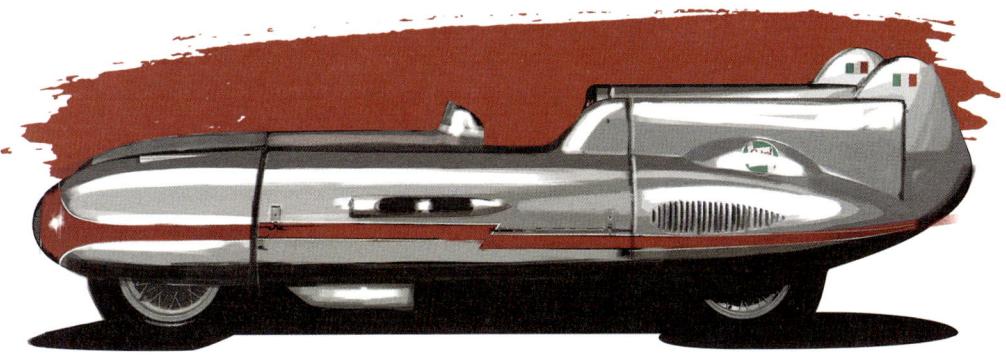

# Tarf II Italcorsa                     1951

As well as being a leading driver, Piero Taruffi is also remembered as the engineering and designer behind some highly original and very successful record-breaking cars. The car he called the Tarf II Italcorsa made experimental use of more than one engine, including a Maserati F1 unit with which in 1951 he set two international records in Class E for cars with engines up to 2000 cc. The Tarf's body was made of two aluminium shells shaped like a *siluro* or torpedo (a name which was used at that time for aerodynamic bodies fitted to racing cars), hence the car's Bisiluro (double torpedo) nickname. The torpedo on the right (the opposite of the arrangement on the Tarf I) contained the driver's seat, with two levers for steering and one for the four-speed gear-change; the left-hand pontoon, connected to its mate via the axles, housed the engine. At the rear were two stabilizing fins fitted with adjustable rudder and faired into the centre of each pontoon; the right fin also served as a head-rest for the driver. The engine was the four-cylinder 16-valve twin-cam from the single-seater Formula 1 Maserati in its most highly-developed form, the 4CL T-50, with the displacement increased from 1490.84 to 1720.20 cc and fitted with two-stage supercharging for a maximum power output of 290 hp at 7000 rpm. Transmission was via a motorcycle chain connected to the rear axle. On the 20TH of March 1951, Taruffi set two flying start world records, recording an average speed of 298.507 kph for the kilometre and 290.553 kph for the mile. A top speed of 313 kph was also recorded. The records set by the Tarf II improved on those previously set on the Bonneville Salt Flats (Utah) over the same distances by the Englishman Alfred Thomas Goldie Gardner at the wheel of a streamlined MG EX-135. Taruffi's records were achieved on the 41 km straight on the Via Appia (Strada Statale n. 7) between Cisterna di Latina and Terracina, commonly known as the "Fettuccia di Terracina".

Monza, 7ᵀᴴ of September 1952, Italian Grand Prix: the Argentine José Froilán Gonzáles tackling the porphyry cobbles at the wheel of his Maserati A6 GCM-51 in which he finished second between the two Ferrari 500 F2s of the winner Alberto Ascari and Gigi Villoresi, third. From the following season the far more competitive A6 GCM-53 was to take to the tracks.

## TECHNICAL SPECIFICATION

**ENGINE**
front, longitudinal, straight six

| | |
|---|---|
| Bore and stroke | 72.6 x 80 mm (1951-52) |
| | 75 x 75 mm (1952) |
| Unitary displacement | 331.17 cc (1951-52) |
| | 331.33 cc (1952) |
| Total displacement | 1978.02 cc (1951-52) |
| | 1988.03 (1952) |
| Valvegear | double overhead camshafts |
| Number of valves | two per cylinder |
| Compression ratio | 13.5:1 (1951-52) |
| Fuel system | three Weber 38DCO3 carburettors (40DCO3) |
| Ignition | single, with Marelli ST95DAS distributor (1951-52) |
| | dual with 2 Marelli magnetos (1952-53) |
| Cooling | water, centrifugal pump and radiator |
| Lubrication | pressurised, with delivery delivery and scavenge pumps |
| Maximum power | 160 hp at 6500 rpm (1951-52) |
| | 180 hp at 7600 rpm (1952) |
| Specific power output | 80.52 hp/litre (1951-52) |
| | 90.54 hp/litre (1952) |

**TRANSMISSION**

| | |
|---|---|
| Driven wheels | rear |
| Clutch | multiple dry-plate |
| Gearbox | 4 speeds + reverse |

**BODYWORK**
single-seater

**ROLLING CHASSIS**

| | |
|---|---|
| Chassis | tubular with longerons and cross members |
| Front suspension | independent, coil springs, Houdaille hydraulic shock absorbers |
| Rear suspension | live axle, leaf springs, Houdaille hydraulic shock absorbers |
| Brakes | hydraulically actuated drums |
| Steering | worm and gear |
| Fuel tank | from 160 to 200 litres (1953) |
| Tyres front | 5.00-15 / 5.50-15 (1951-52) |
| Tyres rear | 6.00-15 / 6.50-15 (1951-52) |

**DIMENSIONS AND WEIGHT**

| | |
|---|---|
| Wheelbase | 2280 mm (1951-52) |
| Tracks front | 1278 mm (1951-52) |
| Tracks rear | 1200 mm (1951-52) |
| Length | – |
| Width | – |
| Height | – |
| Dry weight | 550-560 kg (1951-52) |
| Weight to power ratio | 3.43-3.50 kg/hp (1951-52) / 3.11 (1952) |

**PERFORMANCE AND PRODUCTION**

| | |
|---|---|
| Maximum speed | 250 kph |
| Units produced | 7 |

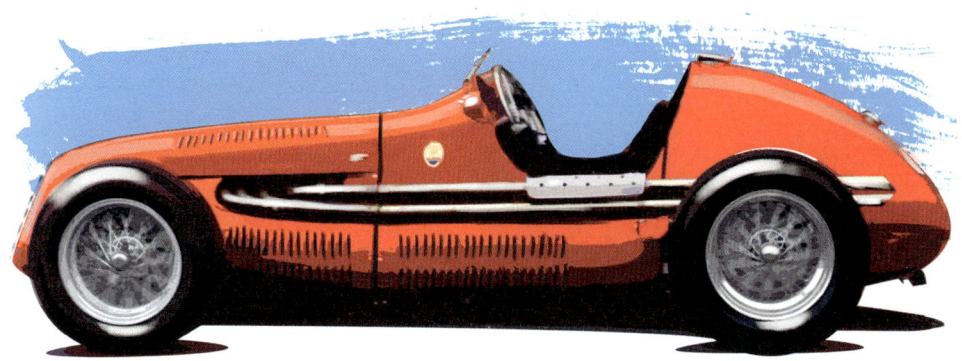

# A6 GCM-51                1951

The excellent results that had been achieved by the A6 GCS encouraged the company to build a car in 1951 specifically designed for circuit racing (which meant that unlike the preceding model, there was no need for it to be converted by removing the mudguards and so on). The project, entrusted to the engineers Alberto Massimino and Vittorio Bellentani, led to the birth of the A6 GCM, a name that can be translated as A for Alfieri Maserati, 6 cylinders, G crankcase made of cast-iron (*ghisa*) even though it was in fact made of aluminium, C racing category (categoria Corsa), M single-seater (monoposto). The only thing the engine had in common with the one from the A6 GCS was the cylinder configuration. It had the same initial displacement (1987.02), although the bore and stroke were changed in 1952 to 75 x 75 mm rather than 72.6 x 80 mm. The fuel supply was naturally aspirated with three twin-choke carburettors; no supercharger was fitted in order to conform to the Formula 2 regulations that only allowed supercharging for engines with a maximum displacement of 500 cc. The valvegear once again used double overhead camshafts, while the compression ratio was raised to 13.5:1 and beyond with a maximum power output that from 1951 to 1952 increased from 160 to 180 hp. Using a similar chassis to that of the 4CL T-48, with a wheelbase shortened from 2500 mm to 2280 mm, Fantuzzi fitted a particularly lightweight body that allowed him to keep the overall weight down to 550-560 kg. Unfortunately, the chassis was not up to the job and it had a negative effect on roadholding. The two cars built during 1951 were never raced and were sold to the Escuderia Bandeirantes owned by the Brazilian driver Chico Landi, however, despite modifications and improvements, they did not achieve any noteworthy successes the following season. The sole victory in 1952 came with the company's chief road-tester Guerino Bertocchi at the wheel of a third modified car in the Riunione dei Primati at the Aerautodromo in Modena.

Another photo of Froilán Gonzáles, this time in action at the wheel of an A6 GCM-53. The setting is the unmistakeable Silverstone track and the 1953 British Grand Prix (18 July). The Prancing Horse and the Trident marques were the undisputed protagonists in the race, with Ascari in a Ferrari 500 F2 winning ahead of Fangio (Maserati) and Farina (Ferrari).

## TECHNICAL SPECIFICATION

### ENGINE
front, longitudinal, straight six

| | |
|---|---|
| Bore and stroke | 76.5 x 72 mm |
| Unitary displacement | 330.93 cc |
| Total displacement | 1985.61 cc |
| Valvegear | double overhead camshafts |
| Number of valves | two per cylinder |
| Compression ratio | 12.1 |
| Fuel system | three Weber 38DCO3 carburettors (40DCO3) |
| Ignition | dual with 2 Marelli magnetos |
| Cooling | water, centrifugal pump and radiator |
| Lubrication | pressurised, with delivery delivery and scavenge pumps |
| Maximum power | 197 hp at 8000 rpm |
| Specific power output | 99.99 hp/litre |

### TRANSMISSION
| | |
|---|---|
| Driven wheels | rear |
| Clutch | multiple dry-plate |
| Gearbox | 4 speeds + reverse |

### BODYWORK
single-seater

### ROLLING CHASSIS
| | |
|---|---|
| Chassis | tubular with longerons and cross members |
| Front suspension | independent, coil springs, Houdaille hydraulic shock absorbers |
| Rear suspension | live axle, leaf springs, Houdaille hydraulic shock absorbers |
| Brakes | hydraulically actuated drums |
| Steering | worm and gear |
| Fuel tank | 200 litres |
| Tyres front | 6.25-16 |
| rear | 6.50-16 |

### DIMENSIONS AND WEIGHT
| | |
|---|---|
| Wheelbase | 2310 mm |
| Tracks front | 1225 mm |
| rear | 1160 mm |
| Length | – |
| Width | – |
| Height | – |
| Dry weight | 570 kg |
| Weight to power ratio | 2.89 kg/hp |

### PERFORMANCE AND PRODUCTION
| | |
|---|---|
| Maximum speed | 250 kph |
| Units produced | 5 (converted to 250 F in 1954) |

# A6 GCM-53                    1953

The unsatisfactory sporting results achieved by the first version of the A6 GCM, despite the continuous modifications made, showed that a radical change of technical direction was required. Towards the end of 1952, Gioachino Colombo took over the job of head of design. He was "father" of both the Alfa Romeo 158-159, winner of the 1950 and 1951 Formula 1 World Championship and the first 12-cylinder Ferrari, destined to enjoy lasting fame. Colombo immediately applied himself to the task of updating the A6 GCM, redesigning the engine that went from square (75x75 mm) to oversquare (76,5x72 mm = 1985.61 cc) and despite reducing the compression ratio from 13.5:1 to 12:1 immediately obtained a power output of 190 hp, rising to 200 hp during the 1953 season. The chassis, which had caused problems of instability in the 1951-52 version, was thoroughly revised by combining the traditional structure of longerons and cross members with a framework made of circular section tubes that substantially increased the resistance to torsional stress. The bodywork stayed the same for the first races in 1953 but from May onwards it was replaced with a much sleeker and more and harmonious design – also the work of Medardo Fantuzzi – easily recognisable by its oval radiator grille with a vertical bar. The A6 GCM-53's palmares included several victories by the Swiss driver Emmanuel De Graffenried (Syracuse GP, Chichester and Lavant Cup at Goodwood and the classic Eifelrennen at the Nürburgring) while Fangio won a hotly disputed edition of the Italian Grand Prix and then the Modena GP too. Further victories came in hillclimbs, again thanks to De Graffenried (Freiburg-Schauinsland), Fangio (Vue des Alpes), Bonetto (Pontedecimo-Giovi) and Gino Bianco (Subida da Tijuca, at Rio de Janeiro), while privateers continued to enjoy success over the following years in Belgium, Switzerland, Australia and the United States.

Mille Miglia, 26TH of April 1953. At 5.11 in the morning, Luigi Musso and Oscar Donatello are about to roll down the starting ramp in their Maserati A6GCS. A broken differential was to put an end to their race between Florence and Bologna.

## TECHNICAL SPECIFICATION

### ENGINE
front, longitudinal, straight six

| | |
|---|---|
| Bore and stroke | 76.5 x 72 mm |
| Unitary displacement | 330.93 cc |
| Total displacement | 1985.61 cc |
| Valvegear | double overhead camshafts |
| Number of valves | two per cylinder |
| Compression ratio | 8.75.1 |
| Fuel system | three Weber 40DCO3 carburettors |
| Ignition | double with Marelli ST65DTEM distributors or Marelli magnetos |
| Cooling | water, centrifugal pump and radiator |
| Lubrication | dry-sump, with delivery delivery and scavenge pumps) |
| Maximum power | 170 hp at 7300 rpm |
| Specific power output | 85.61 hp/litre |

### TRANSMISSION
| | |
|---|---|
| Driven wheels | rear |
| Clutch | multiple dry-plate |
| Gearbox | four speeds + reverse |

### BODYWORK
single-seater

### ROLLING CHASSIS
| | |
|---|---|
| Chassis | tubular with longerons and cross members |
| Front suspension | independent, coil springs, Houdaille hydraulic shock absorbers |
| Rear suspension | live axle, leaf springs, Houdaille hydraulic shock absorbers |
| Brakes | hydraulically actuated drums |
| Steering | worm and gear |
| Fuel tank | 125 l |
| Tyres front | 6.00-16 |
| rear | 6.00-16 |

### DIMENSIONS AND WEIGHT
| | |
|---|---|
| Wheelbase | 2310 mm |
| Tracks front | 1335 mm |
| rear | 1220 mm |
| Length | – |
| Width | – |
| Height | – |
| Dry weight | 740 kg |
| Weight to power ratio / | 4.35 kg/hp |

### PERFORMANCE AND PRODUCTION
| | |
|---|---|
| Maximum speed | 235 kph |
| Units produced | 48 |

# A6 GCS-53 1953

Ahead of the 1953 season, in parallel with the preparation of the Formula 2 A6 GCM, Gioachino Colombo also started work on the revision of the 2000 Sport, or rather the A6 GCS that, as with the single-seater, was also known as the A6 GCS-53. After the experimental use of the new twin-cam engine on two of the older cars, the chassis was also redesigned using a tubular frame and the rear suspension geometry was changed to solve the stability problems of the old A6 GCM. The engine was also thoroughly revised. First and foremost, as the two-seater Sport was going to be competing in road races over very long distances the power output was reduced from 190 to 170 hp. Furthermore, the regulations for road races now called for the use of commercially available petrol that was not compatible with the very high compression ratios instead possible when using a mixture of methyl alcohol, benzene and acetone. The compression ratio was therefore reduced from 12:1 to 8.75:1, which made the engine of the A6 GCS incredibly reliable. Colombo also designed new bodywork that was made by Medardo Fantuzzi (along with a number of examples by Celestino Fiandri). The modern and harmonious lines added to the value of the car and its exceptional sporting character, with the result that no less than 52 cars were made. The A6 GCS-53's competition record is one of the richest and most prestigious of the two-seater racing cars of all times. A total of more than 70 outright victories, in Italy and beyond were achieved by this sparkling Trident Sport in the hands of numerous drivers, some of whom became famous world-wide such as Sergio Mantovani, Luigi Musso, Emmanuel De Graffenried, Cesare Perdisa, Roy Salvadori, Luigi Bellucci, Alfonso De Portago, Maria Teresa de Filippis, Giorgio Scarlatti, Odoardo Govoni and many others.

The Mancini/Dal Cin A6 GCS-53 spider bodied by Vignale at the start of the XXI Mille Miglia (1ST of May 1954). In an edition that saw the Trident marque's car fighting for the leading positions, this crew did not enjoy similar fortunes and retired after passing Rome.

## TECHNICAL SPECIFICATION

### ENGINE

front, longitudinal, straight six

| | |
|---|---|
| Bore and stroke | 76.5 x 72 mm |
| Unitary displacement | 330.93 cc |
| Total displacement | 1985.61 cc |
| Valvegear | double overhead camshafts |
| Number of valves | two per cylinder |
| Compression ratio | 8.75.1 |
| Fuel system | three Weber 40DCO3 carburettors |
| Ignition | double with Marelli ST65DTEM distributors or Marelli magnetos |
| Cooling | water, centrifugal pump and radiator |
| Lubrication | dry-sump, with delivery delivery and scavenge pumps |
| Maximum power | 170 hp at 7300 rpm |
| Specific power output | 85.61 hp/litre |

### TRANSMISSION

| | |
|---|---|
| Driven wheels | rear |
| Clutch | multiple dry-plate |
| Gearbox | four speeds + reverse |

### BODYWORK

single-seater

### ROLLING CHASSIS

| | |
|---|---|
| Chassis | tubular with longerons and cross members |
| Front suspension | independent, coil springs, Houdaille hydraulic shock absorbers |
| Rear suspension | live axle, leaf springs, Houdaille hydraulic shock absorbers |
| Brakes | hydraulically actuated drums |
| Steering | worm and gear |
| Fuel tank | - |
| Tyres front | - |
| rear | - |

### DIMENSIONS AND WEIGHT

| | |
|---|---|
| Wheelbase | - |
| Tracks front | - |
| rear | - |
| Length | - |
| Width | - |
| Height | - |
| Dry weight | - |
| Weight to power ratio | - |

### PERFORMANCE AND PRODUCTION

| | |
|---|---|
| Maximum speed | - |
| Units produced | 1 (rebodied by Scaglietti in 1955) |

# A6 GCS-53 Spider Vignale 1953

One of the first A6 GCS or A6 GCS-53 second series rolling chassis to leave the factory, bearing the number 2049, was assigned to Carrozzeria Vignale, commissioned by Tony Parravano to build a spider based on it. This fascinating character of Italian origin had become a construction magnate in the United States and had indulged his passion for cars by forming a racing team and over the course of the 1950s buying about twenty Ferrari and Maserati sports cars, which were raced by drivers of the calibre of Carroll Shelby, Jack McAfee, Ken Miles, Jimmy Bryan, Pat O'Connor, Masten Gregory and others. Vignale's A6 GCS spider was designed by Giovanni Michelotti and built in a very short space of time to be displayed at the Turin Motor Show in April 1953, where it was greatly admired. Alfredo Vignale, a former panel beater at Pinin Farina, had only had his own workshop for seven years. A combination of his skill and Michelotti's ingenious talent gave rise to a highly original car. What was immediately striking was the compact and sleek body of the car, a characteristic it might be said that was common to all of Vignale's cars. It had an aggressive nose, thrusting forward, with the radiator grille enclosed within an eye-catching chrome frame. Other highly innovative design features included the chrome exhaust pipes that ran along the bottom of the left-hand side, and a parallel raised trim that gradually became more pronounced towards the rear of the car, highlighting the edge of the door and the line of the wheel arch. A raised rib on the bonnet was continued through to the boot lid where it became a stabilizing fin. Two years later the car returned to Italy where it was fitted with new bodywork by Scaglietti, retaining the spider configuration.

A fine exercise in style on the A6 GCS-53 rolling chassis penned by Pietro Frua. The Rome Maserati dealer, Mimmo Dei specifically commissioned the 40-year-old Turinese designer to produce this car with its elegant but aggressive lines and original radiator grille and white longitudinal stripe on the bonnet.

## TECHNICAL SPECIFICATION

### ENGINE
front, longitudinal, straight six

| | |
|---|---|
| Bore and stroke | 76.5 x 72 mm |
| Unitary displacement | 330.93 cc |
| Total displacement | 1985.61 cc |
| Valvegear | double overhead camshafts |
| Number of valves | two per cylinder |
| Compression ratio | 8.75.1 |
| Fuel system | three Weber 40DCO3 carburettors |
| Ignition | double with Marelli ST65DTEM distributors or Marelli magnetos |
| Cooling | water, centrifugal pump and radiator |
| Lubrication | dry-sump, with delivery and scavenge pumps |
| Maximum power | 170 hp at 7300 rpm |
| Specific power output | 85.61 hp/litre |

### TRANSMISSION
| | |
|---|---|
| Driven wheels | rear |
| Clutch | multiple dry-plate |
| Gearbox | four speeds + reverse |

### BODYWORK
single-seater

### ROLLING CHASSIS
| | |
|---|---|
| Chassis | tubular with longerons and cross members |
| Front suspension | independent, coil springs, Houdaille hydraulic shock absorbers |
| Rear suspension | live axle, leaf springs, Houdaille hydraulic shock absorbers |
| Brakes | hydraulically actuated drums |
| Steering | worm and gear |
| Fuel tank | - |
| Tyres front | - |
| rear | - |

### DIMENSIONS AND WEIGHT
| | |
|---|---|
| Wheelbase | - |
| Tracks front | - |
| rear | - |
| Length | – |
| Width | – |
| Height | – |
| Dry weight | - |
| Weight to power ratio | |

### PERFORMANCE AND PRODUCTION
| | |
|---|---|
| Maximum speed | - |
| Units produced | 1 |

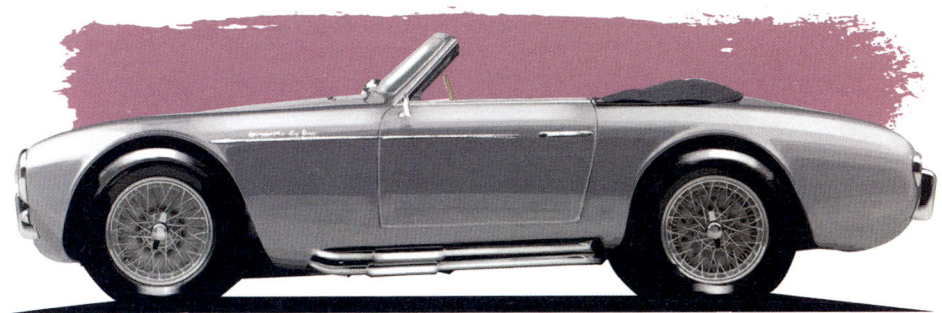

# A6 GCS-53 Spider Frua                    1953

Guglielmo Dei is remembered above all for his work as a sports impresario and founder of the Scuderia Centro-Sud racing team, which was active for a decade between 1956 and 1965 and also as a worthy promoter of many drivers. Less well-known are examples of his inexhaustible spirit of initiative, for example, the way in which he encouraged makers to produce cars which at the time were called *fuori-serie* (one-offs). In 1951, when he was a Maserati dealer in Rome, he commissioned Pietro Frua to build a berlinetta based on the A6G 2000 (incidentally, the car won the Pincio Concours d'Elegance prize in May of that year). Two years later – on the 5[TH] of November 1953, to be precise, as recorded in the Trident factory's records, Dei bought A6 GCS-53 rolling chassis number 2054 and entrusted it to Pietro Frua for the realisation of a new body, this time a spider. The Turin designer produced a car with taut lines that succeeded expressing the car's racing vocation, but without gilding the lily and without sacrificing elegance, on the basis of aesthetic princi-ples that were being established at that time and that would achieve recognition throughout the world: those of the Italian Gran Turismo car. In other words, as has been written: "a car that is both suitable for going to the theatre and for going to a track, taking part in a race and maybe winning it, then going home... still in the same car." The most obvious sign of its racing purpose, apart from the aggressive styling of the front end, is the use of the dual external exhaust pipes running along the left-hand side, above which there is a thin chrome trim aligned with the door handle, with "Maserati 2000 Gran Sport" badging above it. The admirable straight line tracing the shape of the barchetta body then curves gently to reach the front and rear lights. This prototype may be considered to be a precursor of the A6G-54 that would soon see the light of day.

One of the most beautiful cars in Italian automotive history and an authentic icon for Maserati that in styling terms still today draws inspiration for its latest models from this car: the A6 GCS-53 coupé commissioned from Pinin Farina once again by the Mimmo Dei. While today it's standing is undisputed, at the time it was "misunderstood" to the extent that the only four examples ever constructed were soon dismantled.

## TECHNICAL SPECIFICATION

### ENGINE
front, longitudinal, straight six

| | |
|---|---|
| Bore and stroke | 76.5 x 72 mm |
| Unitary displacement | 330.93 cc |
| Total displacement | 1985.61 cc |
| Valvegear | double overhead camshafts |
| Number of valves | two per cylinder |
| Compression ratio | 8.75.1 |
| Fuel system | three Weber 40DCO3 carburettors |
| Ignition | double with Marelli ST65DTEM distributors or Marelli magnetos |
| Cooling | water, centrifugal pump and radiator |
| Lubrication | dry-sump, with delivery and scavenge pumps |
| Maximum power | 170 hp at 7300 rpm |
| Specific power output | 85.61 hp/litre |

### TRANSMISSION
| | |
|---|---|
| Driven wheels | rear |
| Clutch | multiple dry-plate |
| Gearbox | four speeds + reverse |

### BODYWORK
| | |
|---|---|
| coupé Pinin Farina | two doors, two seats |

### ROLLING CHASSIS
| | |
|---|---|
| Chassis | tubular with longerons and cross members |
| Front suspension | independent, coil springs, Houdaille hydraulic shock absorbers |
| Rear suspension | live axle, leaf springs, Houdaille hydraulic shock absorbers |
| Brakes | hydraulically actuated drums |
| Steering | worm and gear |
| Fuel tank | - |
| Tyres front | - |
| rear | - |

### DIMENSIONS AND WEIGHT
| | |
|---|---|
| Wheelbase | 2310 mm |
| Tracks front | – |
| rear | – |
| Length | 3480 mm |
| Width | 1530 mm |
| Height | 860 mm |
| Dry weight | – |
| Weight to power ratio | – |

### PERFORMANCE AND PRODUCTION
| | |
|---|---|
| Maximum speed | – |
| Units produced | 4 |

# A6 GCS-53 Coupé Pinin Farina 1954

As well as the spider he commissioned Frua to build on the A6 GCS-53 rolling chassis, Guglielmo Dei had Pinin Farina build four coupés, the first of which was presented at the Turin Motor Show in the spring of 1954. Pinin Farina had already established a solid working relationship with Ferrari so he was not too happy about designing bodywork for Maserati, whom Enzo Ferrari considered to be "the enemy", but he allowed himself a few exceptions such as this one, blurring the issue by using the formal distinction regarding the name of the company that ordered the car; that is to say, Dei's Scuderia Centro-Sud, rather than Maserati. However, the end-result was extraordinary and it is a shame that there are only photographs to remind us of the car. The protruding front section that created downforce and the size of the bonnet nestling between the wings, the large oval radiator grille set apart from the headlights made for a new and aggressive image that made it obvious at first sight that the car was to be used for racing. One was immediately struck by the sleekness of the car and the extreme nature of stylistic features such as the upper body set well towards the rear and the rounded windscreen with its pillar clearly positioned beyond the halfway point of the wheelbase. The aesthetic tension generated by the whole was attenuated by the design of the rear end, which was sober and compact, using the elegant rounded fastback shape that was to become a classic Pinin Farina feature through to the early Sixties. You might ask yourself what else could be missing from such a seductive coupé, powered by the high-performance two-litre twin-cam engine from the A6 GCS-53, for it to be successful in competition. And the answer is not difficult to find: quite simply a design aimed not just at beauty but the essential functionality needed to compete on the track and on roads too. Judged to be "uncomfortable, suffocating and not sufficiently streamlined", the four marvellous bodyshells were one by one removed from the chassis and exchanged for more practical barchettas made by Medardo Fantuzzi and Celestino Fiandri.

With Pinin Farina dropping out of the Maserati orbit (so as not to enter into a conflict of interests with his great client Ferrari), other names began to play more significant roles. One of these was Pietro Frua who contributed to the successful 2000 GT series, firstly with the creation of a coupé and then with a spider. The mechanical specification was modified with the maximum power output rising to 150 hp.

## TECHNICAL SPECIFICATION

### ENGINE
front, longitudinal, straight six

| | |
|---|---|
| Bore and stroke | 76.5 x 72 mm |
| Unitary displacement | 330.93 cc |
| Total displacement | 1985.61 cc |
| Valvegear | double overhead camshafts |
| Number of valves | two per cylinder |
| Compression ratio | 8:1 |
| Fuel system | three Weber 40DCO3 carburettors (38DC03 - 36DCO4) |
| Ignition | double with Marelli ST111DTEM distributor (ST65 - ST100) |
| Cooling | water, centrifugal pump and radiator |
| Lubrication | pressurized, with delivery pump |
| Maximum power | 150 hp at 6000 rpm |
| Specific power output | 75.54 hp/litre |

### TRANSMISSION
| | |
|---|---|
| Driven wheels | rear |
| Clutch | single dry-plate |
| Gearbox | 4 speeds + reverse |

### BODYWORK
| | |
|---|---|
| coupé Frua | 2 doors, 2+2 seats (also with A6GCS/53 chassis and 2 seat bodywork) |

### ROLLING CHASSIS
| | |
|---|---|
| Chassis | tubular with longerons and cross members |
| Front suspension | independent, coil springs, Houdaille hydraulic shock absorbers |
| Rear suspension | live axle, leaf springs, Houdaille hydraulic shock absorbers |
| Brakes | hydraulically actuated drums |
| Steering | worm and gear |
| Fuel tank | 70 litres |
| Tyres front | 6.00-16 |
| rear | 6.00-16 |

### DIMENSIONS AND WEIGHT
| | |
|---|---|
| Wheelbase | 2550 mm |
| Tracks front | 1360 mm |
| rear | 1220 mm |
| Length | 3900 mm |
| Width | 1650 mm |
| Height | 1280 mm |
| Dry weight | 840 kg |
| Weight to power ratio | 5.6 kg/hp |

### PERFORMANCE AND PRODUCTION
| | |
|---|---|
| Maximum speed | 195-210 kph |
| Units produced | 6 |

# A6G-54 Coupé Frua
# 1954

The success of the Maserati 2000 Sport, in its two versions the A6 GCS and the A6 GCS-53, came mainly in racing, while the road-going versions made by Frua, Vignale and Pinin Farina never enjoyed similar fortunes on the market, penalised by the limited power output of 100-110 hp. The model that took their place - the A6G-54, still called the 2000 Gran Turismo in the catalogue - was designed by Vittorio Bellentani, after Gioachino Colombo had gone to Bugatti. The chassis retained the same tubular structure as before, but the wheelbase was increased from 2310 to 2550 mm, the front suspension was independent and a live axle was used at the rear. The engine benefitted from several modifications to simplify it, especially as regards the valvegear (chain- rather than gear-driven now) and the lubrication system (wet sump instead of dry sump). The power of the sports version was reduced from 170 to 150 hp, but this was still a considerable increase compared to the previous GT cars. Frua, Zagato and Allemano "clothed" this chassis in turn, but not Pinin Farina who was by now tied with a double knot to Maserati's great rival Ferrari. Frua created a coupé that is considered a pre-production model, with the new engine still fitted to a short wheelbase chassis (no. 2063) from the A6 GCS-53 series. The car, shown at the Paris Salon in October 1954, had no innovative features, and reprised the lines that followed the traditional aesthetic canons of the Turin coachbuilder. The overall impression was however one of balance and harmony of proportions, emphasised by the white paintwork. On a number of the cars that followed, Frua abandoned one-colour paintwork and tried combinations of colours that were not always met with approval (above all, it must be said, from critics in the years to follow...), such as, for example, the use of blue for the body of the car and white for the roof, combined with a stripe in the centre of the bonnet and the internal upholstery.

After winning the last round of the 1953 F1 World Championship with the ageing A6GCM, Maserati launched its latest creation, the 250 F. The new car won the Argentinian and Belgian GP with Fangio, before the Argentine moved to Mercedes as per the agreement between the two teams. 1954 saw further six victories in non-championship races. The photo here shows Musso at Pau on the 11TH of April 1955, shortly before his retirement.

## TECHNICAL SPECIFICATION

### ENGINE

front, longitudinal, straight six

| | |
|---|---|
| Bore and stroke | 84 x 75 mm |
| Unitary displacement | 415.63 cc |
| Total displacement | 2493.79 cc |
| Valvegear | double overhead camshafts |
| Number of valves | two per cylinder |
| Compression ratio | 12:1 - 10.8:1 (1958) |
| Fuel system | three Weber 42DCO3 carburettors (45DCO3) (1956: also with direct injection) |
| Ignition | double with two Marelli magnetos double with special distributors (1957) |
| Cooling | water, centrifugal pump and radiator |
| Lubrication | dry-sump, pressurized, with delivery and scavenge pump |
| Maximum power | 240-270 hp at 7200-8000 rpm |
| Specific power output | 96.23 - 108.26 hp/litre |

### TRANSMISSION

| | |
|---|---|
| Driven wheels | rear |
| Clutch | multiple dry-plate |
| Gearbox | in-unit with the differential four speeds + reverse |

### BODYWORK

single-seater

### ROLLING CHASSIS

| | |
|---|---|
| Chassis | tubular with longerons and cross members (from 1957 reticular) |
| Front suspension | independent, coil springs, Houdaille hydraulic shock absorbers |
| Rear suspension | De Dion axle, transverse leaf springs, Houdaille hydraulic shock absorbers |
| Brakes | hydraulically actuated drums |
| Steering | worm and gear |
| Fuel tank | from 200 to 230 l |
| Tyres front | 5.25-16 / 5.50-16 / 6.50-16 |
| rear | 6.50-16 / 7.00-16 / 7.00-17 |

### DIMENSIONS AND WEIGHT

| | |
|---|---|
| Wheelbase | 2280 - 2225 mm (1957) - 2200 (1958) |
| Tracks front/rear | 1300 - 1310 mm (1958) |
| Length | – |
| Width | – |
| Height | – |
| Dry weight | 670-630 - 550 kg (1958) |
| Weight to power ratio | 2.79-2.33 / 2.29-2.03 (1958) |

### PERFORMANCE AND PRODUCTION

| | |
|---|---|
| Maximum speed | 290 kph |
| Units produced | 18 (of which five were converted A6GCMs) |

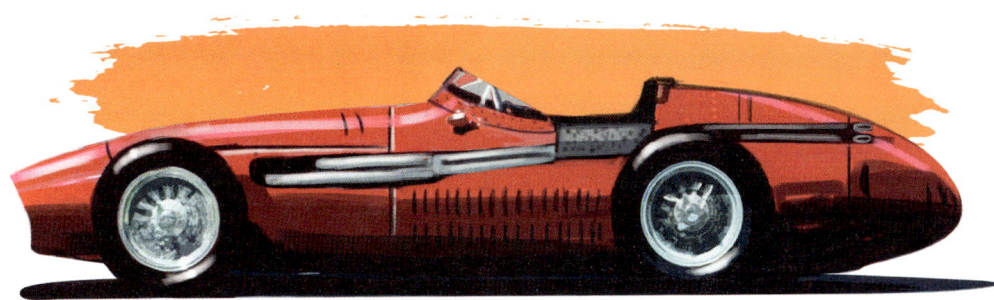

# 250 F                                    1954

In view of the 1954 season, the year the Grand Prix formula was to see increase in the displacement limit for naturally aspirated engines from 2000 to 2500 cc, Maserati decided not to produce a new version of the still competitive A6 GCM and focussed instead on building a new single-seater. Gioachino Colombo designed the engine and when he moved to Bugatti Vittorio Bellentani entrusted the young engineer Giulio Alfieri with responsibility for its development. The chassis, suspension, transmission and braking system were, however, the work of Valerio Colotti. Although it was initially called the 6C 2500, the name 250 F was later used - 250 stood for the two and a half litre displacement and the letter F stood for Formula. Several features were "inherited" from the A6 GCM: the tubular chassis with longerons and cross-members had the same configuration and wheelbase; the engine retained the 6-cylinder architecture, but with the bore and stroke even more over-square - 76.5x72 against 84x75 mm. The power output increased from 197 to 240 hp, approaching 100 hp per litre, a figure that was exceeded in subsequent versions of the car, which was to become one of the most successful F1 single-seaters of all time. This was clear right from the car's debut, with wins for Fangio in the first two Grands Prix (Argentina and Belgium) of the World F1 Championship in 1954. The South American ace had already been signed by Mercedes-Benz but their car was not yet ready for the track, so he was allowed to race with the Maserati, which, thanks to those two wins, entered the World Championship hall of fame, alongside the German marque. The 250 F won on many other occasions in 1954 and in 1955 with Moss, Salvadori, "Bira", Marimón, Musso, Behra, Collins, Simon, Hawthorn and Gerard. Over the first two years of its long career it benefitted from the adoption of a five-speed gearbox and a power increase to 260 hp, a prelude to the thorough update the car was to undergo in 1956.

Maserati participated in the 1954 World Championship for Sports Cars entering a car powered by the 250 F engine installed in an A6 GCS chassis and later equipped with a new tubular chassis, This photos shows the car in action in thre Supercortemaggiore GP with Marimón (paired with Fangio) under attack from the Ferrari 750 Monza of González/ Trintignant. After lying in 2ND place, the 250 S retired with a broken trasnmission.

## TECHNICAL SPECIFICATION

**ENGINE**
front, longitudinal, straight six

| | |
|---|---|
| Bore and stroke | 84 x 75 mm |
| Unitary displacement | 415.63 cc |
| Total displacement | 2493.79 cc |
| Valvegear | double overhead camshafts |
| Number of valves | two per cylinder |
| Compression ratio | 9:1 |
| Fuel system | three Weber 42DCO3 carburettors |
| Ignition | double with Marelli distributors |
| Cooling | water, centrifugal pump and radiator |
| Lubrication | dry-sump, pressurized, with delivery and scavenge pumps |
| Maximum power | 230 hp at 7000 rpm |
| Specific power output | 92.22 hp/litre |

**TRANSMISSION**

| | |
|---|---|
| Driven wheels | rear |
| Clutch | multiple dry-plate |
| Gearbox | 4 or 5 speeds + reverse |

**BODYWORK**
sports two-seater

**ROLLING CHASSIS**

| | |
|---|---|
| Chassis | tubular spaceframe |
| Front suspension | independent, coil springs, Houdaille hydraulic shock absorbers |
| Rear suspension | transverse leaf springs, Houdaille hydraulic shock absorbers, de Dion axle from 1956. |
| Brakes | hydraulically actuated drums |
| Steering | worm and gear |
| Fuel tank | - |
| Tyres front | 5.50-16 |
| rear | 6.00-16 |

**DIMENSIONS AND WEIGHT**

| | |
|---|---|
| Wheelbase | 2310 mm |
| Tracks front/rear | 1300 / 1250 mm |
| Length | – |
| Width | – |
| Height | – |
| Dry weight | 760 kg |
| Weight to power ratio | 3.30 kg/hp |

**PERFORMANCE AND PRODUCTION**

| | |
|---|---|
| Maximum speed | 250 kph |
| Units produced | 1 + 2 engines |

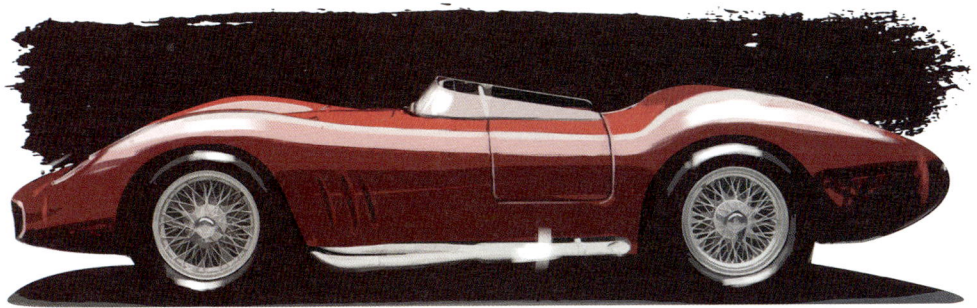

# 250 S (2500 Sport) 1954

The institution, from 1953, of a World Championship for Sports cars, encouraged Maserati to try to compete at a higher level than that of the two-litre displacement, that is to say, in the class in which the A6 GCS was doing particularly well. Their approach was very cautious. A six-cylinder engine from a single-seater Formula 1 car (the 250 F) was installed in an A6 GCS and the car, which never had an official name but can be called the 250 S which is consistent with the way in which cars were named at that time, made its debut in the 1954 Mille Miglia but did not finish the race. In the meantime, the real 250 S was being prepared using a new tubular chassis and all-new bodywork that was aggressively elegant and with the steering wheel on the right, given that in most races the circuits were lapped in a clockwise direction. The 250 F engine was adapted for use with commercial fuel (a rule that was already in force in Sports Car races and which came into force in F1 in 1958) with an inevitable reduction in the compression ratio, from 12 to 9:1. Maximum power was nonetheless fairly high - 230 hp at 7000 rpm - with a top speed of 260 kph. The car's debut on the track came at Monza in the Supercortemaggiore GP in 1954 with Fangio/Marimón at the wheel, while Mantovani/Musso drove the A6 GCS version with the 250 F engine. Even though they were up against rivals with 3-litre engines - Ferrari, Aston Martin and Gordini - the two Maseratis performed honourably, although they suffered under the strain and had to abandon the race. At Modena the firm made a decisive effort to produce a new 3000 cc Sport car, the 300 S, which was destined to see the light of day in 1955. The engine from the 250 S was used again in 1956 in two cars made under an agreement with Talbot, with Campana bodywork being designed by Sergio Reggiani. They were entered in the Le Mans 24 Hours race, but they did not finish and Maserati's collaboration with the French company ended there.

In the mid-1950s the Zagato studio was not restricted to just racing cars: take, for example, this elegant spider based on the A6G-54 rolling chassis presented at the Geneva in 1955, which it caught the eye of the then President of Argentina Juan Domingo Perón. Despite the initial programme, that example was not followed by others and after passing through various hands the car is now frequently participant in concours d'elegance.

## TECHNICAL SPECIFICATION

### ENGINE
front, longitudinal, straight six

| | |
|---|---|
| Bore and stroke | 76.5 x 72 mm |
| Unitary displacement | 330.93 cc |
| Total displacement | 1985.61 cc |
| Valvegear | double overhead camshafts |
| Number of valves | two per cylinder |
| Compression ratio | 8:1 |
| Fuel system | three Weber 40DCO3 carburettors (38DC03 - 36DCO4) |
| Ignition | double with Marelli ST111DTEM distributor (ST65 - ST100) |
| Cooling | water, centrifugal pump and radiator |
| Lubrication | pressurized, with delivery pump |
| Maximum power | 150 hp at 6000 rpm |
| Specific power output | 75.54 hp/litre |

### TRANSMISSION
| | |
|---|---|
| Driven wheels | rear |
| Clutch | single dry-plate |
| Gearbox | four speeds + reverse |

### BODYWORK
| | | |
|---|---|---|
| Zagato | spider | two doors, two seats |

### ROLLING CHASSIS
| | |
|---|---|
| Chassis | tubular with longerons and cross members |
| Front suspension | independent, coil springs, Houdaille hydraulic shock absorbers |
| Rear suspension | live axle, leaf springs, Houdaille hydraulic shock absorbers |
| Brakes | hydraulically actuated drums |
| Steering | worm and gear |
| Fuel tank | 70 l |
| Tyres front | 6.00-16 |
| rear | 6.00-16 |

### DIMENSIONS AND WEIGHT
| | |
|---|---|
| Wheelbase | 2550 mm |
| Tracks front | 1360 mm |
| rear | 1220 mm |
| Length | 3900 mm |
| Width | 1650 mm |
| Height | 1280 mm |
| Dry weight | 840 kg |
| Weight to power ratio | 5.6 kg/hp |

### PERFORMANCE AND PRODUCTION
| | |
|---|---|
| Maximum speed | 195-210 kph |
| Units produced | 1 |

# A6G-54 Spider Zagato               1955

The chance to "clothe" a chassis like that of the A6G-54, which looked like it was going to achieve even greater things in competition than the A6 GCS-53, could not fail to attract the attention of a designer like Zagato, who had always been engaged in making bodywork clearly inspired by racing. Nevertheless, the first car to come out of his workshop based on the rolling chassis of the new two-litre Maserati was a car for "cruising", an extremely elegant spider that was much admired at the 1955 Geneva Motor Show and immediately found a famous buyer: the President of the Republic of Argentina, Juan Domingo Perón, who asked Zagato to make a few changes to improve comfort and to adapt it to his needs. Zagato carried out the work, but when the car was ready, the South American dictator was involved in a political and military upheaval that led to him being overthrown. The spider stayed in the factory and was put on show with a few modifications at the 1958 Paris Motor Show, after which it was sold and had several owners over the years. Finally, it was painstakingly restored and is still the focus of exhibitions and international Concours d'Elegance even today, where it wins prizes as befits a one-off model of this quality. To tell the truth, the front section of this car has been criticised by some. In fact, the formal balance between the bonnet, embedded between the front wings, the headlights and the ellipsoid radiator grille is disturbed by the chrome Trident symbol attached to a chrome baton that divides the radiator in two: the whole thing weighed down by a conspicuous bumper. However, the spider redeems itself when seen from any other point of view, its dynamic shape, the neatness of the lines, the almost sensual harmony of its proportions. Last but not least, is the petrol green paintwork, which replaced the grey of the prototype, complementing the delicate grey velvet of the car's upholstery.

The Coupé by the same stylist enjoyed better fortunes than the Spider A6G-54 Zagato, at least in production terms. A number of examples of this Maserati were built, albeit with variations based on the specific requests of the clients. Worthy of note are the eye-catching graphics of the front end, with the trident badge set off by the chrome trim. On a number of examples Zagato incorporated one of his best known motifs, the double bubble roof.

## TECHNICAL SPECIFICATION

### ENGINE

front, longitudinal, straight six

| | |
|---|---|
| Bore and stroke | 76.5 x 72 mm |
| Unitary displacement | 330.93 cc |
| Total displacement | 1985.61 cc |
| Valvegear | double overhead camshafts |
| Number of valves | two per cylinder |
| Compression ratio | 8:1 |
| Fuel system | three Weber 40DCO3 carburettors (38DC03 - 36DCO4) |
| Ignition | double with Marelli ST111DTEM distributor (ST65 - ST100) |
| Cooling | water, centrifugal pump and radiator |
| Lubrication | pressurized, with delivery pump |
| Maximum power | 150 hp at 6000 rpm |
| Specific power output | 75.54 hp/litre |

### TRANSMISSION

| | |
|---|---|
| Driven wheels | rear |
| Clutch | single dry-plate |
| Gearbox | four speeds + reverse |

### BODYWORK

| | |
|---|---|
| coupé Zagato | two doors, two seats |

### ROLLING CHASSIS

| | |
|---|---|
| Chassis | tubular with longerons and cross members |
| Front suspension | independent, coil springs, Houdaille hydraulic shock absorbers |
| Rear suspension | live axle, leaf springs, Houdaille hydraulic shock absorbers |
| Brakes | hydraulically actuated drums |
| Steering | worm and gear |
| Fuel tank | 70 litres |
| Tyres front | 6.00-16 |
| rear | 6.00-16 |

### DIMENSIONS AND WEIGHT

| | |
|---|---|
| Wheelbase | 2550 mm |
| Tracks front | 1360 mm |
| rear | 1220 mm |
| Length | 3900 mm |
| Width | 1650 mm |
| Height | 1280 mm |
| Dry weight | 840 kg |
| Weight to power ratio | 5.6 kg/hp |

### PERFORMANCE AND PRODUCTION

| | |
|---|---|
| Maximum speed | 195-210 kph |
| Units produced | 20 |

# A6G-54 Coupé Zagato                              1955

Based on an A6G-54 chassis built by Gilco with particularly well-balanced proportions, after building an elegant spider that did not go into production, Zagato created a coupé that was so popular with Maserati's sports car customers that 20 of the cars were built between 1955 and 1956. The coupé's design was inspired by the Fiat 8V Zagato, which had seen the light of day the previous year, but had a sleeker and more compact appearance, which shows how the Milanese coachbuilder always tended to give greatest importance to streamlining and manoeuvrability. And he also tried to make his cars as light as possible too; in fact, this coupé, with its aluminium bodywork and Plexiglas in place of glass, weighed not more than 840 kg. Evidence of this exhaustive quest for functionality could be seen in the passenger compartment too, where the interior design was basic if not spartan, with a conscious rejection of sophisticated details and a complete range of accessories, as was appropriate and still is today for a car intended for use in races. Another feature that was typical of the high level of craftsmanship among coachbuilders of the time and in particular Zagato's engineering practices, was the fact that it is difficult if not impossible to find two identical cars among the 20 A6G-54 coupés produced. Very obvious differences can be seen, above all in the always rather uneasy graphics of the radiator grille, with variations in the style, size and position of the Maserati trident, as well as the shape of the bumpers - either one-piece or two separate pieces, or even with no bumpers at all with the car simply ready to race. But the bodywork of the car was also subject to fairly significant changes: on at least one car the roof had the two unmistakeable "humps" which in those golden years of car production emerged as Zagato's special trademark.

The indirect collaboration between Maserati and Frua continued, thanks once again to the intervention of the Rome dealer Mimmo Dei. It was the patron of the Scuderia Centro Sud who commissioned a series of no less than 10 Spiders based on the Maserati 2000 GT. The first example was delivered to the headquarters of the Scuderia while Dei was preparing to leave for the imminent German Grand Prix five days later.

## TECHNICAL SPECIFICATION

### ENGINE
front, longitudinal, straight six

| | |
|---|---|
| Bore and stroke | 76.5 x 72 mm |
| Unitary displacement | 330.93 cc |
| Total displacement | 1985.61 cc |
| Valvegear | double overhead camshafts |
| Number of valves | two per cylinder |
| Compression ratio | 8:1 |
| Fuel system | three Weber 40DCO3 carburettors (38DC03 - 36DCO4) |
| Ignition | double with Marelli ST111DTEM distributor (ST65 - ST100) |
| Cooling | water, centrifugal pump and radiator |
| Lubrication | pressurized, with delivery pump |
| Maximum power | 150 hp at 6000 rpm |
| Specific power output | 75.54 hp/litre |

### TRANSMISSION
| | |
|---|---|
| Driven wheels | rear |
| Clutch | single dry-plate |
| Gearbox | four speeds + reverse |

### BODYWORK
| | |
|---|---|
| Frua spider | two doors, 2+2 seats (also with A6GCS/53 chassis and two-seater bodywork) |

### ROLLING CHASSIS
| | |
|---|---|
| Chassis | tubular with longerons and cross members |
| Front suspension | independent, coil springs, Houdaille hydraulic shock absorbers |
| Rear suspension | live axle, leaf springs, Houdaille hydraulic shock absorbers |
| Brakes | hydraulically actuated drums |
| Steering | worm and gear |
| Fuel tank | 70 l |
| Tyres front | 6.00-16 |
| rear | 6.00-16 |

### DIMENSIONS AND WEIGHT
| | |
|---|---|
| Wheelbase | 2550 mm |
| Tracks front | 1360 mm |
| rear | 1220 mm |
| Length | 3900 mm |
| Width | 1650 mm |
| Height | 1280 mm |
| Dry weight | 840 kg |
| Weight to power ratio | 5.6 kg/hp |

### PERFORMANCE AND PRODUCTION
| | |
|---|---|
| Maximum speed | 195-210 kph |
| Units produced | 12 |

# A6G-54 Spider Frua                               1955

Towards the end of 1954, Pietro Frua was the first designer to clothe the new Maserati 2000 Gran Turismo, using a rolling chassis that was not yet in definitive form (with a shorter wheelbase than the A6 GCS-53 series of cars). This prototype coupé, considered to be a pre-production model, was later replicated on a further five rolling chassis, while from the beginning of 1956, it was flanked by a spider version. The first of a series of 10 cars was completed on the 30TH of June and delivered on the 30TH of July to Guglielmo Dei, who was by now a well-established customer and a Maserati dealer in Rome; his almost feverish spirit of initiative led to the creation of several one-off *fuoriserie*, as they were called at that time. In its body design the new spider reprised the well-judged lines of the coupé, with its smooth, elongated style, which stood out even more in an open-topped car. The strong flanks of the car ran beneath a belt line that was just slightly curved at either end, towards the headlights and the rear lighting clusters, and was emphasised by a thin chrome trim running from the front wing to the door handle and underlined, as it had done two years before on the A6 GCS-53, the "Maserati 2000 c.c. Gran Sport" badging. As always... the challenging design of the front of the car varied and was revisited on more than one occasion (especially the radiator and the bumpers), but eventually a configuration was found that was both more balanced and aggressive, with an air intake that was lower and wider and the bonnet set lower between the mudguards. The first car, the one built for Guglielmo Dei (chassis number 2104), had a particularly attractive paint finish: the body was painted light blue, with an ivory strip running up the bonnet and light brown interior upholstery. This configuration was used again, using different colour combinations which always created a different and interesting aesthetic effect.

In the second half of the 1950s three coach-builders tackled the A6G-54 theme: Zagato, Frua and Allemano. While the first two created both spider and coupé models, the third focussed on the coupé alone. Compared with the designs of the other two stylists, this version was less race-oriented and 21 examples were produced. Among the features were a conspicuous air intake on the bonnet and a rather emphatic.

## TECHNICAL SPECIFICATION

### ENGINE

front, longitudinal, straight six

| | |
|---|---|
| *Bore and stroke* | 76.5 x 72 mm |
| *Unitary displacement* | 330.93 cc |
| *Total displacement* | 1985.61 cc |
| *Valvegear* | double overhead camshafts |
| *Number of valves* | two per cylinder |
| *Compression ratio* | 8:1 |
| *Fuel system* | three Weber 40DCO3 carburettors (38DC03 – 36DCO4) |
| *Ignition* | dual, with Marelli distributor ST111DTEM (ST65 – ST100) |
| *Cooling* | water, with centrifugal pump and radiator |
| *Lubrication* | pressurised, with delivery pumps |
| *Maximum power* | 150 hp at 6000 rpm |
| *Specific power output* | 75.54 hp/litre |

### TRANSMISSION

| | |
|---|---|
| *Driven wheels* | rear |
| *Clutch* | single dry-plate |
| *Gearbox* | four speeds + reverse |

### BODYWORK

| | |
|---|---|
| *Allemano coupé* | two doors, 2+2 seats |

### ROLLING CHASSIS

| | |
|---|---|
| *Chassis* | tubular, with longerons and cross members |
| *Front suspension* | independent, coil springs, Houdaille hydraulic dampers |
| *Rear suspension* | live axle, leaf springs, Houdaille hydraulic dampers |
| *Brakes* | hydraulically actuated drums |
| *Steering* | worm and gear |
| *Fuel tank* | 70 l |
| *Tyres front/rear* | 6.00-16 / 6.00-16 |

### DIMENSIONS AND WEIGHT

| | |
|---|---|
| *Wheelbase* | 2550 mm |
| *Tracks front/rear* | 1360 / 1220 mm |
| *Length* | 3900 mm |
| *Width* | 1650 mm |
| *Height* | 1280 mm |
| *Dry weight* | 840 kg |
| *Power/weight ratio* | 5.6 kg/hp |

### PERFORMANCE AND PRODUCTION

| | |
|---|---|
| *Maximum speed* | 195-210 kph |
| *Units produced* | 21 |

# A6G-54 Coupé Allemano 1955

Maserati decided to flank its Frua and Zagato spider and coupé models based on the A6G-54 rolling chassis with a less sporting version that would be more attractive to those clients with no racing ambitions but more interested in space, comfort and even luxury. Clients who, with the progressive improvement of the standard of living in Italy and in Europe, were to become more numerous, as intuited by the powers that be at Maserati. The creation of this this new type of car was entrusted to the Turin atelier of Serafino Allemano who, between 1955 and 1957, built 21 examples of a 2+2 coupé destined to establish the styling motifs of reference for the future Trident models. The coachwork inspired an immediate sense of elegance, in harmony with the aesthetic trends of the GT cars of the time: large glazed areas, slim pillars, smooth flanks and a minimal use of chroming. The interpretation of the front end was less convincing in the earliest examples to be produced, with an oval grille that incorporated the auxiliary lights and a conspicuous air intake that encumbered the bonnet. This configuration was the object of successive modifications that with the elimination of the air intake and the fog lights and with a new rectangular grille design with four rounded corners set forward ahead of the radiator itself. Along with the sophisticated trim that embellished the Allemano 2+2, mention has to be made of the undoubted added value of an extensive accessories list that ranged from a Smith heating system to a radio and a set of luggage made to measure for the boot. A total of 60 examples of the A6G-54 were produced over a three-year period subdivded as follows: one spider and 20 coupés by Zagato, 12 spiders and six coupés by Frua and as mentioned above 21 coupés by Allemano.

Giorgio Scarlatti is about to start the 1957 Mille Miglia. He was to finish in 4TH place overall and 3RD in the over 2000 c Sport class, behind the dominant Ferraris. This was one of the last appearances in the World Championship for the 300 S which the previous year had contested through to the final round in Sweden the title with its historic Modenese rival, thanks to earlier victories in Buenos Aires and at the Nürburgring.

## TECHNICAL SPECIFICATION

### ENGINE
front, longitudinal, straight six

| | |
|---|---|
| Bore and stroke | 84 x 90 mm |
| Unitary displacement | 498.75 cc |
| Total displacement | 2992.55 cc |
| Valvegear | double overhead camshafts |
| Number of valves | two per cylinder |
| Compression ratio | 9:1 |
| Fuel system | three Weber 42DCO3 carburettors |
| Ignition | dual, with two Marelli magnetos |
| Cooling | water, with centrifugal pump and radiator |
| Lubrication | dry sump, with delivery and scavenge pumps |
| Maximum power | 245 hp at 6200 rpm |
| Specific power output | 81.86 hp/litre |

### TRANSMISSION
| | |
|---|---|
| Driven wheels | rear |
| Clutch | multiple dry-plate |
| Gearbox | in-unit with differential four speeds + reverse (five in 1958) |

### BODYWORK
two-seater sport

### ROLLING CHASSIS
| | |
|---|---|
| Chassis | tubular spaceframe |
| Front suspension | independent, coil springs, Houdaille hydraulic dampers |
| Rear suspension | transverse leaf-spring, Houdaille hydraulic dampers |
| Brakes | hydraulically actuated drums |
| Steering | worm and gear |
| Fuel tank | 170 l |
| Tyres front/rear | 6.00-16 / 6.50-16 |

### DIMENSIONS AND WEIGHT
| | |
|---|---|
| Wheelbase | 2310 mm |
| Tracks front/rear | 1300 / 1250 mm |
| Length | – |
| Width | – |
| Height | – |
| Dry weight | 780 kg |
| Power/weight ratio | 3.18 kg/hp |

### PERFORMANCE AND PRODUCTION
| | |
|---|---|
| Maximum speed | 290 kph |
| Units produced | 27 |

# 300 S                                     1955

The 250 S's lack of competitiveness persuaded Maserati to develop a new engine with a larger displacement of 2782.61 against 2493.79 cc and with different architecture in which the height of the cylinders was greater than their diameter (81x90 mm against 84x75). The new unit first saw the light of day in the autumn of 1954 and when installed in the 250 S was subjected to a series of tests at Modena and Monza that failed to provide satisfactory results. The 2.8-litre straight six nonetheless went on to power successfully the boat of the racer Liborio Guidotti, while Vittorio Bellentani designed a new three-litre engine, again with a long stroke (84x90 mm), as Maserati's technical director was a great believer in the advantages the configuration offered in terms of torque at low revs and progressive acceleration. Elsewhere the engineering was tried and trusted: three twin-choke carburettors, double overhead camshafts and the gearbox in-unit with the differential. With a compression ratio of 9:1 the maximum power output reached 245 hp at the relatively low engine speed of 6200 rpm. Fantuzzi clothed the spaceframe chassis with a body of undoubted aesthetic impact. Occasional excessively voluminous sections (such as the rear end, which housed the fuel and oil tanks as well as the spare wheel) were subsequently harmonized with the rest of the car which appeared more streamlined. The mechanical specification was the object of continual development making the 300 S one of the most successful Maseratis. As well as allowing the Modenese marque to come close to winning the 1956 World Sports Car Championship, it remained competitive for many years and over the course of a decade (1955-1966) accumulated no less than 58 overall victories in Europe, the United States and South America, in the hands of rapid gentleman drivers and established stars such as Fangio, Moss, Behra, Musso, Shelby, Gregory, Bryan and others.

The private Maserati 159 S entered for the 1956 Mille Miglia by the Belgian crew of Georges Berger and René Foiret. At the finish they were only 145TH overall (but 5TH in the 1300 cc Sport class which saw 2ND place taken by a works 150 S driven by the Frenchman Jean Behra, 20TH overall and 40 minutes behind the OSCA of the winner Giulio Cabianca.

## TECHNICAL SPECIFICATION

### ENGINE

front, longitudinal, straight four

| | |
|---|---|
| Bore and stroke | 81 x 72 mm |
| Unitary displacement | 371.01 cc |
| Total displacement | 1484.06 cc |
| Valvegear | double overhead camshafts |
| Number of valves | two per cylinder |
| Compression ratio | 9:1 |
| Fuel system | two Weber 45DCO3 carburettors |
| Ignition | double, with Marelli or Magneti Marelli distributors |
| Cooling | water, centrifugal pump and radiator |
| Lubrication | dry sump, with delivery and scavenge pumps |
| Maximum power | 140 hp at 7500 rpm |
| Specific power output | 94.33 hp/litre |

### TRANSMISSION

| | |
|---|---|
| Driven wheels | rear |
| Clutch | multiple dry-plate |
| Gearbox | four (or five) speeds + reverse |

### BODYWORK

| | |
|---|---|
| two-seater Sport | a cabriolet GT version was also offered in 1957 |

### ROLLING CHASSIS

| | |
|---|---|
| Chassis | tubular spaceframe |
| Front suspension | independent, coil springs, Houdaille hydraulic dampers |
| Rear suspension | de Dion axle, transverse leaf spring, Houdaille hydraulic dampers |
| Brakes | hydraulically actuated drums |
| Steering | worm and gear |
| Fuel tank | 125 l |
| Tyres front/rear | 5.25-16 / 5.50-16 |

### DIMENSIONS AND WEIGHT

| | |
|---|---|
| Wheelbase | 2150-2250 mm |
| Tracks front/rear | 1250-1200 mm |
| Length | – |
| Width | – |
| Height | – |
| Dry weight | 630 kg |
| Power to weight ratio | 4.5 kg/hp |

### PERFORMANCE AND PRODUCTION

| | |
|---|---|
| Maximum speed | 330 kph |
| Units produced | 25 |

# 150 S                                    1955

By 1953, Vittorio Bellentani had already started work on a 1.5-litre four that Maserati felt might power a new GT car, an idea soon rejected in favour of a Sport model. The project was inspired by the 4C F2 (four cylinders Formula 2) realised in 1952 under the direction of Alberto Massimino. The displacement was reduced from 1994 to 1484 cc while retaining the short stroke configuration, from 88x82 to 81x72 mm, two twin-choke carburettors, double overhead camshafts and dual ignition, in the best Maserati traditions. The power output reached 140 hp at 7500 rpm. The first unit, signed off in the October of 1954, was then sold to the power-boat racer Liborio Guidotti who fitted it to his boat Maria Luisa IV and set a world speed record. With regard to the chassis, the initial intent was to use that of the A6 GCS but Ing. Giulio Alfieri, head of development, made significant modifications to the structure, firstly with the adoption of a de Dion axle and transverse leaf spring in place of the obsolete live axle. The bodywork, similar to that of the 300 S, was created by Celestino Fiandri. The first examples of the 150 S were delivered in the June of 1955 and on the 28TH of August the new Sport, driven by Jean Behra, recorded a stunning victory in the Nürburgring 500 km, beating 13 Porsches and 4 EMW's. While that triumph made the car reasonably popular, it failed to receive the development work its potential deserved, with the factory fully committed to the F1 single-seater and the six-cylinder Sport models. Nonetheless, the 150 S recorded numerous class victories and between 1955 and 1958 also collected a dozen overall wins. A further 23 wins were scored by the English driver Brian Naylor who installed a 150 S engine in a Lotus 11, initiating the practice of assembling racing cars that was to prove to be a successful strategy in the years to come.

The final preparations ahead of the start of the 1957 Mille Miglia, which no one could imagined would be the last edition of that unforgettable race. The Italian manufacturer was represented in the 1500-2000 cc category by four 200 SIs. Unfortunately, not a single example reached the finish in Brescia, including No. 506, seen in the foreground here, driven by Luigi Bellucci of Naples.

## TECHNICAL SPECIFICATION

### ENGINE

front, longitudinal, straight four

| | |
|---|---|
| *Bore and stroke* | 92 x 75 mm |
| *Unitary displacement* | 498.57 cc |
| *Total displacement* | 1994.28 cc |
| *Valvegear* | double overhead camshafts |
| *Number of valves* | two per cylinder |
| *Compression ratio* | 9.8:1 |
| *Fuel system* | two Weber 45DCO3 carburettors |
| *Ignition* | dual, with Marelli or Magneti Marelli distributors |
| *Cooling* | water, centrifugal pump and radiator |
| *Lubrication* | dry sump, with delivery and scavenge pumps |
| *Maximum power* | 190 hp at 7500 rpm |
| *Specific power output* | 95.27 hp/litre |

### TRANSMISSION

| | |
|---|---|
| *Driven wheels* | rear |
| *Clutch* | multiple dry-plate |
| *Gearbox* | four (or five) speeds + reverse |

### BODYWORK

*two-seater Sport*

### ROLLING CHASSIS

| | |
|---|---|
| *Chassis* | tubular spaceframe |
| *Front suspension* | independent, coil springs, Houdaille hydraulic dampers |
| *Rear suspension* | de Dion axle, transverse leaf spring, Houdaille hydraulic dampers (in the first examples, then live axle, semi-cantilever longitudinal leaf springs) |
| *Brakes* | hydraulically actuated drums |
| *Steering* | worm and gear |
| *Fuel tank* | 100 l |
| *Front tyres* | 5.25-16 / 5.50-16 |
| *Rear tyres* | 5.50-16 / 6.00-16 |

### DIMENSIONS AND WEIGHT

| | |
|---|---|
| *Wheelbase* | 2150-2250 mm |
| *Tracks front/rear* | 1250-1200 mm |
| *Length* | – |
| *Width* | – |
| *Height* | – |
| *Dry weight* | 670-660 kg |
| *Power to weight ratio* | 3.52 – 3.47 kg/hp |

### PERFORMANCE AND PRODUCTION

| | |
|---|---|
| *Maximum speed* | 250 kph |
| *Units produced* | 28 |

# 200 S – 200 SI                    1955

In 1954, in parallel with the development of the 150 S, work began on a two-litre engine that was also derived from the 4C F2 (4 cylinders Formula 2) introduced two years earlier. The objective was that of creating a Sport 2000 that would in the future replace the A6 GCS. With respect to that of the 150 S, the new unit differed only in terms of the cylinder dimensions - 92 x 75 mm against 81 x 72 mm – and reprised the configuration of the smaller unit: a fuel system with twin-choke carburettors, double overhead camshafts and dual ignition. The sharp increase in power, from 140 to 190 hp at the same engine sped of 7200 rpm, raised serious handling issues, especially in the early version built in 1955 on an A6 GCS chassis with a live axle. The subsequent adoption of a de Dion axle improved matters, but the 200 S remained a "difficult" car. The tubular chassis, initially built in-house, was then contracted to Gilco, while responsibility for the bodies after the first few examples passed from Fiandri to Fantuzzi. The car went into serial production in 1957 and was renamed as the 200 SI: the letters were the initials of the Sport Internazionale category, to the new regulations of which the car conformed, including the risible requirements for an unusable hood, a wiper for the Plexiglas windscreen and a simulated boot. The 200 SI's competition career between 1956 and 1963 was crowned by numerous wins in the two-litre class and 32 overall victories, in the hands of established drivers such as Behra and others destined for future fame such as Bonnier, Hall and Vaccarella. Moreover, as had been the case with the 150 S, Maserati supplied the 2000 cc four to diverse racer-constructors who installed it in chassis by Cooper, JBW (the initials of John Bryan Naylor and that of the surname of Fred Wilkinson) and WRE (Tony Settember's World Racing Enterprises). Between 1958 and 1963, the drivers of these "hybrids" enjoyed the taste of victory 14 times.

An interesting experiment was conducted on the 250 F in 1955, in an attempt to replicate the success achieved by the streamlined Mercedes-Benzes. The "covered-wheel" Maserati is seen on one of Monza's banked corners during that year's Italian GP. With Jean Behra at the wheel, the car started from the third row and eventually finished 4th, albeit almost four minutes down on the German cars.

## TECHNICAL SPECIFICATION

### ENGINE
front, longitudinal, 60° V12

| | |
|---|---|
| Bore and stroke | 68.7 x 56 mm |
| Unitary displacement | 207.58 cc |
| Total displacement | 2490.99 cc |
| Valvegear | double overhead camshafts per bank |
| Number of valves | two per cylinder |
| Compression ratio | 11.3:1 |
| Fuel system | six Weber 35IDM carburettors |
| Ignition | dual, with two Magneti Marelli magnetos |
| Cooling | water, centrifugal pump and radiator |
| Lubrication | dry sump, pressurised, with delivery and scavenge pumps |
| Maximum power | 310 hp at 10,000 rpm |
| Specific power output | 124.44 hp/litre |

### TRANSMISSION
| | |
|---|---|
| Driven wheels | rear |
| Clutch | multiple dry-plate |
| Gearbox | in-unit with the differential five speeds + reverse |

### BODYWORK
single-seater

### ROLLING CHASSIS
| | |
|---|---|
| Chassis | tubular ladder or reticular frame |
| Front suspension | independent, coil springs, Houdaille hydraulic dampers |
| Rear suspension | de Dion axle, transverse leaf spring, Houdaille hydraulic dampers |
| Brakes | hydraulically actuated drums |
| Steering | worm and gear |
| Fuel tank | 230 l |
| Front tyres | 5.50-16 / 6.50-16 / 5.50-17 |
| Rear tyres | 7.00-16 / 7.00-17 |

### DIMENSIONS AND WEIGHT
| | |
|---|---|
| Wheelbase | 2300 mm |
| Front track | 1310 mm |
| Rear track | 1250 mm |
| Length | – |
| Width | – |
| Height | – |
| Dry weight | 650 kg |
| Weight to power ratio | 2.09 kg/hp |

### PERFORMANCE AND PRODUCTION
| | |
|---|---|
| Maximum speed | 305 kph |
| Units produced | 1 |

# 250 F carenata                                    1955

Most of the myriad improvements made to the 250 F concerned its general mechanical specification. There was, however, a version of the car introduced in 1955, the second year of its long career, that was distinguished by the originality of the aerodynamic research on which it was based. The car was fitted with a fully streamlined body that meant it resembled a sports car in all but the central driving position. Maserati had already experimented with this type of bodywork with the 4CL with which Villoresi at the wheel set the fastest time in qualifying for the Grand Prix of Tripoli in 1939; he then suffered a broken gearbox immediately after the start and had to retire, with the project then being abandoned. In 1955, it was the great efficiency demonstrated by the special bodywork designed by Mercedes-Benz for its single-seaters on high speed tracks that encouraged the development of the aerodynamic body. Medardo Fantuzzi's creation recalled the Stuttgart Strömlinienwagen but differed in at least two conspicuous details: the air vents on the flanks (inspired by the contemporary Maserati 300 S) and the interruption of the panelling in four points that left the upper parts of the wheels exposed to facilitate the cooling of tyres and brakes. Entered with Jean Behra at the wheel for the Italian Grand Prix held on the circuit incorporating the new Alta Velocità curve, the car displayed significant stability issues on the sweeping banked corners, paying the price for hurried development. Behra did manage to finish 4TH in the race, but was almost a lap down on the Mercedes of the winner Fangio. Entrusted to Schell for the successive Syracuse GP, the car finished 5TH and was then used again at Monza for fuel injection testing. The following season, it was again driven by Behra, but with the usual open-wheel bodywork, before being destroyed in a fire at the factory.

Monte Carlo, 13 May 1956: this was a race dominated from start to finish by Stirling Moss in a Maserati 250F, in which he took the most significant victory in the history of the Trident by winning the Monaco Grand Prix. During that season, the British ace achieved another success at Monza, the last round in the World Championship, finishing as runner-up yet again in the title table to Juan Manuel Fangio and confirming himself a king without a crown.

## TECHNICAL SPECIFICATION

### ENGINE

front, longitudinal, straight six

| | |
|---|---|
| Bore and stroke | 84 x 75 mm |
| Unitary displacement | 415.63 cc |
| Total displacement | 2493.79 cc |
| Valvegear | double overhead camshafts |
| Number of valves | two per cylinder |
| Compression ratio | 12:1 – 10.8:1 (1958) |
| Fuel system | three Weber 42DCO3 (45DCO3) carburettors (1956: also indirect fuel injection) |
| Ignition | dual, with two Marelli magnetos dual, with special distributors (1957) |
| Cooling | water, centrifugal pump and radiator |
| Lubrication | dry sump, pressurised, with delivery and scavenge pumps |
| Maximum power | 240-270 hp at 7200-8000 rpm |
| Specific power output | 96.23 – 108.26 hp/litre |

### TRANSMISSION

| | |
|---|---|
| Driven wheels | rear |
| Clutch | multiple dry-plate |
| Gearbox | in-unit with the differential four speeds + reverse (five + reverse from 1955) |

### BODYWORK

single-seater

### ROLLING CHASSIS

| | |
|---|---|
| Chassis | tubular with longerons and cross members (reticular from 1957) |
| Front suspension | independent, coil springs, Houdaille hydraulic dampers |
| Rear suspension | de Dion axle, transverse leaf spring, Houdaille hydraulic dampers |
| Brakes | hydraulically actuated drums |
| Steering | worm and gear |
| Fuel tank | from 200 to 230 litres |
| Front tyres | 5.25-16 / 5.50-16 / 6.50-16 |
| Rear tyres | 6.50-16 / 7.00-16 / 7.00-17 |

### DIMENSIONS AND WEIGHT

| | |
|---|---|
| Wheelbase | 2280 – 2225 (1957) – 2200 (1958) mm |
| Front track | 1300 – 1310 (1958) mm |
| Rear track | 1250 mm |
| Length | – |
| Width | – |
| Height | – |
| Dry weight | 670-630 – 550 kg |
| Weight to power ratio | 2.79–2.33 / 2.29–2.03 (1958) kg/hp |

### PERFORMANCE AND PRODUCTION

| | |
|---|---|
| Maximum speed | 290 kph |
| Units produced | 15 |

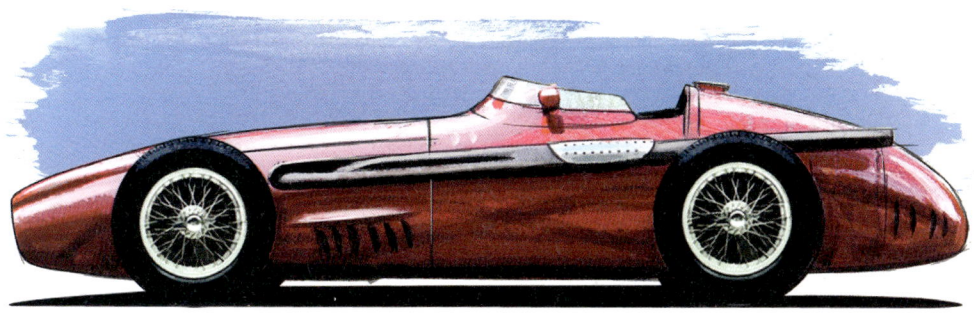

# 250 F                                        1956

The success of the 250 F and its longevity can be explained by the incessant development to which it was subjected over its seven-year career (1954-1960), allowing it to remain competitive. In particular, after the first two years it benefitted from a series of modifications that amounted to a true second series. The engined was inclined through 6° with respect to the longitudinal axis, which allowed the initially central transmission tunnel that ran between the driver's legs to be moved to the left. The driving position and the car's centre of gravity could then be lowered, to the benefit of the already excellent handling. The fuel injection system proved to be unsatisfactory, while after comparison testing drum brakes, one of the 250 F's great strengths, continued to be preferred to discs. Ahead of the 1957 season, a new reticular chassis in small diameter tubes was developed and provided a further saving in weight. The bodywork was also the object of continual development by Fantuzzi, becoming visibly more compact and aerodynamic, with the panelling featuring fewer apertures: a single conspicuous air intake on the right of the bonnet was balanced by the exhausts running into a single pipe along the left flank. The 1956 season, with Mercedes-Benz dropping out of Formula 1, saw Moss return to Maserati and give serious food for thought to Fangio who had in turn moved to Ferrari where he won his fourth world title, beating the Englishman by a handful of points. The following year, Fangio was behind the wheel of the 250 F with which he again triumphed in motorsport's blue ribbon series, a feat that was sadly followed by the announcement of Maserati's withdrawal from direct participation in racing. Nonetheless, for some years to come the Trident's single-seater, now in private hands, continued to embellish its remarkable competition record which boasts no less than 61 victories.

Germany's Hans Herrmann at the start of the 1957 Mille Miglia in the only 350 S entered for the Brescian marathon. The young driver, who gained his experience at Mercedes-Benz until a few years earlier, retired with a broken engine without even crossing the Italian capital. The 3.5-litre V12 put out a maximum of 290 hp at 6000 rpm, which took that spectacular barchetta to a top speed of around 300 kph.

## TECHNICAL SPECIFICATION

### ENGINE

front, longitudinal, straight six
(in 1957 also with the 3490.5 cc 60° V12)

| | |
|---|---|
| *Bore and stroke* | 86 x 100 mm |
| *Unitary displacement* | 580.87 cc |
| *Total displacement* | 3485.27 cc |
| *Valvegear* | double overhead camshafts |
| *Number of valves* | two per cylinder |
| *Compression ratio* | 9.5:1 |
| *Fuel system* | three Weber 45DCO3 carburettors |
| *Ignition* | dual, with Marelli magnetos |
| *Cooling* | water, centrifugal pump and radiator |
| *Lubrication* | dry sump, with delivery and scavenge pumps |
| *Maximum power* | 290 hp at 6000 rpm |
| *Specific power output* | 83.20 hp/litre |

### TRANSMISSION

| | |
|---|---|
| *Driven wheels* | rear |
| *Clutch* | multiple dry-plate |
| *Gearbox* | in-unit with the differential five speeds + reverse |

### BODYWORK

*two-seater Sport*

### ROLLING CHASSIS

| | |
|---|---|
| *Chassis* | tubular spaceframe |
| *Front suspension* | independent, coil springs, dual Houdaille hydraulic dampers |
| *Rear suspension* | de Dion axle, transverse leaf spring, dual Houdaille hydraulic dampers |
| *Brakes* | hydraulically actuated drums |
| *Steering* | worm and gear |
| *Fuel tank* | 150 l |
| *Front tyres* | 6.00-16 / 6.50-16 |
| *Rear tyres* | 7.00-16 / 7.00-17 |

### DIMENSIONS AND WEIGHT

| | |
|---|---|
| *Wheelbase* | 2325 mm |
| *Tracks front/rear* | 1300-1260 mm |
| *Length* | – |
| *Width* | – |
| *Height* | – |
| *Dry weight* | 780 kg |
| *Weight to power ratio* | 2.86 kg/hp |

### PERFORMANCE AND PRODUCTION

| | |
|---|---|
| *Maximum speed* | 300 kph |
| *Units produced* | 3 |

# 350 S                           1956

While the 300 S was enjoying considerable success on many fronts, it frequently found itself at a disadvantage when facing rivals with larger displacements. Maserati attempted to close this gap with the 350 S of which three examples were constructed with varying specifications. The chassis destined to be fitted with the 4.5-litre V8 of the 450 S, fine tuning of which was delayed, was instead mated with the six-cylinder unit of the new 3500 GT, naturally revised in view of its use in racing. The configuration was traditional Maserati with a long stroke, three twin-choke carburettors, double overhead camshafts (chain- rather than gear-driven) and dual ignition. The increase in power was notable - from 245 to 290 hp at 6000 rather than 6200 rpm - and the car was capable of a maximum speed of 300 kph. The coachwork, almost identical to that of the 300 S, was distinguished by a conspicuous bulge on the bonnet required to accommodate the larger engine. Entered for the 1956 Mille Miglia with Moss and Jenkinson, it suffered diverse problems and eventually crashed. Subsequent comparison testing with a 300 S surprisingly revealed that the three-litre car was more competitive and so the 350 S was dismantled and replaced by a second example, with substantial modifications being made to the suspension that improved the roadholding. However, Maserati was by now focussing on the now almost ready 450 S and the 350 S was sold to the driver Luigi Piotti and then, in late 1956, to Tony Parravano's American team, but it never won a race. The third example of the 350 S was equipped with the 3.5-litre six and finished 5[TH] in the 1957 Buenos Aires 1000 Km with Piotti and Bonomi. It was then fitted with a new short stroke (73.8x68 mm) 3490 cc 60° V12 producing 335 hp and a new body built by Fantuzzi to Maserati designs. It competed in the 1957 Mille Miglia with Herrmann (retiring with a broken engine) and was then entered for various races without success.

The photograph at the side is a sort of historic document. The number 537 indicated the time at which the Fantuzzi-bodied Maserati 450 S rolled down the Brescian starting ramp in the 1957 Mille Miglia. Winners two years earlier in a Mercedes-Benz 300 SLR, Moss-Jenkinson's race lasted just a few kilometres. Nobody ever thought for a moment that that 450 S would be the last car to roll down the starting ramp in the entire history of the Mille Miglia.

## TECHNICAL SPECIFICATION

### ENGINE
front, longitudinal, 60° V8

| | |
|---|---|
| Bore and stroke | 93.8 x 81 mm |
| Unitary displacement | 559.73 cc |
| Total displacement | 4477.85 cc |
| Valvegear | double overhead camshafts per bank |
| Number of valves | two per cylinder |
| Compression ratio | 9.5:1 |
| Fuel system | four Weber 45IDM carburettors |
| Ignition | dual, with Marelli magnetos or Marelli distributors |
| Cooling | water, centrifugal pump and radiator |
| Lubrication | dry sump, with delivery and scavenge pumps |
| Maximum power | 400 hp at 7200 rpm |
| Specific power output | 89.32 hp/litre |

### TRANSMISSION
| | |
|---|---|
| Driven wheels | rear |
| Clutch | multiple dry-plate |
| Gearbox | in-unit with the differential five speeds + reverse |

### BODYWORK
two-seater Sport

### ROLLING CHASSIS
| | |
|---|---|
| Chassis | tubular spaceframe |
| Front suspension | independent, coil springs, Houdaille hydraulic dampers |
| Rear suspension | de Dion axle, transverse leaf spring, Houdaille hydraulic dampers |
| Brakes | hydraulically actuated drums |
| Steering | worm and gear |
| Fuel tank | 140 l |
| Front tyres | 6.00-16 |
| Rear tyres | 7.00-16 / 7.00-17 |

### DIMENSIONS AND WEIGHT
| | |
|---|---|
| Wheelbase | 2400 mm |
| Tracks front/rear | 1350-1300 mm |
| Length | – |
| Width | – |
| Height | – |
| Dry weight | 790 kg |
| Weight to power ratio | 1.97 kg/hp |

### PERFORMANCE AND PRODUCTION
| | |
|---|---|
| Maximum speed | 320 kph |
| Units produced | 11 |

# 450 S                                    1956

The research that led to the design and production of the 450 S dated back to 1954, but it was only intermittently pursued due to other commitments Maserati felt had priority, hence the first example of the car only saw the light of day in June 1956. Under the direction of Ing. Giulio Alfieri, Guido Taddeucci designed the engine, while the chassis and transmission, as with the 250 F, were the work of Valerio Colotti. The first chassis used for testing was that of the 350 S damaged by Moss in the Mille Miglia a few weeks earlier. Entered for the Swedish GP, the car ran in practice but was not raced because the formidable 4.5-litre engine was transmitting worrying vibrations. The 90° V8 architecture had a precedent in Maserati history in the form of the Tipo V8 RI from 1935, but this engine had a completely different configuration: a short rather than long stroke (93.8x81 against 84x108 mm), naturally aspirated rather than supercharged and two overhead camshafts per bank instead of one. The unit produced a power output of 400 hp at 7200 rpm and propelled the car to a top speed of 320 kph. Following radical development that included the machining of a new crankshaft, the car made its race debut in the 1957 Sebring 12 Hours which it dominated with Fangio and Behra. There followed a series of failures or minor placings before another victory in the Swedish GP with Moss and Behra put Maserati in a position to challenge for the World Sports Car Championship. Unfortunately, the final race, the GP of Venezuela, saw a catastrophic series of accidents that took out every car entered by the company. The international regulations for 1958 restricted the maximum displacement to 3000 cc and the 450 S was forced to bow out. However, it found further opportunities for success in the United States, in races that were not run to FIA regulations and with private teams and drivers it recorded 23 overall victories between 1957 and 1959 and a further two in Brazil in 1961 and 1964.

Despite the lucky 1 race number that the organisers of the1957 24 Hours of Le Mans had given it, the Zagato-bodied 450 S Coupé crewed by Moss and Schell was unlucky. A retirement in the early part of the race stopped it from any further development. On its return to the garage, it went through the capable hands of the Fantuzzi brothers, who did their best to give it more of a road-going body with a view to it competing in possible future events outside Italy.

## TECHNICAL SPECIFICATION

### ENGINE
front, longitudinal, 60° V8

| | |
|---|---|
| Bore and stroke | 93.8 x 81 mm |
| Unitary displacement | 559.73 cc |
| Total displacement | 4477.85 cc |
| Valvegear | double overhead camshafts per bank |
| Number of valves | two per cylinder |
| Compression ratio | 9.5:1 |
| Fuel system | four Weber 45IDM carburettors |
| Ignition | dual, with Marelli magnetos or Marelli distributors |
| Cooling | water, centrifugal pump and radiator |
| Lubrication | dry sump, with delivery and scavenge pumps |
| Maximum power | 400 hp at 7200 rpm |
| Specific power output | 89.32 hp/litre |

### TRANSMISSION
| | |
|---|---|
| Driven wheels | rear |
| Clutch | multiple dry-plate |
| Gearbox | in-unit with the differential five speeds + reverse |

### BODYWORK
Coupé Zagato

### ROLLING CHASSIS
| | |
|---|---|
| Chassis | tubular spaceframe |
| Front suspension | independent, coil springs, Houdaille hydraulic dampers |
| Rear suspension | de Dion axle, transverse leaf spring, Houdaille hydraulic dampers |
| Brakes | hydraulically actuated drums |
| Steering | worm and gear |
| Fuel tank | 140 l |
| Front tyres | 6.00-16 |
| Rear tyres | 7.00-16 / 7.00-17 |

### DIMENSIONS AND WEIGHT
| | |
|---|---|
| Wheelbase | 2400 mm |
| Tracks front/rear | 1350-1300 mm |
| Length | – |
| Width | – |
| Height | – |
| Dry weight | – |
| Weight to power ratio | – |

### PERFORMANCE AND PRODUCTION
| | |
|---|---|
| Maximum speed | 320 kph |
| Units produced | 1 |

# 450 S Coupé Zagato — 1957

The great potential of the 450 S and its excellent roadholding reinforced Maserati's so far frustrated ambition to win the Le Mans 24 Hours, the most prestigious of the great circuit and endurance races. To improve the cars aerodynamics it was decided to equip it with a closed body and on Stirling Moss's insistence the company drew on the experience of the Englishman Frank Costin, who had worked with Colin Chapman on the first Lotuses and was to go on to create the Vanwalls. Costin's design was "translated" into metal by Zagato, who completed the job in just a few days. The appearance of the resulting coupé was striking for its gently elongated and sleek lines and its downforce inducing and aggressive front end that recalled to some extent the Lotus 11. Unfortunately, however, the lack of available time (the car only left the factory a week before the French race) hardly helped its development. Above all, the closed bodywork and the prudential adoption of elements designed to reinforce the structure led to an increase in weight of 65 kg compared with the spider (from 1118 to 1183 kg). In its new setting the engine tended to overheat and the excess heat with nowhere else to go invaded the cockpit. Lastly, the hoped for advantages in terms of aerodynamics were hard to see: at Le Mans, the fastest time in practice was the 203.530 kph recorded by Fangio, the reserve driver for the Behra/Simon spider that was to retire from the race after 28 laps with a broken axle. The coupé, driven by Moss and Schell, lasted just four laps more before being sidelined with an identical transmission problem. Subjected to radical revision by Fantuzzi ahead of being exported to the United States (where the three-litre limit introduced by the FIA for 1958 International Sports Car races did not apply), the car was more comfortable but never raced again.

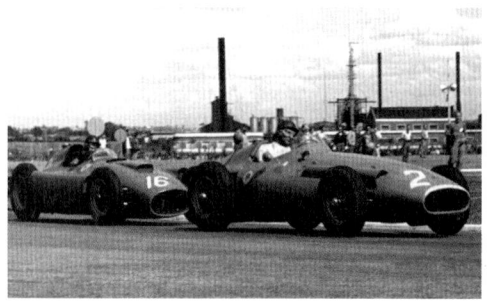

Fangio leads Hawthorn in the Ferrari 801 at the 1957 Grand Prix of Argentina. The South American world champion is driving the glorious 6-cylinder 250 F, but that same year a new 12-cylinder version was developed, although that car had little success. The almost contemporary halt in Maserati factory motor sport activity clipped the wings of this new project.

## TECHNICAL SPECIFICATION

### ENGINE
front, longitudinal, 60° V12

| | |
|---|---|
| Bore and stroke | 68.7 x 56 mm |
| Unitary displacement | 207.58 cc |
| Total displacement | 2490.99 cc |
| Valvegear | double overhead camshafts per bank |
| Number of valves | two per cylinder |
| Compression ratio | 11.3:1 |
| Fuel system | six Weber 35IDM carburettors |
| Ignition | dual, with two Marelli magnetos |
| Cooling | water, centrifugal pump and radiator |
| Lubrication | dry sump, pressurised, with delivery and scavenge pumps |
| Maximum power | 310 hp at 10,000 rpm |
| Specific power output | 124.44 hp/litre |

### TRANSMISSION
| | |
|---|---|
| Driven wheels | rear |
| Clutch | multiple dry-plate |
| Gearbox | in-unit with the differential five speeds + reverse |

### BODYWORK
single-seater

### ROLLING CHASSIS
| | |
|---|---|
| Chassis | tubular ladder or reticular frame |
| Front suspension | independent, coil springs, Houdaille hydraulic dampers |
| Rear suspension | de Dion axle, transverse leaf spring, Houdaille hydraulic dampers |
| Brakes | hydraulically actuated drums |
| Steering | worm and gear |
| Fuel tank | 230 l |
| Front tyres | 5.50-16 / 6.50-16 / 5.50-17 |
| Rear tyres | 7.00-16 / 7.00-17 |

### DIMENSIONS AND WEIGHT
| | |
|---|---|
| Wheelbase | 2300 mm |
| Front track | 1310 mm |
| Rear track | 1250 mm |
| Length | 4350 mm |
| Width | 900 mm |
| Height | 900 mm |
| Dry weight | 650 kg (T3 550 kg) |
| Weight to power ratio | 2.09 kg/hp |

### PERFORMANCE AND PRODUCTION
| | |
|---|---|
| Maximum speed | 305 kph |
| Units produced | 2 T2 + 2 T3 +1 T3 derived from a T2 |

# 250 F T2 – T3                    1957

In 1957, while Fangio was closing in on his fifth World Championship title, providing eloquent testimony as to the surprising competitiveness of the "ageing" 250 F, Maserati was already thinking to the future and the increasingly slim margins for development of the car and in particular its six-cylinder power unit. Since 1955, Ing. Giulio Alfieri had been working on a 12-cylinder design that, in order to be carried forwards would have required the creation of a new chassis, an idea that at least temporarily was shelved due to budgetary restrictions. The new engine was finally built a year later, bench tested in the December of 1956 and then installed in a 250 F chassis. This car (identified in-house with the T2 code given to the 12-cylinder engines) was subjected to intensive testing and entered for numerous races in 1957; however it was long afflicted by fuelling problems due to the difficulty in tuning the six twin-choke Weber carburettors. However, the most serious problem, identified by the drivers, was the delivery of the enormous power output – 310 hp at 10,000 rpm – that was too brusque to be controllable and useful in racing. Only in the Italian Grand Prix at Monza, did the 250 F T2, driven by Behra, show that it was capable of going head-to-head with the domineering Vanwalls, until it was forced to retire with lubrication problems. Maserati's subsequent withdrawal from direct involvement in racing interrupted the development of the 12-cylinder power unit, while Alfieri, with the skeleton racing department staff that remained, turned back to the six-cylinder unit, giving rise to an extreme development of the 1957 version of the car, with its weight reduced from 650 to 550 kg. Three examples of this car, known as the 250 F T3 were constructed, and raced by private teams and drivers with little success. The only result of note was Fangio's 4[TH] place in the French Grand Prix in 1958.

The 250 S, the name of which gives away the car's typology: a 2.5-litre sports racer, but it didn't produce much in terms of the performance of the car that preceded it and by which it was inspired, the 200 SI. Only four of these cars were built, to which another five engines were added and they ended up across the Channel where they were successful in various categories.

## TECHNICAL SPECIFICATION

### ENGINE
front, longitudinal, straight four

| | |
|---|---|
| *Bore and stroke* | 96 x 86 mm |
| *Unitary displacement* | 622.48 cc |
| *Total displacement* | 2489.94 cc |
| *Valvegear* | double overhead camshafts |
| *Number of valves* | two per cylinder |
| *Compression ratio* | 9.75:1 |
| *Fuel system* | two Weber 45DCO3 carburettors (1959: two Weber 48DCO3) |
| *Ignition* | dual, with Marelli distributors or Marelli magnetos |
| *Cooling* | water, centrifugal pump and radiator |
| *Lubrication* | dry sump, with delivery and scavenge pumps |
| *Maximum power* | 196 hp at 7800 rpm (1959: 235 hp at 7200 rpm) |
| *Specific power output* | 78.71 hp/litre (1959: 94.37 hp/litre) |

### TRANSMISSION
| | |
|---|---|
| *Driven wheels* | rear |
| *Clutch* | multiple dry-plate |
| *Gearbox* | four (or five) speeds + reverse |

### BODYWORK
*two-seater Sport*

### ROLLING CHASSIS
| | |
|---|---|
| *Chassis* | tubular spaceframe |
| *Front suspension* | independent, coil springs, Houdaille hydraulic dampers |
| *Rear suspension* | de Dion axle, transverse leaf spring, Houdaille hydraulic dampers |
| *Brakes* | hydraulically actuated drums |
| *Steering* | worm and gear |
| *Fuel tank* | 130 l |
| *Tyres front/rear* | 5.25-16 / 6.50-16 |

### DIMENSIONS AND WEIGHT
| | |
|---|---|
| *Wheelbase* | 2150 mm |
| *Tracks front/rear* | 1250-1200 mm |
| *Length* | – |
| *Width* | – |
| *Height* | – |
| *Dry weight* | 660 kg |
| *Weight to power ratio* | 3.36 kg/hp (1959: 2.80 kg/hp) |

### PERFORMANCE AND PRODUCTION
| | |
|---|---|
| *Maximum speed* | 260 kph |
| *Units produced* | 4 |

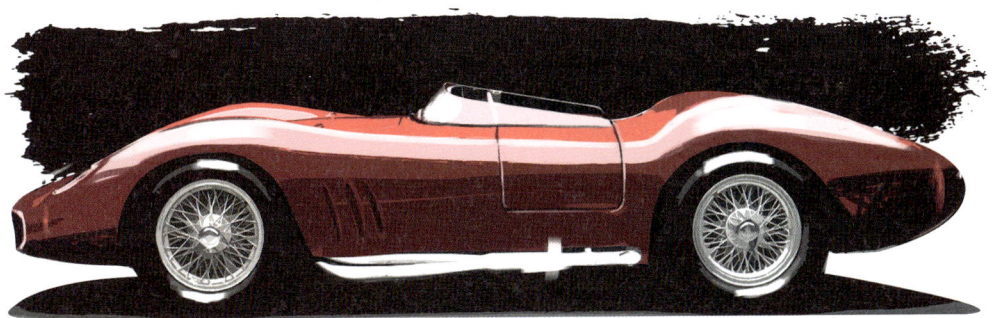

# 250 S 1957

Early in 1957, the new Maserati four-cylinder range was completed with the advent of the 250 S that joined the 150 S and the 200 S/200 SI. The model name clearly indicated that it was a Sport model with a displacement of 2500 cc and it was a works name, only nominally identical to the one that three years earlier had for the sale of convenience distinguished an officially anonymous 2.5-litre model, a very different car based on an A6 GCS chassis and the six-cylinder engine from the 250 F Formula 1 single-seater. The 250 S's four-cylinder engine was instead based on the block from the two-litre engine and equipped with a new crankshaft. The cylinder dimensions were increased from 92x75 mm to 96x86 mm for a total displacement of 2489.94 cc against 1994.28 cc. The chassis was that of the 200 SI and the bodywork was not dissimilar to that of the two-litre model, although it did have a sleeker appearance. Unfortunately, the increase in terms of maximum power was very limited, from 190 to 198 hp, with an identical weight of 660 kg and so understandably the car was never particularly competitive. Four complete examples were built, along with five engines destined for the British and American markets that instead proved to be very successful. In fact, while the car as such obtained no more than four overall victories, the Trident's four-cylinder engines (as had already been the case with those of the 150 S and the 200 S/200 SI) were installed in British Cooper, JBW and Gilby chassis and between 1959 and 1962, won no less than 30 races in England, the United States, Angola and Australia. A number of victories rewarded the installation of the 250 S engine in the Cooper T62, better known as the Cooper Monaco which distinguished itself in a number of sport car races, but the greatest success came in Formula Libre with Brian Naylor's JBW single-seaters playing leading roles between 1959 and 1961.

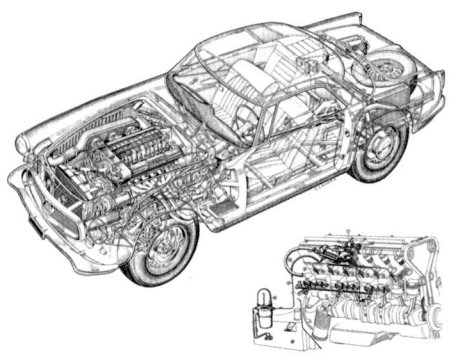

Spring 1957, the Geneva Motor Show: Maserati introduced in its own way a conceptually new model at that prestigious event as the car embodied much of the experience Maserati acquired during its years of racing. It was the 3500 GT, an elegant coupé bodied by Touring on the tubular chassis of the 350 S in which a 6-cylinder in-line power unit that put out 3485.27 cc was installed.

## TECHNICAL SPECIFICATION

### ENGINE
front, longitudinal, straight six

| | |
|---|---|
| Bore and stroke | 86 x 100 mm |
| Unitary displacement | 580.87 cc |
| Total displacement | 3485.27 cc |
| Valvegear | double overhead camshafts |
| Number of valves | two per cylinder |
| Compression ratio | 8.5:1 |
| Fuel system | three Weber 42DCO3 carburettors (1961: a GTI version was also offered with Lucas indirect fuel injection) |
| Ignition | dual, with Marelli distributor |
| Cooling | water, centrifugal pump and radiator |
| Lubrication | pressurised with delivery pump |
| Maximum power | GT: 220 hp at 5500 rpm GTI: 235 hp at 5800 rpm |
| Specific power output | GT: 63.12 hp/litre GTI: 67.42 hp/litre |

### TRANSMISSION
| | |
|---|---|
| Driven wheels | rear |
| Clutch | single dry-plate |
| Gearbox | four speeds + reverse (1960: five speeds + reverse) |

### BODYWORK
| | |
|---|---|
| Touring coupé | two doors, 2+2 seats |

### ROLLING CHASSIS
| | |
|---|---|
| Chassis | tubular |
| Front suspension | independent, coil springs, wishbones, anti-roll bar, telescopic hydraulic dampers |
| Rear suspension | live axle, semi-cantilever leaf springs, telescopic hydraulic dampers |
| Brakes | servo-assisted drums (1959: front discs) |
| Steering | recirculating ball |
| Fuel tank | 75 l |
| Tyres front/rear | 6.50-16 / 6.00-16 |

### DIMENSIONS AND WEIGHT
| | |
|---|---|
| Wheelbase | 2600 mm |
| Tracks front/rear | 1390-1360 mm |
| Length | 4700 mm |
| Width | 1700 mm |
| Height | 1300 |
| Dry weight | 1300 kg |
| Weight to power ratio | 5.90 kg/hp |

### PERFORMANCE
| | |
|---|---|
| Maximum speed | 220 kph |
| Units produced | 1 |

# 3500 GT Coupé Touring «Dama bianca»

## 1957

Maserati's sporting success peaked in 1957 with Fangio's conquest of Formula 1 World Championship title in the 250 F and the marque missing out on the World Sports Car title only because of an almost unbelievable series of negative coincidences. In the meantime, the company's economic difficulties had worsened and at the end of the year it was forced to go into administration and abandon direct participation in racing. From then on, the Trident's presence in competition was to be through the initiatives of private teams and drivers. However, another event that indelibly marked that year was evidence of the Modenese marque's new and more determined commitment to the production of Grand Touring cars: the spring launch of the brand new 3500 GT at the Geneva Motor Show. This was to all intents and purposes a road-going version of the 350 S, with a longer wheelbase tubular chassis (2600 against 2325 mm) and independent front suspension and a live axle at the rear. The engine was the long-stroke, 3.5-litre straight six with reduced maximum power and speed: from 290 to 220 hp and from 300 to 220 kph. The rolling chassis of the Geneva prototype boasted an elegant 2+2 coupé body by Touring, featuring the classic Superleggera technology. The car was admired for its well balanced lines: smooth flanks, slim pillars and discreet chroming. The large oval radiator grille pushed forwards with the Trident at its centre. The richly equipped interior was characterised by luxurious finishing and great comfort. The white paint of the first example earned the car a nickname that was echoed in the newspapers of the period: "Dama Bianca", or "White Lady", as the protagonist of a sentimental affair involving the great racing cyclist Fausto Coppi was known.

Maserati started to rise again with the various versions of the 3500 GT. The Trident's retirement from top level motor sport meant no more front page newspaper coverage; all to the advantage of its rival, Ferrari. But at the same time, the development of the 3500 GT, gave the company leadership in top level road car production, a segment which, from that moment on, meant Maserati became the undisputed leader in the Italian and foreign markets.

## TECHNICAL SPECIFICATION

### ENGINE
front, longitudinal, straight six

| | |
|---|---|
| Bore and stroke | 86 x 100 mm |
| Unitary displacement | 580.87 cc |
| Total displacement | 3485.27 cc |
| Valvegear | double overhead camshafts |
| Number of valves | two per cylinder |
| Compression ratio | 8.5:1 |
| Fuel system | three Weber 42DCO3 carburettors (1961: a GTI version was also offered with Lucas indirect fuel injection) |
| Ignition | dual, with Marelli distributor |
| Cooling | water, centrifugal pump and radiator |
| Lubrication | pressurised with delivery pump |
| Maximum power | GT: 220 hp at 5500 rpm GTI: 235 hp at 5800 rpm |
| Specific power output | GT: 63.12 hp/litre GTI: 67.42 hp/litre |

### TRANSMISSION
| | |
|---|---|
| Driven wheels | rear |
| Clutch | single dry-plate |
| Gearbox | four speeds + reverse (1960: five speeds + reverse) |

### BODYWORK
| | |
|---|---|
| 2+2 coupé or spider | two doors, two or 2+2 seats |
| | (Allemano, Touring, Frua coupés; Touring, Frua, Vignale spiders) |

### ROLLING CHASSIS
| | |
|---|---|
| Chassis | tubular |
| Front suspension | independent, coil springs, wishbones, anti-roll bar, telescopic hydraulic dampers |
| Rear suspension | live axle, semi-cantilever leaf springs, telescopic hydraulic dampers |
| Brakes | servo-assisted drums (1959: front discs) |
| Steering | recirculating ball |
| Fuel tank | 75 l |
| Tyres front/rear | 6.50-16 / 6.00-16 |

### DIMENSIONS AND WEIGHT
| | |
|---|---|
| Wheelbase | coupé: 2600 mm / spider: 2500 mm |
| Tracks front/rear | 1390-1360 mm |
| Length | 4700 mm |
| Width | 1700 mm |
| Height | 1300 mm |
| Dry weight | coupé 1300 kg / spider: 1200 kg |
| Weight to power ratio | GT coupé: 5.90 kg/hp spider: 5.45 kg/hp GTI coupé: 5.53 kg/hp spider: 5.10 kg/hp |

### PERFORMANCE AND PRODUCTION
| | |
|---|---|
| Maximum speed | GT: 220 kph / GTI: 235 kph |
| Units produced | GT, GTI, coupé and spider: 2224 |

# 3500 GT – GTI Coupé – Spider        1957

The Carrozzeria Touring coupé nicknamed the Dama Bianca, presented at the Geneva Motor Show in the spring of 1957, had been preferred to another two variations on the theme, one by Allemano (personalised with a less-than-convincing two-tone paint finish) and the other by Zagato (conceived in view of a sporting use that the deliberately "relaxed" configuration of the car denied from the outset). Months later, two open versions were also seen, neither destined for production, a spider again by Touring, which reprised the styling of the coupé as if it had been shorn of its upper body, and a 2+2 cabriolet by Frua. The serial production of the 3500 GT was to begin in the second half of 1957 and the definitive car showed that with respect to the prototype, numerous mechanical and functional modifications were made as a result of the intensive testing conducted in that period, in the factory and on the road. Over the coming years, just minor changes were made to the bodywork: air intakes, front and rear lighting clusters, glazing, details of a classically configured design. The mechanical specification was instead subject to a constant evolution: the adoption of a limited slip differential and disc brakes (1959), a five-speed gearbox (1960) and fuel injection (1961). This constant research and development reflected the engineering philosophy of Giulio Alfieri and was an important element in the success of the 3500 GT, which achieved production numbers that were unrivalled in Maserati history: of the A6 barely 150 examples were constructed over the previous decade while 2200 examples of the new GT were built in seven years. The fact that the Modenese marque survived the economic difficulties of late 1957 and its vigorous subsequent revival were at least in part made possible by the strong sales of this prestigious car.

One of the unusual images from Maserati history is the Eldorado, as it is commonly known and the car is currently owned by the Panini family. Born on the basics of the 250 F, this single-seater raced just once, at Monza in 1958 and was driven by Stirling Moss. It came fourth and fifth in the first two heats but ended up off the track in the third and was classified seventh even if it didn't cross the finish line.

## TECHNICAL SPECIFICATION

### ENGINE
front, longitudinal, 90° V8

| | |
|---|---|
| Bore and stroke | 93.8 x 75.8 mm |
| Unitary displacement | 523.79 cc |
| Total displacement | 4190.38 cc |
| Valvegear | double overhead camshafts per bank |
| Number of valves | two per cylinder |
| Compression ratio | 12:1 |
| Fuel system | four Weber 46IDM carburettors |
| Ignition | dual, with Marelli magnetos |
| Cooling | water, centrifugal pump and radiator |
| Lubrication | dry sump, with delivery and scavenge pumps |
| Maximum power | 410 hp at 8000 rpm |
| Specific power output | 97.84 hp/litre |

### TRANSMISSION
| | |
|---|---|
| Driven wheels | rear |
| Clutch | multiple dry-plate |
| Gearbox | in-unit with the rear axle two speeds + reverse |

### BODYWORK
single-seater

### ROLLING CHASSIS
| | |
|---|---|
| Chassis | tubular spaceframe |
| Front suspension | independent, coil springs, hydraulic dampers |
| Rear suspension | de Dion axle, transverse leaf spring, dual hydraulic dampers |
| Brakes | hydraulically actuated drums |
| Steering | worm and gear |
| Fuel tank | 250 l |
| Front tyres | 7.60-16 / 8.00-16 |
| Rear tyres | 8.00-18 |

### DIMENSIONS AND WEIGHT
| | |
|---|---|
| Wheelbase | 2400 mm |
| Tracks front/rear | 1300-1250 mm |
| Length | – |
| Width | – |
| Height | – |
| Dry weight | 758 kg |
| Weight to power ratio | 1.84 kg/hp |

### PERFORMANCE AND PRODUCTION
| | |
|---|---|
| Maximum speed | 350 kph |
| Units produced | 1 |

# 420 M-58 Eldorado – 420 M-59     1958

For the Monza 500 Miles instituted in 1957 and named the "Trofeo dei Due Mondi", Maserati prepared two improvised cars that failed to qualify: one was the 420 F, a 250 F with a 3.5-litre, 12-cylinder engine, and a 450 S, the Sport 4.5 with the displacement reduced to 4.2 litres. In 1958, instead, at the second and last edition of the race, despite being in administration Maserati participated with a powerful single-seater commissioned and financed by a private client, Gino Zanetti, owner of the well-known Eldorado ice cream company. This name, conspicuously exhibited on the bodywork, flanked and effectively replaced the factory Tipo 4 or 420 M-58 nomenclature. The tubular chassis was inspired by that of the lightweight 250 F, with oversized suspension elements to cope with both the enormous power output of the engine (410 hp at 8000 rpm) and the stress caused by the speeds of over 200 kph constantly sustained on the banked track paved in concrete slabs that were never perfectly joined. The engine was the 90° V8 of the 450 S with the displacement reduced from 4477.85 to 4190.38 cc with the bored unaltered and the stroke lowered from 81 to 75.8 mm. Given that the track was lapped anti-clockwise, the engine was installed on the left-hand side of the chassis (90 mm off the longitudinal axis) with the cockpit shifted to the right. The gearbox had two speeds, the first used only at the start. The Eldorado competed magnificently in the first two heats of the race, with Stirling Moss driving it to 4TH and 5TH place. In the third, however, the steering broke, throwing the English driver off the track at 260 kph; he was nonetheless classified 7th. Subsequently transformed and renamed as the 420 M-59, the car was entered for the Indianapolis 500 Miles for Ralph Liguori who failed to qualify.

After the 3500 GT's introduction, Bertone took the car's chassis and designed and built a sleek, one-off gritty coupé on it. The project was carried out by the much respected designer Franco Scaglione, who gave it a look similar to other of his recent creations, ranging from the NSU Prinz 4 to the Alfa Romeo Giulietta Sprint Speciale. Perhaps Scaglione drew from a repertoire that was not too familiar to Maserati, which prejudiced the success of this particular version.

## TECHNICAL SPECIFICATION

### ENGINE

front, longitudinal, straight six

| | |
|---|---|
| Bore and stroke | 86 x 100 mm |
| Unitary displacement | 580.87 cc |
| Total displacement | 3485.27 cc |
| Valvegear | double overhead camshafts |
| Number of valves | two per cylinder |
| Compression ratio | 8.5:1 |
| Fuel system | three Weber 42DCO3 carburettors |
| Ignition | dual, with Marelli distributor |
| Cooling | water, centrifugal pump and radiator |
| Lubrication | pressurised with delivery pump |
| Maximum power | 220 hp at 5500 rpm |
| Specific power output | 63.12 hp/litre |

### TRANSMISSION

| | |
|---|---|
| Driven wheels | rear |
| Clutch | single dry-plate |
| Gearbox | four speeds + reverse (1960: five speeds + reverse) |

### BODYWORK

| | |
|---|---|
| Bertone 2+2 coupé | two doors, 2+2 seats |

### ROLLING CHASSIS

| | |
|---|---|
| Chassis | tubular |
| Front suspension | independent, coil springs, wishbones, anti-roll bar, telescopic hydraulic dampers |
| Rear suspension | live axle, semi-cantilever leaf springs, telescopic hydraulic dampers |
| Brakes | servo-assisted drums (1959: front discs) |
| Steering | recirculating ball |
| Fuel tank | 75 l |
| Tyres front/rear | 6.50-16 / 6.00-16 |

### DIMENSIONS AND WEIGHT

| | |
|---|---|
| Wheelbase | 2600 mm |
| Tracks front/rear | 1390-1360 mm |
| Length | – |
| Width | – |
| Height | – |
| Dry weight | 1300 kg |
| Weight to power ratio | 5.90 kg/hp |

### PERFORMANCE AND PRODUCTION

| | |
|---|---|
| Maximum speed | 220 kph |
| Units produced | 1 |

# 3500 GT Coupé Bertone                                    1959

One of the most particular interpretations of the prestigious 3500 GT theme was offered in 1959 by Bertone and in particular by Franco Scaglione, one of the most creative Italian stylists, in what was one of his last jobs as head of design for the Turin coachbuilder which had just moved into its new Grugliasco premises. The car was a coupé destined to remain a one-off, commissioned by Amilcare Martinelli and Aldo Sonvico, owners of the Maserati importers in Switzerland and founders of the popular Lugano racing team of the same name for which numerous drivers from the Canton Ticino competed early in their careers, above all Silvio Moser and Clay Regazzoni. The styling of the car featured a number of the motifs typical of the Tuscan designer, beginning with the compact upper body with the roof line dipping sharply between the rear fins, and recalls on a larger scale the unmistakeable profile of the contemporary NSU Prinz coupé, also referenced by the fins themselves. The sharp crease line of the front wheelarch that almost reaches the door handle (and is then reprised and continued at the rear) is an exaggerated citation of the similar treatment that can be seen on the flanks of the Alfa Romeo Giulietta SS, also presented in 1959. The most original feature of the car can be seen from the front, with the sharp, aggressive nose extending into a large, flat bonnet with a very slim but long air intake. The sensation of longitudinal sleekness was reinforced by the length of the flanks, judged to be somewhat excessive at the rear. What is less convincing in this coupé are in fact the dimensional relationships, the proportions between the elements of which it is composed and which, taken individually, are striking for the originality or successful reprisal but which overall struggle to find or indeed fail to find harmony or compositional equilibrium.

Another possible stylistic development of the 3500 GT for an open top version was entrusted to Pietro Frua. The result was a 2 + 2 cabriolet, which appeared in October 1959 in Paris. It was liked by many people for some of its original aspects, such as the shell that connected the headlights with the radiator grill, the prominent decoration on the sides and the elegant interior. But the idea was not followed up and the Frua example remained an isolated case.

## TECHNICAL SPECIFICATION

### ENGINE
front, longitudinal, straight six

| | |
|---|---|
| Bore and stroke | 86 x 100 mm |
| Unitary displacement | 580.87 cc |
| Total displacement | 3485.27 cc |
| Valvegear | double overhead camshafts |
| Number of valves | two per cylinder |
| Compression ratio | 8.5:1 |
| Fuel system | three Weber 42DCO3 carburettors |
| Ignition | dual, with Marelli distributor |
| Cooling | water, centrifugal pump and radiator |
| Lubrication | pressurised with delivery pump |
| Maximum power | 220 hp at 5500 rpm |
| Specific power output | 63.12 hp/litre GTI: 67.42 hp/litre |

### TRANSMISSION
| | |
|---|---|
| Driven wheels | rear |
| Clutch | single dry-plate |
| Gearbox | four speeds + reverse (1960: five speeds + reverse) |

### BODYWORK
| | |
|---|---|
| Frua 2+2 cabriolet | two doors, 2+2 seats |

### ROLLING CHASSIS
| | |
|---|---|
| Chassis | tubular |
| Front suspension | independent, coil springs, wishbones, anti-roll bar, telescopic hydraulic dampers |
| Rear suspension | live axle, semi-cantilever leaf springs, telescopic hydraulic dampers |
| Brakes | servo-assisted drums (1959: front discs) |
| Steering | recirculating ball |
| Fuel tank | 75 l |
| Tyres front/rear | 6.50-16 / 6.00-16 |

### DIMENSIONS AND WEIGHT
| | |
|---|---|
| Wheelbase | 2500 mm |
| Tracks front/rear | 1390-1360 mm |
| Length | – |
| Width | – |
| Height | – |
| Dry weight | 1300 kg |
| Weight to power ratio | 5.45 kg/hp |

### PERFORMANCE AND PRODUCTION
| | |
|---|---|
| Maximum speed | 220 kph |
| Units produced | 1 |

# 3500 GT Cabriolet 2+2 Frua     1959

At the Paris Motor Show in the October of 1959, Frua presented a 2+2 cabriolet on the Maserati 3500 GT chassis with elegant and delicate two-tone white and turquoise upholstery. The car remained a one-off, never going into serial production, but as a styling project it is remembered for a number of original features. The upper profile of the flanks ran along an almost dead straight section: this choice meant the designer had to forego the soft volumes of the spiders built a few years earlier on the 2000 GT rolling chassis, but foreshadowed a trend that was destined to take hold in the medium term. One particular striking feature was the dual air vents on the flanks with chromed perimeter and finning, a familiar motif (the A6G coupé by Allemano, 1954) but here sharpened and conspicuously accentuated with the upper profile extending uninterrupted through to the tail and carrying the name of the model - Maserati 3500 GT – with the signature of Pietro Frua below, while the lower profile was set almost flush with the door sill and linked the two wheel arches. The front end contrasted even more strongly with the basic configuration - which had in any case given rise to sleek, well-balanced body – dominated as it was by the chroming of the radiator grille with the large trident and the half-bumpers with their large overriders. The sense of strained styling was heightened by the composition of the large air intake on the bonnet, the headlights and the circular indicators as well as well as the rectangular fog lamps; the result was not unattractive in itself, but rather deceptive in the sense that it distracted attention of other details of undoubted interest: for example, the treatment of the headlights with their housing characterised at the bottom by a scoop linking them to radiator, a styling feature that over the years was to reprised successfully on many sports cars.

As production continued of the closed Touring-bodied 3500 GT, another stylist, Alfredo Vignale, had joined the list of Maserati suppliers. The company was commissioned to create a roadster, which followed the Frua cabriolet a few days later which, unlike the Frua car, was considered quite different and of which over 200 cars were built.

## TECHNICAL SPECIFICATION

### ENGINE

front, longitudinal, straight six

| | |
|---|---|
| Bore and stroke | 86 x 100 mm |
| Unitary displacement | 580.87 cc |
| Total displacement | 3485.27 cc |
| Valvegear | double overhead camshafts |
| Number of valves | two per cylinder |
| Compression ratio | 8.5:1 |
| Fuel system | three Weber 42DCO3 carburettors (1961: a GTI version was also offered with Lucas indirect fuel injection) |
| Ignition | dual, with Marelli distributor |
| Cooling | water, centrifugal pump and radiator |
| Lubrication | pressurised with delivery pump |
| Maximum power | GT: 220 hp at 5500 rpm GTI: 235 hp at 5800 rpm |
| Specific power output | GT: 63.12 hp/litre GTI: 67.42 hp/litre |

### TRANSMISSION

| | |
|---|---|
| Driven wheels | rear |
| Clutch | single dry-plate |
| Gearbox | four speeds + reverse (1960: five speeds + reverse) |

### BODYWORK

| | |
|---|---|
| Vignale spider | two doors, two seats |

### ROLLING CHASSIS

| | |
|---|---|
| Chassis | tubular |
| Front suspension | independent, coil springs, wishbones, anti-roll bar, telescopic hydraulic dampers |
| Rear suspension | live axle, semi-cantilever leaf springs, telescopic hydraulic dampers |
| Brakes | servo-assisted drums (1959: front discs) |
| Steering | recirculating ball |
| Fuel tank | 75 l |
| Tyres front/rear | 6.50-16 / 6.00-16 |

### DIMENSIONS AND WEIGHT

| | |
|---|---|
| Wheelbase | coupé: 2600 mm cabriolet: 2500 mm |
| Tracks front/rear | 1390-1360 mm |
| Length | – |
| Width | – |
| Height | – |
| Dry weight | 1200 kg |
| Weight to power ratio | GT: 5.45 kg/hp GTI: 5.10 kg/hp |

### PERFORMANCE AND PRODUCTION

| | |
|---|---|
| Maximum speed | GT: 220 kph GTI: 235 kph |
| Units produced | 242 |

# 3500 GT Spider Vignale                    1959

At the Turin Motor Show of 1959, the standard Touring coupé on the Maserati 3500 GT chassis was flanked by a Vignale spider that followed up the Frua 2+2 cabriolet presented at the Paris Motor Show a few weeks earlier. The Vignale design was the fruit of the talent of Giovanni Michelotti, then at the height of his career as a stylist with all the creative fervour that sustained it. On a rolling chassis with the wheelbase shortened by 100 mm (from 2600 to 2500), at first sight the coach-work invoked a sense of sporting agility not lacking in elegance. The front end was redesigned around the customary elements, but given a more decisive graphic configuration with the radiator grille thrust forwards and with a heavy chrome frame. Either side, the elements of each lighting cluster, headlight, fog lamp and indicator, the points identified of a virtual triangle. The most attractive part of the side view was the upper crease line that ran along two levels with a kick immediately behind the door raising the rear section, while the line ran almost imperceptibly upwards towards the nose before being truncated by the front end which was slightly inclined in parallel with the rear. This treatment of the flanks was to have a certain popularity in that period among the open cars of various marques: it can for example bee seen on the Pinin Farina Ferrari and on Michelotti's interpretations of diverse Fiat, Triumph and BMW models. The Vignale-bodied Maserati 3500 GT spider, already equipped with disc brakes on the front wheels (only optional in 1959 and destined to be standard from 1960) was produced through to 1964 in 242 example and also appeared in a couple of American films, *Two Weeks in Another Town*, by Vincente Minnelli (1962) *The Killers*, by Don Siegel (1964), this last featuring Ronald Reagan, future President of the United States.

The 3500 GT was a success in terms of the number of cars built and at the end of the '50s Maserati added an even more exclusive model to the range, the 5000 GT. This was a sensational car that was powered by the 4.8-litre V8 engine from the 450 S and taken to 5-litres in 1960. Italy's top body stylists of the period produced their versions of this car, first among them Touring, which created the first 5000 GT commissioned by the Shah of Persia, Mohammad Reza Pahlavi.

## TECHNICAL SPECIFICATION

### ENGINE
front, longitudinal, 90° V8

| | |
|---|---|
| Bore and stroke | 98.5 x 81 mm (from 1960: 94 x 89) |
| Unitary displacement | 617.22 cc (from 1960: 617.63) |
| Total displacement | 4837.83 cc (from 1960: 4941.11 cc) |
| Valvegear | double overhead camshafts per bank |
| Number of valves | two per cylinder |
| Compression ratio | 8.5:1 |
| Fuel system | four Weber 45IDM (or 46IDM) carburettors (from 1960: also with Lucas indirect fuel injection) |
| Ignition | dual, with Marelli or Lucas distributors |
| Cooling | water, centrifugal pump and radiator |
| Lubrication | pressurised with delivery pump |
| Maximum power | 325 hp at 5500 rpm (from 1960: 340 hp at 5800 rpm) |
| Specific power output | 67.17 hp/litre (from 1960: 68.81 hp/litre) |

### TRANSMISSION
| | |
|---|---|
| Driven wheels | rear |
| Clutch | dual dry-plate |
| Gearbox | four speeds + reverse (from 1963: five speeds + reverse) |

### BODYWORK
| | |
|---|---|
| Touring coupé | two doors, 2+2 seats |

### ROLLING CHASSIS
| | |
|---|---|
| Chassis | tubular |
| Front suspension | independent, coil springs, wishbones, anti-roll bar, telescopic hydraulic dampers |
| Rear suspension | live axle, semi-elliptical leaf springs, struts, anti-roll bar, telescopic hydraulic dampers |
| Brakes | hydraulically actuated, servo-assisted front discs and rear drums |
| Steering | recirculating ball |
| Fuel tank | 100 l |
| Front tyres | 6.50-16 (from 1963: 205-15) |
| Rear tyres | 6.50-16 (from 1963: 205-15) |

### DIMENSIONS AND WEIGHT
| | |
|---|---|
| Wheelbase | 2600 mm |
| Tracks front/rear | 1390-1360 mm |
| Length | – |
| Width | – |
| Height | – |
| Dry weight | 1500 kg |
| Weight to power ratio | 4.61 kg/hp (from 1960: 4.41 kg/hp) |

### PERFORMANCE AND PRODUCTION
| | |
|---|---|
| Units produced | 3 (+1 renumbered) |

# 5000 GT Coupé 2+2 Touring
# «Scià di Persia»

### 1959

A special client – Mohammed Reza Pahlavi, the last Shah of Persia – after having tested the Maserati 3500 GT, said that he was interested in purchasing one, but feeling that it was not sufficiently exclusive, asked for a version more appropriate to his position to be prepared. Ing. Giulio Alfieri installed the V8 engine from the 450 S in a suitably reinforced 3500 chassis. The bore was increased from 93.8 to 98.5 mm with the stroke of 81 mm remaining unchanged, the displacement therefore increasing from 4.5 to 5 litres (from 4477.85 to 4937.83 cc). The power output was reduced with respect to the racing Sport model from 400 to 325 hp, but despite an increase in weight from 790 to 1500 kg, the top speed dropped only from 320 to 260 kph, making this the world's fastest GT car. The interior was suitably luxurious, with fine leather upholstery, special woods and solid gold fittings. The creation of a body was entrusted to Touring, the firm already responsible for the standard 3500, and the resulting car was not dissimilar to that model: the same smooth flanks, although a little deeper, and a slightly smaller, single-light glasshouse with very slim pillars. The most conspicuous difference came at the front with an ellipsoidal full-width grille incorporating dual headlights and with the upper edge interrupted by a kind of "snout" housing the trident. The overall result was somewhat baroque revealing a degree of creative fatigue in the Milan coachbuilder, with recourse made to rather dated motifs already seen on the Alfa Romeo 1900 C Super Sprint and the Lancia Flaminia GT. Touring constructed three examples of the 5000 GT, after which the following units were entrusted to other stylists. From 1960, the mechanical specification was modified with a displacement of 4941.11 cc obtained via a smaller bore and a significantly longer stroke (94x89 mm) and fuel injection, the power output consequently rising to 340 hp and the top speed to 270 kph.

Even though it had officially left top flight motor sport by the end of the '50s, Maserati soon began to design a brand new model specifically for racing. It was called the Tipo 60, a futuristic barchetta which, due to its original tubular chassis, was given the nickname Birdcage. The car won first time out in France driven by Stirling Moss, which immediately created a rush of sporting customers who wanted to buy one from the Modena factory.

## TECHNICAL SPECIFICATION

### ENGINE
front, longitudinal, straight four

| | |
|---|---|
| Bore and stroke | 93.8 x 72 mm |
| Unitary displacement | 497.53 cc |
| Total displacement | 1990.5 |
| Valvegear | double overhead camshafts |
| Number of valves | two per cylinder |
| Compression ratio | 9.8:1 |
| Fuel system | two Weber 45DCO3 carburettors |
| Ignition | dual, with Marelli distributor or Marelli magnetos |
| Cooling | water, centrifugal pump and radiator |
| Lubrication | dry sump, with delivery and scavenge pumps |
| Maximum power | 200 hp at 7800 rpm |
| Specific power output | 100.49 hp/litre |

### TRANSMISSION
| | |
|---|---|
| Driven wheels | rear |
| Clutch | multiple dry-plate |
| Gearbox | in-unit with the differential five speeds + reverse |

### BODYWORK
two-seater Sport

### ROLLING CHASSIS
| | |
|---|---|
| Chassis | tubular spaceframe |
| Front suspension | independent, coil springs, telescopic hydraulic dampers |
| Rear suspension | de Dion axle, transverse leaf spring, telescopic hydraulic dampers |
| Brakes | hydraulically actuated discs |
| Steering | rack and pinion |
| Fuel tank | 120 l |
| Front tyres | 5.25-16 / 5.50-16 / 6.00-16 |
| Rear tyres | 6.00-16 / 6.50-16 |

### DIMENSIONS AND WEIGHT
| | |
|---|---|
| Wheelbase | 2200 mm |
| Tracks front/rear | 1250-1200 mm |
| Length | – |
| Width | – |
| Height | – |
| Dry weight | 570 kg |
| Weight to power ratio | 2.85 kg/hp |

### PERFORMANCE AND PRODUCTION
| | |
|---|---|
| Maximum speed | 270 kph |
| Units produced | 6 |

# 60                                    1959

In 1959, as the company continued to recover from the difficulties that had sent it into administration, Ing. Giulio Alfieri designed a new sports car that was destined to carve itself a future and to earn a place in history as a kind of swan-song for the front-engined racing car. Alfieri created a tubular spaceframe chassis, perfecting what had already been tested on the last 250 F single-seaters and the 150 S prototype. No less than 200 small diameter 10, 12 and 15 mm tubes welded together formed a structure resembling a large cage: Birdcage was in fact the nick-name by which the Tipo 60 was soon enthusiastically known throughout the racing world. The 250 F T2 supplied the suspension, independent at the front and with a de Dion axle at the rear, and the four-speed gearbox in-unit with the differential. The engine was the straight four from the 200 S, with the displacement reduced from 1994.28 to 1990.15 cc by increasing the bore form 92 to 93.8 mm and reducing the stroke from 75 to 72 mm. The compression ratio was unchanged at 9.8:1, while the naturally aspirated fuel system featured two twin-choke carburettors and dual ignition. The power output rose from 190 to 200 hp (at 7800 rather than 7500 rpm) and the top speed from 250 to 270 kph: this was in part due to the fact that the engine was inclined at 45° to the right which as well was lowering the centre of gravity of the car allowed the cross section of the beautiful, innovative, aluminium two-seater bodywork to be reduced significantly. The Birdcage made its competition debut on the 12th of July 1959, winning the Delamarre-De Boutteville Cup with Stirling Moss at Rouen and generating enormous interest among drivers and teams. However, the company only constructed six examples, focussing on preparing the Tipo 61 with the more competitive three-litre engine. Nonetheless, the 60 raced for seven season – 1959-1965 - recording 55 overall victories.

In 1960, a young Nino Vaccarella takes on the twists and turns of the Targa Florio route in a Tipo 61. He co-drove with veteran Umberto Maglioli, but unfortunately the pair were forced to retire. The car was entered by America'sCamoradi, a name derived from the two first letters of CAsner MOtor RAcing DIvision, a team established by aircraft pilot Lloyd Perry Casner especially to race the Tipo 61.

## TECHNICAL SPECIFICATION

### ENGINE
front, longitudinal, straight four

| | |
|---|---|
| Bore and stroke | 100-92 mm |
| Unitary displacement | 722.56 cc |
| Total displacement | 2890.26 cc |
| Valvegear | double overhead camshafts |
| Number of valves | two per cylinder |
| Compression ratio | 9.8:1 |
| Fuel system | two Weber 45DCO3 carburettors |
| Ignition | dual, with Marelli distributor or Marelli magnetos |
| Cooling | water, centrifugal pump and radiator |
| Lubrication | dry sump, with delivery and scavenge pumps |
| Maximum power output | 250 hp at 6800 rpm |
| Specific power output | 86.49 hp/litre |

### TRANSMISSION
| | |
|---|---|
| Driven wheels | rear |
| Clutch | multiple dry-plate |
| Gearbox | in-unit with the differential five speeds + reverse |

### BODYWORK
two-seater Sport

### ROLLING CHASSIS
| | |
|---|---|
| Chassis | tubular spaceframe |
| Front suspension | independent, coil springs, telescopic hydraulic dampers |
| Rear suspension | de Dion axle, transverse leaf spring, telescopic hydraulic dampers |
| Brakes | hydraulically actuated discs |
| Steering | rack and pinion |
| Fuel tank | 120 l |
| Front tyres | 6.00-16 |
| Rear tyres | 6.50-16 |

### DIMENSIONS AND WEIGHT
| | |
|---|---|
| Wheelbase | 2200 mm |
| Tracks front/rear | 1250-1200 mm |
| Length | – |
| Width | – |
| Height | – |
| Dry weight | 600 kg |
| Weight to power ratio | 2.40 kg/hp |

### PERFORMANCE AND PRODUCTION
| | |
|---|---|
| Maximum speed | 285 kph |
| Units produced | 17 |

# 61 1959

The Birdcage's extraordinary roadholding was immediately appreciated and Maserati received suggestions and pressure from Stirling Moss and especially from the American racing world to mate such a fabulous chassis with a three- rather than two-litre engine so as to be able to compete at a higher level. So it was that work began on the Tipo 61. Alfieri decided to reinforce the gearbox and the de Dion axle and moved onto the creation of the new engine. The four vertical cylinders had the bore and stroke increased from 93.8x72 to 100x92 mm for a total displacement of 2890.26 cc. With the compression ratio unchanged at 9.8:1 the power output rose from 200 to 250 hp at a lower engine speed of 6800 rather than 7800 rpm. The valvegear, fuel system, ignition and lubrication were all unchanged. Racing experience then suggested the adoption of a more robust crankshaft and oversized con-rods, while with regard to the bodywork, which initially was very similar to that of the 60, in view of the 1960 edition of the Le Mans 24 Hours, a version with a long aerodynamic tail, supplementary lighting and a very aerodynamic windscreen was prepared. All this increased the weight of the car from 600 to 689 kg, but allowed the maximum speed to be increased from 285 to 300 kph. All 17 examples of the Tipo 61 produced between the October of 1959 and the February of 1961 had as their first owners US drivers or a US team, Camoradi, which in the early Sixties achieved exceptional popularity thanks to its remarkable success. The most prestigious victories were obtained in two World Sports Car Championship races, the 1960 and 1961 editions of the Nürburgring 1000 Km with Moss and Gurney and Gregory and Casner respectively. However, the 61 took the chequered flag, for the most part in the United States, no less than 88 times; adding a further 12 victories obtained by hybrids with the 61 chassis mated to Ferrari, Ford and Buick engines, the total reaches a round 100.

It has been seen that Pietro Frua's name was often linked to Maserati, as also shown in this interpretation built on the 5000 GT's chassis. The Turin body was requested by another member of the early '60s jet set, Aga Khan Karim IV. It was in that period that the prince fell in love with Italy, making a particular contribution to changing the face of Sardinia and, over the years, turning the Costa Smeralda into one of the most exclusive areas in the Mediterranean.

## TECHNICAL SPECIFICATION

### ENGINE
front, longitudinal, 90° V8

| | |
|---|---|
| Bore and stroke | 94x89 mm |
| Unitary displacement | 617.63 cc |
| Total displacement | 4941.11 cc |
| Valvegear | double overhead camshafts per bank |
| Number of valves | two per cylinder |
| Compression ratio | 8.5:1 |
| Fuel system | four Weber 45IDM (or 46IDM) carburettors or Lucas indirect fuel injection |
| Ignition | dual, with Marelli or Lucas distributors |
| Cooling | water, centrifugal pump and radiator |
| Lubrication | pressurised with delivery pump |
| Maximum power | 340 hp at 5800 rpm |
| Specific power output | 68.81 hp/litre |

### TRANSMISSION
| | |
|---|---|
| Driven wheels | rear |
| Clutch | dual dry-plate |
| Gearbox | four speeds + reverse (from 1963: five speeds + reverse) |

### BODYWORK
| | |
|---|---|
| Frua Coupé / Monterosa Coupé | two doors, 2+2 seats |

### ROLLING CHASSIS
| | |
|---|---|
| Chassis | tubular |
| Front suspension | independent, coil springs, wishbones, anti-roll bar, telescopic hydraulic dampers |
| Rear suspension | live axle, semi-elliptical leaf springs, struts, anti-roll bar, telescopic hydraulic dampers |
| Brakes | hydraulically actuated, servo-assisted front discs and rear drums |
| Steering | recirculating ball |
| Fuel tank | 100 l |
| Front tyres | 6.50-16 (from 1963: 205-15) |
| Rear tyres | 6.50-16 (from 1963: 205-15) |

### DIMENSIONS AND WEIGHT
| | |
|---|---|
| Wheelbase | 2600 mm |
| Tracks front/rear | 1390-1360 mm |
| Length | – |
| Width | – |
| Height | – |
| Dry weight | 1500 kg |
| Weight to power ratio | 4.41 kg/hp |

### PERFORMANCE AND PRODUCTION
| | |
|---|---|
| Maximum speed | 260-270 kph |
| Units produced | 1 Frua Coupé + 1 Monterosa Coupé |

# 5000 GT
## Coupé Frua / Coupé Monterosa

1960

Many clients purchasing the prestigious Maserati 5000 GT were very well-known figures, starting with the very first, the Shah of Persia Reza Pahlavi, who was joined by the President of Mexico Adolfo López Mateos, Saud, the exiled King of Saudi Arabia, Giovanni Agnelli, Ferdinando Innocenti, Briggs Cunningham, the actor Stewart Granger, Basil Read and others, including the young Aga Khan Karim who in 1962 ordered a coupé from Pietro Frua. Drawing on his established aesthetic vocabulary, Frua created a car characterised by styling motifs that were destined to be present in other projects he developed using the mechanical organs from the Modena-based constructor: square-cut lines, taut surfaces, extensive glazing with extravagantly curved glass and a low belt line designed to communicate a sense of dynamic sleekness. The frontal graphics were particularly original, composed of rectangular elements with slightly convex sides, as were the twin main headlights, the indicators and the radiator grille. This last, set rather low, was topped by a small air intake in which the trident was set and which formed a relief feature on the bonnet that widened as its rose to the base of the windscreen. The fairly small rear lighting clusters were set on the sharply truncated tail panel as was the badging with the name of the model – Maserati 5000 GT – and the version, the "Iniezione" script traversing the chrome frame in which another trident was set. For the record it should be added that an interpretation on the 5000 GT theme was also produced by Carrozzeria Monterosa, which in 1960 – around a year before the firm closed - prepared it own coupé, in this case a modest design defined by the critics as "a rather uninspired reworking of the Touring version before the much more successful Allemano one."

This car is a hybrid created to meet Lloyd Casner's request. With the 1960 24 Hours of Le Mans coming up, the car was readied on the basics of a Tipo 60, a sports car the engine of which was given more power and refined aerodynamics. The result was of unquestioned technical value with excellent performance, which enabled the drivers, to convincingly lead the early stages of the race. But it retired after that and slipped into undeserved oblivion.

## TECHNICAL SPECIFICATION

### ENGINE
front, longitudinal, straight four

| | |
|---|---|
| Bore and stroke | 100x92 mm |
| Unitary displacement | 722.56 cc |
| Total displacement | 2890.26 cc |
| Valvegear | double overhead camshafts |
| Number of valves | two per cylinder |
| Compression ratio | 9.8:1 |
| Fuel system | two Weber 45DCO3 carburettors |
| Ignition | dual, with Marelli distributor or Marelli magnetos |
| Cooling | water, centrifugal pump and radiator |
| Lubrication | dry sump, with delivery and scavenge pumps |
| Maximum power | 250 hp at 6800 rpm |
| Specific power output | 86.49 hp/litre |

### TRANSMISSION
| | |
|---|---|
| Driven wheels | rear |
| Clutch | multiple dry-plate |
| Gearbox | in-unit with the differential five speeds + reverse |

### BODYWORK
two-seater Sport

### ROLLING CHASSIS
| | |
|---|---|
| Chassis | tubular spaceframe |
| Front suspension | independent, coil springs, telescopic hydraulic dampers |
| Rear suspension | de Dion axle, transverse leaf spring, telescopic hydraulic dampers |
| Brakes | hydraulically actuated discs |
| Steering | rack and pinion |
| Fuel tank | 120 l |
| Front tyres | 6.00-16 |
| Rear tyres | 6.50-16 |

### DIMENSIONS AND WEIGHT
| | |
|---|---|
| Wheelbase | 2200 mm |
| Tracks front/rear | 1250-1200 mm |
| Length | – |
| Width | – |
| Height | – |
| Dry weight | 689 kg |
| Weight to power ratio | 2.75 kg/hp |

### PERFORMANCE AND PRODUCTION
| | |
|---|---|
| Maximum speed | 300 kph |
| Units produced | 1 |

# 61 coda lunga                    1960

Among the most enthusiastic fans of the Birdcage was the American Lloyd Perry, "Lucky" Casner, a native of Miami, Florida, airline pilot and talented racing driver. He turned up at Maserati in the September of 1959 to purchase a 61, but production of the sought-after sports car had already been sold for that year and the next. Casner insisted and in order to satisfy him the 60 prototype was dusted off, hurriedly adapted and equipped with the three-litre engine. Entered for a number of races (Nassau, Buenos Aires, Sebring), the car, entrusted to Carroll Shelby and Masten Gregory never managed to finish due to a lack of development. In the meantime, Casner had founded the Scuderia Camoradi (an acronym of the names CAsner MOtor RAcing DIvision) and refused to give up, sending the 61 to compete in the 1960 Targa Florio. Driven by Umberto Maglioli and Nino Vaccarella, the car dominated the race until it was sidelined by a stone that holed the fuel tank with all the petrol being lost. Casner then asked Maserati to construct a new body so that he could try his luck in the imminent Le Mans 24 Hours. Ing. Alfieri prepared a new version with a long aerodynamic rear fairing in place of the previous truncated tail, supplementary lighting and a very streamlined windscreen. While the weight rose from 600 to 689 kg, so did the maximum speed from 285 to 300 kph. It was entered at Le Mans for Chuck Daigh and Masten Gregory. At the end of the first lap Gregory was leading and retained his position for a couple of hours, recording the highest speed of 274 kph on the Hunaudières straight and stopping to refuel with a lead of four minutes (a full lap). Unfortunately, a problem with the starter motor meant Daigh was unable to get away from the pits. The repair required an hour and the American restarted in last place. Both he and Gregory made up numerous positions but in the 9TH hour the engine expired, putting an end to the adventure.

Of the wealthy clients who commissioned exclusive models from key Italian body stylists, the top place has to go to Gianni Agnelli, who had already got Pinin Farina to provide some cars on Ferrari mechanics in the '50s. In 1961 Agnelli had his eyes on the Maserati 5000 GT and turned once more to Pinin Farina, who designed the body for another car of the Trident, but without an especially happy result.

## TECHNICAL SPECIFICATION

### ENGINE
front, longitudinal, 90° V8

| | |
|---|---|
| Bore and stroke | 94-89 mm |
| Unitary displacement | 617.63 cc |
| Total displacement | 4941.11 cc |
| Valvegear | double overhead camshafts per bank |
| Number of valves | two per cylinder |
| Compression ratio | 8.5:1 |
| Fuel system | Lucas indirect fuel injection |
| Ignition | dual, with Marelli or Lucas distributors |
| Cooling | water, centrifugal pump and radiator |
| Lubrication | pressurised with delivery pump |
| Maximum power | 340 hp at 5800 rpm |
| Specific power output | 68.81 hp/litre |

### TRANSMISSION
| | |
|---|---|
| Driven wheels | rear |
| Clutch | dual dry-plate |
| Gearbox | four speeds + reverse |

### BODYWORK
| | |
|---|---|
| Pininfarina coupé | two doors, 2+2 seats |

### ROLLING CHASSIS
| | |
|---|---|
| Chassis | tubular |
| Front suspension | independent, coil springs, wishbones, anti-roll bar, telescopic hydraulic dampers |
| Rear suspension | live axle, semi-elliptical leaf springs, struts, anti-roll bar, telescopic hydraulic dampers |
| Brakes | hydraulically actuated, servo-assisted front discs and rear drums |
| Steering | recirculating ball |
| Fuel tank | 100 l |
| Front tyres | 6.50-16 |
| Rear tyres | 6.50-16 |

### DIMENSIONS AND WEIGHT
| | |
|---|---|
| Wheelbase | 2600 mm |
| Tracks front/rear | 1390-1360 mm |
| Length | – |
| Width | – |
| Height | – |
| Dry weight | 1500 kg |
| Weight to power ratio | 4.41 kg/hp |

### PERFORMANCE AND PRODUCTION
| | |
|---|---|
| Maximum speed | 260-270 kph |
| Units produced | 1 |

# 5000 GT Coupé Pininfarina                 1961

A very special car based on the 5000 GT rolling chassis first saw the light of day in 1961, commissioned from Pininfarina by a no less special client, Avvocato Giovanni Agnelli. This car was so obscure and unique that it did not even carry the constructor's badging. In practice, the future president of Fiat had asked the Turin coachbuilder to create a body that replicated the one he had built for him two years earlier, presented at the Turin Motor Show on the Ferrari 400 Superamerica chassis. And a replica was what Pininfarina created, with minor variations due to the different characteristics of the chassis. It has to be said, the result was not among the most memorable: the car had the air of a two-door saloon rather than that of a sports model, which is what one might expect given the eight-cylinder engine with that displacement, power and performance: five litres, 340 hp at 5800 rpm and 270 kph. The front end featured a large quadrangular radiator grille, slightly protruding with respect to the panels that housed twin headlights set above the indicators. The smooth flanks were distinguished by a crease line linking the wheel arches and were topped by a very airy upper body with extensive glazing and a wrap-around windscreen. The bonnet and boot were both large, both being truncated with a slight forward incline. The rear wheel arches terminated with two slim fins at the ends of which vertical lighting clusters were installed. For the record, 1961 was the year in which the first centenary of the Unification of Italy was celebrated and also that in which Battista "Pinin" Farina obtained the right, through a presidential decree, to add his adolescent nickname to his surname, which from then on became Pininfarina for his cars and for his immediate family and descendants.

From the Shah of Persia to Gianni Agnelli to the wealthy William H. Brown. In the early '60s, the mania for a personalised car had exploded and Maserati rode the crest of the wave by having in its price list a model that was already as exclusive as the 5000 GT. On that demanding chassis was also built an Allemano body, which was made in more than one single example, bodying 22 of the 34 5000 GTs that were built.

## TECHNICAL SPECIFICATION

### ENGINE

front, longitudinal, 90° V8

| | |
|---|---|
| Bore and stroke | 94-89 mm |
| Unitary displacement | 617.63 cc |
| Total displacement | 4941.11 cc |
| Valvegear | double overhead camshafts per bank |
| Number of valves | two per cylinder |
| Compression ratio | 8.5:1 |
| Fuel system | four Weber 45IDM (or 46IDM) carburettors or Lucas indirect fuel injection |
| Ignition | dual, with Marelli or Lucas distributors |
| Cooling | water, centrifugal pump and radiator |
| Lubrication | pressurised with delivery pump |
| Maximum power | 340 hp at 5800 rpm |
| Specific power output | 68.81 hp/litre |

### TRANSMISSION

| | |
|---|---|
| Driven wheels | rear |
| Clutch | dual dry-plate |
| Gearbox | four speeds + reverse (from 1963: five speeds + reverse) |

### BODYWORK

| | |
|---|---|
| Allemano coupé | two doors, 2+2 seats |

### ROLLING CHASSIS

| | |
|---|---|
| Chassis | tubular |
| Front suspension | independent, coil springs, wishbones, anti-roll bar, telescopic hydraulic dampers |
| Rear suspension | live axle, semi-elliptical leaf springs, struts, anti-roll bar, telescopic hydraulic dampers |
| Brakes | hydraulically actuated, servo-assisted front discs and rear drums |
| Steering | recirculating ball |
| Fuel tank | 100 l |
| Front tyres | 6.50-16 (from 1963: 205-15) |
| Rear tyres | 6.50-16 (from 1963: 205-15) |

### DIMENSIONS AND WEIGHT

| | |
|---|---|
| Wheelbase | 2600 mm |
| Tracks front/rear | 1390-1360 mm |
| Length | – |
| Width | – |
| Height | – |
| Dry weight | 1500 kg |
| Weight to power ratio | 4.41 kg/hp |

### PERFORMANCE AND PRODUCTION

| | |
|---|---|
| Maximum speed | 260-270 kph |
| Units produced | 22 |

# 5000 GT Coupé Allemano 1961

The first example of the 5000 GT, finished in a sophisticated blue livery, was delivered to Shah Reza Pahlavi in Tehran, in the summer of 1959. A second coupé, also bodied by Touring, finished in green with a cream interior, was exhibited at the Turin Motor Show in the November of that year. The success encountered went beyond all expectations and convinced Maserati to put into limited series production - to order – this extraordinary car that rather than by the official Tipo Am 103 or 5000 GT nomenclature was to go down in history as the Shah of Persia, thanks in part to the extensive media coverage devoted to the original client who had recently divorced his second wife Soraya and was about to marry the third, Farah Diba. The car had a list price of seven and a half million Lire, almost three million more than the 3500 GT. The third example with Touring bodywork appeared at the Geneva Motor Show in 1960 and was the first to be equipped with the new mechanical specification (revised displacement, fuel injection, chain-driven valvegear) after which the task of clothing the prestigious rolling chassis was passed to other stylists. The most successful version was that by Allemano, with 22 of the total number of 34 cars produced. The project, dating from the 30TH of August 1961, was the work of Giovanni Michelotti and appeared to be more of a revision of the Touring coupé rather than a redesign, allowing the doors, the upper body, the glazing and the wheel arches to be reused. The front end was instead new and significantly simpler than its predecessor, with the radiator grille no longer extending the full width and the trident set in the middle, between twin rectangular headlights and above a lighter bumper. The first example constructed by Allemano, finished in grey with a red interior, was completed on the 28TH of September 1961. It had been commissioned by William H. Brown of Pittsburgh and was given the project name "Indianapolis".

Of the stylists that bodied the various versions of the 5000 GT, Ghia could not be left out. The historic Turin atelier, which later worked on the Ghibli, was commissioned by the Florence constructor and owner of his industrial organisation Ferdinando Innocenti, to create an exclusive design of the well-known Modena car. The result wasn't especially brilliant, due to both its heavy front and the disharmony of its rear.

## TECHNICAL SPECIFICATION

### ENGINE
front, longitudinal, 90° V8

| | |
|---|---|
| Bore and stroke | 94 x 89 mm |
| Unitary displacement | 617.63 cc |
| Total displacement | 4941.11 cc |
| Valvegear | double overhead camshafts per bank |
| Number of valves | two per cylinder |
| Compression ratio | 8.5:1 |
| Fuel system | four Weber 45IDM (or 46IDM) carburettors or Lucas indirect fuel injection) |
| Ignition | dual, with Marelli or Lucas distributors |
| Cooling | water, centrifugal pump and radiator |
| Lubrication | pressurised with delivery pump |
| Maximum power | 340 hp at 5800 rpm |
| Specific power output | 68.81 hp/litre |

### TRANSMISSION
| | |
|---|---|
| Driven wheels | rear |
| Clutch | dual dry-plate |
| Gearbox | four speeds + reverse (from 1963: five speeds + reverse) |

### BODYWORK
| | |
|---|---|
| Ghia coupé | two doors, 2+2 seats |

### ROLLING CHASSIS
| | |
|---|---|
| Chassis | tubular |
| Front suspension | independent, coil springs, wishbones, anti-roll bar, telescopic hydraulic dampers |
| Rear suspension | live axle, semi-elliptical leaf springs, struts, anti-roll bar, telescopic hydraulic dampers |
| Brakes | hydraulically actuated, servo-assisted front discs and rear drums |
| Steering | recirculating ball |
| Fuel tank | 100 l |
| Front tyres | 6.50-16 (from 1963: 205-15) |
| Rear tyres | 6.50-16 (from 1963: 205-15) |

### DIMENSIONS AND WEIGHT
| | |
|---|---|
| Wheelbase | 2600 mm |
| Tracks front/rear | 1390-1360 mm |
| Length | – |
| Width | – |
| Height | – |
| Dry weight | 1500 kg |
| Weight to power ratio | 4.41 kg/hp |

### PERFORMANCE AND PRODUCTION
| | |
|---|---|
| Maximum speed | 260-270 kph |
| Units produced | 1 |

# 5000 GT Coupé Ghia 1961

Ferdinando Innocenti, the Tuscan industrialist who owned the Milan-based engineering company of the same name, had begun building cars following the extraordinary success achieved by the popular Lambretta scooter from 1947. The company assembled the Austin A 40 under licence from the British Motor Corporation, with bodywork pressed in the Lambrate factory. At the same time Innocenti had also been authorised to build a new small spider, known as the Innocenti 950, based on the Austin Healey Sprite, presented together with the A 40 and received favourably at the Turin Motor Show that year. The bodywork had been designed by Ghia, whom Innocenti also commissioned to produce a special version of the Maserati 5000 GT, unofficially known as the Shah of Persia after its very well known original client. Ghia created a coupé that reflecting the fashion and tastes of the time but which had considerable character. Presented at the Turin Motor Show in 1961 (where the previous year, among other novelties, the Fiat 2300 S by the same coachbuilder had been launched), the coupé was striking for the sleek longitudinal development of its flanks, above which was set an elegant and airy glasshouse. A crease line and horizontal slots for venting air from the engine bay enlivened the smooth flanks finished in a pale silver grey livery. The space at the front was entirely occupied by the ellipsoidal grille with dual round headlights at either extremity and another ellipse at the centre framing the trident. Less successful were the wrap-around bumpers that reached the wheel arches, a motif repeated in even more eye-catching fashion at the rear where, moreover, the large flat boot lid was poorly matched to the extensive glazing of the rear screen and the compact and truncated tail housing the number plate and the two lighting clusters with paired circular lamps.

Bertone was already a well-known name in the body stylists' world of the early '60s. Less so that of Giorgetto Giugiaro, who was just a promising young designer at the time. The union between the two of them, at least while they worked together, brought to life unquestioned masterpieces in the history of the Italian motor industry. One of them was this 5000 GT: an elegant and bold coupé that anticipated a large number of trends to be found on subsequent Bertone cars.

## TECHNICAL SPECIFICATION

| **ENGINE** | |
|---|---|
| front, longitudinal, 90° V8 | |
| *Bore and stroke* | 94x89 mm |
| *Unitary displacement* | 617.63 cc |
| *Total displacement* | 4941.11 cc |
| *Valvegear* | double overhead camshafts per bank |
| *Number of valves* | two per cylinder |
| *Compression ratio* | 8.5:1 |
| *Fuel system* | four Weber 45IDM (or 46IDM) carburettors or Lucas indirect fuel injection |
| *Ignition* | dual, with Marelli or Lucas distributors |
| *Cooling* | water, centrifugal pump and radiator |
| *Lubrication* | pressurised with delivery pump |
| *Maximum power* | 340 hp at 5800 rpm |
| *Specific power output* | 68.81 hp/litre |

| **TRANSMISSION** | |
|---|---|
| *Driven wheels* | rear |
| *Clutch* | dual dry-plate |
| *Gearbox* | four speeds + reverse (from 1963: five speeds + reverse) |

| **BODYWORK** | |
|---|---|
| *Bertone coupé* | two doors, 2+2 seats |

| **ROLLING CHASSIS** | |
|---|---|
| *Chassis* | tubular |
| *Front suspension* | independent, coil springs, wishbones, anti-roll bar, telescopic hydraulic dampers |
| *Rear suspension* | live axle, semi-elliptical leaf springs, struts, anti-roll bar, telescopic hydraulic dampers |
| *Brakes* | hydraulically actuated, servo-assisted front discs and rear drums |
| *Steering* | recirculating ball |
| *Fuel tank* | 100 l |
| *Front tyres* | 6.50-16 (from 1963: 205-15) |
| *Rear tyres* | 6.50-16 (from 1963: 205-15) |

| **DIMENSIONS AND WEIGHT** | |
|---|---|
| *Wheelbase* | 2600 mm |
| *Tracks front/rear* | 1390-1360 mm |
| *Length* | – |
| *Width* | – |
| *Height* | – |
| *Dry weight* | 1500 kg |
| *Weight to power ratio* | 4.41 kg/hp |

| **PERFORMANCE AND PRODUCTION** | |
|---|---|
| *Maximum speed* | 260-270 kph |
| *Units produced* | 1 |

# 5000 GT Coupé Bertone                    1961

In 1961, at 23 years of age, Giorgetto Giugiaro became head of styling for Carrozzeria Bertone, the company he had joined two years earlier as a draughtsman. Among the talented young designer's first creations was a Maserati 5000 GT coupé that broke away from the standards of the time in a number of areas. The flanks were made more dynamic by the almost imperceptible sculpting of the belt line that united the front and rear lighting clusters and suggested an idea of tapering volumes. Lower down, a broad groove extended from the front wheel arch to the tail, incorporating the air vent from the engine bay, below which the coachbuilder's logo was placed. The upper body harmonized perfectly in this context, with its steeply inclined windscreen mirrored by the rear screen that flowed uninterruptedly into the boot and the tail. The front end was marked by a compositional sobriety: a full width grille with the trident at the centre and rectangular lighting clusters, half emerging above the upper lip of the grille. The bonnet featured a droplet-shaped bulge required to clear the engine. The sharply protruding bumpers were able to house the indicators. The rear was characterised by a similar simplicity, with small, horizontal hexagonal-perimeter lighting clusters and number plate lights set on the bumper. Looking at this interpretation of the 5000 GT with the benefit of hindsight, we are able to identify in the overall composition and in the details certain previews of styling features that were to be developed in future Giugiaro masterpieces. The stylist was never to overlook one of the fundamental principals of the philosophy of contemporary design: form accompanies function but never "prevails" over it and, moreover, has to find within itself an expressive ideal without recourse to embellishment that all too often is more presumed than real.

Two Sebrings on display at a motor show. The 2+2 coupé, construction of which began in 1962, enjoyed reasonable success until 1968, when production ended, 600 cars having been built. Substantially similar to each other, the only difference was in the engines, all 6-cylinders but with three different cubatures, from 3.5, 3.7 and 4-litres.

## TECHNICAL SPECIFICATION

### ENGINE

front, longitudinal, straight six

| | |
|---|---|
| Bore and stroke | 3500: 86x100 mm |
| | 3700: 86x106 mm |
| | 4000: 86x110 mm |
| Unitary displacement | 3500: 580.87 cc |
| | 3700: 615.73 cc |
| | 4000: 669.03 cc |
| Total displacement | 3500: 3485.27 cc |
| | 3700: 3694.39 cc |
| | 4000: 4014.19 cc |
| Valvegear | double overhead camshafts |
| Number of valves | two per cylinder |
| Compression ratio | 8.8:1 |
| Fuel system | Lucas indirect fuel injection |
| Ignition | dual, with distributor |
| Cooling | water, centrifugal pump and radiator |
| Lubrication | pressurised, with delivery pump |
| Maximum power | 3500: 235 hp at 5500 rpm |
| | 3700: 245 hp at 5200 rpm |
| | 4000: 255 hp at 5200 rpm |
| Specific power output | 3500: 67.42 hp/litre |
| | 3700: 66.31 hp/litre |
| | 4000: 63.52 hp/litre |

### TRANSMISSION

| | |
|---|---|
| Driven wheels | rear |
| Clutch | single dry-plate |
| Gearbox | five speeds + reverse |

### BODYWORK

| | |
|---|---|
| Vignale coupé or spider | two doors, 2+2 seats |

### ROLLING CHASSIS

| | |
|---|---|
| Chassis | tubular |
| Front suspension | independent, coil springs, wishbones, anti-roll bar telescopic hydraulic dampers |
| Rear suspension | live axle, semi-cantilevered leaf springs anti-roll bar, trailing arms, telescopic hydraulic dampers |
| Brakes | servo-assisted discs |
| Steering | recirculating ball |
| Fuel tank | 75 l |
| Front tyres | 185-16 / 205-15 |
| Rear tyres | 185-16 / 205-15 |

### DIMENSIONS AND WEIGHT

| | |
|---|---|
| Wheelbase | 2500 mm |
| Tracks front/rear | 1390/1380 mm |
| Length | 4700 mm |
| Width | 1700 mm |
| Height | 1300 mm |
| Dry weight | 1300 - 1350 kg |
| Weight to power ratio | 3500: 5.53 / 5.74 kg/hp |
| | 3700: 5.30 / 5.51 kg/hp |
| | 4000: 5.09 / 5.29 kg/hp |

### PERFORMANCE AND PRODUCTION

| | |
|---|---|
| Maximum speed | 235-245 kph |
| Units produced | 600 |

# Sebring 3,5 – 3,7 – 4,0      1961

While the 3500 GT was crowning its "career" by breaking every previous Maserati production record – 2,225 examples constructed in GT, GTI, coupé and spider forms from 1957 to 1964 – Ing. Giulio Alfieri was working on what was to be its heir, the Sebring. This was the first time that one of the Trident's cars was given a name rather than a number, a tribute to Fangio and Behra's victory with the 450 S in the Sebring 12 Hours in 1957. The prototype, presented at the Torino Motor Show in 1961, encapsulated an evolution in terms of styling and equipment rather than the mechanical specification. The tubular chassis was in fact that of the 3500 GT with the wheelbase shortened from 260 to 2500 mm for the Vignale 2+2 spider version and the engine was the classic long stroke straight six of 3485.27 cc, fitted with fuel injection and boasting a power output of 235 hp 5500 rpm and a maximum speed of 235 kph. These characteristics and performance were enhanced over the following years with the offer of two larger engines: 3694.39 cc (245 hp, 245 kph) and 4014.19 cc (255 hp, 245 kph). The Sebring embodied to perfection the role of the prestige Italian Grand Tourer and was available with automatic transmission, four-wheel disc brakes, wire wheels and –exceptionally for the era – air conditioning. The body-work, designed by the tireless Giovanni Michelotti for Vignale, was characterised by extremely clean styling of the front end and the flanks, an airy upper body with slim pillars, a truncated tail and, more in general, taut, solid surfaces that made a clean break with now dated sinuous curves of Touring's 3500 GT and anticipated a trend that was destined for widespread success and in fact the Sebring was subjected to only minor revisions over the course of its career. Having gone into production in 1962 following the presentation in definitive form at the Turin Motor Show, 600 units were constructed through to 1968.

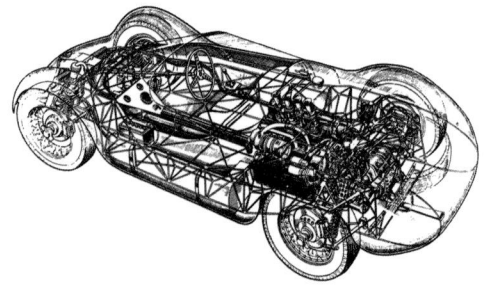

While Maserati continued to achieve major commercial success with its road cars, that which can be called the racing department was selecting new technical developments, one of the most important moving the engine from the front to the rear axle, which British constructors had already successfully pioneered in the mid-'50s. The Tipo 63 was the first Maserati with such a deployment.

## TECHNICAL SPECIFICATION

### ENGINE

rear, longitudinal, straight four
rear, longitudinal, 60° V12

| | |
|---|---|
| Bore and stroke | four cylinders 100x92 mm<br>12 cylinders 70.4x64 mm |
| Unitary displacement | four cylinders: 497.53 cc<br>12 cylinders: 249.12 cc |
| Total displacement | four cylinders: 2890.26 cc<br>12 cylinders: 2989.48 cc |
| Valvegear | four cylinders: double overhead camshafts 12 cylinders: double overhead camshafts per bank |
| Number of valves | two per cylinder |
| Compression ratio | 4 cylinders: 9.8:1<br>12 cylinders: 10:1 |
| Fuel system | 4 cylinders: two Weber 45DCO3 carburettors<br>12 cylinders: six Weber 35DCV or 38IDM carburettors |
| Ignition | dual, with Marelli distributor |
| Cooling | water, centrifugal pump and radiator |
| Lubrication | dry sump, with delivery and scavenge pumps |
| Maximum power | 4 cylinders: 250 hp at 7000 rpm<br>12 cylinders: 320 hp at 8200 rpm |
| Specific power output | 4 cylinders: 86.49 hp/litre<br>12 cylinders: 107.04 hp/litre |

### TRANSMISSION

| | |
|---|---|
| Driven wheels | rear |
| Clutch | multiple dry-plate |
| Gearbox | in-unit with the differential<br>five speeds + reverse |

### BODYWORK

*two-seater Sport*

### ROLLING CHASSIS

| | |
|---|---|
| Chassis | tubular spaceframe |
| Front suspension | independent, coil springs, telescopic hydraulic dampers |
| Rear suspension | de Dion axle, transverse leaf spring telescopic hydraulic dampers |
| Brakes | hydraulically actuated discs |
| Steering | rack and pinion |
| Fuel tank | 120 l |
| Front tyres | four cylinders: 5.25-16 / 5.50-16 / 6.00-16<br>12 cylinders: 6.00-16 / 5.50:16 |
| Rear tyres | four cylinders: 6.00-16 / 6.50-16<br>12 cylinders: 6.00-16 / 6.50-16 |

### DIMENSIONS AND WEIGHT

| | |
|---|---|
| Wheelbase | 2200 mm |
| Tracks front/rear | 4 cylinders: 1250/1200 mm<br>12 cylinders: 1200/1200 mm |
| Length | – |
| Width | – |
| Height | – |
| Dry weight | four cylinders: 600 kg<br>12 cylinders: 730 kg |
| Weight to power ratio | four cylinders: 2.40 kg/hp<br>12 cylinders: 2.28 kg/hp |

### PERFORMANCE AND PRODUCTION

| | |
|---|---|
| Maximum speed | four cylinders: 285 kph<br>12 cylinders: 312 kph |
| Units produced | 9 |

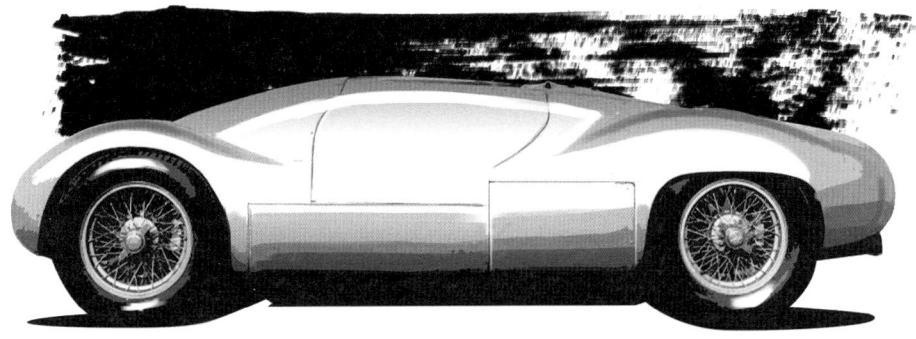

# 63 1961

Towards the end of the 1950s, the trend for engines located at the rear in racing cars was about to make the traditional configuration obsolete. By 1959, the Formula 1 World Championship had been won by Jack Brabham in a Cooper powered by a rear-mounted Coventry-Climax straight four: from then on, the title was to be the exclusive preserve of cars with this mechanical layout. For covered-wheel cars the evolution was in progress: it was to be slower, but equally definitive. At Maserati, this inexorable technical shift had certainly not escaped the attention of Ing. Giulio Alfieri, who was focussing on the design for a more up-to-date sports car. The prototype of the new car was already lapping the Aerautodromo circuit in Modena before the end of 1960. The name of the model – which followed the 60 and 61 – was not the 62 because the number had already been used to distinguish a large eight-cylinder marine engine with a 6.5-litre displacement, but rather the 63. The car was powered by the three-litre engine from the 63, located in a rear-central position and inclined through 58° to the right, which allowed two larger carburettors to be fitted and an increase in power from 250 to 320 hp. This, however, came with the passage from the Tipo 61's straight four to the V12 created for the 250 F T2 in 1957. The chassis was subjected to comprehensive revision from which it emerged even lighter. The 63's international debut came in the 1961 edition of the Le Mans 24 Hours where the Cunningham team's example driven by Pabst and Thompson finished 4th, albeit some way behind the dominant Ferraris. Unfortunately, the car then failed to live up to that early promise: it proved to be rather unreliable, collecting a couple of victories and numerous retirements or delays caused by problems of even a modest nature, evidence of the lack of development and fine tuning as the cars passed through the hands of diverse privateers without the indispensible but impossible coordination on the part of the constructor.

As well as America's Camoradi, other early '60s teams chose to compete with Maserati sports racing cars. Among them was Scuderia Serenissima, which acquired two Tipo 63s in 1961. At the same time the team also competed in Formula 1 with – among other single-seaters - a Cooper powered by a 4-cylinder Maserati, but with scarce success.

## TECHNICAL SPECIFICATION

### ENGINE

rear, longitudinal, straight four
rear, longitudinal, 60° V12

| | |
|---|---|
| Bore and stroke | four cylinders: 100x92 mm<br>12 cylinders: 70.4x64 mm |
| Unitary displacement | 4 cylinders: 497.53 cc<br>12 cylinders: 249.12 cc |
| Total displacement | four cylinders: 2890.26 cc<br>12 cylinders: 2989.48 cc |
| Valvegear | four cylinders: double overhead camshafts 12 cylinders: double overhead camshafts per bank |
| Number of valves | two per cylinder |
| Compression ratio | four cylinders: 9.8:1<br>12 cylinders: 10:1 |
| Fuel system | four cylinders: two Weber 45DCO3 carburettors<br>12 cylinders: six Weber 35DCV or 38IDM carburettors |
| Ignition | dual, with Marelli distributor |
| Cooling | water, centrifugal pump and radiator |
| Lubrication | dry sump, with delivery and scavenge pumps |
| Maximum power | four cylinders: 260 hp at 7000 rpm<br>12 cylinders: 320 hp at 8200 rpm |
| Specific power output | 4 cylinders: 86.49 hp/litre<br>12 cylinders: 107.04 hp/litre |

### TRANSMISSION

| | |
|---|---|
| Driven wheels | rear |
| Clutch | multiple dry-plate |
| Gearbox | in-unit with the differential five speeds + reverse |

### BODYWORK

two-seater Sport

### ROLLING CHASSIS

| | |
|---|---|
| Chassis | tubular spaceframe |
| Front suspension | independent, coil springs, telescopic hydraulic dampers |
| Rear suspension | de Dion axle, transverse leaf spring telescopic hydraulic dampers |
| Brakes | hydraulically actuated discs |
| Steering | rack and pinion |
| Fuel tank | 120 l |
| Front tyres | four cylinders: 5.25-16 / 5.50-16 / 6.00-16<br>12 cylinders: 6.00-16 / 5.50:16 |
| Rear tyres | four cylinders: 6.00-16 / 6.50-16<br>12 cylinders: 6.00-16 / 6.50-16 |

### DIMENSIONS AND WEIGHT

| | |
|---|---|
| Wheelbase | 2200 mm |
| Tracks front/rear | four cylinders: 1250/1200 mm<br>12 cylinders: 1200/1200 mm |
| Length | – |
| Width | – |
| Height | – |
| Dry weight | four cylinders: 600 kg<br>12 cylinders: 730 kg<br>Tipo 64: 640 kg |
| Weight to power ratio | four cylinders: 2.30 kg/hp<br>12 cylinders: 2.28 kg/hp<br>Tipo 64: 2 kg/hp |

### PERFORMANCE AND PRODUCTION

| | |
|---|---|
| Maximum speed | 4 cylinders: 285 kph<br>12 cylinders: 312 kph<br>Tipo 64: 320 kph |
| Units produced | 1 (transformed into Tipo 64) |

# 63 Serenissima                                   1961

In the spring of 1961, Count Giovanni Volpi di Misurata's Scuderia Serenissima acquired two examples of the Tipo 63 barchetta that it entered for the Targa Florio: one, in standard form, was entrusted to Vaccarella and Trintignant and finished in 4TH place, the other was given to Maglioli and Scarlatti after the bodywork had been modified with the addition of a conspicuous rear stabilizing fin that carried the teams's logo. The modification did not bring the hoped for results and the crew finished 5th, a position that was to be the best achieved in the car's brief and modest career largely composed of a disappointing series of retirements. The following June the car was radically updated with the installation – in place of the original three-litre, four-cylinder engine – of the three-litre 60° V12 that had been run in 1957 in the F1 250 F T2 single-seater. The changes brought a sharp rise in the power output, from 260 to 320 hp, while the maximum speed rose from 285 to 312 kph. Unfortunately, the increase in weight from 600 to 730 hp and above all its distribution, by no means ideal in the original version following the shift from the front in the 61 to the rear location of the 63, made the roadholding more precarious and this together with overheating problems had a detrimental effect on reliability and racing performance. Early in 1962 the car was updated to Tipo 64 specification with modifications to the chassis and the engine-gearbox assembly moved forwards; 90 kg was shaved off the weight (6409 against 730 kg) which with the same power output of 320 hp at 8200 rpm meant the maximum speed rose from 312 to 320 kph. Franco Scaglione designed a body with unconventional, strong lines that were well ahead of their time, but the car's performance did not improve and neither did its embarrassing competition record.

Testing took place of the new Tipo 64 at the Modena Autodrome on the cold local Po Valley in mid-January 1962. The veteran test driver Guarino Bertocchi, on the left of the car, observed in readiness to get back to lapping the circuit again while, kneeling at the rear end, are two people who had rendered "Made in Italy" on four wheels great, engineers Giulio Alfieri and Gian Paolo Dallara.

## TECHNICAL SPECIFICATION

### ENGINE

rear, longitudinal, 60° V12

| | |
|---|---|
| Bore and stroke | 70.4x64 mm |
| Unitary displacement | 249.12 cc |
| Total displacement | 2989.48 cc |
| Valvegear | double overhead camshafts per bank |
| Number of valves | two per cylinder |
| Compression ratio | 10:1 |
| Fuel system | six Weber 35DCV or 38IDM carburettors |
| Ignition | dual, with Marelli distributor |
| Cooling | water, centrifugal pump and radiator |
| Lubrication | dry sump, |
| | with delivery and scavenge pumps |
| Maximum power | 320 hp at 8200 rpm |
| Specific power output | 107.04 hp/litre |

### TRANSMISSION

| | |
|---|---|
| Driven wheels | rear |
| Clutch | multiple dry-plate |
| Gearbox | in-unit with the differential five speeds + reverse |

### BODYWORK

two-seater Sport

### ROLLING CHASSIS

| | |
|---|---|
| Chassis | tubular spaceframe |
| Front suspension | independent, coil springs, telescopic hydraulic dampers |
| Rear suspension | de Dion axle, transverse leaf spring telescopic hydraulic dampers |
| Brakes | hydraulically actuated discs |
| Steering | rack and pinion |
| Fuel tank | 120 l |
| Front tyres | 6.00-16 / 5.50:16 |
| Rear tyres | 6.00-16 / 6.50-16 |

### DIMENSIONS AND WEIGHT

| | |
|---|---|
| Wheelbase | 2200 mm |
| Tracks front/rear | 1200/1200 mm |
| Length | – |
| Width | – |
| Height | – |
| Dry weight | 640 kg |
| Weight to power ratio | 2 kg/hp |

### PERFORMANCE AND PRODUCTION

| | |
|---|---|
| Maximum speed | 320 kph |
| Units produced | 2 (Tipo 63 transformations) |

# 64            1961

Rather than a truly new model, the Tipo 64 may be considered as the fruit of the significant updating of two examples of the Tipo 63 that, in view of the 1962 season were sent back to the factory by their owners Briggs Cunningham and Count Giovanni Volpi di Misurata's Scuderia SSS Repubblica di Venezia (formerly Scuderia Serenissima). Ing. Giulio Alfieri made radical modifications to the chassis, with the engine-transmission assembly and the cockpit shifted forwards, given that the adoption of the rear engine configuration had revolutionised the optimal weight distribution that from the outset had been one of the great strengths of the Birdcage. The rear suspension was given a modified de Dion axle that improved the car's handling and also allowed the general geometry to be adapted. The displacement of the 60° V12, derived from the 250 F unit, was unchanged at 2989.48 cc, with bore and stroke dimensions of 70.4x64 mm. Other experimental units were constructed with dimensions of 63.3x68 mm (2989.65 cc) and 75.2x56 mm (2984.65 cc) but the results were very similar. There was a notable saving in weight (640 instead of 730 kg) which had a positive effect on performance, with the top speed rising from 312 to 320 kph while the power output (320 hp at 8200 rpm) and compression ratio (10:1) remained the same. Cunningham's example, which had been damaged in a crash at Laguna Seca in California, had a new, very linear body, with compact volumes, less pronounced wings and a truncated tail. The Scuderia Serenissima car instead boasted innovative styling by Franco Scaglione characterised by futuristic lines of great character. However, neither of the two examples of the 64 that took to the tracks achieved any results of notes.

The 5000 GT had enchanted people across the world. One American, Briggs Cunningham, was a car connoisseur and gentleman racing driver, but especially a constructor of prestige cars. It was he who commissioned Vignale to design and build its interpretation of the 5000 GT that was different from the others; the result was certainly that, like the Cunninghams, which had tried with reasonable results the Le Mans adventure.

## TECHNICAL SPECIFICATION

### ENGINE

front, longitudinal, 90° V8

| | |
|---|---|
| Bore and stroke | 94x89 mm |
| Unitary displacement | 617.63 cc |
| Total displacement | 4941.11 cc |
| Valvegear | double overhead camshafts per bank |
| Number of valves | two per cylinder |
| Compression ratio | 8.5:1 |
| Fuel system | four Weber 45IDM (or 46IDM) carburettors or Lucas indirect fuel injection |
| Ignition | dual, with Marelli or Lucas distributors |
| Cooling | water, centrifugal pump and radiator |
| Lubrication | pressurised with delivery pump |
| Maximum power | 340 hp at 5800 rpm |
| Specific power output | 68.81 hp/litre |

### TRANSMISSION

| | |
|---|---|
| Driven wheels | rear |
| Clutch | dual dry-plate |
| Gearbox | four speeds + reverse (from 1963: five speeds + reverse) |

### BODYWORK

| | |
|---|---|
| Vignale coupé | two doors, 2+2 seats |

### ROLLING CHASSIS

| | |
|---|---|
| Chassis | tubular |
| Front suspension | independent, coil springs, wishbones, anti-roll bar, telescopic hydraulic dampers |
| Rear suspension | live axle, semi-elliptical leaf springs, struts, anti-roll bar, telescopic hydraulic dampers |
| Brakes | hydraulically actuated, servo-assisted front discs and rear drums |
| Steering | recirculating ball |
| Fuel tank | 100 l |
| Front tyres | 6.50-16 (from 1963: 205-15) |
| Rear tyres | 6.50-16 (from 1963: 205-15) |

### DIMENSIONS AND WEIGHT

| | |
|---|---|
| Wheelbase | 2600 mm |
| Tracks front/rear | 1390-1360 mm |
| Length | – |
| Width | – |
| Height | – |
| Dry weight | 1500 kg |
| Weight to power ratio | 4.41 kg/hp |

### PERFORMANCE AND PRODUCTION

| | |
|---|---|
| Maximum speed | 260-270 kph |
| Units produced | 1 |

# 5000 GT Coupé Vignale                         1962

Like other famous personalities, Briggs Cunningham, a rich US businessman, an amateur racer of great talent and a successful racing car constructor (also winning in international races), commissioned a coupé from Vignale on the basis of the 5000 GT. He was particularly fortunate because the design by the inexorably talented Giovanni Michelotti was one of the most original interpretations on the theme of this remarkable car. The first impression it inspires is the satisfying sense of great compositional harmony, the proportions between the elements of an authentically classical whole. The most innovative section of the design concerned the front end, with the elliptical radiator grille that extends the bonnet volume, protruding beyond the line of the wheel arches and featuring the trident at the centre and the two auxiliary lamps either side. The main headlights were concealed behind oval lids that permitted the wings to curve uninterruptedly down to the central body via a streamlined fairing. The indicators were instead located on the bumper. The flanks were taut and smooth, with a slight low crease that from the rear wheel arch reaches the engine bay air vent which itself was divided by finning and above which was set the coachbuilder's badging. Two slim, parallel creases depart from behind the rear wheel arches and run around the tail, emphasising the upper edge of the boot and its base, surrounded by wrap-around bumpers. The compact, truncated tail houses the lighting clusters with twin circular elements either side of the number plate. The upper body, rendered particularly airy by the extensive glazing, is neatly integrated and completes the elegant aesthetic equilibrium of the overall design.

In 1962, Rodolfo Bonetto (known for his celebrated work in other sectors) designed a 2+2 coupé for Carrozzeria Boneschi. The overall result, while anticipating certain features that were to gain currency over time, was not convincing in its treatment of the front end and the stiffness of the flanks and upper body.

## TECHNICAL SPECIFICATION

### ENGINE

front, longitudinal, straight six

| | |
|---|---|
| Bore and stroke | 86x100 mm |
| Unitary displacement | 580.87 cc |
| Total displacement | 3485.27 cc |
| Valvegear | double overhead camshafts |
| Number of valves | two per cylinder |
| Compression ratio | 8.5:1 |
| Fuel system | three Weber 42DCO3 carburettors |
| Ignition | dual, with Marelli distributor |
| Cooling | water, centrifugal pump and radiator |
| Lubrication | pressurised, with delivery pump |
| Maximum power | 220 hp at 5500 rpm |
| Specific power output | 63.12 hp/litre |

### TRANSMISSION

| | |
|---|---|
| Driven wheels | rear |
| Clutch | single dry-plate |
| Gearbox | four speeds + reverse (1960: five speeds + reverse) |

### BODYWORK

| | |
|---|---|
| Boneschi coupé | two doors, 2+2 seats |

### ROLLING CHASSIS

| | |
|---|---|
| Chassis | tubular |
| Front suspension | independent, coil springs, wishbones, anti-roll bar telescopic hydraulic dampers |
| Rear suspension | live axle, semi-cantilevered leaf springs, telescopic hydraulic dampers |
| Brakes | servo-assisted drums (1959: front discs) |
| Steering | recirculating ball |
| Fuel tank | 75 l |
| Front/rear tyres | 6.50-16 / 6.00-16 |

### DIMENSIONS AND WEIGHT

| | |
|---|---|
| Wheelbase | 2600 mm |
| Tracks front/rear | 1390/1360 mm |
| Length | – |
| Width | – |
| Height | – |
| Dry weight | 1300 kg |
| Weight to power ratio | 5.90 kg/hp |

### PERFORMANCE AND PRODUCTION

| | |
|---|---|
| Maximum speed | GT: 220 kph / GTI: 235 kph |
| Units produced | 2 |

# 3500 GT Coupé Boneschi        1962

Among the creations by the Milan coachbuilder Boneschi that have left a trace in the evolution of automotive styling, special mention has to be made of the Maserati 3500 GT coupé presented at the Turin Motor Show in 1962. The Cambiago works bodied industrial, commercial and promotional vehicle to balance the books and occasionally created cars of character that were produced in limited series. Among the most original Boneschi designs was the Amalfi spider built in 1961 on the Lancia Flaminia chassis, which was followed and to a certain extent referenced by the Maserati coupé the next year. Both cars were the fruit of the talented Milanese stylist Rodolfo Bonetto, destined to achieve great fame in other sectors of design. The Maserati 3.5 rolling chassis inspired him to create a shape that was made a clean break with the standards of the day: the coupé in fact had taut lines, flat, angular surfaces, sharp corners and little in the way of fairings that, compared with the traditional aesthetic canons, appeared to be highly provocative. As with all avant-garde proposals, the overall result undoubtedly left room for reservations, but as the most authoritative critics have noted it "marked the impatience with consolidated forms that was evolving and that, shrewdly harnessed by the great studios" was to lead to spectacular results: to mention just two of the prototypes still considered to be milestones in the history of automotive styling, both created in 1968, the Alfa Romeo 33 Carabo by Marcello Gandini for Bertone and the Bizzarrini Manta by Giorgetto Giugiaro for his newly founded Ital Design. Only one further example of Boneschi's Maserati coupé was produced in 1963, characterised by a series of ill-judged modifications and changes that compromised its appearance.

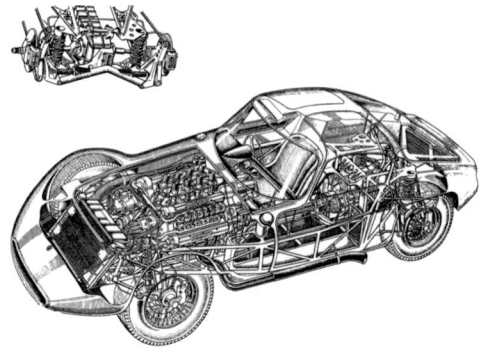

The story of the Tipo 151 is closely linked to that of the 24 Hours of Le Mans, the race for which this car was conceived. A month before its debut the car with chassis number 002 was also entered for the 1000 Km of the Nürburgring. Another two were built, their chassis numbers 004 and 006, and they were entered in various races until the tragic test of 10 April 1965, when Lloyd Casner lost his life aboard 002, bringing to a terrible end the racing story of the Tipo 151.

## TECHNICAL SPECIFICATION

### ENGINE
front, longitudinal, 90° V8

| | |
|---|---|
| Bore and stroke | 91 x 75.8 mm (151/2: 94 x 89 mm) |
| Unitary displacement | 492.99 cc (151/2: 617.63) |
| Total displacement | 3943.95 cc (151/2: 4941.11) |
| Valvegear | double overhead camshafts per bank |
| Number of valves | two per cylinder |
| Compression ratio | 12:1 |
| Fuel system | four Weber 46IDM carburettors |
| Ignition | dual, with Marelli magnetos |
| Cooling | water, centrifugal pump and radiator |
| Lubrication | dry sump, with delivery and scavenge pumps |
| Maximum power | 410 hp (151/2: 430 hp) at 8000 rpm |
| Specific power output | 97.84 hp/litre (151/2: 87.02) |

### TRANSMISSION
| | |
|---|---|
| Driven wheels | rear |
| Clutch | multiple dry-plate |
| Gearbox | in-unit with the rear axle two speeds + reverse |

### BODYWORK
single-seater

### ROLLING CHASSIS
| | |
|---|---|
| Chassis | tubular spaceframe |
| Front suspension | independent, coil springs, hydraulic dampers |
| Rear suspension | de Dion axle, transverse leaf spring, dual hydraulic dampers |
| Brakes | hydraulically actuated discs |
| Steering | worm and gear |
| Fuel tank | 250 l |
| Front tyres | 7.60-16 / 8.00-16 |
| Rear tyres | 8.00-18 |

### DIMENSIONS AND WEIGHT
| | |
|---|---|
| Wheelbase | 2400 mm |
| Tracks front/rear | 1300/1250 mm |
| Length | – |
| Width | – |
| Height | – |
| Dry weight | 895 kg (151/2: 860) |
| Weight to power ratio | 2.18 kg/hp (151/2: 2) |

### PERFORMANCE AND PRODUCTION
| | |
|---|---|
| Maximum speed | 320 kph (151/2: 330) |
| Units produced | 3 |

# 151                                                           1962

In view of the 1962 season, as Maserati could not, like many other manufacturers, participate in the World Championship for Marques, reserved for GT cars (homologated as such only when produced in at least 100 examples), the firm opted to build a prototype, commissioned by the teams of Briggs Cunningham and John Simone (Maserati France), known as the 151 and conceived for the Le Mans 24 Hours. Giulio Alfieri went against the tide with respect to even his own recent racing cars, foregoing the reticular chassis in favour of one with large diameter tubes and moving the engine to the front again. The power unit in question was the 90° V8 from the 450 S of 1956, with the displacement reduced from 4477.85 to 3943.95 cc but with an increase in power (from 400 to 410 hp) and top speed (from 320 to 330 kph). The very streamlined bodywork also recalled that of the 450 S bodied by Zagato but differed in the conspicuous bulge on the bonnet (in correspondence with the large carburettors). Three examples started the French 24 Hours race, but not one finished. Thompson and Kimberly crashed, Trintignant and Bianchi suffered anomalous tyre wear and Hansgen and McLaren were sidelined with a broken piston. A year later, Maserati France tried again with the prototype renamed as the 151/2 and equipped with a new eight-cylinder engine derived from the production 5000: 4941.11 cc, fuel injection, 430 hp and overall weight reduced from 895 to 860 kg. Simon and Casner retired with a broken transmission. The 151/3 was prepared for the 1963 edition of the 24 Hours; significant changes made to the chassis and the bodywork with a lowered bonnet and a very high tail with a vertical rear screen. This time Simon and Trintignant's retirement was caused by an electrical failure. The last attempt, with the 151/4, the fruit of further revision, ended in tragedy in April 1965 with the accident in which Lloyd Casner was killed during practice for the 24 Hours.

Setting aside the single models created by a number of important body stylists, the major production in the successful story of the 3500 GT was shared by Touring and Vignale. Especially Touring, which built over 1,400 cars. In that period, the company also came up with two further styling proposals which they thought would prolong the model's life. But neither was produced.

## TECHNICAL SPECIFICATION

### ENGINE
front, longitudinal, straight six

| | |
|---|---|
| Bore and stroke | 86x100 mm |
| Unitary displacement | 580.87 cc |
| Total displacement | 3485.27 cc |
| Valvegear | double overhead camshafts |
| Number of valves | two per cylinder |
| Compression ratio | 8.5:1 |
| Fuel system | GT: three Weber 42DCO3 carburettors |
| | GTI: Lucas indirect fuel injection |
| Ignition | dual, with Marelli distributor |
| Cooling | water, centrifugal pump and radiator |
| Lubrication | pressurised, with delivery pump |
| Maximum power | GT: 220 hp at 5500 rpm |
| | GTI: 235 hp at 5800 rpm |
| Specific power output | GT: 63.12 hp/litre |
| | (GTI: 67.42 hp/litre) |

### TRANSMISSION
| | |
|---|---|
| Driven wheels | rear |
| Clutch | single dry-plate |
| Gearbox | four speeds + reverse (1960: five speeds + reverse) |

### BODYWORK
| | |
|---|---|
| Touring coupé | two doors, 2+2 seats |

### ROLLING CHASSIS
| | |
|---|---|
| Chassis | tubular |
| Front suspension | independent, coil springs, wishbones, anti-roll bar telescopic hydraulic dampers |
| Rear suspension | live axle, semi-cantilevered leaf springs, telescopic hydraulic dampers |
| Brakes | servo-assisted front discs rear drums |
| Steering | recirculating ball |
| Fuel tank | 75 l |
| Front/rear tyres | 6.50-16 / 6.00-16 |

### DIMENSIONS AND WEIGHT
| | |
|---|---|
| Wheelbase | 2600 mm |
| Tracks front/rear | 1390/1360 mm |
| Length | – |
| Width | – |
| Height | – |
| Dry weight | 1300 kg |
| Weight to power ratio | GT: 5.90 kg/hp / GTI: 5.53 kg/hp |

### PERFORMANCE AND PRODUCTION
| | |
|---|---|
| Maximum speed | GT: 220 kph / GTI: 235 kph |
| Units produced | 1402 |

# 3500 GT – GTI Coupé Touring                    1963

The 3500 GT's great commercial success was due in part if not above all to the constant commitment to development and qualitative improvement both of the mechanical side and driver and passenger comfort in order to satisfy a naturally demanding clientele. This wide-ranging evolutionary research was conducted in-house under the direction and thanks to the inexorable spirit of the engineer Giulio Alfieri. The car benefitted from the gradual adoption of important equipment: a limited slip differential and front disc brakes (optional in 1959 and standard the following year), centre-lock wire wheels and lastly indirect fuel injection in 9160 with a Lucas pump replacing the three twin-choke Weber carburettors. The peak power engine speed rose from 5500 to 5800 rpm, providing an increase in power from 220 to 235 hp, while the top speed also rose from 230 to 240 kph. For its part, Touring worked on both the interior and the exterior of the body, with modifications to the side windows, the air intakes and the lighting clusters that never compromised the styling of the body or its classical configuration. Nonetheless, in parallel with this routine updating, the Milan studio, working on the possibility of a future replacement for the 3500 GT, gave rise to at least two proposals for new coupés. Both were characterised by the abandonment of the single-light upper body in a search for greater light, obtained in part through very slim pillars. They differed in the treatment of the radiator grille: one was similar to that of the standard version but set between twin headlights, in relief with respect to the lowered bonnet; the other had a coarser grille and an oval shape like that of the headlights. Some of these innovations were applied to the production model that was finally dropped in 1964, when many other programmes were about to be launched at Maserati.

As the production of the 3500 Touring coupé continued, Vignale came up with an elegant roadster with a black hood at the 1963 Turin Motor Show. Pairs of circular headlights were set into the grill, air intakes were close to the front wings and the car had a sinuous belt line; just some of the new aspects of this car which, in some areas, was like the future Fiat Dino roadster of 1966.

## TECHNICAL SPECIFICATION

### ENGINE
front, longitudinal, straight six

| | |
|---|---|
| Bore and stroke | 86x100 mm |
| Unitary displacement | 580.87 cc |
| Total displacement | 3485.27 cc |
| Valvegear | double overhead camshafts |
| Number of valves | two per cylinder |
| Compression ratio | 8.5:1 |
| Fuel system | GT: three Weber 42DCO3 carburettors<br>GTI: Lucas indirect fuel injection |
| Ignition | dual, with Marelli distributor |
| Cooling | water, centrifugal pump and radiator |
| Lubrication | pressurised, with delivery pump |
| Maximum power | GT: 220 hp at 5500 rpm<br>GTI: 235 hp at 5800 rpm |
| Specific power output | GT: 63.12 hp/litre<br>(GTI: 67.42 hp/litre) |

### TRANSMISSION
| | |
|---|---|
| Driven wheels | rear |
| Clutch | single dry-plate |
| Gearbox | four speeds + reverse<br>(1960: five speeds + reverse) |

### BODYWORK
| | |
|---|---|
| Vignale spider | two doors, two seats |

### ROLLING CHASSIS
| | |
|---|---|
| Chassis | tubular |
| Front suspension | independent, coil springs, wishbones, anti-roll bar telescopic hydraulic dampers |
| Rear suspension | live axle, semi-cantilevered leaf springs, telescopic hydraulic dampers |
| Brakes | servo-assisted front discs |
| | rear drums |
| Steering | recirculating ball |
| Fuel tank | 75 l |
| Front/rear tyres | 6.50-16 / 6.00-16 |

### DIMENSIONS AND WEIGHT
| | |
|---|---|
| Wheelbase | 2500 mm |
| Tracks front/rear | 1390/1360 mm |
| Length | – |
| Width | – |
| Height | – |
| Dry weight | 1200 kg |
| Weight to power ratio | GT: 5.45 kg/hp<br>GTI: 5.10 kg/hp |

### PERFORMANCE AND PRODUCTION
| | |
|---|---|
| Maximum speed | GT: 220 kph / GTI: 235 kph |
| Units produced | 250 |

# 3500 GTI Spider Vignale $\qquad$ 1963

At the Turin Motor Show that opened in the autumn of 1963 a new Maserati 3500 GT spider was exhibited on the Vignale stand. The Turin coachbuilder, which from 1959 had already constructed in series another spider on the same rolling chassis to designs by Giovanni Michelotti, broke away from the earlier model that had been well received, as was customary with the creations by the talented and prolific designer. Michelotti also fearlessly broke away from what had become established as the typical styling of his open-top cars, characterised by compact volumes, bold lines and racing references. The new spider was based, like its predecessor, on the rolling chassis of the 3.5 GT, shortened by 10 cm (from 260 to 250 cm). It was striking in its simple, elongated and gently sinuous forms that anticipated the styling of other cars, some of them particularly well known such as the Fiat Dino 200 with the Ferrari V6 engine, designed and constructed by Pininfarina from 1966 to 1972. The front end was distinguished by its modern appearance, with the horizontally developed radiator grille shaped by the profile of the overhanging leading edge of the bonnet. At either side were the twin headlights, while the trident was set in the centre, framed in a circular support. The composition was then underlined by the wrap-around bumper. The flanks were smooth and continuous, sharply defined and rendered dynamic by a crease line and the rounded volume of the rear wing. Two indents for the engine bay air vents were topped by the model name badging – Maserati 3500 GTI (with the I indicating the fuel injected engine) – and the coachbuilder's logo. Below, a chromed strip linked the two wheel arches at the height of the hubs. The truncated tail, also embraced by a wrap-around bumper, featured circular lighting clusters: another styling feature that was to prove popular and would continue to be proposed for many years.

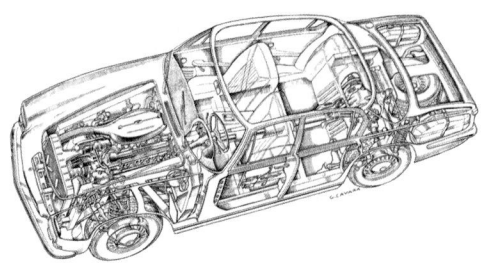

Back in 1963, nobody could ever have imagined that the name to be given to the top-of-the-range Maserati would be Quattroporte and that it would stay alive through to the present day, despite the company's changes of ownership and the alternating fortunes of the company throughout its history. The first Quattroporte was designed by Pietro Frua and built in Turin by Vignale, to remain in production for six years with only minimum changes, so valid was the original project.

## TECHNICAL SPECIFICATION

### ENGINE
front, longitudinal, 90° V8

| | |
|---|---|
| Bore and stroke | 88x85 mm (from 1969: 93.9 x 85) |
| Unitary displacement | 516.98 cc (from 1969: 588.62) |
| Total displacement | 4135.84 cc (from 1969: 4709 cc) |
| Valvegear | double overhead camshafts per bank |
| Number of valves | two per cylinder |
| Compression ratio | 8.5:1 |
| Fuel system | four Weber 38 DCNL5 carburettors |
| Ignition | single, with Marelli distributor |
| Cooling | water, centrifugal pump and radiator |
| Lubrication | pressurised, with delivery pump |
| Maximum power | 260 hp at 5000 rpm 1969: 290 hp at 5200 rpm |
| Specific power output | 62.86 hp/litre (from 1969: 61.58 hp/litre) |

### TRANSMISSION

| | |
|---|---|
| Driven wheels | rear |
| Clutch | single dry-plate |
| Gearbox | five speeds + reverse (automatic optional) |

### BODYWORK
Vignale saloon (designed by Frua) four doors, four-five seats

### ROLLING CHASSIS

| | |
|---|---|
| Chassis | unitary construction with front subframe |
| Front suspension | independent, coil springs, wishbones, anti-roll bar telescopic hydraulic dampers |
| Rear suspension | de Dion axle, semi-cantilevered leaf springs, trailing arms, anti-roll bar, ((from 1966: live axle, semi-elliptical leaf springs and anti-roll bar) telescopic hydraulic dampers |
| Brakes | servo-assisted hydraulically actuated discs |
| Steering | recirculating ball |
| Fuel tank | 90 l |
| Front/rear tyres | 205-15 |

### DIMENSIONS AND WEIGHT

| | |
|---|---|
| Wheelbase | 2750 mm |
| Tracks front/rear | 1390/1403 mm |
| Length | 5000 mm |
| Width | 1720 mm |
| Height | 1360 mm |
| Dry weight | 1650 kg |
| Weight to power ratio | 6.34 kg/hp (from 1969: 5.68 kg/hp) |

### PERFORMANCE AND PRODUCTION

| | |
|---|---|
| Maximum speed | 230 kph |
| Units produced | 776 |

# Quattroporte 4,1 – 4,7        1963

For Maserati, 1963 was a year of extraordinary creative fertility. As well as the launch of the new Sebring, the Turin Motor Show saw the debut of the prototype of the Mistral and that of the Quattroporte, which marked an epochal turning point: this was the fist saloon in the history of the Trident and it presented unique characteristics that ensured it would be a success destined to endure over the decades. Out of Giulio Alfieri's project came a brand new structure that rather than a traditional tubular chassis used a modern unitary construction bodyshell, together with a front subframe carrying the engine-gearbox assembly and the front suspension. This last was fully independent while at the rear there was a de Dion axle, a sophisticated and advanced feature (the most prestigious production cars were to adopt the layout year later). The engine was the V8 from the 5000 GT with the displacement reduced from 4941.11 to 4135.84 cc, although the power output remained an exceptional 260 hp at the relatively low engine speed of 5000 rpm, which permitted the car to achieve a top speed in the order of 240 kph and legitimately claim to be the "fastest production saloon car in the world." This notable level of performance was matched by the mechanical specification and the list of accessories - offered either as standard or as options - including automatic transmission, power steering, all-round servo-assisted disc brakes, air conditioning, electric windows and luxurious trim, thanks to which the car offered a supremely comfortable driving and travelling experience. Built, like the Sebring, by Vignale to the designs of Pietro Frua, the imposing size of the car was balanced by the low belt line with extensive curved glazing, while the broad, smooth surfaces and square-cut volumes lent a degree of dynamism. The first series – which in 1966 was subject to minor changes such as the adoption of twin headlights – was produced through to 1969 in 776 units.

Not many less than 1,000 Mistrals were produced in the six years between 1964 and 1969. And this two-seater boasted stylistic aspects worthy of note: they ranged from the new integrated grill to the bumpers and the bright roof group, which had ample glass surfaces down to the rear, where the fastback profile and the adoption of a hatch back were the most characteristic features.

## TECHNICAL SPECIFICATION

### ENGINE

front, longitudinal, straight six

| | |
|---|---|
| Bore and stroke | 3700: 86x106 mm |
| | 4000: 88x110 mm |
| Unitary displacement | 3700: 615.73 cc |
| | 4000: 669.03 cc |
| Total displacement | 3700: 3694.39 cc |
| | 4000: 4014.19 cc |
| Valvegear | double overhead camshafts |
| Number of valves | two per cylinder |
| Compression ratio | 8.8:1 |
| Fuel system | Lucas indirect fuel injection |
| Ignition | dual, with distributor |
| Cooling | water, centrifugal pump |
| | and radiator |
| Lubrication | pressurised, with delivery pump |
| Maximum power | 3700: 235 hp at 5500 rpm |
| | 4000: 245 hp at 5500 rpm |
| Specific power output | 3700: 63.60 hp/litre |
| | 4000: 61.03 hp/litre |

### TRANSMISSION

| | |
|---|---|
| Driven wheels | rear |
| Clutch | single dry-plate |
| Gearbox | five speeds + reverse |

### BODYWORK

Vignale coupé (designed by Frua) two doors, 2+2 seats

### ROLLING CHASSIS

| | |
|---|---|
| Chassis | tubular |
| Front suspension | independent, coil springs, wishbones, anti-roll bar telescopic hydraulic dampers |
| Rear suspension | live axle, semi-cantilevered leaf springs, anti-roll bar, trailing arms, telescopic hydraulic dampers |
| Brakes | servo-assisted discs |
| Steering | recirculating ball |
| Fuel tank | 75 l |
| Front/rear tyres | 205-15 |

### DIMENSIONS AND WEIGHT

| | |
|---|---|
| Wheelbase | 2400 mm |
| Tracks front/rear | 1390/1364 mm |
| Length | 4500 mm |
| Width | 1650 mm |
| Height | 1300 mm |
| Dry weight | 1350 kg |
| Weight/power ratio | 3700: 5.74 kg/hp |
| | 4000: 5.51 kg/hp |

### PERFORMANCE AND PRODUCTION

| | |
|---|---|
| Maximum speed | 235-255 kph |
| Units produced | 955 |

# Mistral 3,7 – 4,0 1963

While the Sebring was proceeding from the development stage to serial production, the prototype for a new coupé was presented that sparked what was to become a tradition in Maserati nomenclature that is still followed today: naming the cars after various winds. This prototype was given the name Mistral after the French win that blows south from the Rhone valley towards the Mediterranean. The car was born with the objective of flanking the Sebring with a more sporting model, hence the adoption of an even shorter chassis, with the cabin being a strict two-seater rather than the 2+2 configuration. Of the three engines offered in the Sebring - 3500, 3700 and 4000 - the largest was rejected as it offered performance so similar to the other two: 235-245 hp and 235-255 kph. The Mistral's strength was its particularly attractive styling. Built by Vignale to designs by Pietro Frua – to whom the idea for the name should apparently be attributed – it boasted a number of original features, beginning with the front end in which a very sloping bonnet almost hid the radiator grille which became a low, fill width air intake, open below the bumper. The bodywork broke with the classic three-box configuration of the Sebring, gaining admirers thanks to its fastback profile and the exceptionally extensive glazing with its pronounced curves. The rear screen was particularly interesting as it formed a hatch allowing access to the luggage compartment. In 1966, together with a number of minor modifications, the 2+2 configuration was revived. The Mistral, presented at the Turin Motor Sow in 1963, went into production the following year and was constructed through to 1969 in 955 examples. This was the last model to be powered by the glorious straight six, the beating heart of the Maserati GTs for over a decade.

Almost at the same time as the coupé, Maserati unveiled the Mistral Spider. Initial production included a 3.5-litre engine, which was not installed in the coupé. But the unit's cubic capacity was soon dropped in favour of the higher performing 3.7-litre. Two years later, the engine was taken to 4-litres.

## TECHNICAL SPECIFICATION

### ENGINE

front, longitudinal, straight six

| | |
|---|---|
| Bore and stroke | 3500: 86x100 mm |
| | 3700: 86x106 mm |
| | 4000: 88x110 mm |
| Unitary displacement | 3500: 580.87 cc |
| | 3700: 615..73 cc |
| | 4000: 669.03 cc |
| Total displacement | 3500: 3485.27 cc |
| | 3700: 3694.39 cc |
| | 4000: 4014.19 cc |
| Valvegear | double overhead camshafts |
| Number of valves | two per cylinder |
| Compression ratio | 8.8:1 |
| Fuel system | Lucas indirect fuel injection |
| Ignition | dual, with distributor |
| Cooling | water, centrifugal pump and radiator |
| Lubrication | pressurised, with delivery pump |
| Maximum power | 3500: 235 hp at 5500 rpm |
| | 3700: 245 hp at 5500 rpm |
| | 4000: 255 hp at 5500 rpm |
| Specific power output | 3500: 67.52 hp/litre |
| | 3700: 66.31 hp/litre |
| | 4000: 63.42 hp/litre |

### TRANSMISSION

| | |
|---|---|
| Driven wheels | rear |
| Clutch | single dry-plate |
| Gearbox | five speeds + reverse |

### BODYWORK

| | |
|---|---|
| Vignale coupé (designed by Frua) | two doors, 2+2 seats |

### ROLLING CHASSIS

| | |
|---|---|
| Chassis | tubular |
| Front suspension | independent, coil springs, wishbones, anti-roll bar telescopic hydraulic dampers |
| Rear suspension | live axle, semi-cantilevered leaf springs, anti-roll bar, trailing arms, telescopic hydraulic dampers |
| Brakes | servo-assisted discs |
| Steering | recirculating ball |
| Fuel tank | 75 l |
| Front/rear tyres | 205-15 |

### DIMENSIONS AND WEIGHT

| | |
|---|---|
| Wheelbase | 2400 mm |
| Tracks front/rear | 1390/1364 mm |
| Length | 4500 mm |
| Width | 1650 mm |
| Height | 1300 mm |
| Dry weight | 1300 kg |
| Weight/power ratio | 3500: 5.53 kg/hp |
| | 3700: 5.30 kg/hp |
| | 4000: 5.09 kg/hp |

### PERFORMANCE AND PRODUCTION

| | |
|---|---|
| Maximum speed | 235-255 kph |
| Units produced | 125 |
| | 3500: 12 / 3700: 76 / 4000: 37 |

# Mistral Spider 3,5 – 3,7 – 4,0      1963

The coupé version of the Mistral, the prototype of which was presented at the Turin Motor Show in 1963, went into production the following year, while the spider – again built by Vignale to designs by Pietro Frua – first saw the light of day. The rolling chassis was that of the Sebring, with the wheelbase shortened from 2500 to 2400 mm, while the engine, in contrast with the Mistral coupé, was initially only offered in 3.5-litre form. However, a few months after the presentation at the Geneva Motor Show in the spring of 1964, the spider was also equipped with the 3694.39 cc engine that delivered 235 hp at 5500 rpm, good for a maximum speed of 245 kph. From the February of 1966 it was also possible to order the spider with the 4014.19 cc engine, with consequent increases in maximum power (245 hp at the same rev speed) top speed (255 kph). The most significant elements of the mechanical specification remained identical to those of the coupé, from the indirect fuel injection to the five-speed gearbox and the servo-assisted four-wheel disc brakes, while the rear suspension was modified with the coil springs being replaced with more functional semi-elliptical leaf springs. The transformation from closed to open naturally involved the loss of the upper body that so distinguished the coupé with its original fastback configuration and the curving of the extensive glazing. The still very sleek flanks continued at the rear with the boot volume, impeccably designed according to the most traditional canons, as was the truncated tail with its small, rectangular lighting clusters. The overall appearance was in any case that of a sleek, light car even though, compared with the coupé, it did lack a little character. There was also an aesthetically less successful version with a removable hardtop that robbed the design of its elegant levity.

The especially aerodynamic lines of the Tipo 65, the sports racing car hastily built after the Casner's accident in the Tipo 151, so that the company could compete in the 1965 24 Hours of Le Mans. This, too, was an unlucky car in the classic French marathon. After having qualified at more than 30 seconds from the Ford Mk II in pole position, the car left the road on the fourth lap with Swiss driver Siffert at the wheel and it was retired.

## TECHNICAL SPECIFICATION

### ENGINE
rear, longitudinal, 90° V8

| | |
|---|---|
| Bore and stroke | 95x89 mm |
| Unitary displacement | 630.85 cc |
| Total displacement | 5046.8 cc |
| Valvegear | double overhead camshafts per bank |
| Number of valves | two per cylinder |
| Compression ratio | 9:1 |
| Fuel system | Lucas indirect fuel injection |
| Ignition | dual, with two distributors |
| Cooling | water, centrifugal pump and radiator |
| Lubrication | dry sump, with delivery and scavenge pumps |
| Maximum power | 430 hp at 7000 rpm |
| Specific power output | 85.20 hp/litre |

### TRANSMISSION
| | |
|---|---|
| Driven wheels | rear |
| Clutch | multiple dry-plate |
| Gearbox | in-unit with the differential five speeds + reverse |

### BODYWORK
two-seater Sport

### ROLLING CHASSIS
| | |
|---|---|
| Chassis | tubular spaceframe |
| Front suspension | independent, coil springs, telescopic hydraulic dampers |
| Rear suspension | longitudinal torsion bars, telescopic hydraulic dampers |
| Brakes | hydraulically actuated discs |
| Steering | rack and pinion |
| Fuel tank | 160 l |
| Front tyres | 6.00-15 |
| Rear tyres | 6.50-15 |

### DIMENSIONS AND WEIGHT
| | |
|---|---|
| Wheelbase | 2400 mm |
| Tracks front/rear | 1400/1370 mm |
| Length | – |
| Width | – |
| Height | – |
| Dry weight | 960 kg |
| Weight/power ratio | 2.23 kg/hp |

### PERFORMANCE AND PRODUCTION
| | |
|---|---|
| Maximum speed | 350 kph |
| Units produced | 1 |

## 65 — 1965

Following the accident in preliminary practice at Le Mans (10TH April 1965) in which Lloyd Casner was killed at the wheel of a Maserati 151, Colonel John Simone who had entered the car for Maserati France immediately commissioned another. Giulio Alfieri designed a new prototype, abandoning the engineering of the 151 in favour of a rear engine, spaceframe chassis and open-top bodywork, as previously used on the Tipo 63 and 64. The two-seater was prepared in less than two months: a tour de force that was destined to have a detrimental effect on quality. The engine was the V8 from the 151, slightly enlarged from 4941.11 to 5046.8 cc with an increase in power from 410 to 430 hp at 8000 rather than 7000 rpm and a top speed that from 330 kph rose to 350 kph. Installed centrally, but not so far forwards as with the 64, the unit required a redistribution of the weight through the adoption of three fuel tanks, one in the centre, inside the cockpit, and two at the sides. The coachwork had features made familiar by the most recent Maserati racing prototypes, with the engine bay closed by a very large flat cover that terminated in a sharply truncated tail. The size of the engine prevented the adoption rather than the independent rear suspension with torsion bars of a de Dion axle that would have improved the car's handling, judge to be unsatisfactory by the two drivers that raced it at Le Mans on the 20TH of June that year, Joseph Siffert and Jochen Neerpasch. Having set the 21ST fastest time in qualifying, the Maserati crashed out on the 4TH lap. In the months that followed, Alfieri modified the suspension, especially at the rear, replacing the torsion bars with coil springs, but the project was then abandoned. The prototype was sold to the Pellin brothers and reappeared in 1968 with bodywork updated in line with the trends of the time but it raced only very rarely.

A rear view of the Mexico, a four-seater coupé introduced in 1966 that got its name after the prototype body was sold to a Mexican client and installed in 5000 GT chassis that belonged to the president of Mexico, Aldolfo López Mateos. The idea for that name became even more appropriate after John Surtees won the Grand Prix of Mexico in a Cooper-Maserati on 23 October 1966, just a few days after the Paris presentation of the definitive version.

## TECHNICAL SPECIFICATION

### ENGINE
front, longitudinal, 90° V8

| | |
|---|---|
| Bore and stroke | 93.9x85 mm (from 1969 also 88 x 85) |
| Unitary displacement | 588.62 cc (from 1969 also 516.98) |
| Total displacement | 4709 cc (from 1969 also 4135.84) |
| Valvegear | double overhead camshafts per bank |
| Number of valves | two per cylinder |
| Compression ratio | 8.5:1 |
| Fuel system | four Weber 38 DCNL5 carburettors |
| Ignition | single, with Marelli distributor |
| Cooling | water, centrifugal pump and radiator |
| Lubrication | pressurised, with delivery pump |
| Maximum power | 290 hp at 5000 rpm (from 1969 also 260 hp at 5200 rpm) |
| Specific power output | 61.58 hp/litre (from 1969 also 62.86 hp/litre) |

### TRANSMISSION
| | |
|---|---|
| Driven wheels | rear |
| Clutch | single dry-plate |
| Gearbox | five speeds + reverse (automatic optional) |

### BODYWORK
Vignale saloon (designed by Vairo) two doors, four seats

### ROLLING CHASSIS
| | |
|---|---|
| Chassis | unitary construction with front subframe |
| Front suspension | independent, wishbones, coil springs, anti-roll bar, telescopic hydraulic dampers |
| Rear suspension | live axle, semi-cantilevered leaf springs, trailing arms, anti-roll bar, telescopic hydraulic dampers |
| Brakes | servo-assisted hydraulically actuated discs |
| Steering | recirculating ball |
| Fuel tank | 95 l |
| Front/rear tyres | 205-15 |

### DIMENSIONS AND WEIGHT
| | |
|---|---|
| Wheelbase | 2640 mm |
| Tracks front/rear | 1390/1360 mm |
| Length | 4760 mm |
| Width | 1720 mm |
| Height | 1360 mm |
| Dry weight | 1450 kg |
| Weight/power ratio | 5 kg/hp (from 1969 also 5.57 kg/hp) |

### PERFORMANCE AND PRODUCTION
| | |
|---|---|
| Maximum speed | 255 kph (from 1969 also 240 kph) |
| Units produced | 485 |

# Mexico 4,7 – 4,1       1966

The Turin Motor Show of 1965 saw the presentation of a prototype constructed by Vignale to designs by Virginio Vairo, an in-house Maserati stylist also responsible for the Indy. Named the 5000 GT Vignale, the car was based on the rolling chassis of the Quattroporte II, with the wheelbase shortened from 2750 to 2640 mm, while the eight-cylinder engine was drawn from the 5000 range (4941.11 cc). Bodied as an elegant four-seater coupé, the car was so widely admired that it was decided to put it into serial production. The standard configuration was launched in the October of the following year at the Paris Motor Show. The 4709 cc engine was derived from that of the Quattroporte (as was the 4135.84 cc unit offered as an alternative from 1969), mated to a four-speed mechanical gearbox or, on request, a three-speed automatic. The car boasted fuel injection and servo-assisted disc brakes on all four wheels. The Mexico was an harmonious, balanced design, with a sober front end, smooth flanks, an airy glasshouse and little in the way of decoration. The tail was a little controversial, but the most serious criticisms of the overall styling concerned " lack of involvement, a car that failed to arouse the passions: by no means a minor flaw for a Maserati." Nonetheless, the car enjoyed considerable success: 485 examples were constructed and clients included such famous figures as Nino Benvenuti, Virna Lisi and Ronald Reagan, then just an actor. The Vignale prototype was sold in 1965 to a Mexican client, Dìaz Barroso, the owner of the Allemano 5000 GT that had belonged to the President of Mexico, Adolfo López Mateos, and which had been damaged in an accident. Días Barroso asked for the bodywork of the prototype to be installed on the chassis of his wreck and his transformed car was returned to Mexico. Hence the idea to name the model as the Mexico, a decision that was to prove particularly appropriate following John Surtees victory with the Cooper-Maserati in the Mexican GP on the 23[RD] of October 1966, a few days after the Parisian presentation of the definitive version.

Turin, November 1966: the 48TH Turin International Motor Show opened for 10 days and there Maserati introduced, as usual, the best of its own potential. Five cars were on display, the star among them the latest Ghibli, which was surrounded by the rest of the production of the moment made up of the Sebring, Quattroporte, Mexico and Mistral.

## TECHNICAL SPECIFICATION

### ENGINE
front, longitudinal, 90° V8

| | |
|---|---|
| Bore and stroke | 93.9x85 mm (from 1970 Ghibli SS: 93.9x89 mm) |
| Unitary displacement | 588.62 cc (from 1970 Ghibli SS: 616.32 cc) |
| Total displacement | 4709 cc (from 1970 Ghibli SS: 4930.61 cc |
| Valvegear | double overhead camshafts per bank |
| Number of valves | two per cylinder |
| Compression ratio | 8.5:1 |
| Fuel system | four Weber 40 DCNL carburettors |
| Ignition | single, with distributor (from 1969 transistorised) |
| Cooling | water, centrifugal pump and radiator |
| Lubrication | pressurised with delivery and scavenge pumps |
| Maximum power | 340 hp at 5000 rpm (from 1970 Ghibli SS: 330 hp at 5500 rpm) |
| Specific power output | 72.20 hp/litre (from 1970 Ghibli SS: 66.92 hp/litre) |

### TRANSMISSION

| | |
|---|---|
| Driven wheels | rear |
| Clutch | single dry-plate |
| Gearbox | five speeds + reverse (automatic optional) |

### BODYWORK
Ghia coupé (designed by Giugiaro)      two doors, 2+2 seats

### ROLLING CHASSIS

| | |
|---|---|
| Chassis | tubular with front subframe |
| Front suspension | independent, wishbones, coil springs, anti-roll bar, telescopic hydraulic dampers |
| Rear suspension | live axle, cantilevered leaf springs, struts, anti-roll bar, telescopic hydraulic dampers |
| Brakes | servo-assisted hydraulically actuated discs |
| Steering | recirculating ball |
| Fuel tank | 100 l |
| Front/rear tyres | 205-15 |

### DIMENSIONS AND WEIGHT

| | |
|---|---|
| Wheelbase | 2550 mm |
| Tracks front/rear | 1440/1420 mm |
| Length | 4590 mm |
| Width | 1800 mm |
| Height | 1530 mm |
| Dry weight | 1530 - 1680 kg |
| Weight/power ratio | 4.5 kg/hp / Ghibli SS 5.09 kg/hp |

### PERFORMANCE AND PRODUCTION

| | |
|---|---|
| Maximum speed | 265-280 kph |
| Units produced | 1280 |

# Ghibli – Ghibli SS 1967

The Carrozzeria Ghia stand at the Turin Motor Show of 1966 featured a prototype coupé of great aesthetic impact, the Ghibli, named after the Scirocco wind in Libya that blows from the south-east. Born out of a memorable design by Giorgetto Giugiaro, the car caught the eye with its sleek and aggressive lines of sporting inspiration, masterfully harmonized in an overall design of remarkable formal composure. The chassis was derived from that of the Mexico, shortened fro 2640 to 2550 mm, while the engine was the 4.7-litre V8 from the Quattroporte with an important modification: the adoption of dry sump lubrication which allowed the height to be reduced, giving the stylist the chance to create a low, sloping and thrilling attractive bonnet. Below the pop-up headlight, the front end with its all-new graphics presented a slim, full-width air intake with a slightly protruding chromed surround and a small trident at the centre. A crease line ran along the flanks, defining two smooth surfaces interrupted by the curvatures of the wheel arches and the C-pillar. The upper body was perfectly integrated with the overall design and terminated in a single line at the truncated tail, which was also very slim and enclosed by wrap-around bumpers, the only element added to a conceptually pure form. The engine developed a maximum power output of 340 hp, good for a maximum speed of 265 kph. Launched in 1967, the Ghibli was updated in 1970 with modifications that gave rise to the SS version. Changes were made to the lighting clusters (now larger), the instrument panel and the headrests and above all to the mechanical specification, with the adoption of a 4930.61 cc engine that, even though detuned to 330 hp and despite a significant increase in weight (from 1530 to 1680 kg) powered the car to a top speed of 280 kph. Between 1967 and 1972, the Ghibli was constructed in 1280 examples.

In 1968, shortly before entering the Citroën orbit, Maserati commissioned Vignale and Ghia to create a high performance two-door, four-seater saloon. The young Giugiaro designed the Simùn for Ghia, a prototype that remained such. Vignale's proposal, to the designs of Virginio Vairo, instead prefigured the fabulous future Indy model.

## TECHNICAL SPECIFICATION

### ENGINE
front, longitudinal, 90° V8

| | |
|---|---|
| Bore and stroke | 88x85 mm |
| Unitary displacement | 516.98 cc |
| Total displacement | 4135.84 cc |
| Valvegear | double overhead camshafts per bank |
| Number of valves | two per cylinder |
| Compression ratio | 8.5:1 |
| Fuel system | four Weber 38 DCNL5 carburettors |
| Ignition | single, with Marelli distributor |
| Cooling | water, centrifugal pump and radiator |
| Lubrication | pressurised, with delivery pump |
| Maximum power | 260 hp at 5200 rpm |
| Specific power output | 62.86 hp/litre |

### TRANSMISSION
| | |
|---|---|
| Driven wheels | rear |
| Clutch | single dry-plate |
| Gearbox | five speeds + reverse |

### BODYWORK
Ghia saloon (designed by Giugiaro) two doors, four seats

### ROLLING CHASSIS
| | |
|---|---|
| Chassis | unitary construction with front subframe |
| Front suspension | independent, wishbones, coil springs, anti-roll bar, telescopic hydraulic dampers |
| Rear suspension | live axle, semi-cantilevered leaf springs, trailing arms, anti-roll bar, telescopic hydraulic dampers |
| Brakes | servo-assisted hydraulically actuated discs |
| Steering | recirculating ball |
| Fuel tank | 95 l |
| Front/rear tyres | 205-15 |

### DIMENSIONS AND WEIGHT
| | |
|---|---|
| Wheelbase | 2640 mm |
| Tracks front/rear | 1390/1360 mm |
| Length | 4760 mm |
| Width | 1720 mm |
| Height | 1360 mm |
| Dry weight | 1450 kg |
| Weight/power ratio | 5.57 kg/hp |

### PERFORMANCE AND PRODUCTION
| | |
|---|---|
| Maximum speed | 240 kph |
| Units produced | 1 |

# Simùn Ghia 1968

In the late Sixties, Maserati decided to create a high performance four-seater and commissioned Ghia to develop the project. The resulting prototype was previewed at the Turin Motor Show in 1968 and named – as had been the case with the Mistral (1963) and Ghibli (1966) – after a wind, the Simùn that blows in the Algerian Sahara. The chassis was a modified version of that of the Mexico, with the 90° V8 engine in 4.2-litre, 260 hp form mated to a five-speed mechanical gearbox. The suspension geometry was traditional, independent at the front and a live axle at the rear. The car boasted a top speed of 240 kph. Giorgetto Giugiaro was responsible for the bodywork styling, the last project the great stylist was to undertake for third parties given that in that same year he was to open his own Italdesign firm. The Simùn, a large two-door saloon with four seats and sophisticated fittings and finish was striking with its sleek, elongated lines, the bonnet with pop-up headlights and the original rear end. It showed innovative touches in the air vents from the engine bay on the wings and the low belt line that rose above the rear wheel arches, but in the end it was not entirely convincing. "The Simùn", as the most attentive criticism reads, "is not one of Giugiaro's most memorable designs but testifies to the capacity that has accompanied him throughout his very long career to produce ever-consistent and extremely professional designs, realised with great control of the volumes and the surfaces, so that the result is always of a high level even when the inspiration is somewhat lacking." In conclusion, the prototype remained as such and Maserati choose a contemporary proposal by Vignale for what would become one of its most appealing products, the Indy, serial production of which was to begin the following year.

The move from a coupé to a roadster version of a model like the Ghibli, a car that was a fundamental contribution to the history of design and not just of Maserati, couldn't be simple. Yet the result is still well worthy of note, with a tight, slender lined car of great style, which was well received by the public and the motor industry, and produced in 125 units.

## TECHNICAL SPECIFICATION

### ENGINE
front, longitudinal, 90° V8

| | |
|---|---|
| Bore and stroke | 93.9x85 mm (from 1970 Ghibli SS Spider: 93.9x89 mm) |
| Unitary displacement | 588.62 cc (from 1970 Ghibli SS Spider: 616.32 cc) |
| Total displacement | 4709 cc (from 1970 Ghibli SS Spider: 4930.61 cc) |
| Valvegear | double overhead camshafts per bank |
| Number of valves | two per cylinder |
| Compression ratio | 8.5:1 |
| Fuel system | four Weber 40 DCNL carburettors |
| Ignition | single, with distributor (from 1969 transistorised) |
| Cooling | water, centrifugal pump and radiator |
| Lubrication | pressurised with delivery and scavenge pumps |
| Maximum power | 340 hp at 5000 rpm (from 1970 Ghibli SS Spider: 330 hp at 5500 rpm) |
| Specific power output | 72.20 hp/litre (from 1970 Ghibli SS Spider: 66.92 hp/litre) |

### TRANSMISSION
| | |
|---|---|
| Driven wheels | rear |
| Clutch | single dry-plate |
| Gearbox | five speeds + reverse (automatic optional) |

### BODYWORK
| | |
|---|---|
| Ghia spider | two doors, 2+2 seats |

### ROLLING CHASSIS
| | |
|---|---|
| Chassis | tubular with front subframe |
| Front suspension | independent, wishbones, coil springs, anti-roll bar, telescopic hydraulic dampers |
| Rear suspension | live axle, cantilevered leaf springs, struts, anti-roll bar, telescopic hydraulic dampers |
| Brakes | servo-assisted hydraulically actuated discs |
| Steering | recirculating ball |
| Fuel tank | 100 l |
| Front/rear tyres | 205-15 |

### DIMENSIONS AND WEIGHT
| | |
|---|---|
| Wheelbase | 2550 mm |
| Tracks front/rear | 1440/1420 mm |
| Length | 4590 mm |
| Width | 1800 mm |
| Height | 1530 mm |
| Dry weight | 1630 kg Ghibli SS Spider: 1680 kg |
| Weight/power ratio | 4.79 kg/hp Ghibli SS Spider 5.09 kg/hp |

### PERFORMANCE AND PRODUCTION
| | |
|---|---|
| Maximum speed | 265-280 kph |
| Units produced | 125 (of which 20-25 Ghibli SS Spider) |

# Ghibli Spider – Ghibli SS Spider 1969

In 1969, while the Ghibli was establishing itself on the international markets as one of the most successful coupés, it was flanked by a spider version also built by Ghia. The transformation from a closed to an open-top car led to a change in the personality of the model: while the elimination of the roof in a three-box car is a relatively simple procedure, the same is not the case with a fastback coupé in which the roof panel is integrated with the rear end and its removal involves structural modifications and the consequent need to reconstruct ex-novo a cover for the luggage compartment. This problem presented itself with the Ghibli's transformation from coupé to spider, but Ghia succeeded in creating a visually attractive design, with the low, flat rear section well integrated within the overall design. Instead this was not the case with the hardtop version, which proved to be less successful given the inevitable need to install mounts for the removable roof. The mechanical specification mirrored that of the coupé, with the 4.7-litre V8 engine and from 1970, the 4.9-litre alternative of the SS version with a maximum power output of 340 hp and a top speed of 270 kph. The suspension was unchanged, independent at the front and a live axle at the rear, dual circuit servo-assisted disc brakes, a five-speed mechanical gearbox (a three-speed automatic was available on request) and a limited slip differential. The trim and equipment levels reflected the traditional Maserati quality and class. Over the course of the five years the model was on sale, 125 units were constructed, around 20-25 of which in SS form, and it is still particularly sought-after on the classic car market, to the point where diverse Ghiblis born as coupés have successively been transformed into spiders.

Previously, Maserati had often used the names of winds by which to call their cars: Mistral, Ghibli and Simùn are some examples. But for the new 1969 coupé called Indy the choice fell on the celebrated Indiana motor racing circuit, home of the 500 Miles of Indianapolis, which Maserati won in 1939 and 1940.

## TECHNICAL SPECIFICATION

### ENGINE

front, longitudinal, 90° V8

| | |
|---|---|
| Bore and stroke | 4.1: 88x85 mm<br>4.7: 93.9x85 mm<br>4.9: 93.9x89 mm |
| Unitary displacement | 4.1: 516.98 cc - 4.7: 588.62 cc<br>4.9: 616.32 cc |
| Total displacement | 4.1: 4135.84 cc - 4.7: 4709 cc<br>4.9: 4930.61 cc |
| Valvegear | double overhead camshafts<br>per bank |
| Number of valves | two per cylinder |
| Compression ratio | 8.5:1 |
| Fuel system | four Weber 42 DCNF carburettors |
| Ignition | single, with distributor<br>and transistor<br>(from 1970, Bosch electronic) |
| Cooling | water, centrifugal pump<br>and radiator |
| Lubrication | pressurised, with delivery pump |
| Maximum power | 4.1: 260 hp at 5500 rpm<br>4.7: 290 hp at 5500 rpm<br>4.9: 335 hp at 5500 rpm |
| Specific power output | 4.1: 62.86 hp/litre<br>4.7: 61.58 hp/litre<br>4.9: 67.94 hp/litre |

### TRANSMISSION

| | |
|---|---|
| Driven wheels | rear |
| Clutch | single dry-plate |
| Gearbox | five speeds + reverse<br>(automatic optional) |

### BODYWORK

*Vignale coupé (designed by Vairo)*      two doors, 2+2 seats

### ROLLING CHASSIS

| | |
|---|---|
| Chassis | unitary construction |
| Front suspension | independent, wishbones,<br>coil springs, anti-roll bar,<br>telescopic hydraulic dampers |
| Rear suspension | live axle, cantilevered leaf springs,<br>trailing arms, anti-roll bar,<br>telescopic hydraulic dampers |
| Brakes | servo-assisted hydraulically<br>actuated discs |
| Steering | recirculating ball<br>(from 1973 power steering<br>on request) |
| Fuel tank | 95 l |
| Front/rear tyres | 205-14 (from 1973 205-15) |

### DIMENSIONS AND WEIGHT

| | |
|---|---|
| Wheelbase | 2600 mm |
| Tracks front/rear | 1480/1434 mm |
| Length | 4740 mm |
| Width | 1760 mm |
| Height | 1220 mm |
| Dry weight | 4.1: 1500 kg<br>4.7: 1500 kg<br>4.9: 1650 kg |
| Weight/power ratio | 4.1: 5.76 kg/hp<br>4.7: 5.17 kg/hp<br>4.9: 4.92 kg/hp |

### PERFORMANCE AND PRODUCTION

| | |
|---|---|
| Maximum speed | 250-280 kph |
| Units produced | 1104 |

# Indy 4,1 – 4,7 – 4,9 1969

The prototype of a brand-new Maserati model destined to replace the Mexico coupé was exhibited on the Carrozzeria Vignale stand at the 1968 Turin Motor Show. The definitive version was seen at the Geneva Show in 1969, where it was presented with a name celebrating the 8C TF's victory in the Indianapolis 500 Miles 30 years earlier: Indy. Built by Vignale to designs by Virginio Vairo, as had been the case with the Mexico, the car offered four comfortable seats in an imposing coupé with well-balanced forms. From the large, sloping bonnet, less aggressive than that of the Ghibli, rose the steeply sloping windscreen that flowed into the car's fastback pro-file, with the flanks marked by a robust B-pillar, the very large glazed rear hatch and the truncated tail. The Indy's streamlined shape was also accentuated by it height, significantly lower than the Mexico: 1220 against 1360 mm. The wheelbase was also shortened while the tracks were instead increased and the weight remained unchanged (1500 kg, although this was destined to rise to 1650 with the subsequent mechanical modifications). For the first year of production the car was offered with the 4135.84 cc V8 engine producing 260 hp and good for a top speed of 250 kph. In 1970, as had been the case with the Mexico, the Indy was also offered with the 4709 cc engine (290 hp, 265 kph) and was officially renamed as the Indy America. From 1971, the engine range was practically unified with the five-litre (4930.61 cc) unit from the Ghibli SS (335 hp, 280 kph). Produced through to 1975, the Indy enjoyed great success: 1104 units were constructed against the 1280 of well established Ghibli. Between the creation of the first and the second of these two cars, in the January of 1968, the Orsi family sold its shareholding in the company to Citroën. The Ghibli was therefore the last car to be launched with the Modenese industrialists at the helm. The Indy was the first to be born under the new management.

Once again the name of a wind was used for the Bora, a new Maserati that first appeared in 1971. This agile and quick sports coupé had many new developments and improvements, its only defect being that it was conceived at the start of a crisis that proved complex for sports cars, which were penalised by the oil crisis of the early '70s, which hit sales.

## TECHNICAL SPECIFICATION

### ENGINE
rear, longitudinal, 90° V8

| | |
|---|---|
| Bore and stroke | 4.7: 94x895 mm |
| | 4.9: 93.9x89 mm |
| Unitary displacement | 4.7: 589.88 cc |
| | 4.9: 616.32 cc |
| Total displacement | 4.7: 4719,04 cc |
| | 4.9: 4930.61 cc |
| Valvegear | double overhead camshafts per bank |
| Number of valves | two per cylinder |
| Compression ratio | 8.5:1 |
| Fuel system | four Weber 42 DCNF carburettors |
| Ignition | single, Bosch electronic |
| Cooling | water, centrifugal pump and radiator |
| Lubrication | pressurised with delivery and scavenge pumps |
| Maximum power | 4.7: 310 hp at 5000 rpm |
| | 4.9: 320 hp at 6000 rpm |
| Specific power output | 4.7: 65.69 hp/litre |
| | 4.9: 64.90 hp/litre |

### TRANSMISSION
| | |
|---|---|
| Driven wheels | rear |
| Clutch | single dry-plate |
| Gearbox | five speeds + reverse |

### BODYWORK
| | |
|---|---|
| Italdesign coupé | two doors, two seats |

### ROLLING CHASSIS
| | |
|---|---|
| Chassis | unitary construction |
| Front suspension | independent, wishbones coil springs, anti-roll bar, telescopic hydraulic dampers |
| Rear suspension | independent, wishbones coil springs, anti-roll bar, telescopic hydraulic dampers |
| Brakes | servo-assisted hydraulically actuated discs |
| Steering | recirculating ball (later rack and pinion) |
| Fuel tank | 100 l |
| Front/rear tyres | 215-70 VR-15 |

### DIMENSIONS AND WEIGHT
| | |
|---|---|
| Wheelbase | 2600 mm |
| Tracks front/rear | 1470/1447 mm |
| Length | 4335 mm |
| Width | 1768 mm |
| Height | 1134 mm |
| Dry weight | 1400 kg |
| Weight/power ratio | 4.7: 4.51 kg/hp |
| | 4.9: 4.37 kg/hp |

### PERFORMANCE AND PRODUCTION
| | |
|---|---|
| Maximum speed | 280 kph |
| Units produced | 530 |

# Bora 4,7 – 4,9                                    1971

As early as 1969 Maserati had commissioned Giorgetto Giugiaro's youthful Italdesign to produce a high performance model destined to replace the Ghibli. Following a trend that had yet to establish itself – apart from Porsche, there were two precedents of note: the Lamborghini Miura (1966) and the Dino 206 GT (1967) – Giugiaro located the engine in a rear central position, design a compact, monolithic body fitted to a brand-new unitary construction chassis. The new coupé, named the Bora after the strong European wind blowing from the north-east, made its debut at the Geneva Motor Show in 1971. Its slim nose, set below the sloping bonnet with pop-up headlights, was characterised by an air intake divided into two rectangles with chromed frames either side of the trident. The perfectly smooth flanks featured a black running along the centre and linking the wheel arches. The profile was characterised by a conspicuous B-pillar to which were attached the original stainless steel roof panel contrasting with the body colour and the vertical glass screen that separated the cockpit from the engine bay. The engine itself was visible through the extensive glazing of the rear hatch. Two tried and trusted engines were offered: the 4.7- and (from 1975) the 4.9-litre V8s offering 210 and 320 hp and top speeds over 280 kph. Among the mechanical innovations were independent suspension all round. Apart form its outright performance, the Bora was noted for its roadholding, handling, cockpit sound-damping and its luggage capacity. Regrettably, the car's by no means indifferent commercial potential – was with all GTs at the time – was compromised by the oil crisis sparked in 1973 by the Yom Kippur war between Egypt, Syria and Israel and the lacerating political and social disputes that followed. Nonetheless, over the course of its eight-year production career, 530 examples of the Bora were constructed.

Designed by Giorgetto Giugiaro and his Italdesign in 1972, the Boomerang was an extreme exercise in creativity, conceived around the concept of a car in the shape of a wedge, similar to that which Bertone, for example, had already elaborated at the end of the previous decade with models like the 1968 Carabo and Pininfarina's 1970 Modulo. These were concept cars in the purest sense, which left a substantial mark on the history of car design.

## TECHNICAL SPECIFICATION

### ENGINE
rear, longitudinal, 90° V8

| | |
|---|---|
| Bore and stroke | 4.7: 94x85 mm |
| Unitary displacement | 4.7: 589.88 cc |
| Total displacement | 4.7: 4719.04 cc |
| Valvegear | double overhead camshafts per bank |
| Number of valves | two per cylinder |
| Compression ratio | 8.5:1 |
| Fuel system | four Weber 42 DCNF carburettors |
| Ignition | single, Bosch electronic |
| Cooling | water, centrifugal pump and radiator |
| Lubrication | pressurised with delivery and scavenge pumps |
| Maximum power | 310 hp at 5500 rpm |
| Specific power output | 65.69 hp/litre |

### TRANSMISSION
| | |
|---|---|
| Driven wheels | rear |
| Clutch | single dry-plate |
| Gearbox | five speeds + reverse |

### BODYWORK
| | |
|---|---|
| Italdesign coupé | two doors, two seats |

### ROLLING CHASSIS
| | |
|---|---|
| Chassis | unitary construction |
| Front suspension | independent, wishbones coil springs, anti-roll bar, telescopic hydraulic dampers |
| Rear suspension | independent, wishbones, coil springs, anti-roll bar, telescopic hydraulic dampers |
| Brakes | servo-assisted hydraulically actuated discs |
| Steering | recirculating ball (later rack and pinion) |
| Fuel tank | – |
| Front/rear tyres | 215-70 VR-15 |

### DIMENSIONS AND WEIGHT
| | |
|---|---|
| Wheelbase | 2600 mm |
| Tracks front/rear | 1475/1445 mm |
| Length | 4342 mm |
| Width | 1860 mm |
| Height | 1070 mm |
| Dry weight | – |
| Weight/power ratio | – |

### PERFORMANCE AND PRODUCTION
| | |
|---|---|
| Maximum speed | 280 kph |
| Units produced | 1 |

# Boomerang Italdesign                                   1972

In the early Seventies, automotive design abandoned the fluid lines and softly rounded volumes in vogue in the post-war period in favour of the geometric lines and square-cut masses that were to dominate the scene for 20 years. Leading the way in this drastic change of direction were numerous prototypes, but two in particular have to be recognised as having been historical precursors and trend-setters, for the names of their creators as well as the spectacular innovative charge of their styling: Bertone's Carabo (based on the Alfa Romeo 33 from 1968) and Pininfarina's Modulo (Ferrari 512 S, 1970). To these can be added the Boomerang coupé, created by Italdesign on the basis of the Maserati Bora 4.7 and presented as a epoxy resin model at the Turin Motor Show in 1972 and as a rolling prototype five months later at the Geneva Show in 1973. Giorgetto Giugiaro had already designed diverse concept cars developing the nascent aesthetic of angular surfaces: take for example certain names that have become icons in the history of automotive design such as the Iguana (1969), the Tapiro (1970) and the Caimano (1971) and at least one that made it into serial production: the stunning Lotus Esprit (1971). However, it was with the Boomerang coupé that he took this formal research to the extreme, exaggerating the wedge-shaped profile, the corners folds and the angular folds. The car is still sensational in appearance today: however, it had never had, and could never have had, any production follow-up; in effect it was an incredibly stimulating work of sculpture. Giugiaro himself has admitted as much: "In the search for the new one risks taking the wrong path. That pushing on towards ever more graphic forms is excessive here: the Boomerang may be attractive as a form, but it is contradictory from the point of view of aerodynamics, almost a degeneration of the square-cut shapes. It had a sense of provocation when it was created; today it is simply a nice museum piece."

For no fewer than 11 years – a kind of record for Maserati – the Merak remained in production in its various forms. That period coincided with a new change of ownership to the company and the exit of Citröen as the major shareholder in Maserati after which De Tomaso took over.

## TECHNICAL SPECIFICATION

### ENGINE
rear, longitudinal, 90° V6

| | |
|---|---|
| *Bore and stroke* | Merak and Merak SS: 91.6 x 75 mm |
| *Unitary displacement* | Merak and Merak SS: 494.24 cc |
| *Total displacement* | Merak and Merak SS: 2965.46 cc |
| *Valvegear* | double overhead camshafts per bank |
| *Number of valves* | two per cylinder |
| *Compression ratio* | Merak: 8.75:1<br>Merak SS: 9:1 |
| *Fuel system* | Merak: three Weber 42 DCNF carburettors<br>Merak SS: three Weber 44 DCNF carburettors |
| *Ignition* | single, electronic |
| *Cooling* | water, centrifugal pump and radiator |
| *Lubrication* | pressurised, with delivery pump |
| *Maximum power* | Merak: 190 hp at 6000 rpm<br>Merak SS: 208 hp at 6500 rpm |
| *Specific power output* | Merak: 64.07 hp/litre<br>Merak SS: 70.14 hp/litre |

### TRANSMISSION
| | |
|---|---|
| *Driven wheels* | rear |
| *Clutch* | single dry-plate |
| *Gearbox* | five speeds + reverse |

### BODYWORK
| | |
|---|---|
| *Italdesign coupé* | two doors, 2+2 seats |

### ROLLING CHASSIS
| | |
|---|---|
| *Chassis* | unitary construction |
| *Front suspension* | independent, wishbones, coil springs, anti-roll bar, telescopic hydraulic dampers |
| *Rear suspension* | independent, wishbones, coil springs, anti-roll bar, telescopic hydraulic dampers |
| *Brakes* | servo-assisted hydraulically actuated discs |
| *Steering* | rack and pinion |
| *Fuel tank* | 85 l |
| *Front tyres* | Merak: 185 VR-15 (then 195 VR-15)<br>Merak SS: 195/70 VR-15 |
| *Rear tyres* | Merak: 205 VR-15 (then 215 VR-15)<br>Merak SS: 215/70 VR-15 |

### DIMENSIONS AND WEIGHT
| | |
|---|---|
| *Wheelbase* | 2600 mm |
| *Tracks front/rear* | 1470/1440 mm |
| *Length* | 4330 mm |
| *Width* | 1770 mm |
| *Height* | 1130 mm |
| *Dry weight* | Merak: 1350 kg<br>Merak SS: 1180 kg |
| *Weight/power ratio* | Merak: 7.10 kg/hp<br>Merak SS: 5.67 kg/hp |

### PERFORMANCE AND PRODUCTION
| | |
|---|---|
| *Maximum speed* | Merak: 240 kph<br>Merak SS: 250 kph |
| *Units produced* | 1619 (626 Merak, 993 Merak SS) |

# Merak – Merak SS                                        1972

The promising success of the Bora prior to the devastating effects of the oil crisis on the global economy encouraged Maserati to produce a model accessible to a broader clientele attracted by the lower price, extra interior space and less daunting performance. Presented at the Paris Motor Show in 1972, the car was named as the Merak after one of the stars in the Big Dipper. Savings on design and production costs were achieved by using the floorpan and part of the bodywork from the Bora and the Tipo C.114 90° V6 engine produced in 1970 for the Citroën SM. By increasing the bore from 87 to 91.6 mm and retaining the same stroke of 75 mm, the displacement was increased from 2675.10 to 2965.46 cc. The maximum power output increased from 170 to 190 hp at 6000 rpm as well as the top speed, from 220 to 240 kph. This much more compact unit allowed Giugiaro to modify the cabin, finding room for two extra seats and making the Merak one of the first examples of a mid-engined 2+2 coupé. The tail was redesigned, eliminating the glazing around the engine bay, now covered by a horizontal steel cover with four grilles set against the vertical rear screen. In order to avoid what has been defined as the risk of a "pick-up effect", Giugiaro added two flying buttresses linking the tail to the roof (now body-coloured instead of unpainted as on the Bora) that became an unmistakeable feature of the Merak. Inside, clearly forcing the issue, components from the Citroën SM were used, the dashboard, steering wheel and instruments, later replaced by Alejandro De Tomaso as soon as he arrived at Maserati in 1975. At the 1975 Geneva Show, the standard Merak was flanked by the SS version, with 208 hp and a top speed of 250 kph, performance in line with that of its Porsche 911 and Dino 246 rivals.

Starting from the chassis of the successful Indy, in 1974 Italdesign created this single 2+2 coupé, built on the AM 124 chassis number 002. The coupé used a tuned version of the Indy's 4.9-litre engine that was also installed longitudinally at the front. The wedge shape of the front, the rear fastback volume and the stubby tail are aspects of this prototype.

## TECHNICAL SPECIFICATION

### ENGINE
front, longitudinal, 90° V8

| | |
|---|---|
| *Bore and stroke* | 93.9 x 89 mm |
| *Unitary displacement* | 616.32 cc |
| *Total displacement* | 4930.61 cc |
| *Valvegear* | double overhead camshafts per bank |
| *Number of valves* | two per cylinder |
| *Compression ratio* | 8.5:1 |
| *Fuel system* | four Weber 42 DCNF carburettors |
| *Ignition* | single, Bosch electronic |
| *Cooling* | water, centrifugal pump and radiator |
| *Lubrication* | pressurised with delivery and scavenge pumps |
| *Maximum power* | 320 hp at 6000 rpm |
| *Specific power output* | 64.90 hp/litre |

### TRANSMISSION
| | |
|---|---|
| *Driven wheels* | rear |
| *Clutch* | single dry-plate |
| *Gearbox* | five speeds + reverse |

### BODYWORK
| | |
|---|---|
| *Italdesign coupé* | two doors, 2+2 seats |

### ROLLING CHASSIS
| | |
|---|---|
| *Chassis* | unitary construction |
| *Front suspension* | independent, wishbones, coil springs, anti-roll bar, telescopic hydraulic dampers |
| *Rear suspension* | independent, wishbones, coil springs, anti-roll bar, telescopic hydraulic dampers |
| *Brakes* | servo-assisted hydraulically actuated discs |
| *Steering* | recirculating ball (later rack and pinion) |
| *Fuel tank* | – |
| *Front/rear tyres* | 215-70 VR-15 |

### DIMENSIONS AND WEIGHT
| | |
|---|---|
| *Wheelbase* | 2600 mm |
| *Tracks front/rear* | 1510/1440 mm |
| *Length* | 4680 mm |
| *Width* | 1870 mm |
| *Height* | 1230 mm |
| *Dry weight* | – |
| *Weight/power ratio* | – |

### PERFORMANCE AND PRODUCTION
| | |
|---|---|
| *Maximum speed* | 280 kph |
| *Units produced* | 1 |

# Coupé 2+2 Italdesign 1974

Using the rolling chassis of the Indy with the most powerful version of the 90° V8 (4930.61 cc, 335 hp, 280 kph) mounted longitudinally at the front, Italdesign prepared a four-seater coupé for the 1974 Turin Motor Show with which it intended to translate into feasible terms earlier styling concepts that had been either too extreme or too advanced. The reference to the Boomerang that Giorgetto Giugiaro had proposed two years earlier was by no means casual: this prototype – which remained known simply as the 2+2 Coupé – also clearly favoured formal geometric tension but the attempt to produce a less extreme version resulted in a compromise that Giugiaro himself admitted was less than successful. The body, which may enclosed within a parallelepiped, was lightened by a very sharp nose that represented the most attractive part of the coupé: with no radiator grille, it was topped by a large bonnet with pop-up headlights that linked it to a very sleek pyramidal upper body. The low, taut flanks were marked by a sharp crease along the belt line, from which rose perhaps the least convincing part of the car, the side windows. They were framed by a polygon with too many sides, the shorter of which, at the front and rear, gave origins to two air intakes that recalled those of the Ghibli but did not appear to be so elegantly integrated with the design as a whole. The fastback profile sloped down to the compact, truncated and well balanced tail that contained six lighting units, although this area too was not immune from criticism, above all due to its "excessive" similarity to that of the Lotus Esprit, penned by Giugiaro three years earlier. The interior was neither original nor particularly refined and all in all the Coupé 2+2 was one of the least successful expressions of the great Italian stylist's talent. The example exhibited in Turin in 1974 remained a one-off that never went into production.

The Coupé 2+2 was joined by a revolutionary prototype, again penned by Giorgetto Giugiaro, that while retaining a sporting connotation, did cast an eye in the direction of other market segments that had yet to be explored by the Trident marque. In the case of the Medici, the idea was to create ample space in the rear passenger compartment that would house four seats facing each other in pairs. Once again the concept never went beyond the prototype stage.

## TECHNICAL SPECIFICATION

### ENGINE

front, longitudinal, 90° V8

| | |
|---|---|
| Bore and stroke | 93.9 x 89 mm |
| Unitary displacement | 616.32 cc |
| Total displacement | 4930.61 cc |
| Valvegear | double overhead camshafts per bank |
| Number of valves | two per cylinder |
| Compression ratio | 8.5:1 |
| Fuel system | four Weber 42 DCNF carburettors |
| Ignition | single, Bosch electronic |
| Cooling | water, centrifugal pump and radiator |
| Lubrication | pressurised with delivery and scavenge pumps |
| Maximum power | 320 hp at 5500 rpm |
| Specific power output | 64.90 hp/litre |

### TRANSMISSION

| | |
|---|---|
| Driven wheels | rear |
| Clutch | single dry-plate |
| Gearbox | five speeds + reverse |

### BODYWORK

| | |
|---|---|
| Italdesign saloon | four doors, six seats (Medici II: four seats) |

### ROLLING CHASSIS

| | |
|---|---|
| Chassis | unitary construction |
| Front suspension | independent, wishbones, coil springs, anti-roll bar, telescopic hydraulic dampers |
| Rear suspension | independent, wishbones, coil springs, anti-roll bar, telescopic hydraulic dampers |
| Brakes | servo-assisted hydraulically actuated discs |
| Steering | recirculating ball (later rack and pinion) |
| Fuel tank | – |
| Front/rear tyres | 215-70 VR-15 |

### DIMENSIONS AND WEIGHT

| | |
|---|---|
| Wheelbase | 3100 mm |
| Tracks front/rear | 1510/1470 mm |
| Length | 5220 mm |
| Width | 1860 mm |
| Height | 1370 mm |
| Dry weight | – |
| Weight/power ratio | – |

### PERFORMANCE AND PRODUCTION

| | |
|---|---|
| Maximum speed | 280 kph |
| Units produced | 2 |

# Medici I – Medici II Italdesign 1974

At the 1974 edition of the Turin Motor Show, alongside the controversial Coupé 2+2, Italdesign presented another prototype using the same underpinnings, those of the Indy with the most powerful engine: the 4930.61 cc, 90° V8 with 335 hp, good for 280 kph. The theme proposed by Giugiaro was that of a large flagship saloon capable of offering accommodation and great comfort for six people without giving the impression of a mastodontic vehicle. This apparently utopian brief was resolved by foregoing the traditional three-box configuration in favour of a fastback profile with a truncated tail with a degree of sporting style. This car, given the Medici name in honour of the famous Florentine family renowned for its business sense and love of art and culture, had a compact appearance and was a half metre shorter than the average American limousine. The overall design recalled another attractive Giugiaro creation, the Asso di Picche four-seater coupé realised a year earlier on the basis of the Audi 80. The design featured almost all the styling motifs typical of Italdesign concept car projects and those destined for production: flat, taut planes, square-cut, well integrated surfaces, a prismatic upper body and extensive glazing. However, leaving aside the exterior, the car was striking in its exploitation of interior space, with the four rear seats arranged in salon-fashion with two individual seats face-to-face with the bench seat. The glass roof and light velour upholstery exalted the airiness of the passenger compartment. This prototype was followed by a restyled version that was less sporting, more classical, known as the Medici II and presented the Paris Motor Show in 1976: a less inclined nose, a grille with twin headlights in place of the pop-up lights, four rather six seats and leather rather than velour upholstery. Both cars remained at the one-off prototype stage.

The last model constructed under Citroën management, the Khamsin coupé was also the last to see the light under the technical direction of Ing. Giulio Alfieri. It was produced in 430 examples, of whcih just under half were destined for the North American market.

## TECHNICAL SPECIFICATION

### ENGINE
front, longitudinal, 90° V8

| | |
|---|---|
| *Bore and stroke* | 93.9 x 89 mm |
| *Unitary displacement* | 616.32 cc |
| *Total displacement* | 4930.61 cc |
| *Valvegear* | double overhead camshafts per bank |
| *Number of valves* | two per cylinder |
| *Compression ratio* | 8.5:1 |
| *Fuel system* | four Weber 42 DCNF carburettors |
| *Ignition* | single, Bosch electronic |
| *Cooling* | water, centrifugal pump and radiator |
| *Lubrication* | pressurised with delivery and scavenge pumps |
| *Maximum power* | 280 hp at 5500 rpm |
| *Specific power output* | 56.78 hp/litre |

### TRANSMISSION
| | |
|---|---|
| *Driven wheels* | rear |
| *Clutch* | single dry-plate |
| *Gearbox* | five speeds + reverse (automatic optional) |

### BODYWORK
| | |
|---|---|
| *coupé* | two doors, 2+2 seats |

### ROLLING CHASSIS
| | |
|---|---|
| *Chassis* | tubular |
| *Front suspension* | independent, wishbones, coil springs, anti-roll bar, telescopic hydraulic dampers |
| *Rear suspension* | independent, wishbones, coil springs, anti-roll bar, telescopic hydraulic dampers |
| *Brakes* | servo-assisted hydraulically actuated discs |
| *Steering* | rack and pinion |
| *Fuel tank* | 90 l |
| *Front/rear tyres* | 215-70 VR-15 |

### DIMENSIONS AND WEIGHT
| | |
|---|---|
| *Wheelbase* | 2550 mm |
| *Tracks front/rear* | 1400/1468 mm |
| *Length* | 4400 mm |
| *Width* | 1804 mm |
| *Height* | 1140 mm |
| *Dry weight* | 1680 kg |
| *Weight/power ratio* | 6 kg/hp |

### PERFORMANCE AND PRODUCTION
| | |
|---|---|
| *Maximum speed* | 270 kph |
| *Units produced* | 430 |

# Khamsin                    1974

The Ghibli (1967-1972) was replaced by an elegant 2+2 coupé designed by Bertone and presented at the Paris Motor Show in 1973 but only put into production a year later, as soon as there was a hint of an improvement in the global energy crisis. The new car was named Khamsin after a wind that blows from the south-east across North-East Africa and the Arabian peninsula. For the record, khamsīn in Arabic means fifty, the number of consecutive days in which the wind is traditionally said to blow with a certain continuity. The mechanical specification of the coupé was that of the Ghibli, with the 4930.61 cc V8 engine producing 280 hp and propelling the car to a speed of 270 kph. What was instead new was the unitary construction bodyshell in place of the tubular chassis and, for the first time on a front-engined Maserati, independent suspension all round. Certain components (such as the high pressure braking system and the progressive assisted power steering) were of Citroën provenance, but this was not an invasive presence and in any case mechanically sophisticated and appropriate to the quality of the car. A coupé with strong, compact lines, the Khamsin was distinguished by its agile fastback profile with a rear hatch and a sweeping crease line running the length of the flanks. The windscreen and roof traced the pyramidal form of the slim upper body that sloped down in a single plane to the transparent truncated tail, with the original lighting clusters set directly into the glass panel. The simple, aggressive front end was also well judged, with pop-up headlights and characteristics asymmetric air vents on the bonnet. Built in 430 examples, this was the last Maserati model to be launched under the technical direction (after over 20 years) of Ing. Giulio Alfieri, the creator of engines and racing and road cars that marked an entire era in the history of the automobile. The Khamsin was also the last Maserati built under Citroën management.

The intention was good but the result was not for various reasons. With the 1976 Maserati Quattroporte II, the company dropped the sporty appearance of all its recent production to try once again to build a tight-lined, squarer top-of-the-range car styled by Bertone. A completely new direction, which would characterise almost all the company's cars in a few years.

## TECHNICAL SPECIFICATION

### ENGINE
front, longitudinal, 90° V6

| | |
|---|---|
| Bore and stroke | 91.6 x 75 mm |
| Unitary displacement | 494.24 cc |
| Total displacement | 2965.46 cc |
| Valvegear | double overhead camshafts per bank |
| Number of valves | two per cylinder |
| Compression ratio | 8.5:1 |
| Fuel system | four Weber 42DCNF carburettors |
| Ignition | single, electronic |
| Cooling | water, centrifugal pump and radiator |
| Lubrication | pressurised, with delivery pump |
| Maximum power | 210 hp at 5500 rpm |
| Specific power output | 70.81 hp/litre |

### TRANSMISSION
| | |
|---|---|
| Driven wheels | front |
| Clutch | single dry-plate |
| Gearbox | manual 5 speeds + reverse |

### BODYWORK
| | |
|---|---|
| Saloon (Bertone design) | 4 doors, 5 seats |

### ROLLING CHASSIS
| | |
|---|---|
| Chassis | Unitary construction |
| Front suspension | hydropneumatic, independent with telescopic hydraulic shock absorbers |
| Rear suspension | hydropneumatic, independent with telescopic hydraulic shock absorbers |
| Brakes | servoassisted hydraulically actuated disks |
| Steering | rack and pinion |
| Fuel tank | 70 l |
| Tyres front | 6.00-16 |
| rear | 6.00-16 |

### DIMENSIONS AND WEIGHT
| | |
|---|---|
| Wheelbase | 2550 mm |
| Tracks front | 1360 mm |
| rear | 1220 mm |
| Length | 3900 mm |
| Width | 1650 mm |
| Height | 1280 mm |
| Dry weight | 840 kg |
| Weight to power ratio | 5.6 kg/hp |

### PERFORMANCE AND PRODUCTION
| | |
|---|---|
| Maximum speed | 195-210 kph |
| Units produced | 12 |

# Quattroporte II                1976

With the aim of blowing the cobwebs off the Quattroporte (776 cars were made between 1963 and 1969), in 1976 production began of a second series of the prestigious saloon car, which shared little more than a name with the first. The chassis was in fact that of the Citroën SM, lengthened from 2950 to 3070 mm, as was the engine, the 1974 three-litre (2965.46 cc) version of the 90° V6, with fuel injection and double overhead cams for each bank of cylinders. Power was increased from 180 to 210 hp, but with a lower rev limit: 5500 against 6250 rpm. The car featured front-wheel drive (a decision that was criticised by the hard-line Maserati "purists") with a cantilevered gearbox at the front end and all four wheels boasting independent hydropneumatic suspension. The top speed - 200 kph compared to 230 kph of the first series - was also considered to be inadequate, although this can be considered a "nominal" rather than a practical consideration, given the decidedly by no means sporting vocation of the car, let alone the speed limits in force on almost all roads. The bodywork, designed by Bertone, was admired for its well-balanced and modern lines, with a comfortable, quiet, well-equipped passenger compartment, which was very suitable for long journeys. Unfortunately, the energy restrictions of the time, Maserati's debts and Citroën's withdrawal from the deal, which coincided with the model's presentation had a detrimental effect, to the extent that the European Community homologation procedure was not even completed. During its three-year production career, only 12 cars were sold, all going to buyers in Arab countries. The Quattroporte II had been preceded by the preparation of design prototypes by both Italdesign (Medici I and II) and Frua, the designer of the Quattroporte I. Neither of the proposals based on the rolling chassis of the Indy with a more powerful engine (90° V8, 4930.61 cc, 335 hp, 280 kph), was ever put into production.

After the Sebring, Mexico and Indy, out came another model that took its name from a racing circuit: Kyalami, the South African track at which a Maserati engine scored its last victory in an international race nine years earlier. It was the first Formula 1 World Championship GP of the 1967 season, which was won by Pedro Rodríguez in a Cooper-Maserati.

## TECHNICAL SPECIFICATION

### ENGINE

front, longitudinal, 90° V8

| | |
|---|---|
| Bore and stroke | 4.1: 88 x 85 mm |
| | 4.9: 93.9 x 89 |
| Unitary displacement | 4.1: 516.98 cc |
| | 4.9: 616.32 |
| Total displacement | 4.1: 4135.84 cc |
| | 4.9: 4930.61 cc |
| Valvegear | double overhead camshafts per bank of cylinders |
| Number of valves | two per cylinder |
| Compression ratio | 8.5:1 |
| Fuel system | four Weber 42DCNF carburettors |
| Ignition | single, electronic |
| Cooling | water, centrifugal pump and radiator |
| Lubrication | pressurised, with delivery pump |
| Maximum power | 4.1: 225 hp at 6000 rpm |
| | 4.9: 280 hp at 5600 rpm |
| Specific power output | 54.42 / 56.78 hp/litre |

### TRANSMISSION

| | |
|---|---|
| Driven wheels | rear |
| Clutch | single dry-plate |
| Gearbox | manual 5 speeds + reverse (automatic on request) |

### BODYWORK

| | |
|---|---|
| coupé Frua | two doors, 2 + 2 seats |
| (design Tjaarda) | |

### ROLLING CHASSIS

| | |
|---|---|
| Chassis | load-bearing body shell |
| Front suspension | independent, with double wishbones and coil springs telescopic hydraulic shock absorbers |
| Rear suspension | independent, anti-roll bars, upper and lower wishbones, trailing arms, telescopic hydraulic shock absorbers |
| Brakes | servoassisted hydraulically actuated disks |
| Steering | rack and pinion |
| Fuel tank | 100 l |
| Tyres front/rear | 215-70 VR-15 |

### DIMENSIONS AND WEIGHT

| | |
|---|---|
| Wheelbase | 2600 mm |
| Tracks front | 1530 mm |
| rear | 1530 mm |
| Length | 4580 mm |
| Width | 1850 mm |
| Height | 1270 mm |
| Dry weight | 1700 kg |
| Weight to power ratio / | 7.55 / 6.07 kg/hp |
| Weight to power ratio | 4.1: 7.55 kg/hp / 4.9: 6.07 |

### PERFORMANCE AND PRODUCTION

| | |
|---|---|
| Maximum speed | 4.1: 235 kph / 4.9: 245 kph |
| Units produced | 200 |

# Kyalami                                                         1976

In March 1975, Citroën, which was already sailing in troubled waters, (leading to control of the company being transferred from Michelin to Peugeot, with the formation of the PSA group) decided to close down Maserati. Afflicted by historical narrow-mindedness and damaged by the fuel crisis like many other companies, the Trident was saved from a real risk of bankruptcy by a financial operation conducted by Alejandro De Tomaso that while criticised was effective and financed by Gepi (Società per le Gestioni e Partecipazioni Industriali), a publicly-funded company. As soon as the company took control of Maserati in August of the same year, the dynamic Argentinian entrepreneur was determined to provide evidence that the company was alive and well. The 1976 Geneva Motor Show was therefore the setting for the presentation of the 2+2 Kyalami coupé. The name derived from the circuit where Pedro Rodríguez won the South African Grand Prix in 1967, at the wheel of a Cooper powered by the 12-cylinder Maserati engine. The Kayalami was prepared in record time, using the chassis from the De Tomaso Longchamp fitted with a choice of the tried and trusted eight-cylinder 4.1- or 4.9-litre engines with maximum power outputs of 225 and 280 hp, allowing top speeds of 235 and 245 kph respectively. The gearbox was a five-speed manual or while automatic transmission was optional, the suspension was independent all round and servo-assisted disc brakes were fitted. The original bodywork, designed by Tom Tjaarda, was reworked by Frua who created a classic, well-balanced saloon car, albeit one somewhat lacking in character. The very linear front end saw the trident in the middle of the radiator grille, set between dual circular headlights, with the sidelights and indicators mounted in the bumpers. The rear lighting clusters, following a practice not uncommon among small-scale car manufacturers of the time, were borrowed from a car by another firm, in this case the Fiat 130 Coupé by Pininfarina. The Kyalami was in production from 1976 to 1983 but enjoyed only limited success: in fact, only 200 cars were made.

In the '70s the motor industry was plagued by strikes, the oil crisis that affected all of the western world, as well as questionable legislative decisions in Italy, among which was more tax that had to be paid for a car of more than 2-litres. In that difficult situation Maserati proposed a less powerful version of the Merak to be called the 2000 that was powered by a 6-cylinder in line 1999.55 cc engine.

## TECHNICAL SPECIFICATION

### ENGINE
front, longitudinal, 90° V6

| | |
|---|---|
| Bore and stroke | 80 x 66.3 mm |
| Unitary displacement | 333.25 cc |
| Total displacement | 1999.55 cc |
| Valvegear | double overhead camshafts per bank |
| Number of valves | two per cylinder |
| Compression ratio | 9:1 |
| Fuel system | three Weber 42DCNF carburettors |
| Ignition | single, electronic |
| Cooling | water, centrifugal pump and radiator |
| Lubrication | pressurised, with delivery pump |
| Maximum power | 170 hp at 7000 rpm |
| Specific power output | 85.01 hp/litre |

### TRANSMISSION
| | |
|---|---|
| Driven wheels | rear |
| Clutch | single dry-plate |
| Gearbox | 5 speeds + reverse |

### BODYWORK
| | |
|---|---|
| coupé Italdesign | 2 doors, 2+2 seats |

### ROLLING CHASSIS
| | |
|---|---|
| Chassis | unitary construction |
| Front suspension | independent with wishbones, coil springs, roll bar, telescopic hydraulic shock absorbers |
| Rear suspension | independent with unequal length A-arms, coil springs, roll bar, telescopic hydraulic shock absorbers |
| Brakes | servo-assisted hydraulically actuated disks |
| Steering | rack and pinion |
| Fuel tank | 85 l |
| Tyres front | 185-70 VR-15 |
| rear | 205-70 VR-15 |

### DIMENSIONS AND WEIGHT
| | |
|---|---|
| Wheelbase | 26000 mm |
| Tracks front | 1474 mm |
| rear | 1474 mm |
| Length | – |
| Width | – |
| Height | – |
| Dry weight | 1330 kg |
| Weight to power ratio | 7.82 kg/hp |

### PERFORMANCE AND PRODUCTION
| | |
|---|---|
| Maximum speed | 220 kph |
| Units produced | 195 |

# Merak 2000                    1977

The fuel crisis that followed the Kippur war, which broke out in 1973, caused an increase in the price of fuel that had drastic consequences for sales of all cars and also for the planning of new models, conditioned by a unprecedented need for fuel economy. In Italy, fiscal law fixed tax rates that were particularly punitive for vehicles powered by engines of over two litres: VAT of 38% was applied rather than the 19% on smaller capacity cars. Within this context, in 1977 Maserati produced a version of the Merak with an engine of under 2000 cc which was thus able to avoid being penalized by the tax increase that naturally discouraged people from buying larger cars. Mounted in the same unitary construction body, the Merak's 90° V6 went into production in 1972, with a bore and stroke reduced from 91.6 x 75 mm to 80 x 66.3 mm, for a total displacement that dropped from 2965.46 to 1999.55 cc. The maximum power output was reduced from 190 to 159 hp at 7100 rpm while the top speed fell from 240 to 220 kph. The average fuel consumption, which in those years even began to be declared by the manufacturers of Gran Turismo cars, proved to be 9.2 litres per 100 km. In 1980, a number of changes were made to the mechanical specification of the car, the most important being the adoption of new disc brakes in place of those previously supplied by Citroën. The bodywork differed with respect to that of the three-litre model in the use of black rather than chromed front and rear bumpers, a black grille between the headlights and a broad black band running along the sides. The front spoiler was removed from the standard version but was available as an optional extra. Only two colours were available, both metallic: silver and light blue. The Merak 2000 remained in production from 1977 to 1983 and 195 cars were made out of a total of 1830 for the entire range.

Despite his latest designed for Maserati that didn't seem especially brilliant, Giorgetto Giugiaro returned and became Maserati's top designer. This time, he kept to the classical and came up with the third version of the Quattroporte, which reflected how the choice of equipment (electric rear mirrors and a mini-bar) the new company line was decidedly less sporty and more oriented towards comfort for both the driver and passengers.

## TECHNICAL SPECIFICATION

### ENGINE

front, longitudinal, 90° V8

| | |
|---|---|
| Bore and stroke | 4.1: 88 x 85 mm<br>4.9: and Royale: 93.9 x 89 |
| Unitary displacement | 4.1: 516.98 cc<br>4.9 and Royale: 616.32 |
| Total displacement | 4.1: 4135.84 cc<br>4.9 and Royale: 4930.61 cc |
| Valvegear | double overhead camshafts per bank |
| Number of valves | two per cylinder |
| Compression ratio | 8.5:1 |
| Fuel system | fourWeber 42DCNF carburettors |
| Ignition | single, Bosch electronic |
| Cooling | water, centrifugal pump<br>and radiator<br>Royale: liquid, pressurised,<br>sealed circuit |
| Lubrication | pressurised, with delivery pump |
| Maximum power | 4.1: 225 hp at 6000 rpm<br>4.9: 280 hp at 5600 rpm<br>Royale: 300 hp at 5600 rpm |
| Specific power output | 4.1: 61.65 hp/litre<br>4.9: 56.78 hp/litre<br>Royale: 60.84 hp/litre |

### TRANSMISSION

| | |
|---|---|
| Driven wheels | rear |
| Clutch | single dry-plate |
| Gearbox | manual five speeds + reverse<br>or automatic |

### BODYWORK

| | |
|---|---|
| Italdesign saloon | four doors, 5 seats |

### ROLLING CHASSIS

| | |
|---|---|
| Chassis | load-bearing body shell |
| Front suspension | independent, double wishbones<br>and coil springs telescopic<br>hydraulic shock absorbers |
| Rear suspension | independent, anti-roll bar,<br>upper and lower wishbones,<br>coil springs, telescopic hydraulic<br>shock absorbers |
| Brakes | servo-assisted hydraulically<br>actuated disks |
| Steering | rack and pinion |
| Fuel tank | 100 l |
| Tyres front/rear | 215-70 VR-15<br>Royale: 225-70 VR-15 |

### DIMENSIONS AND WEIGHT

| | |
|---|---|
| Wheelbase | 2800 mm |
| Tracks front | 1520 mm |
| rear | 1520 mm |
| Length | 4910 mm |
| Width | 1890 mm |
| Height | 1380 mm |
| Dry weight | 1780 kg / Royale: 1900 kg |
| Weight to power ratio | 4.1: 6.98 kg/hp<br>4.9: 6.35 kg/hp<br>Royale: 6.33 kg/hp |

### PERFORMANCE AND PRODUCTION

| | |
|---|---|
| Maximum speed | 4.1: 220 kph<br>4.9 and Royale: 230 kph |
| Units produced | 2155 |

# Quattroporte III 1979

The second series of the Quattroporte had struggled to establish itself in the market both as a result of the international economic crisis and because of the "hybrid" nature of the product, in which mechanical components from Citroën – the chassis from the SM, front-wheel drive transmission, hydropneumatic suspension – were in conflict with a similar number of key features of the Maserati tradition. Alejandro De Tomaso, who had only recently taken the helm of the Trident marque, had no hesitation in commissioning Giugiaro to produce the third edition of the large flagship saloon and the designer created a prototype that was exhibited at the Turin Motor Show in 1976. The chassis, which retained the same wheelbase of 2800 mm, could be fitted with either the 4.1- or the 4.9-litre 90° V engines from the Kyalami, with maximum power outputs of 255 and 289 hp, and top speeds of 220 and 230 kph respectively. Giugiaro – after the unsatisfactory experience with the Medici I and II that never went into production – opted for a return to a classic three-box configuration. The front of the car had a trapezoidal radiator grille that extended forward beyond the plane of the dual rectangular headlights, with both features having chromed surrounds. A groove ran along the side of the car linking the front and rear bumpers and parallel to this, level with the door handles, there was a slight crease line that also helped to lend the sides of the car a degree of dynamism. The interior, with leather upholstery and walnut and velvet trim, offered a high level of comfort, heightened by a accessories that are very common today even on utility cars but which at the time were only found flagship models: electric rear-view mirrors, central locking, electric seat-height adjustment, air conditioning for the rear seats and a minibar. The Quattroporte III was the President of the Republic Sandro Pertini's favourite means of transport. The car went into production in 1979, with 2,155 examples being made through to 1990.

The third series of the Quattroporte had already been on sale for some years when, in 1986, Autocostruzioni SD of Turin built a limited series of examples that to some extent followed the established fashion, especially in North America, for three-light flagships equipped with every comfort for wealthy clients. The Diomante limousine was priced at just 210 million of the old lire.

## TECHNICAL SPECIFICATION

### ENGINE

front, longitudinal, 90° V8

| | |
|---|---|
| Bore and stroke | 4.1 88 x 85 mm<br>4.9: 93.9 x 89 |
| Unitary displacement | 4.1: 516.98 cc<br>4.9: 616.32 |
| Total displacement | 4.1: 4135.84 cc<br>4.9: 4930.61 cc |
| Valvegear | double overhead camshafts<br>per bank of cylinders |
| Number of valves | two per cylinder |
| Compression ratio | 8.5:1 |
| Fuel system | four Weber 42DCNF carburettors |
| Ignition | single, Bosch electronic |
| Cooling | water, centrifugal pump<br>and radiator |
| Lubrication | geared pump |
| Maximum power | 4.1: 225 hp at 6000 rpm<br>4.9: 280 hp at 5600 rpm |
| Specific power output | 4.1: 61.65 hp/litre<br>4.9: 56.78 hp/litre |

### TRANSMISSION

| | |
|---|---|
| Driven wheels | rear |
| Clutch | single dry-plate |
| Gearbox | Chrysler automatic |

### BODYWORK

| | |
|---|---|
| saloon | four doors, five seats |

### ROLLING CHASSIS

| | |
|---|---|
| Chassis | load-bearing body shell |
| Front suspension | independent, double wishbones<br>and coil springs, telescopic<br>hydraulic shock absorbers |
| Rear suspension | independent, anti-roll bar,<br>upper and lower wishbones,<br>coil springs, telescopic hydraulic<br>shock absorbers |
| Brakes | servo-assisted hydraulically<br>actuated disks |
| Steering | rack and pinion |
| Fuel tank | 100 l |
| Tyres front/rear | 215-70 VR-15 |

### DIMENSIONS AND WEIGHT

| | |
|---|---|
| Wheelbase | – |
| Tracks front | – |
| rear | – |
| Length | 5560 mm |
| Width | – |
| Height | 1400 mm |
| Dry weight | 1780 kg |
| Weight to power ratio | 4.1: 6.98 kg/hp<br>4.9: 6.35 kg/hp |

### PERFORMANCE AND PRODUCTION

| | |
|---|---|
| Maximum speed | 4.1: 220 kph<br>4.9: 230 kph |
| Units produced | – |

# Limousine Diomante 1986

While the third edition of the Quattroporte was enjoying increasing success and was about to annihilate the production record of the original model, almost tripling the numbers sold – from 776 to 2,155 cars – the Turin company SD (initials of the owner Salvatore Diomante), prepared a number of examples of a special version of the car, known as the Limousine. The name was an explicit reference to the type of bodywork, which was 65 cm longer and 2 cm taller than the standard model. It was naturally an imposing car but retained the essential features of the classical square-cut proportions of the Giugiaro design. On the mechanical side, the 90° V8 4.1- and 4.9-litre engines from the Quattroporte III were unchanged (maximum power outputs of 255 and 280 hp) and provided top speeds of 220 and 230 kph respectively with the Chrysler A727 Torqueflite automatic three-speed transmission in place of the Borg-Warner unit originally used. The interior was completely redesigned, luxuriously upholstered in white leather, with generous use of walnut and equipped with exclusive accessories. The front passenger seat could be rotated through 180°, thereby creating a true living room mode allowing the passenger to talk to the rear seat passengers face to face. Two writing desks were hidden in the panels of the rear doors, while a video recorder and a stereo system were integrated into the backs of the front seats. The Limousine was put on sale at 210 million Lire. Other special editions of the Quattroporte III were made in the 1980s by the Milan-based Carrozzeria Pavesi: these were armoured cars, one of which, built in 1983, painted "Evening Blue" and known as "Calliope", became especially famous as it was used for state visits by the President of the Republic Sandro Pertini.

When the Diomante limousine came out, Maserati understood that the base model Quattroporte needed to be restyled. That is the reason why a saloon with a new styling footprint came out at the start of 1987. It was the Royale which, in the mind of its conceiver Alejandro De Tomaso, should reach a production of 120 cars, built only to order. In reality, four years later, when it went out of production, just under half that number had been sold.

## TECHNICAL SPECIFICATION

### ENGINE
front, longitudinal, 90° V8

| | |
|---|---|
| Bore and stroke | 93.9 x 89 |
| Unitary displacement | 616.32 |
| Total displacement | 4930.61 cc |
| Valvegear | double overhead camshafts per bank of cylinders |
| Number of valves | two per cylinder |
| Compression ratio | 8.5:1 |
| Fuel system | four Weber 42DCNF carburettors |
| Ignition | single, Bosch electronic |
| Cooling | liquid, pressurised, sealed circuit |
| Lubrication | geared pump |
| Maximum power | 300 hp at 5600 rpm |
| Specific power output | 60.84 hp/litre |

### TRANSMISSION
| | |
|---|---|
| Driven wheels | rear |
| Clutch | single dry-plate |
| Gearbox | manual five speeds + reverse or automatic |

### BODYWORK
| | |
|---|---|
| saloon | four doors, five seats |

### ROLLING CHASSIS
| | |
|---|---|
| Chassis | load-bearing body shell |
| Front suspension | independent, double wishbones and coil springs telescopic hydraulic shock absorbers |
| Rear suspension | independent, anti-roll bar, upper and lower wishbones, coil springs, telescopic hydraulic shock absorbers |
| Brakes | servo-assisted hydraulically actuated disks |
| Steering | rack and pinion |
| Fuel tank | 100 l |
| Tyres front/rear | 225-70 VR-15 |

### DIMENSIONS AND WEIGHT
| | |
|---|---|
| Wheelbase | 2800 mm |
| Tracks front | 1520 mm |
| rear | 1520 mm |
| Length | 4910 mm |
| Width | 1890 mm |
| Height | 1380 mm |
| Dry weight | 1900 kg |
| Weight to power ratio | 6.33 kg/hp |

### PERFORMANCE AND PRODUCTION
| | |
|---|---|
| Maximum speed | 230 kph |
| Units produced | 53 |

# Royale 1986

On the 14TH of December 1986, in Modena, celebrating the 60TH anniversary of the first Maserati car, the Tipo 26, Alejandro De Tomaso presented a luxurious version of the Quattroporte, called the Royale, the name being a deliberate and ambitious reference to Ettore Bugatti's superb creation of the same name. Although the Trident's prestigious flagship saloon had very little competition in the market, it had begun to look a little old-fashioned so it was subjected to attentive restyling. It principally aimed at rounding off the rather angular bodywork so that it would be able to keep up with the new trends in car design. It should be remembered that the Quattroporte III design dated from ten years earlier (the Giugiaro prototype was presented at the 1976 Turin Motor Show). Among the distinguishing features of the exterior of the Royale were the elegant new light alloy wheels and the silver bands embellishing the lower part of the sides. However, the most significant changes were to the passenger compartment, which was completely redesigned with a new dashboard and four electrically adjustable seats. The extensive use of high quality materials, from the leather upholstery to the walnut and velvet trim gave the space an air of great refinement, further enhanced by standard equipment that included small retractable tables concealed in the rear doors, a minibar and a radiotelephone integrated in the central console which at the time was an authentic rarity. The engine, the 4.9-litre 90° V8, had had its power output increased from 280 to 300 hp, but without an increase in top speed, which was limited to 230 kph like the standard version of the flagship car. The Royale was built to order and De Tomaso announced that it was expected they would build a limited series of 120 cars, but when production came to an end in 1990 only 53 cars had left the factory.

With the Biturbo, Maserati reached a production peak that had never previously been imagined by its managements in almost 60 years. The right car in commercial terms which, because of its instant success, experienced teething troubles that were overlooked during pre-production testing, but soon damaged the car's credibility.

## TECHNICAL SPECIFICATION

### ENGINE

front, longitudinal, 90° V6

| | |
|---|---|
| Bore and stroke | 82 x 63 mm |
| Unitary displacement | 332.70 cc |
| Total displacement | 1996.22 cc |
| Valvegear | double overhead camshafts per bank of cylinders |
| Number of valves | three per cylinder |
| Compression ratio | Biturbo: 7.8:1 |
| | Biturbo S: 8.2:1 |
| Fuel system | Weber 36 DCNVH carburettor |
| | (from 1986 fuel injection) |
| Ignition | single, electronic |
| Cooling | liquid, pressurised |
| Lubrication | pressurised, with delivery pump |
| Maximum power | Biturbo: 180 hp at 6000 rpm |
| | Biturbo S: 205 hp at 6000 rpm |
| | Biturbo i: 188 hp at 6000 rpm |
| | Biturbo Si: 223 hp at 6260 rpm |
| Specific power output | Biturbo: 9017 hp/litre |
| | Biturbo S: 102.69 hp/litre |
| | Biturbo i: 94.17 hp/litre |
| | Biturbo Si: 111.71 hp/litre |

### TRANSMISSION

| | |
|---|---|
| Driven wheels | rear |
| Clutch | single dry-plate |
| Gearbox | five speeds + reverse (automatic on request) |

### BODYWORK

coupé ( designed by Andreani) two doors, five seats

### ROLLING CHASSIS

| | |
|---|---|
| Chassis | unitary construction |
| Front suspension | independent, coil springs, anti-roll bar, telescopic hydraulic dampers |
| Rear suspension | independent with longitudinal arms, coil springs, anti-roll bar, telescopic hydraulic dampers |
| Brakes | servo-assisted hydraulically actuated discs |
| Steering | rack and pinion |
| Fuel tank | 161 litres |
| Tyres front | Biturbo: 195-60 HR-14 |
| | Biturbo S: 205-55 VR-14 |
| | Biturbo Si: 205-60 VR-14 |

### DIMENSIONS AND WEIGHT

| | |
|---|---|
| Wheelbase | 2514 mm |
| Tracks front | 1420 mm |
| rear | 1431 mm |
| Length | 4153 mm |
| Width | 1714 mm |
| Height | 1086 mm |
| Dry weight | Biturbo: 1175 kg |
| | Biturbo S: 1216 kg |
| | Biturbo Si: 1210 kg |
| Weight to power ratio | 7.82 kg/hp |

### PERFORMANCE AND PRODUCTION

| | |
|---|---|
| Maximum speed | Biturbo: 215 kph |
| | Biturbo S: 225 kph |
| | Biturbo i: 220 kph |
| | Biturbo Si: 228 kph |
| Units produced | 11,919 |
| | (Biturbo 9,206 / Biturbo S 1,038 / Biturbo i 683 / Biturbo Si 992) |

# Biturbo                     1982

On the 14TH of December 1981, Alejandro De Tomaso presented to the press a new car that was to enjoy enormous initial success. Named the Biturbo in reference to the fuel supply system that featured two turbochargers the car was equipped with a light alloy 90° V6 engine with a displacement of 1996.22 cc derived from the classic Tipo C 114 from the Citroën SM (which had also been used on the Merak), brought up to date with modern technology. The maximum power output was 180 hp at 6000 rpm and the top speed was 215 kph. The engine displacement, intentionally kept below 2 litres, made it possible to avoid the higher tax band (19% instead of 38% VAT) and to put it on sale at an incredibly low list price: 16.7 million lire, that is to say almost half the price of a Porsche 911 SC. "Incredibly" because with the lire prey to galloping inflation, by April 1982 that figure had already gone beyond 19 million to settle at 22,236,000 Lire on the 18TH of June, before deliveries had even begun, an operation that was postponed to the following December. The engine was built in Modena while the bodywork was fabricated in the Innocenti factory in Milan. The styling of the Biturbo was the work of Pierangelo Andreani and along with the mechanical specification and the price that was still competitive was one of the car's strong suits. The model was sleek and compact, with certain styling features reminiscent of the Quattroporte, of which it also reprised the wealth of standard equipment and interior elegance. Over the course of 1983, the first full year of production, more than 5,000 cars were made. Unfortunately, because the development period had been rather hurried, reliability problems arose and that same 1983, with the Biturbo S, was marked by the introduction of the first of numerous improved and more powerful versions that placed original car at the head of a dynasty. By 1989, at the end of its career, 11,919 examples had been made.

The 425 was a recycled version of the Biturbo, especially as far as its engine was concerned, a car that Maserati was offering to foreign markets. Modification both to the inside and the outside the body were interesting. The car was a reasonable sales success, testifying to the fact that, under the management of Alejandro De Tomaso, the Trident had taken a new direction that was less sporty and more commercial.

## TECHNICAL SPECIFICATION

### ENGINE
front, longitudinal, 90° V6

| | |
|---|---|
| Bore and stroke | 91.6 x 63 mm |
| Unitary displacement | 415.16 cc |
| Total displacement | 2490.99 cc |
| Valvegear | double overhead camshafts per bank of cylinders |
| Number of valves | three per cylinder |
| Compression ratio | 7.8:1 |
| Fuel system | Weber twin-choke vertical carburettor two IHI turbocompressors |
| Ignition | electronic |
| Cooling | liquid, pressurised |
| Lubrication | pressurised, with delivery pump |
| Maximum power | 200 hp at 5500 rpm |
| Specific power output | 80.28 hp/litre |

### TRANSMISSION
| | |
|---|---|
| Driven wheels | rear |
| Clutch | single dry-plate |
| Gearbox | fivespeeds + reverse (automatic on request) |

### BODYWORK
| | |
|---|---|
| coupé (Andreani design) | four doors, five seats |

### ROLLING CHASSIS
| | |
|---|---|
| Chassis | unitary construction |
| Front suspension | independent, coil springs, anti-roll bar, telescopic hydraulic dampers |
| Rear suspension | independent with longitudinal arms, coil springs, anti-roll bar, telescopic hydraulic dampers |
| Brakes | servo-assisted hydraulically actuated discs |
| Steering | rack and pinion |
| Fuel tank | 161 l |
| Tyres front | 195-60 HR-14 (on request, 205-60 VR-14) |

### DIMENSIONS AND WEIGHT
| | |
|---|---|
| Wheelbase | 2514 mm |
| Tracks front | 1420 mm |
| rear | 1431 mm |
| Length | – |
| Width | – |
| Height | – |
| Dry weight | 1180 kg |
| Weight to power ratio | 5.90 kg/hp |

### PERFORMANCE AND PRODUCTION
| | |
|---|---|
| Maximum speed | 220 kph |
| Units produced | 2372 |

# 425                                 1984

By 1984 the third series of the Quattroporte (1979-1990) was consolidating Maserati's enviable position of the prestige saloon sector when the 425 came on the scene. The car sat alongside the Quattroporte as a slightly less imposing and less expensive alternative, but one that was still admired for its elegance and quality. The mechanical specification was the same as the Biturbo, with the 90° V6 engine increased to 2.5 litres, thanks to an increase in the bore from 82 mm to 91.6 mm while the stroke remained the same (63 mm). This version was originally intended for foreign markets where there were no tax disadvantages for cars over 2000 cc. The maximum power output rose from 180 to 200 hp at 5500 rpm rather than 6000 rpm and the top speed increased from 215 kph to 220 kph, notable performance, especially taking into consideration that the weight had increased by almost 100 kg (from 1086 kg to 1180 kg). The gearbox was the customary five-speed ZF manual, with automatic transmission available on request. The bodywork, designed for the Biturbo two years earlier by Pierangelo Andreani, was naturally adapted to the objectives of the project, with a lengthening of the wheelbase by 86 mm, the addition of rear doors and the rear volume extended to make a boot. The car's length went from 4153 to 4400 mm, the width from 1712 to 1730 mm and the height from 1305 to 1360 mm. Overall the design retained the original car's harmonious proportions and the Maserati family feeling. The interior, with elegant velour upholstery by Missoni, was similar to that of the two-door model but with a redesigned dashboard and seven circular elements on the instrument panel. On the road, the 425 proved to be markedly superior to the Biturbo, above all because it overcame the unreliability of the earlier model, which had been the object of severe criticism. Between 1984 and 1987, 2372 examples were constructed.

The 425's first number indicates how many doors the car had and the other two its cubic capacity. That was followed by the 420, which was powered by a 2-litre 6-cylinder engine. After that, other versions appeared, right up to the most powerful of them all, the 4.24v, which put out 245 hp from its Biturbo.

## TECHNICAL SPECIFICATION

### ENGINE
front, longitudinal, 90° V6

| | |
|---|---|
| Bore and stroke | 82 x 63 mm |
| Unitary displacement | 332.70 cc |
| Total displacement | 1996.22 cc |
| Valvegear | single overhead camshaft per bank / 4.24v: double |
| Number of valves | three per cylinder / 4.24v.:4 per cylinder |
| Compression ratio | 7.8:1 / 4.24v.: 7.6:1 |
| Fuel system | 420: Weber 34 DAT 23/150 carburettor (from 1986, also electronic fuel injection) |
| | 420 S: Weber 36 DCNVH/26 carburettor |
| | 422 / 4.18v. / 4.24v.: electronic fuel injection |
| | all versions: two IHI turbocompressors |
| Ignition | electronic |
| Cooling | liquid, pressurised |
| Lubrication | pressurised, with delivery pump |
| Maximum power | 420: 200 hp at 5500 rpm |
| | 420 S: 205 at 6500 / 422 and 4.18v.: 223 at 6250 / 4.24v.: 245 at 6200 |
| Specific power output | 420: 100.18 hp/litre |
| | 420 S: 102.69 / 422 and 4.18v.: 111.71 / 4.24v.: 122,73 hp/litre |

### TRANSMISSION
| | |
|---|---|
| Driven wheels | rear |
| Clutch | single dry-plate |
| Gearbox | five speeds + reverse (automatic on request) |

### BODYWORK
| | |
|---|---|
| saloon | four doors, five seats |

### ROLLING CHASSIS
| | |
|---|---|
| Chassis | load-bearing body shell |
| Front suspension | independent, coil springs, roll bar, telescopic hydraulic shock absorbers |
| Rear suspension | independent with longitudinal arms, coil springs, roll bar, telescopic hydraulic shock absorbers |
| Brakes | servo-assisted hydraulically actuated discs |
| Steering | rack and pinion |
| Fuel tank | 80 l |
| Tyres front | 420 / 420 S / 422: 205-60 VR-14 4.18v.: 205+55 VR-14 4.24v.: 205-45 R-16 85 Z |

### DIMENSIONS AND WEIGHT
| | |
|---|---|
| Wheelbase | 420 / 420 S / 422 / 4.18v: 2600 mm 4.24v: 2514 mm |
| Tracks front/ rear | 420 / 420 S: 1420 mm 422 / 4.18v: 1442 / 4.24v: 1458 420 / 420 S: 1431 mm 422 / 4.18v: 1450 / 4.24v: 1454 |
| Length | - |
| Width | - |
| Height | - |
| Dry weight | 420 / 420 S / 422: 1275 KG 4.18v: 1395 / 4.24v: 1370 |
| Weight to power ratio | 420: 6.37 kg/hp 420 S: 6.21 / 422: 5.71 / 4.18v.: 6.25 / 4.24v.: 5.59 |

### PERFORMANCE AND PRODUCTION
| | |
|---|---|
| Maximum speed | 420: 220 kph 420 S e 422: 218 / 422 e 4.18v.: 225 / 4.24v.: 230 |
| Units produced | 6151 (420: 2810 / 420 S: 254 / 420 i: 1124 / 420 Si: 524 / 422: 978 / 4.18v.: 77 / 4.24v.: 384) |

# 420 – 422 – 4.24v.      1985

In 1985, a year after its launch, the 425, or rather the four-door version of the Biturbo, was joined by a two-litre version, the 420, homologated especially for the Italian market that was still blighted by the tax burden on cars over 2000 cc - double rate VAT (38% rather than 19%) and the cars classified as luxury models making it impossible for companies to claim tax relief on them. Between 1986 and 1993, six different versions of the 420 were made. 1986 saw the launch of the 420 S. It differed from the 420 in the use of two NACA ducts on the bonnet (like those on the Biturbo S), a different design for the radiator grille and grey bands along the sides. In the same year the 420 S was also offered with fuel injection as the 420i, which was then joined by the 420 Si in 1987. This car also had NACA ducts on the bonnet and an opening roof was available on request. It had a power output of 205 hp compared to the 200 hp of the carburettor version, although it was a little slower: 218 kph rather than 220 kph. In 1988, it was the 422's turn, again featuring a two-litre engine and with the same aesthetic changes introduced on the 222 coupé, as the year before the original Biturbo had been renamed, with the 422 returning the same performance figures. In 1991, the 4.18v was added to the Maserati catalogue. The engine had 18 valves, three per cylinder and developed 223 hp with a top speed of 225 kph. The car was fitted with ABS and only 77 were made by the end of 1992. Between 1990 and 1993, the 4.24v was the top of the range (recognisable externally by virtue of its rectangular headlights), powered by a new biturbo six-cylinder fuel-injected engine, with two overhead camshafts per bank and four valves per cylinder (hence the name 4.24v). With a power output of 245 hp at 6200 rpm, it could power the car to a top speed of 230 kph. Between 1985 and 1993, the overall production figures for the whole range for the Italian market totalled 6151 cars.

Of all the Biturbo variants with their various engine sizes, special mention should be made of the Spyder. Thirteen years after the Ghibli, last topless Maserati, the company offered the market a roadster, produced by Zagato supported by a Turin company for the production of the bodyshells: over 3,000 cars were manufactured in a decade.

## TECHNICAL SPECIFICATION

### ENGINE

front, longitudinal, 90° V6

| | |
|---|---|
| Bore and stroke | Spyder: 82 x 63 mm / Spyder 2500: 91.60 x 63 / Spyder 2800: 94 x 67 |
| Unitary displacement | Spyder: 332.70 cc / Spyder 2500: 415.16 / Spyder 2800: 464.96 |
| Total displacement | Spyder: 1996.22 cc / Spyder 2500: 2490.99 / Spyder 2800: 2789.78 |
| Valvegear | Spyder: single overhead camshaft per bank / Spyder 2.0 4v: double overhead camshafts per bank |
| Number of valves | three per cylinder |
| | Spyder 2.0 4v.: four per cylinder |
| Compression ratio | Spyder e i: 7.8:1 / 2500: 8.1:1 / 2.0 4v.: 8.5:1 / 2800i: 7.41:1 |
| Fuel system | electronic fuel injection |
| | 2 IHI turbochargers |
| Ignition | electronic |
| Cooling | liquid, pressurised |
| Lubrication | pressurised, with delivery pump |
| Maximum power | Spyder: 180 hp at 6000 rpm / 2500: 192 at 5800 / i: 223 at 6250 / 2.8i: 224 at 5500 / 2.0 / 4v.: 241 at 6500 |
| Specific power output | Spyder: 90.17 hp/litre / 2500: 77.07 / i: 89.52 / 2.8i: 80.29 / 2.0 4v.: 120.72 |

### TRANSMISSION

| | |
|---|---|
| Driven wheels | rear |
| Clutch | single dry-plate |
| Gearbox | five speeds + reverse (automatic on request) |

### BODYWORK

| | |
|---|---|
| cabriolet | two doors, four seats |

### ROLLING CHASSIS

| | |
|---|---|
| Chassis | unitary construction |
| Front suspension | independent, coil springs, anti-roll bar, telescopic hydraulic shock absorbers then oleopneumatic |
| Rear suspension | independent with longitudinal arms, coil springs, anto-roll bar, telescopic hydraulic shock absorbers then oleopneumatic |
| Brakes | servo-assisted hydraulically actuated disks |
| Steering | rack and pinion |
| Fuel tank | Spyder: 61 l / Spyder 2500 e 2800: 80 |
| Tyres front/rear | Spyder: 195-60 HR-14 - 2500: 195-60 VR-14 - i: 205-50 R-15 85V - 2800 i: front 205-55 ZR-15 / rear 225-50 ZR-15 |

### DIMENSIONS AND WEIGHT

| | |
|---|---|
| Wheelbase | 2400 mm |
| Tracks front / rear | Spyder: 1420 mm / 1431 mm |
| | Spyder i: 1454 / 1458 mm |
| | Spyder 2.8 i: 1458 / 1460 mm |
| Length | – |
| Width | – |
| Height | – |
| Dry weight | Spyder: 1041 kg - 2500: 1086 / i: 1251 / 2.8 i: 1345 / 2.0 4v.: 1370 |
| Weight to power ratio | Spyder: 5.78 kg/hp - 2500: 5.65 / i: 5.60 / 2.0 4v.: 5.68 / 2.8i: 6.00 |

### PERFORMANCE AND PRODUCTION

| | |
|---|---|
| Maximum speed | Spyder: 215 kph - i: 220 / 2.0 4v: 225 / 2.8 i: 230 / 2.0 4v.: 225 |
| Units produced | 3076 (Spyder: 276 / 2.5: 1049 / i: 606 / i 2.8: 725 / 2.0 4v.: 200 / Spyder 2.8: 220) |

# Biturbo Spyder                                            1985

In the mid-1980s Maserati decided to revive a tradition from the past, whereby a spider would be sold alongside every coupé (the last example was the Ghibli between 1969 and 1972). The company decided to produce an open-topped car based on the Biturbo chassis. The project was given to Zagato, who used a floorpan shortened by 114 mm (the wheelbase reduced from 2514 to 2400 mm) to create a car with elegant lines and a wedge-shaped profile that was naturally reminiscent of the saloon version. The Biturbo Spyder went into production in 1985 and it followed the aesthetic and mechanical evolution of the model from which it was derived. In 1987, the carburettor fuel system was replaced with fuel injection while a version produced for the American market was equipped with a 2.5-litre engine in place of the standard two-litre unit. In 1990, the soft-top car was subjected to restyling like the rest of the Biturbo range. The front end was now more compact, the radiator grille lower, the headlights were of a new design and there was an extra black grille located below the bumpers, flanked by fog lights. The light alloy wheels from the Shamal were also used. A model powered by a catalysed 2790 cc engine mated to an automatic four-speed gearbox was prepared mainly for the export market. The following year, the Spyder (the official name had by now dropped the word Biturbo) was fitted with a quad-cam, four valves per cylinder engine giving a maximum power output of 241 hp at 6500 rpm that propelled the car to a top speed of 225 kph - a little under the 230 kph the Spyder could achieve when fitted with the 2.8i three valves per cylinder engine even though it was less powerful (224 hp). A total of 3076 examples of the Spyder were manufactured over a period of ten years, from 1985 to 1994.

While the Maserati name started to be seen on the world's roads in greater number, including in Italy, due to the increased production, the Biturbo saga continued in 1987, when the umpteenth model appeared and was called the 228. But it was not a particularly successful model and fewer than 500 were sold in five years.

## TECHNICAL SPECIFICATION

### ENGINE

front, longitudinal, 90° V6

| | |
|---|---|
| Bore and stroke | 94 x 67 mm |
| Unitary displacement | 464.96 cc |
| Total displacement | 2789.78 cc |
| Valvegear | single overhead camshaft per bank (222 4v.:2) |
| Number of valves | 3 per cylinder (222 4v.:double OHC per bank) |
| Compression ratio | 7.4:1 |
| Fuel system | electronic fuel injection |
| Ignition | electronic |
| Cooling | liquid, pressurised |
| Lubrication | pressurised, with delivery pump |
| Maximum power | 228: 255 hp at 5600 rpm / 222 SR: 224 a 5500 / 222 4v.: 279 a 5500 |
| Specific power output | 228: 91.40 hp/litre / 222 SR: 80.29 / 222 4v.: 100.00 |

### TRANSMISSION

| | |
|---|---|
| Driven wheels | rear |
| Clutch | single dry-plate |
| Gearbox | five speeds + reverse (automatic on request) |

### BODYWORK

| | |
|---|---|
| coupé | two doors, five seats |

### ROLLING CHASSIS

| | |
|---|---|
| Chassis | load-bearing body shell |
| Front suspension | independent, coil springs, anti-roll bar, telescopic hydraulic shock absorbers then oleopneumatic |
| Rear suspension | independent with longitudinal arms, coil springs, anti-roll bar, telescopic hydraulic shock absorbersthen oleopneumatic |
| Brakes | servo-assisted hydraulically actuated discs |
| Steering | rack and pinion |
| Fuel tank | 80 l |
| Tyres front | 228: 205-55 VR-15 / 222 SR: 205-50 R-15 Z / 222 4v.: 205-45 R-16 Z |
| Tyres rear | 228: 225-50 VR-15 (on request, 205-60 VR-14) / 222 SR: 205-50 R-15 Z / 22 4v.: 225-45 ZR-16 |

### DIMENSIONS AND WEIGHT

| | |
|---|---|
| Wheelbase | 228: 2514 mm |
| | 222 SR / 222 4v.: 2514 |
| Tracks front/ rear | 228: 1458 / 1454 mm / 222 SR: 1442 / 1450 / 222 4v.: 1450 / 1462 |
| Length | - |
| Width | - |
| Height | - |
| Dry weight | 228: 1210 kg / 222 SR: 1308 / 222 4v.: 1315 |
| Weight to power ratio | 228: 4,74 kg/hp / 222 SR: 5,83 / 222 4v.: 4,71 |

### PERFORMANCE AND PRODUCTION

| | |
|---|---|
| Maximum speed | 228: 235 kph / 222 SR: 220 / 222 4v.: 255 |
| Units produced | 809 (228: 469 / 222 4v.: 130 / 222 SR: 210) |

# 228 – 222 4v. – 222 SR 1987

When the 228 went into production in the summer of 1987, it emphasised Maserati's determination to keep pace with the other European marques such as BMW and Mercedes-Benz that dominated the category. The car was intended for export to countries where tax laws did not punish cars with displacements of over two litres and it was fitted with a 2790 cc single overhead cam, fuel-injected 90° V6 using two turbochargers and developing 255 hp at 5600 rpm, good for a top speed of 235 kph and a flying kilometre time of 26.3". The bodywork had been redesigned and while it was still reminiscent of the Biturbo, it was also very different thanks to the rounding off of the sharp edges, which made the car look less aggressive, softer and more reassuring. Standard equipment included power-steering, light alloy wheels, central locking, electric windows and hand-stitched leather upholstery. There were just two optional extras: ABS and headlight washers. The mechanical specification was changed in 1991 with the launch of the 222 4v with an engine that still had a displacement of 2.8 litres but had four valves per cylinder (hence the 4v in the name) and double overhead camshafts for each cylinder bank. It had a five-speed manual gearbox (automatic on request). The maximum power output was 279 hp at 5500 rpm and the top speed was 255 kph. The 222 SR was launched at the same time as the 222 4v. Presented at the Geneva Motor Show in 1991 and only intended for the export market, it was powered by the 2.8-litre engine with a single overhead camshaft per bank and three valves per cylinder, leading to a considerable reduction in power (224 hp at the same rpm, 5500) but retaining a high top speed of 220 kph. Between 1987 and 1993, a total of 809 of the three cars were made, subdivided as follows: 469 (228). 130 (222 4v.), 210 (222 SR).

From the 425 to the 430. That was the natural evolution of a model which, despite it only having been in production for three years, was a step forward. Of the new 430, which was also powered by the 2.8-litre engine, two versions were created: the basic and the 4-valves per cylinder, which appeared in 1991.

## TECHNICAL SPECIFICATION

### ENGINE

front, longitudinal, 90° V6

| | |
|---|---|
| Bore and stroke | 94 x 67 mm |
| Unitary displacement | 464.96 cc |
| Total displacement | 2789.78 cc |
| Valvegear | 430: single overhead camshaft per bank of cylinders<br>430 4v.: DOHC per bank |
| Number of valves | 430: three per cylinder<br>430 4v.: four |
| Compression ratio | 7.4:1 |
| Fuel system | electronic fuel injection<br>two IHI RHB turbochargers |
| Ignition | electronic |
| Cooling | liquid, pressurised |
| Lubrication | pressurised, with delivery pump |
| Maximum power | 430: 248 hp at 5600 rpm<br>430 catalysed (from 1991): 224 at 5500<br>430 4v.: 279 at 5500 |
| Specific power output | 430: 88.89 hp/litre<br>430 catalysed (from 1991): 80.29<br>430 4v.: 100.00 |

### TRANSMISSION

| | |
|---|---|
| Driven wheels | rear |
| Clutch | single dry-plate |
| Gearbox | five speeds + reverse<br>(from 1990 automatic four speeds + reverse) |

### BODYWORK

| | |
|---|---|
| saloon | four doors, five seats |

### ROLLING CHASSIS

| | |
|---|---|
| Chassis | unitary construction |
| Front suspension | independent, coil springs, anti-roll bar, telescopic hydraulic shock absorbers |
| Rear suspension | independent with longitudinal arms, coil springs, anti-roll bar, hydro-pneumatic shock absorbers |
| Brakes | servo-assisted hydraulically actuated discs |
| Steering | rack and pinion |
| Fuel tank | 80 l |
| Tyres front | 430: 205-55 R-15 87 Z<br>430 4v.: 205-45 R-16 Z |
| Tyres rear | 430: 205-55 R-15 87 Z<br>430 4v.: 225-45 ZR-16 |

### DIMENSIONS AND WEIGHT

| | |
|---|---|
| Wheelbase | 2600 mm |
| Tracks front | 1442 mm |
| rear | 1450 mm |
| Length | – |
| Width | – |
| Height | – |
| Dry weight | 430: 1407 kg<br>430 4v.: 1420 |
| Weight to power ratio | 430: 5,67 kg/hp<br>430 catalysed (from1991): 6.28<br>430 4v.: 5.08 |

### PERFORMANCE AND PRODUCTION

| | |
|---|---|
| Maximum speed | 430: 240 kph<br>430 catalysed (from1991): 233<br>430 4v.: 255 |
| Units produced | 1286 (430: 995 / 430 4v.: 291) |

# 430 – 430 4v.                    1987

As soon as the 425 went out of production, the 430 was introduced in 1987, taking its place as the flagship model in the Biturbo range. The 2.5-litre 90° V6 engine had been replaced with a 2.8-litre unit with single overhead camshafts per bank and fuel injection that was also to be fitted to the soon to be launched Karif. It provided an increase in power from 200 to 248 hp, while the peak power speed rose by just 100 rpm from 5500 to 5600 rpm. The top speed increased from 220 kph to 240 kph. Amongst the most significant updates were an optional opening roof, digital electronic ignition, adjustable driver's seat and steering-wheel and, above all, a limited slip differential that improved the car's road manners by preventing the wheel spin otherwise easily induced by the powerful engine. In 1991, the 430 was joined by, and from the following year, replaced by the 430 4v., powered by a 90° V6 of the same size but with four valves per cylinder actuated by double overhead camshafts per cylinder bank. Compared to the previous version there was a considerable increase in maximum power, from 248 to 279 hp at 5500 rpm, with a top speed of 255 kph, the kind of performance to be expected from an aggressive sports car but surprising in an elegant four-door saloon. The bodywork had a new look, bringing it into line with the restyling the whole Biturbo range had been subjected to from 1990 onwards. The front end displayed a series of features which, taken together, gave it a more compact appearance, with a lower and more slender radiator grille, newly designed headlamps (no longer rectangular but the two external ones round and the two internal ones ellipsoidal) and finally a new black grille, located beneath the bumper with fog lights on either side. Between 1987 and 1994 the total production of the two amounted to 1286 cars, 995 for the 430 and 291 for the 430 4v.

The 222 continued the long journey of cars derived from the Biturbo. The car had a reasonable commercial success, equally divided between two versions, the 222 and the subsequent 2.24v, which hit the market about a year later. For this model, too, evolution continued with numerous aesthetic and mechanical changes and improvements.

## TECHNICAL SPECIFICATION

### ENGINE
front, longitudinal, 90° V6

| | |
|---|---|
| *Bore and stroke* | 82 x 63 mm |
| *Unitary displacement* | 332.70 cc |
| *Total displacement* | 1996.22 cc |
| *Valvegear* | 222: single overhead camshaft per bank 2.24v.: double overhead camshafts per bank |
| *Number of valves* | 3 per cylinder 2.24v.: 4 per cylinder |
| *Compression ratio* | 222: 7.8:1 2.24v.: 7.6:1 |
| *Fuel system* | electronic fuel injection 2 IHI turbochargers |
| *Ignition* | electronic |
| *Cooling* | liquid, pressurised |
| *Lubrication* | pressurised, with delivery pump |
| *Maximum power* | 222: 223 hp at 6250 rpm 2.24v.: 245 at 6200 |
| *Specific power output* | 222: 111.71 hp/litre 2.24v.: 122.73 |

### TRANSMISSION
| | |
|---|---|
| *Driven wheels* | rear |
| *Clutch* | single dry-plate |
| *Gearbox* | five speeds + reverse |

### BODYWORK
| | |
|---|---|
| *coupé* | two doors, four seats |

### ROLLING CHASSIS
| | |
|---|---|
| *Chassis* | load-bearing body shell |
| *Front suspension* | independent, coil springs, anti-roll bar, telescopic hydraulic shock absorbers |
| *Rear suspension* | independent with longitudinal arms, coil springs, anti-roll bar, hydro-pneumatic shock absorbers |
| *Brakes* | servo-assisted hydraulically actuated disks |
| *Steering* | rack and pinion |
| *Fuel tank* | 80 l |
| *Tyres front* | 222: 205-55 VR-14 2.24v.: 205-50 R-15 85, after 205-50 85Z-16V |

### DIMENSIONS AND WEIGHT
| | |
|---|---|
| *Wheelbase* | 2514 mm |
| *Tracks front* | 222: 1442 mm 2.24v.: 1458 mm |
| *rear* | 222: 1450 mm 2.24v.: 1454 mm |
| *Length* | - |
| *Width* | - |
| *Height* | - |
| *Dry weight* | 222: 1210 kg 2.24v.: 1300 |
| *Weight to power ratio* | 222: 5.42 kg/hp 2.24v.: 5.30 |

### PERFORMANCE AND PRODUCTION
| | |
|---|---|
| *Maximum speed* | 222: 225 kph 2.24v.: 230 |
| *Units produced* | 2303 (222: 1156 / 2.24v.: 1147) |

# 222 – 2.24v.                    1988

The last Biturbo to be fitted with the two-litre engine - the patriarch of the genealogy - had already been put on sale before it was presented at the Turin Motor Show in 1988. Renamed the 222, in the same way as other models of the range whose names consisted of numbers, it had undergone restyling thanks to which it now had a new radiator grille and the bonnet no longer featured NACA ducts, while the rear spoiler which increased downforce at the rear of the car was retained. The single cam 90° V6 that powered it, developed a maximum power output of 233 hp at 6250 rpm which allowed it to reach a top speed of 225 kph. The car boasted a comprehensive range of accessories and a passenger compartment trimmed in luxurious materials including velvet, leather and burr walnut. Driving and ride comfort were assured by, amongst other things, electrically adjustable seats and an air-conditioning system. In 1989, the engine was subjected to a radical reworking of the cylinder heads with the number of valves per cylinder being increased from three to four, actuated by two overhead camshafts per bank, giving rise to the creation of the 2.24v. model. The fuel system, pressurised by means of the usual twin turbochargers, featured integrated electronic ignition and multipoint electronic fuel injection, with two progressive aperture throttle valves. The maximum power was thereby increased to 245 hp at 6200 rpm and the top speed was now 230 kph. Further styling changes were made to the bodywork in 1992, the last year of production, when a front end identical to that of the Shamal was adopted with rectangular headlights. The Biturbo era, which marked an unforgettable period in the history of Maserati, came to an end in 1992, ten years after the model's launch. Production figures for the last two versions came to 2303 cars, 1156 for the 222 and 1147 for the 2.24v.

When the Karif reached the Maserati concessionaires, the company was undergoing yet another change of hands, this time to Fiat. The Karif, which once more took its name from an African wind, was the umpteenth result of the long Biturbo genealogy as it was also equipped with the 90° 6-cylinder 2.8-litre engine. It didn't do as well as expected and the 221 produced in four years testify to that.

## TECHNICAL SPECIFICATION

### ENGINE
front, longitudinal, 90° V6

| | |
|---|---|
| Bore and stroke | 94 x 67 mm |
| Unitary displacement | 464.96 cc |
| Total displacement | 2789.78 cc |
| Valvegear | single overhead camshaft per bank of cylinders |
| Number of valves | three per cylinder |
| Compression ratio | 7.4:1 |
| Fuel system | electronic fuel injection two IHI RHB 52 turbochargers |
| Ignition | electronic |
| Cooling | liquid, pressurised |
| Lubrication | pressurised, with delivery pump |
| Maximum power | Karif: 248 hp at 5600 rpm Karif catalyzed (from1990): 224 at 5500 |
| Specific power output | Karif: 88.89 hp/litre Karif catalyzed (from1990): 80.29 |

### TRANSMISSION
| | |
|---|---|
| Driven wheels | rear |
| Clutch | single dry-plate |
| Gearbox | five speeds + reverse (four-speed automatic on request) |

### BODYWORK
| | |
|---|---|
| coupé | two doors, two seats |

### ROLLING CHASSIS
| | |
|---|---|
| Chassis | unitary construction |
| Front suspension | independent, coil springs, anti-roll bar, telescopic hydraulic shock absorbers |
| Rear suspension | independent with longitudinal arms, coil springs, anti-roll bar, gas shock absorbers |
| Brakes | servo-assisted hydraulically actuated disks |
| Steering | rack and pinion |
| Fuel tank | 82 l (80 from 1990) |
| Tyres front | 205-50 ZR-15 / 225-50 VR-15 |

### DIMENSIONS AND WEIGHT
| | |
|---|---|
| Wheelbase | 2400 mm |
| Tracks front | 1458 mm |
| rear | 1460 mm |
| Length | - |
| Width | - |
| Height | - |
| Dry weight | 1335 kg (1346 from 1990) |
| Weight to power ratio | 5.38 kg/hp (6.00 from 1990) |

### PERFORMANCE AND PRODUCTION
| | |
|---|---|
| Maximum speed | 223 kph (230 from 1990) |
| Units produced | 221 |

# Karif

1988

The Karif is a warm wind blowing from the south-west across the Gulf of Aden between Somalia and Yemen, and whose name Maserati gave to a saloon car that marked the revival of a tradition which began with the Mistral and continued with Ghibli, Simùn, Bora and Khamsin before being discontinued. Presented at the Geneva Motor Show in 1988, the Karif was fitted with the well-proven 2.8 litre 90° V6 with single overhead camshaft valve gear and three valves per cylinder, electronic multipoint fuel injection and integrated ignition management. The turbocharging was also electronically managed. The twin turbochargers were equipped with air/air heat exchangers and water-cooled turbines. The maximum power output was 248 hp at 5600 rpm, a figure destined to be reduced to 224 hp on the catalysed version, which was in production from 1990. The top speed was originally 233 kph, which dropped to 230 kph as a result of the catalyser being fitted and of the weight increase from 1335 kg to 1346 kg. The bodywork was based on the spider designed by Zagato onto which a roof section was grafted. The overall appearance, with a much shorter wheelbase than the other saloons, was compact and sporty. The interior, with room for two people, in typical Maserati style was very well finished, featuring high quality materials (burr walnut and natural leather) and it was particularly well-equipped. The Karif remained in production between 1988 and 1991, with 221 cars being built. In the meantime storm clouds were gathering over the future of the Modena company, which in the year that this car was presented suffered losses of 37 billion lire, with a turnover of just over 200 billion. Alejandro De Tomaso was obliged to come to a financial, industrial and commercial agreement with the Fiat Group, to whom he conceded 49% of the firm's capital.

While not given the name of a wind like other Maseratis, Chubasco was still associated with a certain South American climatic condition of wind and rain. With this futuristic prototype, created by Marcello Gandini, a further addition was made to Maserati's long history of concept cars. The model was introduced at the end of 1990 and remained a prototype without mechanics. Today, it is part of the Panini collection in Modena

## TECHNICAL SPECIFICATION

### ENGINE
front, longitudinal, 90° V8

| | |
|---|---|
| Bore and stroke | 80 x 80 mm |
| Unitary displacement | 402.12 cc |
| Total displacement | 3216.98 cc |
| Valvegear | double overhead camshafts per bank |
| Number of valves | fourper cylinder |
| Compression ratio | 7.5:1 |
| Fuel system | electronic fuel injection two IHI RHB 52 turbochargers |
| Ignition | electronic |
| Cooling | liquid, pressurised |
| Lubrication | pressurised, with delivery pump |
| Maximum power | 430 hp at 6500 rpm |
| Specific power output | 100.09 hp/litre |

### TRANSMISSION
| | |
|---|---|
| Driven wheels | rear |
| Clutch | single dry-plate |
| Gearbox | six speeds + reverse |

### BODYWORK
| | |
|---|---|
| coupé/spider | two doors, two seats |
| targa Gandini | |

### ROLLING CHASSIS
| | |
|---|---|
| Chassis | load-bearing central beam |
| Front suspension | independent, coil springs, anti-roll bar, telescopic hydraulic shock absorbers |
| Rear suspension | independent with longitudinal arms, coil springs, anti-roll bar, gas shock absorbers |
| Brakes | servo-assisted hydraulically actuated disks |
| Steering | rack and pinion |
| Fuel tank | 80 l |
| Tyres front/rear | 245-45 ZR-16 225-50 VR-15 |

### DIMENSIONS AND WEIGHT
| | |
|---|---|
| Wheelbase | 2310 mm |
| Tracks front | 1640 mm |
| rear | 1660 mm |
| Length | 4365 mm |
| Width | 2014 mm |
| Height | 1124 mm |
| Dry weight | – |
| Weight to power ratio | – |

### PERFORMANCE AND PRODUCTION
| | |
|---|---|
| Maximum speed | 300 kph |
| Units produced | 1 |

# Chubasco Coupé Gandini                    1990

The Chubasco never went into production but certainly deserves a place in the history of car design. It was presented as a static prototype on the 14TH of December 1990. Its wedge shape, created by the designer Marcello Gandini, was very striking with a low and streamlined profile, a windscreen that was fitted at the same angle as the bonnet, the flat and vertical sides, the one-piece glazing, the oblique angle of the rear wheel arch and the large spoiler mounted on the tail section. The roof could be retracted allowing the car to be used both as a coupé and open as a "targa-topped" car. The chassis was to be built around a central beam (a concept introduced in 1964 by Alessandro De Tomaso on his Vallelunga car), with a load-bearing engine/gearbox assembly, the body-shell suspended on damping supports and push-rod suspension. If it had gone beyond the concept car stage - which did not happen as a result of potentially excessive production costs - the 90° V8 aluminium engine from the Shamal (of which deliveries had just begun) would have been fitted in a rear-central position. Twin turbochargers would have been used along with four valves per cylinder actuated by double overhead camshafts per cylinder bank, which would have enabled the engine to achieve a power output of 430 hp at 6500 rpm, compared to the 322 hp at 6000 rpm of the new saloon car and it would have been able to reach a top speed of around 300 kph. The experience gained with the Chubasco was not lost, however, as it inaugurated a new design path that would be explored two years later with the Barchetta. The name of the car requires an explanation: *chubasco* in Spanish means rain-storm with strong gusts of wind. The same word in the Latin-American dictionary calls it a violent storm with thunder and lightning, a fairly frequent phenomenon in the rainy season along the Pacific Coast, from Mexico to Central and South America. The word is derived from the Portuguese *chuva*, rain.

This model was also inserted into the Maserati Biturbo family. The company intended it to represent a sort of extreme version, of higher performance than the veteran coupé. The engine generated 283 hp, 40 more than the quick 2.24v, and it was no coincidence that the motoring press talked about this car as the most powerful production 2-litre in the world. The chosen name was Racing and the car had every right to join such thoroughbred sports cars.

## TECHNICAL SPECIFICATION

### ENGINE
front, longitudinal, 90° V6

| | |
|---|---|
| Bore and stroke | 82 x 63 mm |
| Unitary displacement | 332.70 cc |
| Total displacement | 1996.22 cc |
| Valvegear | double overhead camshafts per bank of cylinders |
| Number of valves | four per cylinder |
| Compression ratio | 7.6:1 |
| Fuel system | electronic fuel injection two IHI turbochargers |
| Ignition | electronic |
| Cooling | liquid, pressurised |
| Lubrication | pressurised, with delivery pump |
| Maximum power | 283 hp at 6250 rpm |
| Specific power output | 141.76 hp/litre |

### TRANSMISSION
| | |
|---|---|
| Driven wheels | rear |
| Clutch | single dry-plate |
| Gearbox | five speeds + reverse |

### BODYWORK
| | |
|---|---|
| coupé | two doors, four seats |

### ROLLING CHASSIS
| | |
|---|---|
| Chassis | unitary construction |
| Front suspension | independent, coil springs, anti-roll bar, telescopic hydraulic shock absorbers |
| Rear suspension | independent with longitudinal arms, coil springs, anti-roll bar, gas shock absorbers |
| Brakes | servo-assisted hydraulically actuated discs |
| Steering | rack and pinion |
| Fuel tank | 80 l |
| Tyres front | 205-45 R-16 85Z 225-45 ZR-16 |

### DIMENSIONS AND WEIGHT
| | |
|---|---|
| Wheelbase | 2514 mm |
| Tracks front | 1458 mm |
| rear | 1458 / 1454 mm |
| Length | - |
| Width | - |
| Height | - |
| Dry weight | 1323 kg |
| Weight to power ratio | 4.67 kg/hp |

### PERFORMANCE AND PRODUCTION
| | |
|---|---|
| Maximum speed | 256 kph |
| Units produced | 230 |

# Racing                                          1990

Presented in December 1990 and put on sale in May 1991, the Racing, initially only intended for the Italian market, represented the most extreme development of the Biturbo and preceded the advent of the second series of the Ghibli. In appearance it was similar to the Shamal in certain features such as the front end and the aerodynamic spoiler at the bottom of the windscreen, but the rest of the body was still derived from the first Biturbo (1982). A noteworthy development was however to be found in the engine which, although still a two-litre 90° V6, was now made completely of aluminium, with a redesigned crankshaft, new combustion chambers, lightened con-rods, forged rather than cast pistons, sodium valves and a camshafts with new profiles. The usual twin turbochargers were used, albeit modified to suit the new mechanical configuration, and the engine was fitted with four valves per cylinder actuated by double overhead camshafts per bank. Maximum power output was 283 hp at 6250 rpm with a specific power output of 141.76 hp/litre, figures that made it the most powerful production 2000 in the world, able to reach a top speed of 256 kph, to accelerate from 0-100 kph in 5.9" and cover a kilometre from a standing start in 25.9". Also new were the Getrag five-speed gearbox and the active suspension units developed by Koni. Offered as an option on the 2.24, they were included as standard equipment for the first time. Each wheel, by means of sensors, transmitted impulses generated by bumps in the road surface to a control unit that governed the shock absorbers. The versatility of the system was ensured by a four-position control that allowed the driver to adjust the suspension settings according to the conditions. In order to emphasise its aggressive nature, the Racing was supplied in only two colours: red or black. Between 1990 and 1992, 230 examples were made.

While the Racing was introduced in 1990, in the same period the sold Shamals were handed over to clients at the factory. It was a year after the potent car's presentation, equipped with a 90° V8 aluminium engine. About 50 cars a year were built, a good result for a rather exclusive car.

## TECHNICAL SPECIFICATION

**ENGINE**

front, longitudinal, 90° V8

| | |
|---|---|
| Bore and stroke | 80 x 80 mm |
| Unitary displacement | 402.12 cc |
| Total displacement | 3216.98 cc |
| Valvegear | double overhead camshaft per bank of cylinders |
| Number of valves | four per cylinder |
| Compression ratio | 7.5:1 |
| Fuel system | electronic fuel injection two IHI RHB 52 turbochargers |
| Ignition | electronic |
| Cooling | liquid, pressurised |
| Lubrication | pressurised, with delivery pump |
| Maximum power | 322 / 326 hp at 6000 rpm |
| Specific power output | 100.09 / 101.33 hp/litre |

**TRANSMISSION**

| | |
|---|---|
| Driven wheels | rear |
| Clutch | single dry-plate |
| Gearbox | six speeds + reverse |

**BODYWORK**

| | |
|---|---|
| coupé/spider | two doors, two seats |
| Gandini design | |

**ROLLING CHASSIS**

| | |
|---|---|
| Chassis | load-bearing central beam |
| Front suspension | independent, coil springs, anti-roll bar, telescopic hydraulic shock absorbers |
| Rear suspension | independent with oblique arms, coil springs, gas shock absorbers |
| Brakes | servo-assisted hydraulically actuated discs |
| Steering | rack and pinion |
| Fuel tank | 80 l |
| Tyres front | 245-45 ZR-16 225-50 VR-15 |

**DIMENSIONS AND WEIGHT**

| | |
|---|---|
| Wheelbase | 2400 mm |
| Tracks front | 1512 mm |
| rear | 1550 mm |
| Length | - |
| Width | - |
| Height | - |
| Dry weight | 1290/1355 kg |
| Weight to power ratio | 4.00 / 4.15 kg/hp |

**PERFORMANCE AND PRODUCTION**

| | |
|---|---|
| Maximum speed | 260 / 270 kph |
| Units produced | 369 |

# Shamal 1990

At the traditional Maserati press conference on the 14ᵀᴴ of December 1989, a static model of a coupé was presented, the result of a radical revision of the Biturbo. Named as the Shamal, after a warm, dry wind blowing from the north or north-west across Iran, Iraq and the Arab peninsula, causing great sand storms, the car went into production a year later. The bodywork, designed by Marcello Gandini, retained some parts from the Spyder, such as the doors and the windscreen and there was therefore some resemblance to the Karif. However, certain original features differentiated it, like the design of the rear wheel arch (which was reminiscent of the Lamborghini Espada, also designed by Gandini), the moulding running along the bottom of the flanks, the central beam that served as a roll-bar (with a chrome-plated Shamal script), the small rear spoiler and the wide elegantly-designed alloy wheels. The engine was all new – a perfectly square (bore and stroke 80 mm) aluminium, 3.2-litre, 90° V8. It had electronic ignition and was fuelled by twin turbochargers, had four valves per cylinder actuated by two overhead camshafts per cylinder bank and put out 322 hp (later 326) at 6000 rpm. There was a six-speed manual gearbox and the suspension was equipped with an active control system that allowed the driver to adapt the handling of the car according to the needs of roadholding and comfort. The top speed was 260 kph (later increased to 270) and the car could sprint from 0-100 kph in 5.3" and cover a kilometre form a standing start in 24.9". The interior, even though it was less luxurious than that of the Ghibli II series, was of top quality both with regard to the standard equipment and the materials used for the trim. Between 1990 and 1996, 369 examples of the Shamal were produced.

The Maserati Barchetta lasted only two years from 1992-1993 and was the star of two mono-marque championships of first six and then 10 races respectively. It was the first suggestion of Maserati's return to its roots, it having been established first and foremost for racing. It was significant that, as early as the late '80s, Ferrari had gone back to promoting such initiatives with models like the F40 in 1987 and the 348 TB two years later.

## TECHNICAL SPECIFICATION

### ENGINE

front, longitudinal, 90° V6

| | |
|---|---|
| Bore and stroke | 82 x 63 mm |
| Unitary displacement | 332.70 cc |
| Total displacement | 1996.22 cc |
| Valvegear | double overhead camshafts per bank |
| Number of valves | four per cylinder |
| Compression ratio | 8.5:1 |
| Fuel system | electronic fuel injection two IHI turbochargers |
| Ignition | electronic |
| Cooling | liquid, pressurised |
| Lubrication | pressurised, with delivery pump |
| Maximum power | 315 hp at 7200 rpm |
| Specific power output | 157.79 hp/litre |

### TRANSMISSION

| | |
|---|---|
| Driven wheels | rear |
| Clutch | single dry-plate |
| Gearbox | six speeds + reverse |

### BODYWORK

| | |
|---|---|
| competition spider | two doors, two seats |

### ROLLING CHASSIS

| | |
|---|---|
| Chassis | load-bearing central beam |
| Front suspension | independent wishbones, push rods, telescopic hydraulic shock absorbers |
| Rear suspension | independent wishbones, pull rods, telescopic hydraulic shock absorbers |
| Brakes | servo-assisted hydraulically actuated discs |
| Steering | rack and pinion |
| Fuel tank | 40 l |
| Tyres front | 245-40 ZR-18 285-35 ZR-18 |

### DIMENSIONS AND WEIGHT

| | |
|---|---|
| Wheelbase | 2600 mm |
| Tracks front | 1610 mm |
| rear | 1580 mm |
| Length | - |
| Width | - |
| Height | - |
| Dry weight | 775 kg |
| Weight to power ratio | 2.46 kg/hp |

### PERFORMANCE AND PRODUCTION

| | |
|---|---|
| Maximum speed | 300 kph |
| Units produced | 17 |

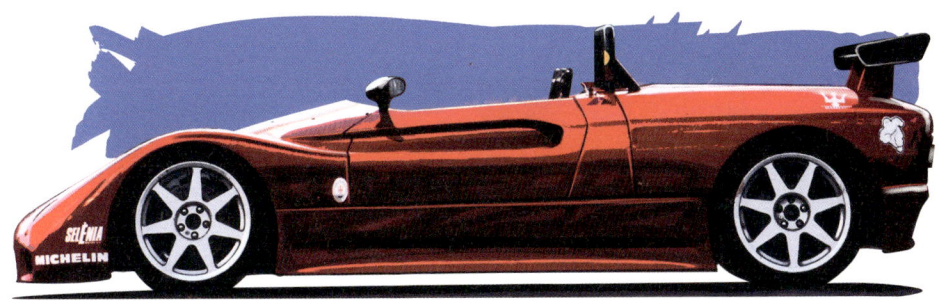

# Barchetta 1992

The idea of setting up and running a single-marque trophy series of races for gentleman drivers, which would help would revive Maserati's sporting tradition, led to the design and production of the Barchetta. Using the central load bearing beam that had been experimented in 1990 on the Chubasco concept car as a starting point, the designer Carlo Gaino of the Synthesis Design studio created an extremely low-slung (845 mm) two-seater, characterised by a large air intake on the bonnet and a dynamic rear wing. The aggressive lines of the bodywork seemed to blend into the softly-flowing surfaces, giving rise to an original result that had no negative effect on aerodynamic efficiency. The generous use of aluminium, carbon fibre and composite materials kept the weight down to 775 kg. The engine, fitted in a rear-central position, was the two-litre 90° V6 from the Biturbo in its most sophisticated guise, fed by electronic fuel injection and supercharged via two IHI turbochargers, with four valves per cylinder actuated by double overhead cams per bank of cylinders. With a compression ratio of 8.5:1 the maximum power output was 315 hp at 7200 rpm. The gearbox was a manual six-speed and the independent suspension, developed from Formula 1, was equipped with push rods at the front and pull rods at the rear. With a top speed of approximately 300 kph, and thanks in part to the very low weight permitting excellent acceleration and braking values, for two years (1992 and 1993) the Barchetta brought to life a trophy that consisted of races not without their spectacular moments, but which attracted fewer drivers prepared to buy the car than had been hoped. 17 cars were built compared to the 25 Maserati had expected to produce and the experiment came to an end. The idea of making a road-going version never went beyond the preparation of a static model.

The glorious Ghibli name was brought out again in the mid-'90s while waiting for the Fiat re-launch programme of the entire Modena complex. A new model which, to tell the truth, was little like the spectacular coupé that appeared in 1967. The Ghibli would still remain in production for seven years.

## TECHNICAL SPECIFICATION

### ENGINE

front, longitudinal, 90° V6

| | |
|---|---|
| Bore and stroke | Ghibli: 82 x 63<br>Ghibli 2.8: 94 x 67 mm |
| Unitary displacement | Ghibli: 332.70<br>Ghibli 2.8: 464.96 cc |
| Total displacement | Ghibli: 1996.22<br>Ghibli 2.8: 2789.78 cc |
| Valvegear | double overhead camshaft per bank |
| Number of valves | four per cylinder |
| Compression ratio | Ghibli: 7.6:1<br>Ghibli 2.8: 7.4:1<br>Ghibli 2.0 Cup, Open Cup and<br>Primatist: 7.6:1 |
| Fuel system | electronic fuel injection<br>two IHI RHB turbochargers |
| Ignition | electronic |
| Cooling | liquid, pressurised |
| Lubrication | pressurised, with delivery pump |
| Maximum power | Ghibli: 306 hp at 6250 rpm /<br>Ghibli 2.8: 281 at 6500 / Ghibli<br>2.0 Open Cup: 330 at 6500 /<br>Ghibli 2.0 Primatist: 306 at 6500 |
| Specific power output | Ghibli: 153.28 hp/litre / Ghibli<br>2.8: 100.72 / Ghibli 2.0 Open<br>Cup: 165.31 / Ghibli 2.0 Prima-<br>tist: 153.28 |

### TRANSMISSION

| | |
|---|---|
| Driven wheels | rear |
| Clutch | single dry-plate |
| Gearbox | six speeds + reverse (Ghibli 2.8:<br>five speeds + reverse) |

### BODYWORK

| | |
|---|---|
| coupé | two doors, five seats |

### ROLLING CHASSIS

| | |
|---|---|
| Chassis | unitary construction |
| Front suspension | independent, coil springs, anti-<br>roll bar, gas shock absorbers. |
| Rear suspension | independent with oblique arms,<br>coil springs, anti-roll bar, gas<br>shock absorbers. |
| Brakes | servo-assisted hydraulically<br>actuated disks |
| Steering | rack and pinion |
| Fuel tank | 82 l |
| Tyres front | Ghibli: 205-50 ZR-16 / Ghibli 2.0<br>Cup e 2.0 Open Cup: 215-45 ZR-17 |
| Tyres rear | Ghibli: 205-50 ZR-16 / Ghibli 2.8:<br>225-50 ZR-16 / Ghibli 2.0 Cup e<br>2.0 Open Cup: 245-45 ZR-17 |

### DIMENSIONS AND WEIGHT

| | |
|---|---|
| Wheelbase | 2514 mm |
| Tracks front/ rear | 1515 mm |
| Length | - |
| Width | - |
| Height | - |
| Dry weight | 1365 kg |
| Weight to power ratio | Ghibli: kg/hp 4.46 / Ghibli 2.8:<br>4.85 / Ghibli 2.0 Open Cup: 4.13<br>/ Ghibli 2.0 Primatist: 4.46 |

### PERFORMANCE AND PRODUCTION

| | |
|---|---|
| Maximum speed | Ghibli: 265 kph / Ghibli 2.0 Cup<br>e 2.0 Open Cup: 270 |
| Units produced | 2303 (Ghibli: 1157 / Ghibli<br>2.8+GT+Primatist: 1063 / Ghibli<br>2.0 Cup: 60 / Ghibli 2.0 Open<br>Cup: 23) |

# Ghibli – Ghibli 2,8 – 2,0 Cup
# 2,0 GT - 2,0 Open Cup – 2,0 Primatist

### 1992

Ten years after the launch of the Biturbo, Maserati made yet another version that looked very similar, but had a radically different mechanical design. The name Ghibli was dusted off, as it retained an aura associated with the coupé produced from 1967 to 1972 and still universally admired. Several cars were removed from the catalogue including the 222, 2.24v, 4.24v., 430 and Spider when the new model was presented at the Turin Motor Show in 1992 and put on sale the following June. The engine was the by now very familiar twin cam 90° V6 with two turbochargers, but was radically different compared to the original. Two displacements were offered, two litres for Italy and 2.8 litres for export markets. The all-aluminium unit was fuelled via electronic fuel injection, had a compression ratio of 7.6:1 (7.4:1 for the 2.8) and developed 306 hp (281 for the 2.8) at 6250 rpm which allowed the car to reach a top speed of 265 kph. The interior had new and more complete instrumentation, including a thermometer that displayed the external temperature, a feature considered to be very advanced at the time. Over the following years the Ghibli benefitted from a wide range of improvements and revisions. In 1993, static ignition was introduced, while 1994 saw an optional automatic gearbox and ABS. In 1995, the Ghibli Cup version was introduced, featuring a more powerful 330 hp engine and 17" wheels, built to take part in the single-marque championship of the same name. The Open Cup version looked even more race-orientated and aggressive (roll-bar, a single anatomic seat), while the GT underwent fewer aesthetic changes and had slightly less power (306 hp). Finally, in 1997, the Primatist was produced in a limited series of 60 cars, taking its name from the world powerboat record established by Bruno Abbate in a boat driven by a Maserati engine. The following year production of the Ghibli ended after 2303 cars had been produced (the official figure was an incomprehensible 2216).

In 1997, Maserati passed under the aegis of its old "enemy" Ferrari. Among the first changes was a massive restyling of the Quattroporte, with the models that closed the series being called, not surprisingly, Evolution.

## TECHNICAL SPECIFICATION

### ENGINE

2.0i V6 e 2,8i V6: front, longitudinal, 90°V6
3.2i V8 (from 1996) 90°V8

| | |
|---|---|
| Bore and stroke | 2.0i V6: 82 x 63 mm / 2.8i V6: 94 x 67 / 3.2i V8: 80 x 80 |
| Unitary displacement | 2.0i V6: 332.70 cc / 2.8i V6: 464.96 cc / 3.2i V8: 402.12 cc |
| Total displacement | 2.0i V6: 1996.22 cc / 2.8i V6: 2789.78 cc / 3.2i V8: 3216.98 cc |
| Valvegear | double overhead camshafts per bank |
| Number of valves | four per cylinder |
| Compression ratio | 2.0i V6: 7.6:1 2.8i V6 and 2.8i V6 Evoluzione: 7.4:1 / 3.2i V8: 7.51 / 3.2i V8 Evoluzione 7.3:1 |
| Fuel system | electronic fuel injection two IHI turbochargers |
| Ignition | electronic |
| Cooling | liquid, pressurised |
| Lubrication | pressurised |
| Maximum power | 2.0i V6: 287 hp at 6500 rpm 2.8i V6 and 2,8i V6 Evoluzione: 284 hp at 6000 rpm / 3.2i V8: 335 at 6400 rpm |
| Specific power output | 2.0i V6: 143.77 hp/litre / 2.8i V6 and 2.8i V6 Evoluzione: 101.80 hp/litre / 3.2i V8: 104.13 hp/litre |

### TRANSMISSION

| | |
|---|---|
| Driven wheels | rear |
| Clutch | single dry-plate |
| Gearbox | 2.0i V6: manual five speeds + reverse / 2.8i and 3.2i: automatic four speeds + reverse |

### BODYWORK

| | |
|---|---|
| saloon | four doors, five seats |

### ROLLING CHASSIS

| | |
|---|---|
| Chassis | unitary construction |
| Front suspension | independent, McPherson type struts, coil springs, anti-roll bar, electronically-controlled dampers |
| Rear suspension | independent with trailing arms, anti-roll bar, electronically-controlled dampers |
| Brakes | servo-assisted hydraulically actuated disks |
| Steering | rack and pinion |
| Fuel tank | 82 or 105 li |
| Tyres front/rear | 205-55 ZR-16 / 225-50 ZR-16 |

### DIMENSIONS AND WEIGHT

| | |
|---|---|
| Wheelbase | 2650 mm |
| Tracks front/ rear | 1522 mm /1502 |
| Length | - |
| Width | - |
| Height | - |
| Dry weight | 2.0i V6: 1543 kg / 2.8i V6 and 3.2i V8: 1560 / 2.8i V6 and 3.2i V8 automatic gearbox: 1584 |
| Weight to power ratio | 2.0i V6: 5.37 kg/hp / 2.8i V6 e 3.2i V8: 5.49 kg/hp / 3.2i V8: 4.65 kg/hp / 2.8i V6 / 3.2i V8 automatic gearbox: 5.57 / 4.72 kg/hp |

### PERFORMANCE AND PRODUCTION

| | |
|---|---|
| Maximum speed | 2.0i V6, 2.8i V6, 2.8 V6 Evoluzione: 260 kph / 3.2i V8 and 3.2i V8 Evoluzione: 270 kph |
| Units produced | 2400 (2.0i V6 24v.: 587 / 2.8i V6 24v.: 668 / 3.2i V8 32v.: 415 / 2.0i V6 Evoluzione: 200 / 2.8i V6 Evoluzione: 190 / 3.2i V8 Evoluzione: 340) |

# Quattroporte IV 2,0i – 2,8i – 3,2i                    1994
# 2,0i-2,8i – Evoluzione

The fourth series of the Quattroporte (which followed those of 1963, 1976 and 1979) was presented at the Turin Motor Show in 1994. The bodywork, redesigned by Marcello Gandini, was undeniably elegant but the use of the Biturbo floorpan, with its 2650 wheelbase (compared to 2800 of previous versions) restricted passenger space in the rear seats. The saloon was offered with a choice of two engines: two litres for the Italian market - where larger displacements still suffered under the tax laws - and 2.8 litres for the foreign market. The engine was the immortal 90° V6 with two turbochargers in its most advanced form: made completely of aluminium, electronic fuel injection and four valves per cylinder actuated by double overhead camshafts per bank. With a compression ratio of 7.6:1 (7.4:1 for the 2.8) it produced 287 hp at 6500 rpm (284 hp at 6000 for the 2.8), allowing the car to reach a top speed of 260 kph, sprint from 0-100 kph in 5.9" and cover the standing start kilometre in 25.9". The gearbox was a manual six-speed or automatic four-speed, and independent suspension with electronically managed shock absorbers was fitted. In 1996, the range was expanded with a version powered by an eight-cylinder 3.2 litre engine with a power output of 335 hp at 6400 rpm and a top speed of 270 kph. From 1998, all three versions were subjected to a thorough revision that affected 400 out of 800 components and the word Evolution was added to the name of all the cars. This was a move on the part of Maserati's new owners, Ferrari S.p.A., to whom Fiat had transferred 50% of the Trident's shares in July 1997. The exterior of the car still looked a little dated, but the newly-refurbished passenger compartment offered refinement and comfort of the highest order. The Quattroporte went out of production in May 2001 after 2400 cars had been produced.

The return of Maserati to less squared lines came from the hands of Giorgetto Giugiaro, who has been the creator of a number of the Trident's cars. More than 20 years after the Merak, Giugiaro became the stylist who re-launched the marque, which was promoted by both Fiat and Ferrari. The veteran stylist created the 3200 GT coupé, a car of bold and elegant lines and one that projected the styling elements of the past in a modern way.

## TECHNICAL SPECIFICATION

### ENGINE
front, longitudinal, 90° V8

| | |
|---|---|
| Bore and stroke | 80 x 80 mm |
| Unitary displacement | 402.12 cc |
| Total displacement | 3216.98 cc |
| Valvegear | double overhead camshaft per bank of cylinders |
| Number of valves | four per cylinder |
| Compression ratio | 8:1 |
| Fuel system | electronic fuel injection two IHI turbochargers |
| Ignition | electronic |
| Cooling | liquid, pressurised |
| Lubrication | pressurised, with delivery pump |
| Maximum power | 368 hp at 6250 rpm |
| Specific power output | 114.39 hp/litre |

### TRANSMISSION
| | |
|---|---|
| Driven wheels | rear |
| Clutch | single dry-plate |
| Gearbox | six speeds + reverse (from 1999 automatic on request) |

### BODYWORK
| | |
|---|---|
| coupé Italdesign | two doors, four seats |

### ROLLING CHASSIS
| | |
|---|---|
| Chassis | unitary construction |
| Front suspension | independent, coil springs, anti-roll bar, lectronically controlled telescopic hydraulic shock absorbers |
| Rear suspension | independent with longitudinal arms, coil springs, anti-roll bar, electronically controlled telescopic hydraulic shock absorbers |
| Brakes | servo-assisted hydraulically actuated disks |
| Steering | rack and pinion |
| Fuel tank | 90 l |
| Tyres front | 245-235-40 ZR-18 265-35 ZR-18 |

### DIMENSIONS AND WEIGHT
| | |
|---|---|
| Wheelbase | 2660 mm |
| Tracks front | 1525 mm |
| rear | 1538 mm |
| Length | 4510 mm |
| Width | 1822 mm |
| Height | 1305 mm |
| Dry weight | 1590 kg |
| Weight to power ratio | 4.32 kg/hp |

### PERFORMANCE AND PRODUCTION
| | |
|---|---|
| Maximum speed | 280 kph (270 with automatic gearbox) |
| Units produced | 4795 |

# 3200 GT                                      1998

Within the context of a renewal of not only the model range but above all the Maserati image, production of the 3200 GT in 1998 was a particularly significant step forward. The bodywork design was the work of Giorgetto Giugiaro, who had already designed the Ghibli (1966), the Bora (1971) and the Merak (1972) for the Trident. The 3200 GT was admired for its compact appearance, emphasized by the soft and sensual shapes that were perfectly in tune with the tastes of the time, with the flat and angular surfaces from the distant past that had survived for too long during the Biturbo dynasty finally being abandoned. Amongst the technical and stylistic innovations, the boomerang-shaped rear light units stood out, as this was one of the first times that LED technology had been used on a production car. The engine, located at the front, was the eight-cylinder 3.2-litre unit with two turbochargers that had been seen before on the Shamal (1990) and the Quattroporte (1994). Its exceptional power output of 368 hp at 6250 rpm allowed the car, weighing 1590 kg, to reach a top speed of 280 kph, to sprint from 0 to 100 kph in 5.12" and to cover the standing start kilometre in 24.2". The painstaking care that went into the developing the car's mechanical specification finally guaranteed the reliability that over the years had been the object of wide-spread criticism and complaints, even though it had improved more recently. In 1999 the 3200 GT was also offered with an automatic and renamed as the 3200 GT Automatica or 3200 GTA. In March 2001, at the Geneva Motor Show, a new version was presented known as the Assetto Corsa, which from June of the same year was sold alongside the standard 3200 GT. The car was built in a limited series (56 for Italy and 194 for the rest of the world) and it was designed for customers who wanted a race-oriented set up that was even more extreme. Total production output for the 3200 GT came to 4795 cars.

Giugiaro's Italdesign was commissioned to design a large two-volume car and high performance. But the result didn't please the press and motor industry experts, perhaps because the model's style didn't match a marque like Maserati, which had always projected its sporty tradition. Only this example of the Buran, unveiled at the 2000 Geneva Motor Show, remains.

## TECHNICAL SPECIFICATION

| ENGINE | |
|---|---|
| front, longitudinal, 90° V8 | |
| Bore and stroke | 80 x 80 mm |
| Unitary displacement | 402.12 cc |
| Total displacement | 3216.98 cc |
| Valvegear | double overhead camshaft per bank of cylinders |
| Number of valves | four per cylinder |
| Compression ratio | 8:1 |
| Fuel system | electronic fuel injection |
| | two IHI turbochargers |
| Ignition | electronic |
| Cooling | liquid, pressurised |
| Lubrication | pressurised, with delivery pump |
| Maximum power | 368 hp at 6250 rpm |
| Specific power output | 114.39 hp/litre |

| TRANSMISSION | |
|---|---|
| Driven wheels | permanent four-wheel drive |
| Clutch | single dry-plate |
| Gearbox | six speeds + reverse (automatic on request) |

| BODYWORK | |
|---|---|
| berlina Italdesign | four doors, five seats |

| ROLLING CHASSIS | |
|---|---|
| Chassis | unitary construction |
| Front suspension | independent, coil springs, anti-roll bar, electronically controlled telescopic hydraulic shock absorbers |
| Rear suspension | independent with longitudinal arms, coil springs, anti-roll bar, electronically controlled telescopic hydraulic shock absorbers |
| Brakes | serv-oassisted hydraulically actuated disks |
| Steering | rack and pinion |
| Fuel tank | |
| Tyres front | 235-40 ZR-18 / 265-35 ZR-18 |

| DIMENSIONS AND WEIGHT | |
|---|---|
| Wheelbase | 2930 mm |
| Tracks front | – |
| rear | – |
| Length | 4983 mm |
| Width | 1950 mm |
| Height | 1630 mm |
| Dry weight | – |
| Weight to power ratio | – |

| PERFORMANCE AND PRODUCTION | |
|---|---|
| Maximum speed | 250 kph |
| Units produced | 1 |

# Buran Italdesign                          2000

At the 2000 Geneva Motor Show, a studio prototype presented by Giorgetto Giugiaro of Ital Design attracted a lot of attention and opinions, not all of them positive. The Buran (named after a strong cold wind that blows north-east across the Sarmatian plain, west of the Urals, often bringing snow storms), had an ambitious and fascinating aim: the creation of a high-performance flagship car with large hatchback bodywork. The body of the car was striking for its boldness and size, as it was almost 5 metres long, 1950 mm wide and, above all, 1630 mm high. For some time Giugiaro had been conducting research and extensive experiments specifically on the use of vertical interior space on two of his famous prototypes - the Alfa Romeo New York Taxi (1976) and the Lancia Megagamma (1978) - the results of which he was able to translate, it might be said, into a smaller and cheaper form in the passenger compartment of the revolutionary Fiat Panda (1980). The philosophy of functionality applied to the extensive space of the Buran (which used a floorpan developed from the Audi A8 in view of a possible agreement with the German company that subsequently came to nothing) was motivated by the chance to provide a range of applications that went from the office to the living room, with sophisticated facilities, the highest level of technological equipment and refined and elegant decor. The Maserati engine, chosen to power the Buran and fitted lengthwise at the front, was the 3.2 litre 90° V8 from the 3200 GT. Fuelled via electronic fuel injection, with two turbochargers, four valves per cylinder actuated by two double overhead camshafts per bank, it developed a maximum power output of 335 hp at 6400 rpm and was mated to a transmission system with permanent four-wheel drive. The prototype remained just that and was never went into production, however its contribution to the evolution of car design has not been lost.

Who knows what the Maserati brothers, the Orsi family and perhaps even Alejandro De Tomaso would have thought if they could have attended the 2001 Frankfurt Motor Show and seen the new Maserati Spyder with its 90° V8, 4-litre engine derived from one of… Ferrari's. A major turning point, a technical outpouring absolutely unthinkable just a few years earlier, but at the time essential to the re-launch of the marque.

## TECHNICAL SPECIFICATION

### ENGINE
front, longitudinal, 90° V8

| | |
|---|---|
| Bore and stroke | 90 x 79.8 mm |
| Unitary displacement | 530.48 cc |
| Total displacement | 4243.84 cc |
| Valvegear | double overhead camshaft per bank |
| Number of valves | four per cylinder |
| Compression ratio | 11.1:1 |
| Fuel system | electronic fuel injection |
| Ignition | electronic |
| Cooling | liquid, pressurised |
| Lubrication | pressurised, with delivery pump |
| Maximum power | 390 hp at 7000 rpm |
| Specific power output | 114.39 hp/litre |

### TRANSMISSION
| | |
|---|---|
| Driven wheels | rear |
| Clutch | single dry-plate |
| Gearbox | six speeds + reverse (Cambio-corsa electro-activated) |

### BODYWORK
| | |
|---|---|
| spider Italdesign | two doors, two seats |

### ROLLING CHASSIS
| | |
|---|---|
| Chassis | load-bearing body |
| Front suspension | independent, coil springs, anti-roll bar, steel one-setting shock absorbers |
| Rear suspension | independent with longitudinal arms, coil springs, anti-roll bar, steel one-setting shock absorbers |
| Brakes | servo-assisted hydraulically actuated disks |
| Steering | rack and pinion |
| Fuel tank | 88 l |
| Tyres front | 235-40 Z-18 / 265-35 Z-18 |

### DIMENSIONS AND WEIGHT
| | |
|---|---|
| Wheelbase | 2440 mm |
| Tracks front | 1525 mm |
| rear | 1538 mm |
| Length | 4523 mm |
| Width | 1822 mm |
| Height | 1305 mm |
| Dry weight | 1630 kg (Cambiocorsa 1655) |
| Weight to power ratio | 4.17 kg/hp (cambiocorsa 4.24) |

### PERFORMANCE AND PRODUCTION
| | |
|---|---|
| Maximum speed | 283 kph |
| Units produced | – |

# Spyder

# 2001

The burst of innovatory energy that had guided Maserati production since Fiat transferred 50% of its shares to Ferrari in 1997 bore its first real fruit in 2001 when the Spyder was presented at the Frankfurt Motor Show. Apart from the debatable inclusion of that "y" in the name - a marketing orientated quirk not confined to Italy - this was a high-quality product, which gave the Trident marque a touch of authentic prestige, giving the company access to the international market and initiating a period of great successes. The bodywork, the engine, the gearbox and the transmission were all new on this seductive open-topped two-seater. Giugiaro worked on the chassis of the 3200 GT, shortening the wheelbase from 2660 to 2440 mm and designing low and compact bodywork with clean, dynamic lines and an elegant and comfortable cockpit that was equipped with all the accessories one might wish for. The mechanical design marked a historic turning point, because the use of twin turbochargers powered by exhaust gases was abandoned after being used on Maserati engines since 1982 and the debut of the Biturbo. The engine was a Ferrari over square (bore 92 mm, stroke 79.8 mm) 4244 cc naturally aspirated 90° V8, with four valves per cylinder actuated by twin overhead camshafts per bank that gave a maximum power output of 390 hp at 7000 rpm. The gearbox was mounted at the back in-unit with the differential and was available as a six-speed manual or in the robotized form as used on the Ferrari 360 Modena that benefitted from the experience gained in Formula 1 and which inspired the Spyder Cambio-corsa version, with four different modes. The top speed that the car could attain was 280 kph and it could sprint from 0 to 100 kph in less than 5 seconds.

Contemporaneously with the Spyder's presentation, another Maserati newborn appeared; it was the Coupé GT, which was also powered by a Ferrari engine. As well as the road-going version, out came a racer, which found its natural outlet in a mono-marque championship called the Trofeo Maserati. Started as a European series in 2003, seven years later in came the Granturismo MC.

## TECHNICAL SPECIFICATION

### ENGINE

front, longitudinal, 90° V8

| | |
|---|---|
| Bore and stroke | 90 x 79.8 mm |
| Unitary displacement | 530.48 cc |
| Total displacement | 4243.84 cc |
| Valvegear | double overhead camshaft per bank of cylinders |
| Number of valves | four per cylinder |
| Compression ratio | 11.1:1 |
| Fuel system | electronic fuel injection |
| Ignition | electronic |
| Cooling | liquid, pressurised |
| Lubrication | pressurised, with delivery pump |
| Maximum power | 368 hp at 6250 rpm (Maserati Trofeo: 420 hp at 6500 rpm) |
| Specific power output | 114.39 hp/litre (Maserati Trofeo: 98.96 hp/litre) |

### TRANSMISSION

| | |
|---|---|
| Driven wheels | rear |
| Clutch | single dry-plate |
| Gearbox | six speeds + reverse (Cambiocorsa electro-activated) |

### BODYWORK

| | |
|---|---|
| coupé Italdesign | two doors, 2 + 2 seats |

### ROLLING CHASSIS

| | |
|---|---|
| Chassis | load-bearing body |
| Front suspension | independent, coil springs, anti-roll bar, steel single-setting shock absorbers |
| Rear suspension | independent with longitudinal arms, coil springs, anti-roll bar, steel single-setting shock absorbers |
| Brakes | servo-assisted hydraulically actuated disks |
| Steering | rack and pinion |
| Fuel tank | 88 l |
| Tyres front | 235-40 Z-18 / 265-35 Z-18 |

### DIMENSIONS AND WEIGHT

| | |
|---|---|
| Wheelbase | 2660 mm |
| Tracks front | 1525 mm |
| rear | 1538 mm |
| Length | 4523 mm |
| Width | 1822 mm |
| Height | 1305 mm |
| Dry weight | 1590 kg (Cambiocorsa 1341) Maserati Trofeo: 1341 kg |
| Weight to power ratio | 4.67 kg/hp (Cambiocorsa 4.70) Maserati Trofeo: 3.19 kg/hp |

### PERFORMANCE AND PRODUCTION

| | |
|---|---|
| Maximum speed | 283 kph |
| Units produced | – |

# 4200 GT – Coupé GT                    2001

When the Spyder was launched at the 2001 Frankfurt Motor Show, the coupé 3200 GT was also updated, mainly through the adoption of an engine that came from Ferrari and the definitive abandonment of the last glorious but obsolete turbocharged engine distantly related to the Biturbo unit from 1982. Named as the 4200 GT and later the Coupé GT, the new car took up the elegant style of the 3200 GT with a few refinements, one of which was the design of the rear lighting clusters, restyled by Giugiaro with larger dimensions (and no longer boomerang-shaped) so that they conformed to United States regulations. The engine was the same Ferrari unit fitted to the open-topped car, that is, an over square (bore 92 mm, stroke 79.8 mm) all-aluminium 4244 cc naturally aspirated 90° V8, with four valves per cylinder actuated by two overhead camshafts per bank, dry sump lubrication and a maximum power output of 390 hp at 7000 rpm. The gearbox was mounted at the back in a transaxle configuration in-unit with the differential and was available as a six-speed manual or in robotized form as also used on the Ferrari 360 Modena that benefitted from the experience gained in Formula 1 and which inspired the Coupé Cambiocorsa version, with four different modes. The top speed was over 280 kph and the 0 to 100 kph time was 5" with a standing start kilometre time of 23.9". In 2003, a special version of the Coupé Cambiocorsa, the Maserati Trofeo, was produced and later took part in a single-marque international championship with great success. The engine had benefitted from having its electronic management unit remapped and a new exhaust system that raised the output to 420 hp. With its weight reduced by 249 kg compared to the production models (1341 compared to 1590) the car had a 0 to 100 time of 4".

In 2003, out came another Giugiaro creation that was a prototype with an exotic Indonesian name: Kubang. The project included collaboration with Germany's Audi, which would have been a winner. But unfortunately, the choice of the German group blocked the way and the two companies took different paths, abandoning a promising market segment in top-class SUVs which were to rival Porsche and BMW.

## TECHNICAL SPECIFICATION

### ENGINE
front, longitudinal, 90° V8

| | |
|---|---|
| Bore and stroke | 80 x 80 mm |
| Unitary displacement | 402.12 cc |
| Total displacement | 3216.98 cc |
| Valvegear | double overhead camshaft per bank of cylinders |
| Number of valves | four per cylinder |
| Compression ratio | 8:1 |
| Fuel system | electronic fuel injection two IHI turbochargers |
| Ignition | electronic |
| Cooling | liquid, pressurised |
| Lubrication | pressurised, with delivery pump |
| Maximum power | 368 hp at 6250 rpm |
| Specific power output | 114.39 hp/litre |

### TRANSMISSION
| | |
|---|---|
| Driven wheels | permanent four-wheel drive |
| Clutch | single dry-plate |
| Gearbox | six speeds + reverse |

### BODYWORK
| | |
|---|---|
| GT Wagon concept Italdesign | four doors, four seats |

### ROLLING CHASSIS
| | |
|---|---|
| Chassis | load-bearing body |
| Front suspension | independent, coil springs, anti-roll bar, electronically controlled telescopic hydraulic shock absorbers |
| Rear suspension | independent with longitudinal arms, coil springs, anti-roll bar, electronically controlled telescopic hydraulic shock absorbers |
| Brakes | servo-assisted hydraulically actuated disks |
| Steering | rack and pinion |
| Fuel tank | - |
| Tyres front | - |

### DIMENSIONS AND WEIGHT
| | |
|---|---|
| Wheelbase | 3064 mm |
| Tracks front | - |
| rear | - |
| Length | 4984 mm |
| Width | 1942 mm |
| Height | 1650 mm |
| Dry weight | - |
| Weight to power ratio | - |

### PERFORMANCE AND PRODUCTION
| | |
|---|---|
| Maximum speed | 255 kph |
| Units produced | 1 |

# Kubang Italdesign 2003

At the Detroit Motor Show in 2003, Italdesign presented a static model of a prototype named the Kubang - in Indonesian *Kumbang* – after a dry wind that blows from the south or south-west on the northern coast of the island of Java. Combining the refinement of Maserati Gran Turismo cars with the SUV format that was beginning to become popular at that time was an objective the Trident was pursuing in view of a model produced in collaboration with Audi. The floorpan for which the bodywork was designed was, in fact, like the one used on Italdesign's Buran three years earlier, based on the Audi 8 and would use 4x4 transmission (which was being investigated at the same time for the new edition of the Quattroporte). The engine destined to power this innovative car was the Maserati 90° V8 from the 3200 GT, the last descendant of the Biturbo family, with fuel injection and twin turbochargers with four valves per cylinder actuated by two overhead camshafts per cylinder bank, and a power output of 368 hp at 6250 rpm. In all probability, had the project been finished and taken through to the production stage, as had been the case with the top models of the range, the Spyder and Coupé, the power unit would have been swapped for the Ferrari twin cam 4244 cc 90°V8, which was naturally aspirated and had a maximum power output of 390 hp at 7000 rpm. Giugiaro really believed in this project (for which he had coined the name "GT Wagon") but the agreement with Audi was never sealed. Maserati was obliged to update and enrich its own products by investing its resources in other directions. Therefore the Kubang was a styling exercise that went no further. It deserved better as it would have appeared before other cars that only a short time later would successfully put the same philosophy into practice: the Porsche Cayenne and BMW X6 above all.

In 2003, the Quattroporte had reached its fifth incarnation and in production terms had reached results never previously achieved, with 24,000 cars being produced in a single decade. In parallel to the company's commercial successes, the Maserati triumphed in motor sport's 2011 international SuperStars series due to the talent of its racing and test driver Andrea Bertolini.

## TECHNICAL SPECIFICATION

### ENGINE

front, longitudinal, 90° V8

| | |
|---|---|
| Bore and stroke | 4.2: mm 92 x 79.8<br>4.7 S and 4.7 Sport GT S: 94 x 84.50 mm |
| Unitary displacement | 4.2: 530.47 cc<br>4.7 S and 4.7 Sport GT S: 586.41 cc |
| Total displacement | 4.2: 4243.83 cc<br>4.7 S and 4.7 Sport GT S: 4691.42 cc |
| Valvegear | double overhead camshafts per bank |
| Number of valves | four per cylinder |
| Compression ratio | 11:1 |
| Fuel system | electronic |
| Ignition | electronic |
| Cooling | liquid, pressurised circuit |
| Lubrication | pressurised |
| Maximum power | 4.2: 400 hp at 7000 rpm<br>4.7 S: 430 hp at 7000 rpm<br>4.7 Sport GT S: 439 hp at 7000 rpm |
| Specific power output | 4.2: 94.25 hp/litre<br>4.7 S: 91.65 hp/litre<br>4.7 Sport GT S: 93.57 hp/litre |

### TRANSMISSION

| | |
|---|---|
| Driven wheels | rear |
| Clutch | single dry-plate |
| Gearbox | sequential automatic, six speeds + reverse |

### BODYWORK

*saloon, styled by Pininfarina*   four doors, five seats

### ROLLING CHASSIS

| | |
|---|---|
| Chassis | unitary construction |
| Front suspension | independent, wishbones, transverse arms, anti-roll bar electronically controlled dampers |
| Rear suspension | independent, semi-trailing arms, coil springs, anti-roll bar, electronically controlled dampers |
| Brakes | hydraulically assisted discs |
| Steering | rack and pinion |
| Fuel tank | 90 l |
| Tyres front/rear | 245-45 ZR-18 / 285-40 ZR-18 |

### DIMENSIONS AND WEIGHT

| | |
|---|---|
| Wheelbase | 3063 mm |
| Tracks front/rear | 1587 / 1560 mm |
| Length | 5052 mm (5097 restyling) |
| Width | 1895 mm |
| Height | 1438 mm |
| Dry weight | 1930 kg |
| Power to weight ratio | 4.2: 4.82 kg/hp<br>4.7 S: 4.48 kg/hp<br>4.7 Sport GT S: 4.39 kg/hp |

### PERFORMANCE AND PRODUCTION

| | |
|---|---|
| Maximum speed | 4.2: 275 kph<br>4.7 S: 280 kph<br>4.7 Sport GT S: 285 kph |
| Units produced | 24.000 |

# Quattroporte V                    2003

The Trident flagship had been produced and updated over four successive editions: 1963, 1976, 1979 and 1994. Moreover, in 1998 it had been subjected to an in-depth revision that earned it the name Quattroporte Evoluzione. When this version went out of production in 2001, the fifth series was on the drawing board and was presented at the Frankfurt Motor Show in 2003. This was clearly a model that shared only a name with its predecessors. The steel platform that constituted its underpinnings had been specially designed for the new saloon, but with characteristics of modularity and flexibility that allowed it to be sued for other models, both in-house (GranTurismo and GranCabrio) and for Alfa Romeo (8C Competizione and 8C Spider). With respect to the previous series with biturbo power, the engine was new: a 4.2-litre Ferrari V8 designed to be used with different configurations by both marques. The new unit provided the 1860-kg car with 400 hp and a top speed of 275 kph. The coachwork was designed by Pininfarina, the company that had styled the A6 1500 in 1947, the very first Maserati Grand Touring model. The saloon designed by the Turin-based stylist had simple lines that emphasised the imposing dimensions and the demands for interior space (5.052 metres long, with a wheelbase of 3.063 metres) but created a sleek, dynamic and softly harmonious whole. Over the following years the Quattroprote was offered in various special forms: Executive GT and Sport GT (2005) and Sport GT S (2007). In 2008 it was subjected to a restyling operation with a few aesthetic modifications and a 4.7-litre, 440 hp engine for the GT S version. Further limited editions models were introduced in 2008 (Collezione Cento), 2009 (Centurion Edition) and 2010 (Sport GT S Awards Edition). Between 2003 and 2012, the Quattroporte was produced in 24,000 examples and received 57 international awards.

To officially compete in the motor racing championships run by FIA, Maserati had to build a minimum number of road-going versions of the car that planned to race in the GT series. So that gave rise to the MC12 road car, the racing version of which achieved outstanding results on the circuits of the world, with overall race wins and world championships.

## TECHNICAL SPECIFICATION

### ENGINE
rear-central, longitudinal, 65° V12

| | |
|---|---|
| Bore and stroke | 92 x 75.2 mm |
| Unitary displacement | 499.89 cc |
| Total displacement | 5998.79 cc |
| Valvegear | double overhead camshafts per bank |
| Number of valves | four per cylinder |
| Compression ratio | 11.2:1 |
| Fuel system | electronic fuel injection |
| Ignition | electronic, integrated with the injection system |
| Cooling | liquid, pressurised circuit |
| Lubrication | dry sump |
| Maximum power | 630 hp at 7500 rpm |
| Specific power output | 105.02 hp/litre |

### TRANSMISSION
| | |
|---|---|
| Driven wheels | rear |
| Clutch | dual dry-plate |
| Gearbox | mechanical, six speeds + reverse |

### BODYWORK
| | |
|---|---|
| two-seater targa, Italdesign | two doors, two seats |

### ROLLING CHASSIS
| | |
|---|---|
| Chassis | monocoque in carbonfibre, composite materials and aluminium |
| Front suspension | wishbones with push-rod configuration coaxial coil springs and single setting dampers |
| Rear suspension | wishbones with push-rod configuration coaxial coil springs and single setting dampers |
| Brakes | hydraulically actuated discs |
| Steering | rack and pinion |
| Fuel tank | 115 l |
| Tyres front/rear | 245-35 ZR-19 345-35 ZR-19 |

### DIMENSIONS AND WEIGHT
| | |
|---|---|
| Wheelbase | 2800 mm |
| Tracks front/rear | 1660 / 1650 mm |
| Length | 5143 mm |
| Width | 2096 mm |
| Height | 1205 mm |
| Dry weight | 1335 kg |
| Power to weight ratio | 2.11 kg/hp |

### PERFORMANCE AND PRODUCTION
| | |
|---|---|
| Maximum speed | 300 kph |
| Units produced | 50 |

# MC12 Stradale
# 2004

Maserati's return to international competition came in 2004 with a car with "targa" bodywork (a coupé-spider with a removable roof) designed by Giugiaro and a mechanical specification developed in collaboration with Dallara: the MC12, an acronym for Maserati Corse 12 cylinders. The monocoque chassis was built in carbonfibre and composite materials, with some components in aluminium. The Ferrari-derived engine was the 65° V12 from the Enzo, with a displacement of 5998 cc and a power output of 630 hp at 7500 rpm. Installed centrally, it was developed to permit both sporting use and driving in everyday traffic. With a weight of 1335 kg, thanks to the great efficiency of the bodywork aerodynamics, the car could achieve a top speed of 300 kph, accelerate from 0 to 100 kph in 3.8 seconds and cover a kilometre from a standing start in 20.1 seconds. The car's race debut came in 2004, ahead of homologation for the FIA GT category that required the construction of 25 examples and the same number the following year. With two MC12s entered by the private team AF Corse came the first victories in Germany (Oschersleben) and China (Zhuhai). In 2005, the entire FIA GT1 championship was disputated, with Vitaphone Racing winning the team cup. Over the following years came four consecutive team titles for the Vitaphone outfit and four drivers' titles for: Michael Bartels/Andrea Bertolini (2006), Thomas Biagi (2007) and Bartels/Bertolini (2008 and 2009). In 2010 FIA GT championship earned "World" status, becoming the FIA GT1 World Series. Once again the individual and team titles went to the Maserati of Bartels/Bertolini and Vitaphone Racing. The MC12's competition record is impressive: in short, six team titles, five drivers' titles and 22 victories in the FIA GT series along with three overall victories in the Spa 24 Hours.

To mark the 75TH anniversary of Pininfarina, the celebrated Turin stylist unveiled a futuristic restyling of the most famous sporting Maserati, the Birdcage. That is the name of a new concept car created under the supervision of the then head of Pininfarina styling Lorenzo Ramaciotti. This visual result is certainly full of impact, some futuristic concepts of which will be extended to the company's entire production.

## TECHNICAL SPECIFICATION

### ENGINE

rear-central, longitudinal, 65° V12

| | |
|---|---|
| *Bore and stroke* | 92 x 75.2 mm |
| *Unitary displacement* | 499.89 cc |
| *Total displacement* | 5998.79 cc |
| *Valvegear* | double overhead camshafts per bank |
| *Number of valves* | four per cylinder |
| *Compression ratio* | 11.2:1 |
| *Fuel system* | electronic fuel injection |
| *Ignition* | electronic, integrated with the injection system |
| *Cooling* | liquid, pressurised circuit |
| *Lubrication* | dry sump |
| *Maximum power* | 700 hp at 7500 rpm |
| *Specific power output* | 116.69 hp/litre |

### TRANSMISSION

| | |
|---|---|
| *Driven wheels* | rear |
| *Clutch* | dual dry-plate |
| *Gearbox* | mechanical, six speeds + reverse |

### BODYWORK

| | |
|---|---|
| two-seater, *Pininfarina* | access via the canopy-type roof, two seats |

### ROLLING CHASSIS

| | |
|---|---|
| *Chassis* | monocoque in carbonfibre, composite materials and aluminium |
| *Front suspension* | wishbones with push-rod configuration coaxial coil springs and single setting dampers |
| *Rear suspension* | wishbones with push-rod configuration, coaxial coil springs and single setting dampers |
| *Brakes* | hydraulically actuated discs |
| *Steering* | rack and pinion |
| *Fuel tank* | 115 l |
| *Tyres front/rear* | 275-30-20 / 295-35-22 |

### DIMENSIONS AND WEIGHT

| | |
|---|---|
| *Wheelbase* | 2800 mm |
| *Tracks front/rear* | 1660 / 1650 mm |
| *Length* | 5143 mm |
| *Width* | 2096 mm |
| *Height* | 1205 mm |
| *Dry weight* | around 1500 kg |
| *Power to weight ratio* | around 2.14 kg/hp |

### PERFORMANCE AND PRODUCTION

| | |
|---|---|
| *Maximum speed* | 350 kph |
| *Units produced* | 1 |

# Birdcage 75ᵀᴴ Pininfarina                    2005

In order to celebrate the marque's 75ᵀᴴ anniversary, Pininfarina came up with a concept car of great emotive impact that was presented at the Geneva Motor Show. The Birdcage name reprised that of a classic Maserati from the 1960s, while the chassis and mechanicals were all Maserati with a carbonfibre monocoque and the 12-cylinder six-litre engine from the MC12 GT1 (derived from that of the Ferrari Enzo, 700 hp at 7500 rpm, 300 kph). The coachwork was futuristic yet still managed to reference styling masterpieces from the past and was the fruit of six months work by a five-man team: Lorenzo Ramaciotti, head of styling at Pininfarina (who was to leave the company after 20 years on the launch of the Birdcage), Lowie Vermeersch, who was to take his place, the creative director Ken Okuyama and the chief designers Jason Castriota and Giuseppe Randazzo. Ramaciotti described the Birdcage 75ᵀᴴ project in his own words: "It's a tribute, like the Mythos was, to the visionary prototypes of the great Italian coachbuilding era, between 1965 and 1972, when every show would see the presentation of something that pushed the boundaries of research and dated what had thrilled us at the previous show. In the Birdcage 75ᵀᴴ the Maserati character is represented by the voluminous wings applied to the slim central body, traversed by a transparent band. The cockpit aperture is a clear reference to the 512 S and Modulo prototypes. The ring-form front and rear lighting clusters and the design of the wheels foreshadowed shapes and graphics later defined for the GranTurismo coupé (2007) and the shape of the air intake was inspired by the Ghibli." The interior featured an innovative interactive communication system between vehicle and user developed by Motorola, with the dashboard, controls and instrument panel replaced with a projection on a transparent panel. The Birdcage 75ᵀᴴ was judged, as the Mythos had been in 1989, as the most attractive concept car presented that year.

The MC12 Corsa was highly unusual in that it was neither homologated for competition nor road use and could only be driven in unofficial races between clients eager to give free rein to their sporting instincts. Derived from the MC12 Stradale (which despite the name, collected world GT titles), it was even more powerful: 755 hp against 630. 15 examples were constructed between 2006 and 2007, 12 being sold at 1 million Euros and three used for testing and promotional purposes..

## TECHNICAL SPECIFICATION

### ENGINE

rear-central, longitudinal, 65° V12

| | |
|---|---|
| Bore and stroke | 92 x 75.2 mm |
| Unitary displacement | 499.89 cc |
| Total displacement | 5998.79 cc |
| Valvegear | double overhead camshafts per bank |
| Number of valves | four per cylinder |
| Compression ratio | 11.2:1 |
| Fuel system | electronic fuel injection |
| Ignition | electronic, integrated with the injection system |
| Cooling | liquid, pressurised circuit |
| Lubrication | dry sump |
| Maximum power | 755 hp at 8000 rpm |
| Specific power output | 125.85 hp/litre |

### TRANSMISSION

| | |
|---|---|
| Driven wheels | rear |
| Clutch | dual dry-plate |
| Gearbox | Electrically actuated Cambio-corsa, six speed + reverse |

### BODYWORK

| | |
|---|---|
| two-seater targa, Italdesign | two doors, two seats |

### ROLLING CHASSIS

| | |
|---|---|
| Chassis | monocoque in carbonfibre, composite materials and aluminium |
| Front suspension | wishbones with push-rod configuration coaxial coil springs and single setting dampers |
| Rear suspension | wishbones with push-rod configuration, coaxial coil springs and single setting dampers |
| Brakes | hydraulically actuated discs |
| Steering | rack and pinion |
| Fuel tank | 115 l |
| Tyres front/rear | 650-325-18 705-325-18 |

### DIMENSIONS AND WEIGHT

| | |
|---|---|
| Wheelbase | 2800 mm |
| Tracks front/rear | 1660 / 1650 mm |
| Length | 5143 mm |
| Width | 2096 mm |
| Height | 1205 mm |
| Dry weight | 1150 kg |
| Power to weight ratio | 1.52 kg/hp |

### PERFORMANCE AND PRODUCTION

| | |
|---|---|
| Maximum speed | 330 kph |
| Units produced | 15 |

# MC12 Corsa
# 2006

Maserati constructed a remarkable car in 15 examples between 2006 and 2007. Named as the MC12 Corsa, it clearly derived from the MC12 Stradale but was homologated for neither racing nor road use: it could only be driven on the track in unofficial races amongst clients eager to satisfy their passion for speed away from the traffic. For this reason the car has been compared to the Ferrari FXX, another competition model associated with another car and not homologated for road use although, for the record, the Ferrari FXX was also used for testing new technologies and recording telemetric statistics. The mechanical configuration was the same as that of the MC12 GT1, with the six-cylinder 65° V12 engine of Ferrari derivation but lacking the flange on the intake manifold (imposed by the regulations for the FIA GT championship), hence with a compression ratio of 11.2:1 it developed a maximum power output of 755 hp at 8000 rpm, 125 hp more than the 630 of the Stradale. Installed in a rear-central location, it was naturally aspirated, with four valves per cylinder actuated by double overhead camshafts per bank and dry sump lubrication. The gearbox, mounted in-unit with the differential, was a semi-automatic, six-speed Maserati Cambiocorsa. The braking system in steel and carbonfibre was of competition specification and therefore lacking ABS. The coupé-spider bodywork designed by Giugiaro was also that of the MC12 Stradale, with a targa-style removable roof. With a weight of 1150 kg, it could reach a top speed of 330 kph. At a price of around 1 million Euros, 12 examples were sold to clients who participated in track days at which Maserati was responsible for maintenance. A further three cars were reserved for testing and advertising initiatives.

The spectacular GranTurismo, which was introduced in 2007, is more than ever a child of its time, a time in rapid evolution. The first version was powered by a Ferrari-derived engine, a 4.2-litre 8-cylinder. Soon afterwards, out came the S version with an engine that was almost 4.7-litres, the same as the one installed in the Alfa Romeo 8C Competizione.

## TECHNICAL SPECIFICATION

### ENGINE
front, longitudinal, 90° V8

| | |
|---|---|
| Bore and stroke | 92 x 79.8 mm<br>Gran Turismo Sport: 94 x 84.50 mm |
| Unitary displacement | 530.48 cc<br>Gran Turismo Sport: 586.41 mm |
| Total displacement | 4243.84 cc<br>Gran Turismo Sport: 4691.28 cc |
| Valvegear | double overhead camshafts per bank |
| Number of valves | four per cylinder |
| Compression ratio | 11.1:1 |
| Fuel system | electronic fuel injection |
| Ignition | electronic |
| Cooling | liquid, pressurised circuit |
| Lubrication | pressurised, with delivery pump |
| Maximum power | 405 hp at 7100 rpm<br>Gran Turismo S: 440 hp<br>Gran Turismo Sport: 460 hp at 7000 rpm |
| Specific power output | 95.43 hp/litre<br>Gran Turismo S: 103.67 hp/litre<br>Gran Turismo Sport: 98.06 hp/litre |

### TRANSMISSION
| | |
|---|---|
| Driven wheels | rear |
| Clutch | single dry-plate |
| Gearbox | six speeds + reverse<br>ZF automatic or DuoSelect robotized system |

### BODYWORK
| | |
|---|---|
| Pininfarina coupé | two doors, 2+2 seats |

### ROLLING CHASSIS
| | |
|---|---|
| Chassis | unitary construction |
| Front suspension | independent, coil springs anti-roll bar electronically controlled hydraulic dampers |
| Rear suspension | independent, trailing arms, coil springs, anti-roll bar, electronically controlled hydraulic dampers |
| Brakes | hydraulically assisted discs |
| Steering | rack and pinion |
| Fuel tank | 86 l |
| Tyres front/rear | 245-40 R-19 / 285-40 R-19<br>Gran Turismo Sport: 245-35 R-20 / 285/35 R-20 |

### DIMENSIONS AND WEIGHT
| | |
|---|---|
| Wheelbase | 2942 mm |
| Tracks front/rear | 1586 / 1590 mm |
| Length | 4881 mm |
| Width | 1847 mm |
| Height | 1353 mm |
| Dry weight | 1880 / 1780 kg |
| Power to weight ratio | 4.67 /4.39 / 4.27 kg/hp |

### PERFORMANCE AND PRODUCTION
| | |
|---|---|
| Maximum speed | 285 kph<br>Gran Turismo S: 295 kph<br>Gran Turismo Sport: 300 kph |
| Units produced | – |

# GranTurismo – GT – S – Sport 2007

The expansion of the range reached a particularly significant stage with the presentation at the Geneva Motor Show of 2007 of a new version of the coupé, a car in which Maserati believed to the point of giving it what might have been seen as a generic name – GranTurismo – but which actually defined it as "the" GT par excellence. The mechanical underpinnings were the platform of the fifth series Quattroporte (2003) with the same 4.2-litre 90° V8 engine of Ferrari origins, with a block in aluminium and silicon, mated to a ZF six-speed automatic gearbox with a torque converter or a DuoSelect robotized box, again with six speeds. This naturally aspirated unit with four valves per cylinder actuated by double overhead camshafts per bank developed a maximum power output of 405 hp at 7100 rpm, capable of propelling the car weighing 1880 kg to a maximum speed of 285 kph and accelerating from 0 to 100 kph in 5.2 seconds. The magnificent Pininfarina-designed bodywork caught the eye with its wedge-shaped profile and a glasshouse set between the wheelarches, the large bonnet and the triangular C-pillar that merged into a small boot: the overall effect subtley referenced the shapes of the racing Maseratis from the 1960s as well as the recent Birdcage 75th. The spacious four-seater interior provided particularly sophisticated elegance and comfort. 2008 saw the launch of a significantly more sporting version, the GranTurismo S, powered by the same 4.7-litre, 90° V8 engine as the Alfa Romeo 8C Competizione with a power output of 440 hp and even stronger performance: a maximum speed of 298 kph, acceleration from 0 to 100 kph in 4.9 seconds. The GranTurismo S was replaced in 2012 by the GranTurismo Sport characterised by minor styling revisions and a more powerful engine (460 hp), a top speed of 300 kph and acceleration from 0 to 100 kph in 4.7 seconds.

Two years after the introduction of the GranTurismo, Maserati brought out an elegant and lively open version of the car. The name was transformed into Gran-Cabrio, so it was a roomy 2+2 cabriolet. Like all the latest generation Maseratis, the new car benefitted from all kinds of electronic driving assistance, permitting the driver to be at the wheel in full safety and at the limit.

## TECHNICAL SPECIFICATION

### ENGINE

front, longitudinal, 90° V8

| | |
|---|---|
| *Bore and stroke* | 92 x 79.8 mm<br>GranCabrio S: 94x 84.5 mm |
| *Unitary displacement* | 530.48 cc<br>GranCabrio S: 586.41 cc |
| *Total displacement* | 4243.84 cc<br>GranCabrio S: 4691.28 cc |
| *Valvegear* | double overhead camshafts per bank |
| *Number of valves* | four per cylinder |
| *Compression ratio* | 11.1:1 |
| *Fuel system* | electronic fuel injection |
| *Ignition* | electronic |
| *Cooling* | liquid, pressurised circuit |
| *Lubrication* | pressurised, with delivery pump |
| *Maximum power* | 430 hp at 7000 rpm<br>GranCabrio S: 450 hp at 7000 rpm |
| *Specific power output* | 101.32 hp/litre<br>GranCabrio S: 95.92 cc |

### TRANSMISSION

| | |
|---|---|
| *Driven wheels* | rear |
| *Clutch* | single dry-plate |
| *Gearbox* | sequential automatic, six speeds + reverse |

### BODYWORK

| | |
|---|---|
| *Maserati style cabriolet* | two doors, 2+2 seats |

### ROLLING CHASSIS

| | |
|---|---|
| *Chassis* | unitary construction |
| *Front suspension* | independent, coil springs anti-roll bar single-setting steel dampers |
| *Rear suspension* | independent, trailing arms, coil springs, anti-roll bar, single-setting steel dampers |
| *Brakes* | hydraulically assisted discs |
| *Steering* | rack and pinion |
| *Fuel tank* | 75 l |
| *Tyres front/rear* | 245-35 ZR-20 / 285-35 ZR-20 |

### DIMENSIONS AND WEIGHT

| | |
|---|---|
| *Wheelbase* | 2942 mm |
| *Tracks front/rear* | 1586 / 1590 mm |
| *Length* | 4881 mm |
| *Width* | 2056 mm |
| *Height* | 1353 mm |
| *Dry weight* | 1887 kg |
| *Power to weight ratio* | 4.38 kg/hp (Cambiocorsa 4.70)<br>GranCabrio S: 4.19 kg/hp |

### PERFORMANCE AND PRODUCTION

| | |
|---|---|
| *Maximum speed* | 283 kph<br>GranCabrio S: 285 kph |
| *Units produced* | – |

# GranCabrio                    2009

As per the consolidated tradition, two years after the presentation of the Gran-Turismo coupé the 2009 Frankfurt Motor Show saw the launch of the open-top version named the GranCabrio. This was not so much a spider, but as the name suggested a cabriolet that retained the comfortable four-seater configuration, a quality among those that had decreed the success of the coupé that was by no means negligible. The wheelbase of 2942 cm was in fact retained, a decision that required major reinforcement of the substantially modified bodyshell to ensure the necessary torsional and flexural rigidity. The bodywork instead adapted well to the conversion, retaining the sleek lines and overall compactness that disguised the almost fives metres length of the car. The multi-layer fabric hood had already been successfully employed on the Spyder and folded electrically into the boot in just 28 seconds at speeds of up to 30 kph. Interior space was reduced slightly by the presence of the hood compartment yet there was still room for four occupants who enjoyed the same fittings, luxury and comfort as in the coupé. Initially powered by the 4.2-litre, 430 hp V8 from the Spyder and Coupé GT, the car was subsequently fitted with the 4.7-litre, 450 hp version in S trim that provided a top speed of 285 kph and acceleration from 0 to 100 kph in 5.2 seconds. Among the safety features fitted to the car was the Maserati Stability Programme, an electronic stability control system capable of correcting slides by reducing engine torque and operating in a fully integrated manner with the ABS and the EBD brake bias systems. The GranCabrio was exported to the United States as the Maserati GranTurismo Convertible given that the term cabrio is rarely used on the other side of the Atlantic.

Kubang - the name is the same as eight years earlier as was the attempt to offer a car to join the ever-expanding SUV high range market segment. But the project, created in the Maserati Styling Centre under the supervision of Lorenzo Rama-ciotti, once again remained just a styling exercise which was neither produced nor sold on a vast scale.

## TECHNICAL SPECIFICATION

### ENGINE
front, longitudinal, 90° V8

| | |
|---|---|
| Bore and stroke | 92 x 79.8 mm |
| Unitary displacement | 530.48 cc |
| Total displacement | 4243.84 cc |
| Valvegear | double overhead camshafts per bank |
| Number of valves | four per cylinder |
| Compression ratio | – |
| Fuel system | electronic fuel injection |
| Ignition | electronic |
| Cooling | liquid, pressurised circuit |
| Lubrication | pressurised, with delivery pump |
| Maximum power | 390 hp at 7000 rpm |
| Specific power output | 91.89 hp/litre |

### TRANSMISSION
| | |
|---|---|
| Driven wheels | permanent four-wheel drive with torque control |
| Clutch | dual disc with electronic control |
| Gearbox | sequential automatic, eight speeds + reverse |

### BODYWORK
| | |
|---|---|
| GT wagon, Maserati style | five doors, five seats |

### ROLLING CHASSIS
| | |
|---|---|
| Chassis | unitary construction |
| Front suspension | independent, coil springs anti-roll bar, single-setting steel dampers |
| Rear suspension | independent, trailing arms, coil springs, anti-roll bar, single-setting steel dampers |
| Brakes | hydraulically assisted discs |
| Steering | rack and pinion |
| Fuel tank | – |
| Tyres front/rear | – |

### DIMENSIONS AND WEIGHT
| | |
|---|---|
| Wheelbase | – |
| Tracks front/rear | – |
| Length | 4984 mm |
| Width | 1942 mm |
| Height | 1650 mm |
| Dry weight | – |
| Power to weight ratio | – |

### PERFORMANCE AND PRODUCTION
| | |
|---|---|
| Maximum speed | 255 kph |
| Units produced | 2 |

# Kubang Centro Stile Maserati     2011

The name Kubang, derived from that of a wind blowing across the island of Java and used for the prototype realised by Giugiaro in collaboration with Maserati in 2003, was reprised eight years later to identify another concept car, presented at the Frankfurt Motor Show but sharing little or nothing with the earlier model. The repetition of the name was due in part to a desire to recall that Maserati had been the first company to propose the sports crossover formula then successfully taken up by other constructors. Over the following years many things changed, from the end of the collaboration between Maserati and Italdesign (which then came within the Volkswagen orbit) to the acquisition of Chrysler by the Fiat Group, which brought new resources and opportunities for synergy and opened up vast potential for expansion on the North American market. The new Kubang project was based on the Jeep Grand Cherokee platform to which the Maserati Styling Centre under the direction of Lorenzo Ramaciotti added a highly original body characterised by a large front grille onto which converged muscular shapes that were disguised by fluid fairings and soft, attractive curves that previewed the styling motifs that were to the Trident's cars distinguish about to be launched on the market: the references to the Quattroporte (the treatment of the flanks and the lateral glazing) and the Ghibli (front lighting clusters, the general configuration of the rear end and the dashboard) were to become clear a couple of years later. In the wake of considerable polemics there was also a change of direction regarding the platform destined to form the basis of the future heir to the Kubang, the Levante SUV: not that of the Jeep Cherokee, but rather that of the Ghibli. The engine was being designed by the Fiat Group's Powertrain division, under the direction of Paolo Martinelli and the project provided for its assembly by Ferrari at Maranello.

With this model, the Quattroporte reached its sixth generation. New mechanics, a new 8-cylinder engine, an 8-speed gearbox and the opportunity to have four-wheel drive were its strong points. Likewise the car's new styling content, which were once again developed under the direction of Lorenzo Ramaciotti.

## TECHNICAL SPECIFICATION

### ENGINE

| | |
|---|---|
| front, longitudinal | 3.0 Biturbo, Biturbo S, Biturbo S Q4: 60° V6 3.8 Biturbo GTS: 90° V8 3.0 Diesel 250 and 275: 60° V6 |
| Bore and stroke | 3.0 Biturbo, Biturbo S, Biturbo S Q4: 86.5 x 84.5 mm / 3.8 Biturbo GTS: 86.5 x 80.8 mm / 3.0 Diesel 250 and 275: 83 x 92 mm |
| Unitary displacement | 3.0 Biturbo, Biturbo S, Biturbo S Q4: 496.56 mm 3.8 Biturbo GTS: 474.82 cc 3.0 Diesel 250 and 275: 497.77 cc |
| Total displacement | 3.0 Biturbo, Biturbo S, Biturbo S Q4: 2979.40 mm 3.8 Biturbo GTS: 3798.59 cc 3.0 Diesel 250 and 275: 2986.65 cc |
| Valvegear | double overhead camshafts per bank |
| Number of valves | four per cylinder |
| Compression ratio | 9.5: 1 (Diesel: 16.5:1) |
| Fuel system | electronic direct fuel injection two turbochargers |
| Ignition | electronic |
| Cooling | liquid, pressurised circuit |
| Lubrication | pressurised |
| Maximum power | 3.0 Biturbo: 330 hp / 3.0 Biturbo S: 410 hp / 3.0 Biturbo Q4: 410 hp / 3.8 Biturbo GTS: 530 hp at 6500 rpm / 3.0 Diesel 250: 250 hp / 3.0 Diesel 275: 275 hp |
| Specific power output | 3.0 Biturbo: 110.76 hp/litre / 3.0 Biturbo S: 137.61 hp/litre / 3.0 Biturbo Q4: 137.61 hp/litre / 3.8 Biturbo GTS: 139.52 hp/litre / 3.0 Diesel 250: 83.7 hp/litre / 3.0 Diesel 275: 92.07 hp/litre |

### TRANSMISSION

| | |
|---|---|
| Driven wheels | rear |
| Clutch | multiple disc with electronic control |
| Gearbox | ZF automatic eight speeds + reverse |

### BODYWORK

| | |
|---|---|
| saloon, Maserati styling | four doors, five seats |

### ROLLING CHASSIS

| | |
|---|---|
| Chassis | unitary construction |
| Front suspension | independent, double wishbones, continuously variable electronically controlled damping |
| Rear suspension | independent, multilink with five arms continuously variable electronically controlled damping |
| Brakes | hydraulically assisted discs |
| Steering | rack and pinion |
| Fuel tank | 80 l |
| Tyres front/rear | 245-40 R-20 / 285-35 R-20 |

### DIMENSIONS AND WEIGHT

| | |
|---|---|
| Wheelbase | 3171 mm |
| Tracks front/rear | 1634 / 1647 mm |
| Length | 5260 mm |
| Width | 1948 mm |
| Height | 1481 mm |
| Dry weight | 1900 kg |
| Power to weight ratio | 3.0 Biturbo: 5.75 kg/hp / 3.0 Biturbo S: 4.63 kg/hp / 3.0 Biturbo Q4: 4.63 hp / 3.8 Biturbo GTS: 3.58 kg/hp / 3.0 Diesel 250: 7.6 kg/hp / 3.0 Diesel 275: 6.9 kg/hp |

### PERFORMANCE AND PRODUCTION

| | |
|---|---|
| Maximum speed | 3.0 Biturbo: 263 kph / 3.0 Biturbo S: 285 kph / 3.0 Biturbo Q4: 283 kph / 3.8 Biturbo GTS: 307 kph / 3.0 Diesel 250: 240 kph / 3.0 Diesel 275: 250 kph |
| Units produced | – |

# Quattroporte VI                    2013

The sixth series of the Maserati flagship was announced in the November of 2012 with a virtual presentation and the opening of a dedicated web site and shown in the flesh at the Detroit Motor Show in the January of 2013, the year it went into production. Completely revised with respect to the preceding model, the sixth series Quattroporte was realised on a new dedicated floorpan that provided for the installation of six types of engine, four petrol units and two diesels (also new designs) as well as two- and four-wheel drive. The bodywork designed by the newly created Maserati Centro Stile, under the direction of Marco Tencone and the supervision of Lorenzo Ramaciotti, was inspired by the canons of harmony and simplicity, with certain stylistic references to the Kubang presented two years earlier that could be seen in the treatment of the flanks and, more in general, a family feeling that led back to the refined and exclusive latest generation Maseratis. The car was 5260 mm long, 208 mm more than the Quattroporte V but, thanks to the extensive use of aluminium in the bodyshell, its weight had been reduced by almost 100 kg, from 1990 to 1900 kg. Drag was also reduced by 20% and fuel consumption by a similar proportion. The most powerful engine, realised like all the others in collaboration with Ferrari and built at Maranello, was a 3.8-litre 90° V8 biturbo fitted to the most extreme version, the GTS, where it developed 530 hp and made the Quattroporte the world's fastest saloon: maximum speed of 307 kph, acceleration from 0-100 kph in 4.7 seconds. This version was flanked by three 3.0-litre, six-cylinder biturbo models: the S (410 hp, 285 kph), the Q4, with four-wheel drive (410 hp, 246 kph) and one detuned to 330 hp (263 kph) reserved for the Chinese market. The range was completed with two diesel versions with 3.0-litre, six-cylinder biturbo engines producing 250 and 275 hp (240 and 250 kph respectively).

In 2013, the name Ghibli became fashionable again, the name of the iconic coupé that first made its appearance during the '60s. This time, the name was adopted by a saloon of undoubted fascination which was immediately well received, literally becoming one of the marque's biggest sellers. The car completed the company's range, which also included the GranTurismo, GranCabrio and the Quattroporte.

## TECHNICAL SPECIFICATION

### ENGINE

| | |
|---|---|
| front, longitudinal | Ghibli, Ghibli S, Ghibli S Q4 Diesel 250 and 275: 60° V6 |
| Bore and stroke | Ghibli, Ghibli S, Ghibli S Q4: 86.5 x 84.5 mm Diesel 250 and 275: 83 x 92 mm |
| Unitary displacement | Ghibli, Ghibli S, Ghibli S Q4: 496.56 cc Diesel 250 and 275: 497.77 cc |
| Total displacement | Ghibli, Ghibli S, Ghibli S Q4: 2979.40 cc Diesel 250 and 275: 2986.65 cc |
| Valvegear | double overhead camshafts per bank |
| Number of valves | four per cylinder |
| Compression ratio | 9.5: 1 (diesel: 16.5:1) |
| Fuel system | electronic direct fuel injection two turbochargers |
| Ignition | electronic |
| Cooling | liquid, pressurised circuit |
| Lubrication | pressurised |
| Maximum power | Ghibli: 330 hp Ghibli S: 410 hp Ghibli S Q4: 410 hp Diesel 250: 250 hp Diesel 275: 275 hp |
| Specific power output | Ghibli: 110.76 hp/litre Ghibli S: 137.61 hp/litre Ghibli S Q4: 137.61 hp/litre Diesel 250: 83.70 hp/litre Diesel 275: 92.07 hp/litre |

### TRANSMISSION

| | |
|---|---|
| Driven wheels | rear (Ghibli S Q4: four-wheel drive) |
| Clutch | multiple disc with electronic control |
| Gearbox | ZF automatic eight speeds + reverse |

### BODYWORK

| | |
|---|---|
| saloon, Maserati styling | four doors, five seats |

### ROLLING CHASSIS

| | |
|---|---|
| Chassis | unitary construction |
| Front suspension | independent, double wishbones, continuously variable electronically controlled damping |
| Rear suspension | independent, multilink with five arms continuously variable electronically controlled damping |
| Brakes | hydraulically assisted discs |
| Steering | rack and pinion |
| Fuel tank | 80 l |
| Tyres front/rear | 235-50 R-18 / 275-45 R-18 |

### DIMENSIONS AND WEIGHT

| | |
|---|---|
| Wheelbase | 2998 mm |
| Tracks front/rear | 1635 / 1653 mm |
| Length | 4971 mm |
| Width | 1945 mm |
| Height | 1461 mm |
| Dry weight | 1810 kg |
| Power to weight ratio | Ghibli: 5.48 kg/hp Ghibli S: 4.41 kg/hp Ghibli S Q4: 4.41 kg/hp 3.8 Biturbo GTS: 3.58 kg/hp 3.0 Diesel 250: 7.24 kg/hp 3.0 Diesel 275: 6.58 kg/hp |

### PERFORMANCE AND PRODUCTION

| | |
|---|---|
| Maximum speed | Ghibli: 263 kph Ghibli S: 285 kph Ghibli S Q4: 284 kph Diesel 250: 240 kph Diesel 275: 250 kph |
| Units produced | – |

# Ghibli 2013

In the April of 2013, the Shanghai Motor Show was the setting for the presentation of a new saloon to flank the Quattroporte VI series launched in Detroit three months earlier. The new car was named the Ghibli, in honour of unforgotten glories. However, this was no longer the coupé of the past, seductive but produced in numbers no longer sufficient to meet the ambitions of the Trident marque, which was now looking at totals of between 10,000 and 50,000 cars a year. Almost five metres long, with four doors and room for five occupants, the new Ghibli represented a proud challenge to the top of the range models from the German manufacturers. The front end was aggressive with the trapezoidal grille and long bonnet with the classic Maserati V panel lines. The typically set-back upper body united the front with the high, short tail with the boot-lid tipped by a slight aerodynamic spoiler. The interior offered an environment that in contrast with the rarefied atmosphere of the Quattroporte was characterised by the snug contours of a "car to be driven" as was written. A choice of three petrol and two diesel engines was offered: the S version, fitted with a 3.0-litre, 60° V6 biturbo producing 410 CV and capable of 285 kph, with acceleration from 0 to 100 kph in 5.0 seconds, the S Q4, with four-wheel drive, which with the same power output (but weighing 1870 instead of 1810 kg) could reach 284 kph and accelerated from 0 to 100 kph in 4.8 seconds and a detuned version with 330 hp (263 kph) reserved for the Chinese market, as with the Quattroporte. The 3.0-litre V6 biturbo diesel engines had power outputs of 250 and 275 hp and provided maximum speeds of 240 and 250 kph respectively. All engines were mated to an eight-speed ZF automatic gearbox that allowed manual selection of gears through the so-called "sequential function".

One hundred years after the foundation of Officine Maserati, in Viale Ciro Menotti in Moderna, during which various people and groups have followed each other as the owners during that century, founder Alfieri Maserati is not forgotten. His memory has been honoured by a superb 2+2 coupé prototype, which will not go into production.

## TECHNICAL SPECIFICATION

### ENGINE
front, longitudinal, 90° V8

| | |
|---|---|
| Bore and stroke | 94 x 84.50 mm |
| Unitary displacement | 586.41 cc |
| Total displacement | 4691.28 cc |
| Valvegear | double overhead camshafts per bank |
| Number of valves | four per cylinder |
| Compression ratio | 11.1:1 |
| Fuel system | electronic fuel injection |
| Ignition | electronic |
| Cooling | liquid, pressurised circuit |
| Lubrication | pressurised, with delivery pump |
| Maximum power | 460 hp at 7000 rpm |
| Specific power output | 98.05 hp/litre |

### TRANSMISSION
| | |
|---|---|
| Driven wheels | rear |
| Clutch | single dry-plate |
| Gearbox | MC Shift sequential automatic, six speeds + reverse |

### BODYWORK
| | |
|---|---|
| coupé, Maserati styling | two doors, 2+2 seats |

### ROLLING CHASSIS
| | |
|---|---|
| Chassis | unitary construction |
| Front suspension | independent, wishbones telescopic struts, oblique arms anti-roll bar, electronically controlled damping |
| Rear suspension | independent, semi-trailing arms, coil springs, anti-roll bar, electronically controlled damping |
| Brakes | hydraulically assisted discs |
| Steering | rack and pinion |
| Fuel tank | – |
| Tyres front/rear | – / – |

### DIMENSIONS AND WEIGHT
| | |
|---|---|
| Wheelbase | 2700 mm |
| Tracks front/rear | mm – / – |
| Length | 4590 mm |
| Width | 1930 mm |
| Height | 1280 mm |
| Dry weight | – |
| Power to weight ratio | – |

### PERFORMANCE AND PRODUCTION
| | |
|---|---|
| Maximum speed | – |
| Units produced | 1 |

# Alfieri Centro Stile Maserati 2014

In the year in which the centenary of the foundation of Maserati was celebrated, the company presented a very special concept car at the Geneva Motor Show. Realised in part to preview future developments from the company, it was named Alfieri after the founder of Officine Maserati in 1914. The car is a 2+2 coupé with overtly sporting styling and character. Designed at the Maserati Styling Centre in Turin, under the guidance of Marco Tencone and with the supervision of Lorenzo Ramaciotti, the Alfieri proposed an extreme interpretation of the "Italian-style GT" theme and was placed in a very different segment to the GranTurismo production model. The very aggressive, spare coachwork presented a wide, low front end ahead of a bonnet that defined the traditional relief V and muscular flanks topped by a glasshouse that merged into a very compact tail. The interior, described by the constructor as inspired by "simplicity and minimalism" transmitted sensations of comfort and above all a sporting not to say racing atmosphere. Constructed on the chassis of the GranTurismo Sport, it was no less than 24 cm shorter. The mechanical organs were borrowed from the same model, with the Ferrari-derived, naturally aspirated, 4.7-litre, 90° V8 with an aluminium and silicon block producing 460 hp at 7000 rpm, mated to an MC Shift electrically actuated six-speed sequential gearbox mounted in a transaxle layout in-unit with the differential. Production is planned to start in 2017 and a later spider version is likely, along with new mechanical options such as a V6 biturbo engine and four-wheel drive. In 2014 the Alfieri was awarded in Geneva the prestigious "Concept Car of the Year" prize and the "Design Award for Concept Cars & Prototypes" at the Villa d'Este Concours d'Elegance.

After two attempts with the Kubang which didn't bear fruit, Maserati could well go to the market with a luxury SUV in 2016. Levante, the umpteenth name of a type of wind, is the challenge of the future for the Trident which, in production terms, is now being produced in tens of thousands per year. The vehicle has various engines, including the historic marque's first diesel, which was in the Quattroporte VI of 2013.

TECHNICAL SPECIFICATION  HYPOTHETICAL SPECIFICATIONS BASED ON THOSE OF THE KUBANG PROTOTYPE FROM 2011

### ENGINE
front, longitudinal, 90° V8

| | |
|---|---|
| Bore and stroke | 92 x 79.8 mm |
| Unitary displacement | 530.48 cc |
| Total displacement | 4243.84 cc |
| Valvegear | double overhead camshafts per bank |
| Number of valves | four per cylinder |
| Compression ratio | – |
| Fuel system | electronic fuel injection |
| Ignition | electronic |
| Cooling | liquid, pressurised circuit |
| Lubrication | pressurised, with delivery pump |
| Maximum power | 390 hp at 7000 rpm |
| Specific power output | 91.89 hp/litre |

### TRANSMISSION
| | |
|---|---|
| Driven wheels | permanent four-wheel drive with torque control |
| Clutch | dual disc with electronic control |
| Gearbox | sequential automatic, eight speeds + reverse |

### BODYWORK
| | |
|---|---|
| GT wagon, Maserati styling | five doors, five seats |

### ROLLING CHASSIS
| | |
|---|---|
| Chassis | unitary construction |
| Front suspension | independent, coil springs anti-roll bar, single-setting steel dampers |
| Rear suspension | independent, trailing arms, coil springs, anti-roll bar, single-setting steel dampers |
| Brakes | hydraulically assisted discs |
| Steering | rack and pinion |
| Fuel tank | – |
| Tyres front/rear | – |

### DIMENSIONS AND WEIGHT
| | |
|---|---|
| Wheelbase | – |
| Tracks front/rear | – |
| Length | 4984 mm |
| Width | 1942 mm |
| Height | 1650 mm |
| Dry weight | – |
| Power to weight ratio | – |

### PERFORMANCE AND PRODUCTION
| | |
|---|---|
| Maximum speed | 255 kph |
| Units produced | – |

# Levante                                      2016

As this book goes to press, what is known about the Maserati Levante is the fruit of journalistic indiscretions and photographs taken of camouflaged prototypes spotted during road testing. It is known that the car's debut is scheduled for the Detroit Motor Show in 2016 with production and then marketing beginning in the March of that year; a base price of around 70,000 has been suggested. This luxury SUV is destined to compete directly with the segment leaders, the BMW X6, the Mercedes-Benz GL Coupé and the Porsche Cayenne. The bodywork, designed as has become the norm, by the Maserati Styling Centre, will be inspired by that of the Kubang prototype presented at Frankfurt in 2011, with styling references to the Alfieri, the concept car seen at the Geneva Show in 2014. Developed on the Ghibli platform, it be offered was to exclusively with Q4 four-wheel drive and the eight-speed automatic gearbox. Maserati is likely to offer six engine options – which also power the various Quattroporte and Ghibli versions: The first three will be the 3.0-litre, 60° V6 biturbo (realised like all the other latest generation power units in collaboration with Ferrari) in 350 and 425 hp versions and the 3.8-litre, 90° V8 biturbo (the 590 hp engine from the Ferrari California T). The diesel versions will be the 3.0-litre V6 in 250 and 275 hp units along with a new 340 hp biturbo currently on the drawing board. The Trident's new crossover will have an exceptionally important mission for the Maserati marque that is focussing on increasing production and expanding its presence on the overseas markets, particularly those of the United States and China. By 2018, the company aims to be constructing 75,000 cars a year, with 50% represented by the Levante model.

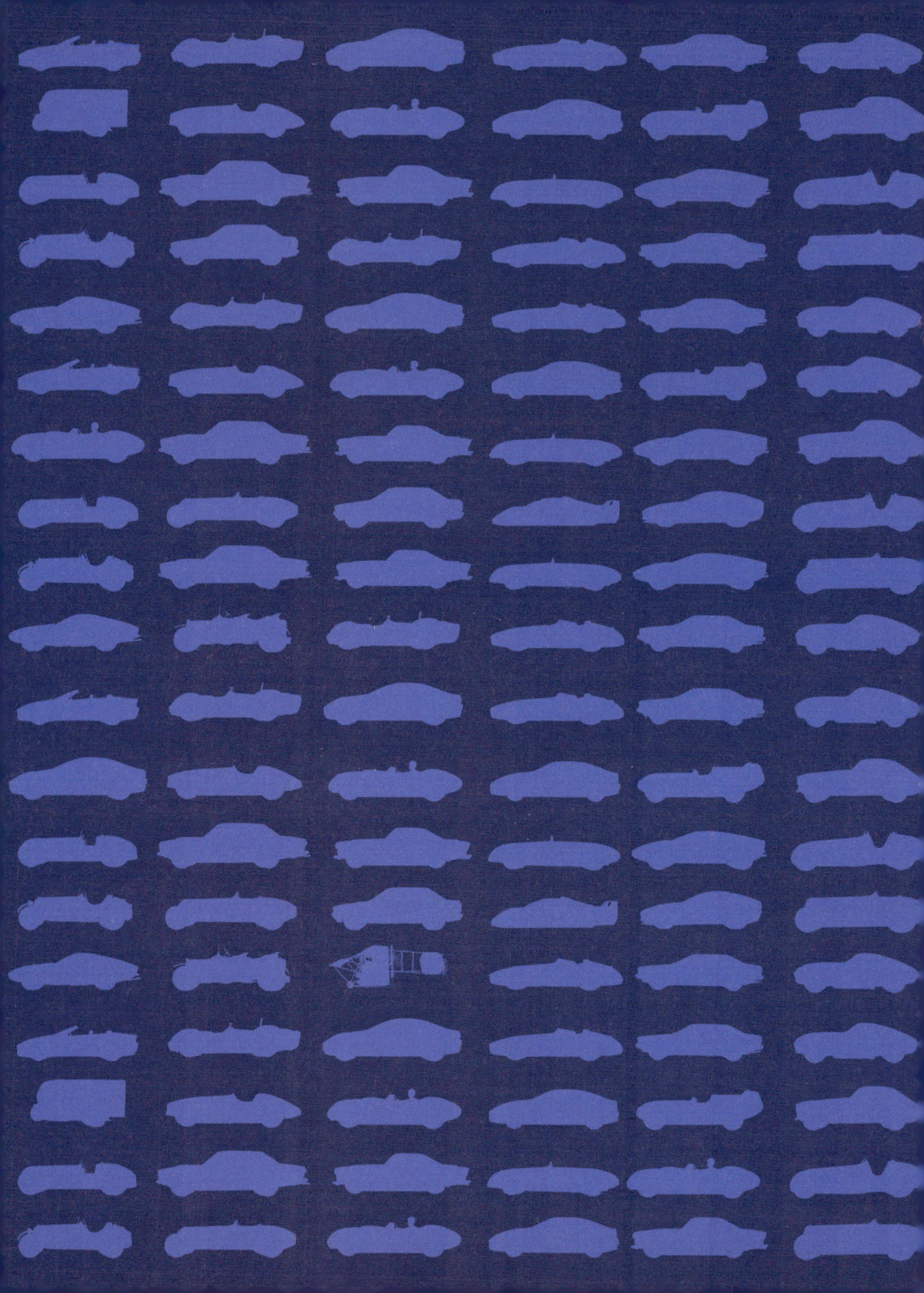

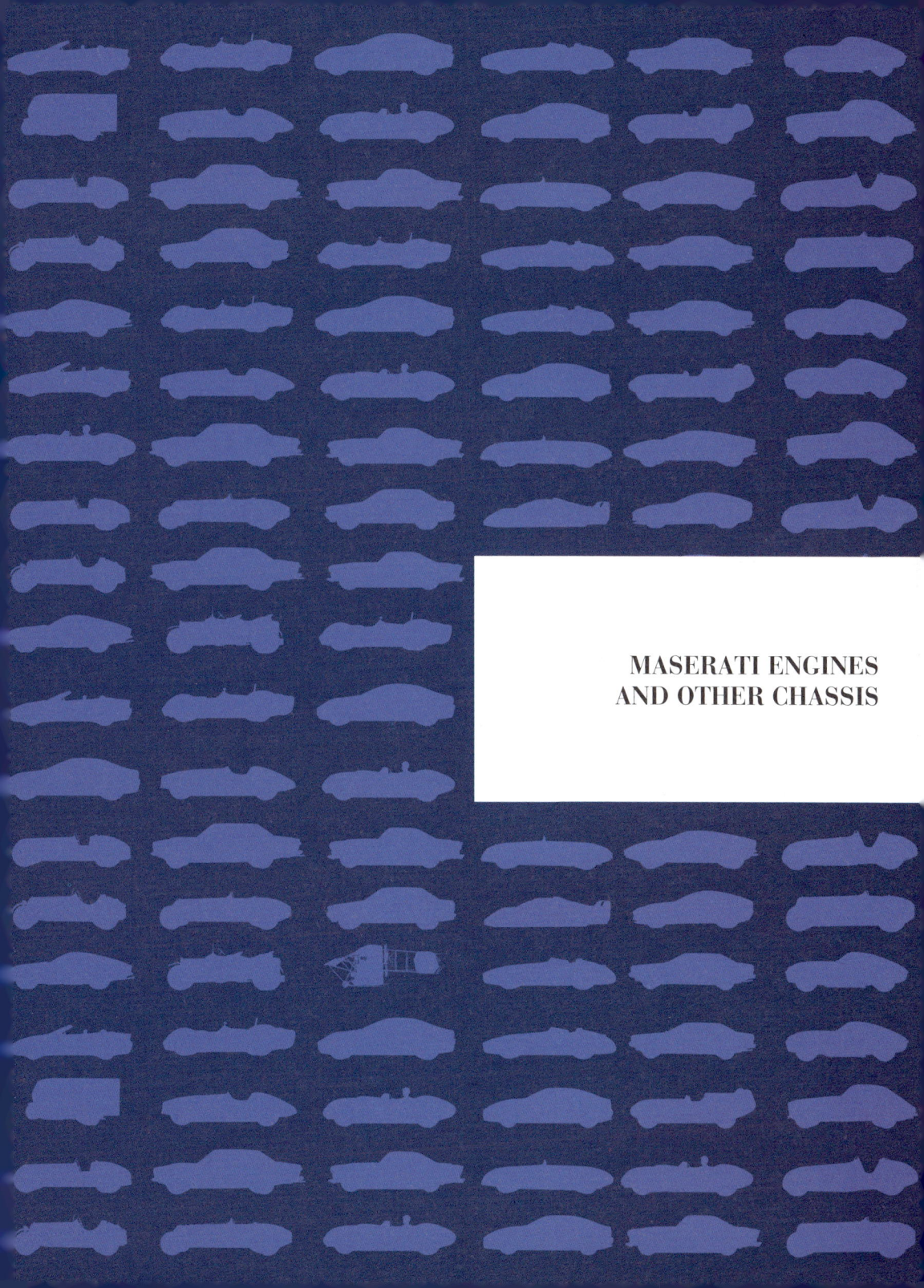

MASERATI ENGINES
AND OTHER CHASSIS

# 4CF2 engine 1952

| Number and configuration of cylinders | straight four |
| --- | --- |
| Bore and stroke | 88 x 82 mm |
| Unitary displacement | 498.73 cc |
| Total displacement | 1994.93 cc |
| Valvegear | double overhead camshafts |
| Number of valves | four per cylinder |
| Compression ratio | 13.5:1 |
| Fuel system | two Weber DCO carburettors |
| Ignition | dual, with Marelli magnetos |
| Cooling | water, with centrifugal pump and radiator |
| Lubrication | dry sump, pressurised with delivery and scavenge pumps |
| Maximum power | 195 hp at 7500 rpm |
| Specific power output | 97.74 hp/litre |

As an alternative to the six-cylinder unit destined for the A6GCM realised in 1951, Ing. Alberto Massimino designed a two-litre, twin-cam four that was loosely inspired by the 4CL, but was in reality significantly different, above all in terms of its oversquare architecture (with a bore of 88 mm and a stroke of 82 mm), but also its light alloy crankcase, detachable cylinder head with four valves per cylinder, multiple piece crankshaft and dual ignition. Despite developing 195 bhp at 7500 rpm (10 more than the Ferrari 500 F2 that twice won the World Championship with Ascari) the project was shelved by Massimino's replacement Gioachino Colombo who designed another six-cylinder unit. The 4CF2 (four-cylinder Formula 2) was used for internal testing of direct injection fuel systems conducted together with Bosch (with unsatisfactory results) under the direction of Ing. Giulio Alfieri, the new technical director from 1953.

# 2500 Sport engine    1954 and 1956

| | |
|---|---|
| Number and configuration of cylinders | straight six |
| Bore and stroke | 84 x 75 mm |
| Unitary displacement | 415.63 cc |
| Total displacement | 2493.79 cc |
| Valvegear | double overhead camshafts |
| Number of valves | two per cylinder |
| Compression ratio | 9:1 |
| Fuel system | three Weber 42 DCO3 carburettors |
| Ignition | dual with two Marelli distributors |
| Cooling | water, with centrifugal pump and radiator |
| Lubrication | dry sump, pressurised with delivery and scavenge pumps |
| Maximum power | 230 hp at 7000 rpm |
| Specific power output | 92.22 hp/litre |

The 2.5-litre, twin-cam straight-six that was fitted to the Formula 1 250 F was revised in view of the 1954 season with modifications that allowed it to power a sports car that would race using commercial petrol as required by the new international regulations. The high compression ratio was reduced from 12 to 9:1 without significantly affecting the maximum power output, which dropped from 240 to 230 hp at 7000 rpm. Initially installed in an A6GCS in place of the standard two-litre engine and then in a new tubular chassis with brand-new bodywork, the unit performed well but the comparison with its three-litre rivals - Aston Martin, Ferrari, Gordini - left no room for doubt and it was shelved. It was used again in 1956, in two cars built at the behest of Talbot in Italy (Carrozzeria Campana, designed by Sergio Reggiani) and entered in the Le Mans 24 Hours, although neither was to finish the race.

# Tipo 59 engine

| | |
|---|---|
| *Number and configuration of cylinders* | 60° V8 |
| *Bore and stroke* | 103 x 85 mm |
| *Unitary displacement* | 708.24 cc |
| *Total displacement* | 5665.95 cc |
| *Valvegear* | double overhead camshafts per bank |
| *Number of valves* | two per cylinder |
| *Compression ratio* | 10.6:1 |
| *Fuel system* | four Weber 45IDM carburettors |
| *Ignition* | dual, with Marelli magnetos and one Marelli distributor |
| *Cooling* | water centrifugal pump and radiator |
| *Lubrication* | pressurised |
| *Maximum power* | 520 hp at 7000 rpm |
| *Specific power output* | 91.77 hp/litre |
| *Weight* | 390 kg |

From 1958, the World Sports Car Championship was run for cars with engine of up to three litres, which sidelined the 450 S except in the United States, where the regulations did not impose a maximum displacement for national races and where the powerful berlinetta was able to race successfully for a number of years. In 1959, Maserati decided to use its eight-cylinder twin-cam engine for nautical purposes, expanding the displacement from 4477.85 cc to 5665.95 cc by increasing the bore and stroke dimensions from 93.8x81 mm to 103x85 mm. Increasing the compression ratio from 9.5:1 to 10.6:1 (and fitting four Weber carburettors, twin-spark ignition and pressurised lubrication) allowed the power output to be increased from 400 to 520 hp at 7000 rpm, 200 less than the car, with a specific power output that rose from 89.32 to 91.77 hp. Between 1959 and 1961, six examples of the engine were constructed before it was replaced by the Tipo 62 the following year.

# Tipo 6 engine

| | |
|---|---|
| Number and configuration of cylinders | straight four |
| Bore and stroke | 81 x 72 mm |
| Unitary displacement | 371.01 cc |
| Total displacement | 1484.06 cc |
| Valvegear | double overhead camshafts |
| Number of valves | two per cylinder |
| Compression ratio | 10.5:1 |
| Fuel system | two Weber 45DCO3 carburettors |
| Ignition | dual with Marelli distributors |
| Cooling | water, centrifugal pump and radiator |
| Lubrication | dry sump with delivery and scavenge pump |
| Maximum power | 165 hp at 8500 rpm |
| Specific power output | 111.18 hp/litre |

When the Formula 1 regulations reduced the maximum displacement for naturally aspirated engines from 2500 to 1500 cc in 1961, Maserati decided to adapt the four-cylinder engine from the 150 S (1955-57) to the new technical specifications, subjecting it to a profound revision and rebaptising it as the Tipo 6. The cylinder head was redesigned and the compression was raised from 9 to 10.5:1, achieving an increase in power from 140 to 165 hp at 8500 rpm, while retaining the same Weber 45 DCO3 twin-choke carburettors. The use of diverse components in Elektron permitted the weight of the unit to be kept down to 130 kg, a further contribution to competitiveness that attracted the interest of drivers such as the Englishman Brian Naylor and private teams such as Centro Sud from Italy which installed the unit in Cooper, Lotus, Emeryson and ENB chassis. The Tipo 6 engine proved to be successful in competition and between 1960 and 1961, 10 examples were built.

# Tipo 62 - 201 - 202 engine          1962-1965

| | | | |
|---|---|---|---|
| Number and configuration of cylinders | 60° V8 | Cooling | water, centrifugal pump and radiator |
| | | Lubrication | pressurised with filter and oil cooler |
| Bore and stroke | Tipo 62: 110 x 85 mm  Tipo 201: 103 x 81 mm  Tipo 202: 94 x 89 mm | Maximum power | Tipo 62: 580 hp at 5500 rpm  (400 hp from 1963)  Tipo 201: 420 hp at 5500 rpm  Tipo 202: 330 hp at 6000 rpm |
| Unitary displacement | Tipo 62: 807.78 cc  Tipo 201: 674.91 cc  Tipo 202: 617.63 cc | Specific power output | Tipo 62: 89.75 hp/litre  (89.34 from 1963)  Tipo 201: 77.78 hp/litre  Tipo 202: 66.78 hp/litre |
| Total displacement | Tipo 62: 6462.25 cc  (4477 from 1963)  Tipo 201: 5399.31 cc  Tipo 202: 4941.11 cc | Weight (including reduction gearing) | 390 kg |
| Valvegear | Double overhead camshafts per bank | | |
| Number of valves | two per cylinder | | |
| Compression ratio | 10:1 | | |
| Ignition | dual with Marelli distributor and a magneto | | |

Maserati's commitment to supplying competition engines for nautical use was rewarded with consistent success. Of particular importance was the Tipo 59 (1959-61), derived from the eight-cylinder, 4.5-litre twin-cam unit from the 450 S, developed and uprated to the point where in 1962 it was decided to build new large displacement engines (4477, 4941, 5399 and 6462 cc) with remarkable power outputs (330, 400, 420, 580 hp). For years the Maserati engines were victorious in boats that were almost always Italian and driven by the likes of Gian Luigi Crivelli, Nando Dell'Orto, Ermanno Marchisio, Lino Spagnoli, as well as by the Guidotti brothers, winners in Timossi boats of numerous world titles, through to the threshold of the 1970s. Among the many, particularly memorable was the world record set for the 1200 kg class by Oscar Scarpa who, in 1961, on the waters of the Idroscalo in Milan, recorded an average speed of 235.889 kph in an Abbate boat powered by a Tipo 59 5.7-litre Maserati engine.

# Tipo 8 engine

# 1962

| | |
|---|---|
| *Number and configuration of cylinders* | 60° V12 |
| *Bore and stroke* | 55.2 x 52 mm |
| *Unitary displacement* | 124.44 cc |
| *Total displacement* | 1493.31 cc |
| *Valvegear* | double overhead camshafts per bank |
| *Number of valves* | two per cylinder |
| *Compression ratio* | 12:1 |
| *Fuel system* | naturally aspirated |
| *Ignition* | dual, with distributors |
| *Cooling* | water centrifugal pump and radiator |
| *Lubrication* | dry sump, pressurised with delivery and scavenge pumps |
| *Maximum power* | 200 hp at 12,000 rpm |
| *Specific power output* | 133.93 hp/litre |
| *Weight* | 140 kg |

Towards the end of 1961, Ing. Giulio Alfieri decided to replace with Tipo 6 four-cylinder engine that powered a number of F1 cars run by private teams and drivers, giving rise to a new and more competitive unit. He therefore took in hand the 250 F T2 project from 1957, reducing the displacement of the 12-cylinder 2.5-litre engine to 1500 cc (by reducing the bore and stroke dimensions from 68,7 x 56 mm to 52,2 x 52 mm), with the new version producing 200 bhp at 12,000 hp, a significant advance over the 165 hp of the Tipo 6. Original features included the transverse rear location planned for the engine, which aroused considerable interest in sporting circles. However, insufficient resources were devoted to the project and Alfieri himself was heavily involved with Maserati's production models and time passed in vain. The Tipo 8 was only considered ready to take to the track at the end of 1964 when the 1500 displacement Formula 1 regulations had just a year to run and the project was abandoned.

23 October 1966, Grand Prix of Mexico, John Surtees is on his way to victory in a Cooper-Maserati. Behind him in the photograph and on the podium is Jack Brabham in a Brabham-Repco ahead of his teammate Denny Hulme. Farther back can be seen the other Cooper-Maserati of Jochen Rindt, who was forced to retire before the halfway point of the race with a broken engine.

## TECHNICAL SPECIFICATION

| | |
|---|---|
| *Number and configuration of cylinders* | 60° V12 |
| *Bore and stroke* | 70.4 x 64 mm<br>68 x 68 mm |
| *Unitary displacement* | 249.12 cc<br>246.95 cc |
| *Total displacement* | 2989.48 cc<br>2963.44 cc |
| *Valvegear* | double overhead camshafts per bank |
| *Number of valves* | two per cylinder |
| *Compression ratio* | 10:1 |
| *Fuel system* | twin-choke Weber carburettors<br>Lucas indirect fuel injection |
| *Ignition* | dual, transistorised<br>with distributors<br>(electronic from 1966) |
| *Cooling* | water, two centrifugal pumps<br>and radiator |
| *Lubrication* | dry sump, pressurised<br>with single delivery pump<br>and two scavenge pumps |
| *Maximum power* | 340 hp at 9000 rpm<br>(360 with fuel injection in 1966) |
| *Specific power output* | 113.73/114.73 hp/litre<br>(with fuel injection: 120.42 / 121.48) |

# Cooper T81-Maserati 9      1965

In view of the new Formula 1 regulations for 1966 that were to raise the maximum displacement for naturally aspirated engines from 1500 to 3000 cc, the Chipstead Group, the Maserati importers for Great Britain that had taken over the Cooper Car Company, commissioned a three-litre engine from the Modenese manufacturer. Ing. Giulio Alfieri returned to the 250 F/T2, realised in 1957 was a possible development of Fangio's World Championship winning single-seater but shelved following the Trident company's decision to abandon direct participation in racing. The engine was a large 60° V12 with a displacement of 2490.9 cc that was increased to 2989.5 cc in the new unit known as the Tipo 9, with two valves per cylinder and indirect fuel injection. Capable of producing 360 hp at 9,000 rpm, the engine allowed the car to reach a top speed of over 300 kph. The Cooper T81-Maserati, which used the first monocoque chassis in the English company's history, was exhibited ahead of its debut at the London Racing Car Show in the January of 1966. The works team would be composed of Jochen Rindt and - with a special permit from Honda, which was not yet ready to take to the track – Richie Ginther. With private teams it was to be driven by Joseph Siffert (Rob Walker Racing Team), Joakim Bonnier (Anglo Swiss Racing Team) and Guy Ligier as a privateer. Following an unhappy debut at Monte Carlo (four cars starting, none finishing), Rindt was second in the Belgian GP and fourth in France where he was flanked, in place of Ginther who had returned to Honda, by John Surtees, who had just divorced from Ferrari and finished second ahead of Rindt in Germany. Another podium came at Watkins Glen (this time with Rindt second ahead of Surtees) and finally a triumph in Mexico, with Surtees winning and finishing second in the Driver's Championship and Cooper-Maserati third in the Constructors' Championship.

If the 1966 Formula 1 World Championship came to an end with John Surtees' victory in the Grand Prix of Mexico the 1967 season opened with another Cooper-Maserati success, by Pedro Rodríguez in the South African GP at Kyalami. At the same time, the Mexican scored his first win in a world championship Grand Prix. He was followed home by John Love in a Lotus-Climax and John Surtees, who had recently joined Honda.

TECHNICAL SPECIFICATION

| | |
|---|---|
| *Number and configuration of cylinders* | 60° V12 |
| *Bore and stroke* | 75.2 x 56 mm |
| *Unitary displacement* | 248.72 cc |
| *Total displacement* | 2984.65 cc |
| *Valvegear* | double overhead camshafts per bank |
| *Number of valves* | three per cylinder |
| *Compression ratio* | 11.8:1 |
| *Fuel system* | Lucas indirect fuel injection |
| *Ignition* | dual, transistorised |
| *Cooling* | water, two centrifugal pumps and radiator |
| *Lubrication* | dry sump, pressurised with one delivery and two scavenge pumps |
| *Maximum power* | 380 hp at 9800 rpm |
| *Specific power output* | 127.31 hp/litre |

# Cooper T81-Maserati 10      1967

For the Maserati-powered Cooper the 1967 Formula 1 season began just as triumphantly as the previous season had finished: victory at Kyalami in the South African Grand Prix going to Pedro Rodríguez, who had just joined the team alongside Richie Ginther, in place of Surtees, the winner two months earlier at Mexico City who had moved on to Honda. Those two consecutive victories served to placate the disputes that had arisen during the course of the first season between the chassis manufacturer and the engine supplier regarding the alternating fortunes of the car. However, the new season continued with disappointing results: not a single podium, with the best results being 4TH, 5TH and 6TH places. Nonetheless, the points accumulated here and there again allowed the team to finish third in the Constructors' Championship and Rodríguez and Rindt to place 6TH and 11TH respectively in the drivers' standings. Cooper had experimented with an evolution of the T81 (T81B) and then the new T86, designed by Derek White, like the previous car, but the early results were less than convincing. For its part, Maserati had prepared a new version of the engine (known as the Tipo 10), with a displacement of 2984.65 cc against the 2989.48 cc of the Tipo 9 thanks to an increase in bore from 70.4 to 75.2 mm and a reduction in the stroke from 64 to 56 mm. The engine featured three valves per cylinder, had a compression ratio of 11.8:1 rather than 10:1 and was capable of producing 380-390 hp at 9800-10,000 rpm. The form also experimented at length with triple rather than double ignition but, from one race to another a persistent fragility emerged, together with doubts over the chassis handling and other technical problems that while minor were together sufficient to cause dropped points and numerous retirements with reciprocal accusations and recriminations. For these reasons, at the end of the year the contract between Cooper and Maserati was not renewed.

During the time that Citröen owned the Maserati marque, there were many opportunities for technical interchange between the two companies. To equip a new top-of-the-range model, the French executives decided to use an engine made in Italy by Maserati. The result of this joint venture was the Citröen SM-Maserati C.114, a 2+2 coupé that was powered by a 2675 cc V6 unit.

TECHNICAL SPECIFICATION

| | |
|---|---|
| *Number and configuration of cylinders* | 90° V6 |
| *Bore and stroke* | 87 x 75 mm<br>from 1974: 91.6 x 75 mm |
| *Unitary displacement* | 445.85 cc<br>from 1974: 494.24 cc |
| *Total displacement* | 2675.10 cc<br>from 1974: 2965.46 cc |
| *Valvegear* | double overhead camshafts<br>per bank |
| *Number of valves* | two per cylinder |
| *Compression ratio* | 9:1 |
| *Fuel system* | three Weber 42 DCNF<br>carburettors<br>from 1972: indirect Bosch<br>electronic fuel injection |
| *Ignition* | single |
| *Cooling* | water, centrifugal pump<br>and radiator |
| *Lubrication* | gear pump, filter on main circuit |
| *Maximum power* | 180 hp at 6250 rpm |
| *Specific power output* | 67.28 hp/litre<br>from 1974: 60.69 hp/litre |

# Citroën SM-Maserati C.114     1970

Shortly after Maserati was acquired by Citroën, Ing. Giulio Alfieri was asked to create an engine for a new prestige car the French company was planning. The designer opted for a 2.7-litre 90° V6 baptised as the C.114, which in the spring of 1968 underwent initial road testing. In 1970, the car was presented at the Geneva Motor Show as the Citroën SM. Designed by Rober Opron, it was a large 2+2 coupé, with two doors and a rear hatch, hydropneumatic suspension – a Citroën classic – and front wheel drive. The Maserati engine in its initial 2675.10 cc configuration was fed by three Weber twin choke carburettors, with two valves per cylinder being actuated by double overhead camshafts per bank. With a compression ratio of 9:1, it had a maximum power output of 180 hp at 6250 rpm and was capable of propelling the car to 220 kph. In 1972, a Bosch fuel injection system was introduced and from 1974 the displacement was increased to 2965.46 cc thanks to an increase in bore from 87 to 91.6 mm and an unvaried stroke of 75 mm. The power output rose to 190 hp while due to the increase in weight from 1460 to 1520 kg, the top speed remained unchanged. The SM's performance was exceptional: through to 1983 and the introduction of the Audi 200, it was the fastest mass-produced front-wheel drive car ever built. Its competition record began with a victroy in the Rally of Morocco in 1971 (crewed by Deschazeaux/Plassard) but the performance was not to be repeated even though a 3rd place was obtained in the Rally of Portugal in 1972 and a 6th in the Bandama Rally in 1973 with a short wheelbase version. When it was dropped in 1975, 12,920 examples of the SM had been constructed, including all the special versions and variant produced in France: the Présidentielle, Opéra, Mylord and Espace, and those assembled by Ligier.

The 1974 1000 Km of Monza was the last to take place on the regular date of 25 April. The picture shows one of the two Ligier JS2s powered by 2.6-litre, 6-cylinder Maserati engine. In the Italian race, the opening round in the world championship, Jacques Laffite alternating with Alain Serpaggi in car number 12, which started from the seventh row on the grid and finished eighth.

## TECHNICAL SPECIFICATION

| | |
|---|---|
| *Number and configuration of cylinders* | 90° V6 |
| *Bore and stroke* | 87 x 75 mm<br>from 1974: 91.6 x 75 mm |
| *Unitary displacement* | 445.85 cc<br>from 1974: 494.24 cc |
| *Total displacement* | 2675.10 cc<br>from 1974: 2965.46 cc |
| *Valvegear* | double overhead camshafts per bank |
| *Number of valves* | two per cylinder |
| *Compression ratio* | 9:1 |
| *Fuel system* | three Weber 42 DCNF carburettors<br>from 1972: indirect Bosch electronic fuel injection |
| *Ignition* | single |
| *Cooling* | water, centrifugal pump and radiator |
| *Lubrication* | gear pump, filter on main circuit |
| *Maximum power* | 180 hp at 6250 rpm |
| *Specific power output* | 67.28 hp/litre<br>from 1974: 60.69 hp/litre |

# Ligier JS2-Maserati C.114                1972

In 1968, the French driver Guy Ligier designed a berlinetta conceived for racing in the Sport category. The car was presented at the Paris Motor Show in 1961 as the JS1, in which the letters JS – since found on all the marque's cars – were the initials of Jo Schlesser, Ligier's great friend who was killed in the French GP in 1968. The very light car (790 kg) was fitted with a 1.6-litre Ford Cosworth V6 located centrally and a polyester two-seater body by Pietro Frua. In 1970, Ligier adopted the Ford Cosworth 1.8 but decided the performance potential was insufficient and opted for the engine-gearbox assembly from the Citroën SM. The adaptation of the Maserati C.114 90° V6 required considerable time and deliveries only started in the early months of 1972. On the track, the JS2 immediately proved to be competitive and attracted the interest of Maserati who supplied Ligier with the three-litre fuel injected version of the engine. In 1974, moreover, the unit was fitted with four valves per cylinder heads that provided a power output of 195 hp at 5500 rpm that allowed the berlinetta to reach a top speed of over 240 kph and to cover the standing start kilometre in 27.2 seconds. The JS2's competition record features numerous category and class wins and two international overall victories: in the 1974 Le Mans 4 Hours, with Guy Chasseuil and in the Tour de France Automobile of the same year with Gérard Larrousse, Jean-Pierre Nicolas and Johnny Rives. No less prestigious was the second place achieved in the 1975 Le Mans 24 Hours with Jean-Louis Lafosse and Guy Chasseuil. A total of 225 examples of the JS2 were produced through to 1975 when Citroën was acquired by Peugeot and Maserati was sold off.

MASERATI VICTORIES

# Maserati Victories

## Edited by Alessandro Silva

Three separate lists comprise the overall victories in racing from 1926 to 2012 of Maserati cars, cars equipped with Maserati engines and cars with Maserati chassis, that is to say, the lists of first places in the overall standings for autonomous races. Multiple races at the same meeting and support races at Grands Prix are also considered to be autonomous races. The heats for races with a final, the single heats in races with overall classifications given by the aggregate times and qualification sessions of any kind are not considered to be autonomous races. Class and Category victories (for instance the Sports car Category) in races with separate category standings have not been considered. In this case only those category winners who also set the fastest time of the day appear in the lists.

Sprint races over distances of less than a mile with restricted entries and not of at least national standing have not been considered. No distinction has instead been made regarding certain races of this kind held in the early years of the marque. Finally, races for historical cars and single-marque races have not been considered. Class and category limits have been indicated for the single races in the same meeting, in the absence of specific denominations, and for the support races where it has the same name as the main race.

Unofficial denominations have been used for certain cars as an aid to identification. CS: special sports cars from the immediate post-war period with naturally aspirated 1.5-litre, six-cylinder engines.

4CLT: a transitional example between the 4CL, of which it retains the lines, but fitted with a new tubular chassis, and the 4CLT/48.

A6GCS/53: to distinguish the later series with enclosed bodywork from the A6GCS "monofaro".

A6G/54: to identify the second series of the coupé A6G Gran Turismo. 470S and 570S: 450S chassis equipped with V8 engines, respectively rebored to 4700cc and for use in power boats.

300V12: three-litre engine used in Formula 1 installed in Cooper chassis in 1966/67.

The "transitional" cars between the Tipo 26, 26B, 26M and 8CM have been indicated by 8C-2800 and 8C-3000 although it is not clear if this was their official name. The names 200S and 200SI for the Tipo 52 are used interchangeably in the sources. It has been indicated that used more often in each case.

---

**LEGEND
NATIONS**

| | | | |
|---|---|---|---|
| A | Austria | MA | Morocco |
| ANG | Angola | MC | Monaco |
| AUS | Australia | NL | The Netherlands |
| B | Belgium | NZ | New Zealand |
| BHM | Bahamas | P | Portugal |
| BR | Brasile | RA | Argentina |
| C | Cuba | RO | Romania |
| CH | Switzerland | S | Sweden |
| CN | China | SF | Finland |
| CS | Czechoslovakia | TN | Tunisia |
| D | Germany | TR | Turkey |
| E | Spain | UK | United Kingdom |
| F | France | YU | Yugoslavia |
| H | Hungary | YV | Venezuela |
| IRL | Ireland | ZA | South Africa |

**LEGEND
AMERICAN STATES (USA)**

| | | | |
|---|---|---|---|
| Al. | Alabama | Mn. | Minnesota |
| Az. | Arizona | Mo. | Missouri |
| Ca. | California | Ne. | Nevada |
| Co. | Colorado | NJ | New Jersey |
| Ct. | Connecticut | NY | New York |
| Fl. | Florida | Ok. | Oklahoma |
| Ga. | Georgia | Pa. | Pennsylvania |
| Hi. | Hawaii | SC | Carolina del Sud |
| Il. | Illinois | Tx. | Texas |
| In. | Indiana | Va. | Virginia |
| Ks. | Kansas | Vt. | Vermont |
| Ky. | Kentucky | Wi. | Wisconsin |
| La. | Louisiana | | |
| Md. | Maryland | | |
| Ma. | Massachussets | | |

# Maserati Victories

## 1926

13 June
Bologna
Flying kilometre
Ernesto Maserati
26

1 August
Rimini
Flying kilometre
Emilio Materassi
26

3 October
Bologna
Rastignano-Loiano
Alfieri Maserati
26

## 1927

6 January
Bologna-Colle dell'Osservanza
Luigi Masi
26

3 July
Vittorio Veneto-Cansiglio
Diego De Sterlich
26B

10 July
Terni-Passo della Somma
Baconin Borzacchini
26

21 August
Pistoia
Coppa della Collina
Baconin Borzacchini
26

20 September
Trento-Bondone
Diego De Sterlich
26B

2 October
Roma
Vermicino-Rocca di Papa
Diego De Sterlich
26B

20 November
Nave, Brescia
Colle di S. Eusebio
Aymo Maggi
26B

## 1928

15 April
Circuito di Caserta
Pietro Brunori
26MM

20 May Catania
Coppa Etna
Baconin Borzacchini
26B

22 July
Trento-Bondone
Cesare Pastore
26

30 September
Tolentino-Colle Paterno
Luigi Fagioli
26

21 October
Roma
Vermicino Rocca di Papa
Baconin Borzacchini
26B

## 1929

22 September
Opatija (Abbazia)
Abbazia-Monte Mayre
Cesare Pastore
26/2100

28 September
Cremona
Flying 10 km
Baconin Borzacchini
V4

6 October
Tolentino-Colle Paterno
Luigi Fagioli
26R

## 1930

23 March
Tripoli
Grand Prix of Tripoli
Baconin Borzacchini (batteria e finale)
V4

25 May
Roma, Tre Fontane
Premio Reale di Roma (Vetturette)
Alfieri Maserati
26C

25 May
Roma, Tre Fontane
Premio Reale di Roma
Luigi Arcangeli
26M

6 July
Avellino
Coppa Principe di Piemonte
Luigi Fagioli
26M

3 August
Livorno
Circuito del Montenero
Luigi Fagioli
26M

3 August
Rimini
Flying Km
Luigi Randazzo
26B

17 August
Pescara
Coppa Acerbo
Achille Varzi
26M

7 September
GP Monza
Achille Varzi
26M

5 October
San Sebastián, E
GP de España
Achille Varzi
26M
(first international GP victory)

25 October
Frascati
Coppa Castelli Romani
Luigi Fagioli/Giuseppe Furmanik
26M

26 October
Roma
Vermicino-Rocca di Papa
Luigi Fagioli
26M

# 1931

22 March
Verona
Corsa alle Torricelle
Cesare Pastore
26M Sport

28 March
Carthage, TN
6 Heures de Tunis
Luigi Castelbarco/René Dreyfus
26M

7 June
Roma,
Autodromo del Littorio
Premio Reale di Roma
Ernesto Maserati (batteria e finale)
V4

28 June
Genova
Pontedecimo-Giovi
Pietro Ghersi
26M
ex-aequo Nuvolari (Alfa Romeo)

16 August
St.-Gaudens, F
GP du Comminges (Vetturette)
Louis Joly
26

23 August
Viterbo
Coppa del Cimino
Umberto Klinger
26M

6 September
Monza
GP Monza
Luigi Fagioli
8C-2800

27 September
Napoli
Coppa Autunno Napoletano
Flying Km
Otello Bava
26B

17 October
Brooklands, UK
Mountain Championship
Henry "Tim" Birkin
26M

25 October
Roma
Autodromo del Littorio
Campionato Sociale AC Roma
Giuseppe Savi
26R

# 1932

24 April
Roma
Autodromo del Littorio
Premio Reale di Roma
Luigi Fagioli (batteria e finale)
V5

25 June
Nancy-Seichamps, F
GP de Lorraine (Vetturette)
Pierre Veyron
26

26 June Tangeri, MA
Djebel Mokra
Jean de Maleplane
26M

3 July
Buenos Aires, AR
Costanera
GP de la Ciudad de Buenos Aires
Juan Malcolm
26B

31 July
Livorno
Circuito del Montenero (Vetturette)
Domenico Rosso di Cerami
4CM

14 August
St.-Gaudens, F
GP du Comminges (Vetturette)
Pierre Veyron
26

21 August
Circuito di Senigallia
Luigi Fagioli
8C 2800

# 1933

8 January
Mar del Plata, RA
GP de Mar del Plata
(Consolation Race)
Juan Malcolm
T26B

17 April
Brooklands, UK
1st Addlestone Mountain Handicap
Whitney Straight
26M

17 April Brooklands, UK
2nd Addlestone Mountain Handicap
Whitney Straight
26M

11 June
Montlhéry, F
GP de l'ACF
Giuseppe Campari
8C 3000

9 July
Spa Francorchamps, B
GP de Belgique
Tazio Nuvolari
8CM

30 July
Livorno
Circuito del Montenero
Tazio Nuvolari
8CM

30 July
Livorno
Circuito del Montenero (Vetturette)
Nando Barbieri
4CM

6 August
Nice, F
GP de Nice
Tazio Nuvolari
8CM

3 September
Mont Ventoux, F
Mont Ventoux
Whitney Straight
26M

30 September
Shelsley Walsh, UK
Shelsley Walsh "Autumn"
Whitney Straight
26M

21 October
Brooklands, UK
Mountain Championship
Whitney Straight
26M

22 October
Ile-de-France, F
Gometz-le-Châtel
Hans Ruesch
8CM

# 1934

3 March
Brooklands, UK
Fourth Walton Sprint Handicap
R.F. "Dickie" Oats
26M

27 March
Nice, F
500 mètres lancés
Hans Ruesch
8CM

28 April
Brooklands, UK
JCC International Trophy
Whitney Straight
8CM

27 May
Péronne, F
GP de Picardie
Benoît Falchetto
8CM

3 June
Nürburgring, D
Eifelrennen (Vetturette)
Luigi Castelbarco
4CM

11 June
Shelsley Walsh, UK
Shelsley Walsh "Spring"
Whitney Straight
8CM

29 June
Napoli
Targa del Vesuvio (Pugliano-Eremo)
Giovanni Rocco
T26B

1 July
Kanton St. Gallen, CH
Rheineck-Walzenhausen-Lachen
Hans Ruesch
8CM

7 July
Brooklands, UK
Third Long Handicap
Adrian H. Boyd
26M

7 July
Brooklands, UK
Scratch Sprint Race A
Adrian H. Boyd
26M

22 July Albi, F
GP d'Albi
Buddy Featherstonhaugh
26M

22 July
Dieppe, F
GP de Dieppe
Philippe Etancelin
8CM

22 July
Livorno
Circuito del Montenero (Vetturette)
Romano Malaguti
4CS

9 September
Montlhéry, F
Grand Prix de l'U.M.F
Benoît Falchetto
8CM

30 September
Brno, CS
Masaryk v okruh (Vetturette)
Nino Farina
4CM

6 October
Donington, UK
Donington Park Trophy
Whitney Straight
8CM

13 October
Brooklands, UK
Mountain Championship
Whitney Straight
8CM

14 October
Circuito di Modena
Tazio Nuvolari
6C-34

21 October
Circuito di Napoli
Tazio Nuvolari
6C-34

27 December
East London, ZA
Prince George Circuit
South African GP
Whitney Straight
8CM

# 1935

17 March
Génève, CH
Grand-Saconnex (sprint)
Hans Ruesch
6C-34

26 May
Avignon, F
Les Alpilles
Raymond Albert Chambost
8CM

23 June
Sorrento-Sant'Agata
Giovanni Rocco
4CS

30 June
Coppa Ascoli
Piero Taruffi
8CM

21 July
Circuito di Varese (Sport 1100)
Ettore Bianco
4CS

21 July
Circuito di Varese (Sport 2000)
Giovanni Lurani
4CS

4 August
Livorno
Circuito del Montenero (Vetturette)
Giuseppe Tuffanelli
4CM

11 August
Haut-Limousin, F
Eymoutiers
Marcel Lehoux
6C-34

24 August
Bern, CH
Bremgarten
Preis von Bremgarten
Max Christen
26B

15 September
Circuito di Modena (Vetturette)
Ippolito Berrone
4CM

6 October
Cluji-Brasov, RO
Feleac
László Hartmann
8CM

# 1936

1 March
Pau, F
GP de Pau
Philippe Etancelin
V8Ri

4 April
Donington Park, UK
British Empire Trophy
Richard Seaman
8CM (ridotta 2.7L)

14 June
Nürburgring, D
Eifelrennen (Vetturette)
Carlo Felice Trossi
6CM

28 June
Milano, Parco Sempione
Circuito di Milano (Vetturette)
Carlo Felice Trossi
6CM

2 August
Livorno
Circuito del Montenero (Vetturette)
Carlo FeliceTrossi
6CM

30 August
Sinaia, RO
Iorgu Ghica
8CM

6 September
Circuito di Lucca
Carlo FeliceTrossi
4CM

20 September
Circuito di Modena (Vetturette)
Carlo FeliceTrossi
6CM

1 November
Bucureşti, RO
GP Bucureşti
Iorgu Ghica
8CM

# 1937

25 April
Napoli
Posillipo
Coppa Principessa di Piemonte
(Vetturette)
Carlo FeliceTrossi
6CM

1 May
Brooklands, UK
Campbell Trophy
Prince "Bira"
8CM

2 May
Lecco
Coppa Valsassina (Lecco-Barzio)
Franco Bertani
4CS/4CM

23 May
Palermo
Favorita
Targa Florio
Francesco Severi
6CM

30 May
Genova
Circuito della Superba (Vetturette)
Aldo Marazza
4CS

13 June
Circuito di Firenze
René Dreyfus
6CM

20 June
Milano
Parco Sempione
Circuito di Milano (Vetturette)
Eugenio Siena
4CM

25 July
Montreux, CH
Montreux-Caux
Max Christen
26B

25 July
Circuito di Sanremo
Achille Varzi (batteria e finale)
4CM

15 August
Pescara
Coppa Acerbo (Vetturette)
Giovanni Rocco
6CM

18 September
Lucca
Coppa Edda Ciano
Carlo Felice Trossi
4CM

25 September
Roosevelt Raceway, Long Island,
NY USA
ARCA Grand Prix
George Rand/Enzo Fiermonte
V8RI

26 September
Brno, CS
Brno Mesto Trofej
Luigi Villoresi
6CM

26 September
Circuito di Campione d'Italia
Giovanni Rocco (batteria e finale)
6CM

17 October
Dobogókö, H
Dobogókö
Ernö Festetics
8CM

# 1938

22 May
Palermo
Favorita
Targa Florio
Giovanni Rocco
6CM

26 June
Napoli
Posillipo
Coppa Principessa di Piemonte
Aldo Marazza
6CM

26 June
Kanton St. Gallen, CH
Rheineck-Walzenhausen-Lachen,
Hans Keßler
6CM

10 July
Albi, F
GP d'Albi
Luigi Villoresi (batteria e finale)
6CM

17 July
Circuito di Varese
Franco Cortese
6CM

14 August
Pescara
Coppa Acerbo (Vetturette)
Luigi Villoresi
6CM

21 August
Bern, CH
Bremgarten
Prix de Berne
Armand Hug
4CM

28 August
La Baule, F
GP de La Baule
Armand Hug
4CM

4 September
Lucca
Coppa Edda Ciano
Luigi Villoresi
6CM

18 September
Circuito di Modena
Franco Cortese
6CM

25 December
Asmara
Circuito Eritreo
Coppa del Governatore
Ferdinando Gay
4CS

# 1939

1 January
East London, ZA
South African GP
Luigi Villoresi
6CM

14 January
Capetown, ZA
Grosvenor Grand Prix
Franco Cortese
6CM

6 May
Brooklands, UK
JCC International Trophy
Prince " Bira"
8CM

7 May
Addis Abeba
Corsa in salita
Alberto Panerai
8C-3000

14 May
Palermo
Favorita
Targa Florio
Luigi Villoresi
4CL

28 May
Napoli
Posillipo
Coppa Principessa di Piemonte
Johnny Wakefield
4CL

30 May
Indianapolis, In. USA
500 Miles Sweepstakes
Wilbur Shaw
8CTF [Boyle Spl]

11 June
Péronne, F
GP de Picardie
Johnny Wakefield (batteria e finale)
4CL

14 June
Valangin, CH
Vue des Alpes
Bernard Blancpain
4CM

25 June
Kanton St. Gallen, CH
Rheineck-Walzenhausen-Lachen,
Bernard Blancpain
4CM

9 July
Reims, F
Coupe de la Commission Sportive
Armand Hug
4CM/4CL

9 July
Circuito di Abbazia
Luigi Villoresi
4CL

16 July
Albi, F
GP d'Albi
Johnny Wakefield (batteria e finale)
4CL

23 July
Canton Jura, CH
Develier-Les Rangiers
Bernard Blancpain
4CM

30 July
Livorno
Circuito del Montenero (Cat. Isolati)
Edoardo Teagno
6CM

13 August
Pescara
Coppa Acerbo (Cat. Isolati)
Guido Barbieri
6CM

19 August
Bern, CH
Bremgarten
Prix du Bremgarten
Emmanuel de Graffenried
6C-34

29 October
Rio de Janeiro, BR

Gávea
Circuito de Gávea Nacional
Manuel de Teffé
6CM

# 1940

20 April
Cape Province, ZA
Camps Bay
Sal Chiappini
26M

23 May
Palermo
Favorita
Targa Florio
Luigi Villoresi
4CL

30 May
Indianapolis, In. USA
500 Miles Sweepstakes
Wilbur Shaw
8CTF [Boyle Special]

6 July
Montauck, NY USA
ARCA Montauck GP
George Rand
V8Ri

# 1941

27 April
Rio de Janeiro, BR
Subida da Tijuca
Manuel de Teffé
6CM

# 1945

9 September
Paris, F
Bois de Boulogne
Coupe de la Libération
Henri Louveau
6CM

# 1946

22 April
Nice, F
GP de la Ville de Nice
Luigi Villoresi
4CL

12 May
Marseille, F
Prado
GP de Marseille
Raymond Sommer
6CM/4CL

19 May
Andrézieux, F
GP du Forez
Raymond Sommer
6CM/4CL

2 June
Rio de Janeiro, BR
Rio de Janeiro-Petrópolis
Gino Bianco
8CM 64-34

9 June
St. Cloud, F
Coupe René Le Bègue
Raymond Sommer
6CM/4CL

15 June
Gransden Lodge, UK
Gransden Lodge
Invitational Meeting
(Corsa 1101-1500)
Reg Parnell
4CL

14 July
Albi, F
GP d'Albi
Tazio Nuvolari
4CL

29 July
Nantes, F
GP des 24hrs du Mans
"Raph"
6CM

24 August
Maloja Pass, CH
Maloja Nationales Rennen
Emmanuel De Graffenried
4CL

25 August
Maloja Pass, CH
Maloja Internationales Rennen
Arialdo Ruggeri
4CL

25 August Lille, F
Circuit des Trois Villes du Nord
Raymond Sommer/Henri Louveau
8CL

2 September Pike's Peak, Co. USA
Pike's Peak
Louis Unser
8CTF

6 October
Paris, F
Bois de Boulogne
GP du Salon
Raymond Sommer
4CL

6 October
Circuito di Mantova (Cat. Sport)
Guido Barbieri
CS

6 October
Circuito di Mantova (Finale handicap)
Guido Barbieri
CS

13 October
Circuito di Voghera
Luigi Villoresi
CS

27 October Barcelona, E
Pedralbes
GP de la Peña Rhin
Giorgio Pelassa
4CL

# 1947

9 February
Buenos Aires, RA
Circuito Retiro
GP de la Ciudad de Buenos Aires
(gara I)
Luigi Villoresi
4CL

16 February
Buenos Aires, RA
Circuito Retiro
GP de la Ciudad de Buenos Aires
(gara II)
Luigi Villoresi
4CL

7 April Pau, F
GP de Pau
Nello Pagani
4CL

8 May St.Helier, UK
Jersey Road Race
Reg Parnell
4CL

11 May
Circuito di Piacenza (Sport oltre
1100)
Guido Barbieri
CS

11 May
Coppa Città di Perugia
Aldo Marchetti
4CM

25 May
Chimay, B
GP des Frontières
"B Bira"
4CL

1 June
Nîmes, F
GP de Nîmes
Luigi Villoresi
4CL

6 June
Bern, CH
Bremgarten
Preis von Bremgarten
Ernst Hürzeler
4CL

5 July
Maloja Pass, CH
Nationales Rennen
Ernst Hürzeler
4CL

6 July
Reims, F
GP de Reims
Christian Kautz
4CL

6 July Maloja Pass, CH
Internationales Rennen
Ernst Hürzeler
4CL

20 July
Nice, F
GP de la Ville de Nice
Luigi Villoresi
4CL

20 July
Canton Jura, CH
Develier-Les Rangiers
Ernst Hürzeler
4CL

3 August
Strasbourg, F
GP d'Alsace
Luigi Villoresi
4CL

10 August
Baden-Württemberg, D
Eggberg
Leonard Joa
4CM

17 August
Kanton St. Gallen, CH
Rheineck-Walzenhausen-Lachen
Ernst Hürzeler
4CL

31 August
Circuito di Novara
Guido Barbieri
CS

1 September
Rio de Janeiro, BR
Subida da Tijuca
Gino Bianco
6C-34

1 September
Pike's Peak, Co. USA
Pike's Peak
Louis Unser
8CTF

28 September
Circuito di Modena
Alberto Ascari
A6GCS

5 October
Lausanne, CH
La Blècherette
GP de Lausanne
Luigi Villoresi
4CL

5 October
Circuito di Voghera (Sport oltre 1100)
Guido Barbieri
CS

7 December
Rio de Janeiro, BR
Circuito da Quinta de Boavista
Benedicto Lopes
4CM/2500

# 1948

17/18 January
Buenos Aires, RA
Circuito Palermo
GP General Juan Perón
y de la Ciudad de Buenos Aires
Luigi Villoresi (batteria e finale)
4CL

25 January
Mar del Plata, RA
GP Internacional General San Martín
Nino Farina
8CL

14 February
Buenos Aires, RA
Circuito Palermo
GP Dalmiro Varela Castex
Luigi Villoresi
4CL

29 March
Pau, F
GP de Pau
Nello Pagani
4CL

2 May
Génève, CH
GP des Nations
Nino Farina
4CLT

16 May
MonteCarlo, MC
GP de Monaco
Nino Farina
4CLT

23 May
Kanton St. Gallen, CH
Rheineck-Walzenhausen-Lachen
Emmanuel de Graffenried
4CL

30 May
Köln, D
Kölner Kurs
Kurt Kiefer
26M

6 June
Valangin, CH
Vue des Alpes
Emmanuel de Graffenried
4CL

13 June
Corsa all'Asmara
Ettore G. Salvatori
4CM Spl.

27 June
Biella-Oropa
Giovanni Bracco
A6GCS

27 June
Circuito di Sanremo
Alberto Ascari
4CLT/48

4 July
Bolzano-Mendola
Giovanni Bracco
A6GCS

4 July
Petrópolis, BR
Circuito Cidade de Petrópolis
Benedicto Lopes
4CL

11 July Cortina d'Ampezzo
Coppa d'Oro delle Dolomiti
Giovanni Bracco
A6GCS

1 August
St.-Gaudens, F
GP du Comminges
Luigi Villoresi
4CLT/48

7 August Zandvoort, NL
Grote Prijs van Zandvoort
"B Bira"
4CL

8 August
Erlen, CH
GP de la Suisse Orientale
Emmanuel de Graffenried
4CL

15 August
Circuito di Pescara
Alberto Ascari/Giovanni Bracco
A6GCS

22 August
Maloja Pass, CH
Nationales Rennen
Emmanuel de Graffenried
4CL

29 August
Albi, F
GP d'Albi
Luigi Villoresi
4CLT/48

18 September
Goodwood, UK
Goodwood Trophy
Reg Parnell
4CLT 48

2 October
Silverstone, UK
R.A.C. Grand Prix
Luigi Villoresi
4CLT/48

31 October
Barcelona, E
Pedralbes
GP de la Peña Rhin
Luigi Villoresi
4CLT/48

16 November Rio de Janeiro, BR
Subida da Tijuca
Antonio Fernandes da Silva
4CL

24 November
Asmara, Eritrea
Riunione all'Asmara
Ettore G. Salvatori
4CM

# 1949

30 January
Buenos Aires, RA
Circuito Palermo
GP General Juan Perón
y de la Ciudad de Buenos Aires
Alberto Ascari
4CLT/48

27 February
Mar del Plata, RA
GP Internacional General San
Martín Juan Manuel Fangio
4CLT/48

6 March
São Paulo, BR
Circuito do Pacaembu
"Chico" Landi
4CL

6 March
Barcelona, E
Montjuich
Premio Para Turismos
Luis Sereix
A6G

20 March
São Paulo, BR
Interlagos
GP da Cidade de São Paulo
Gigi Villoresi
4CLT/48

27 March
Rio de Janeiro, BR
Gávea
GP da Cidade de Rio de Janeiro
Gigi Villoresi
4CLT/48

3 April
Circuito di Sanremo
Juan Manuel Fangio
4CLT/48

18 April
Pau, F
GP de Pau
Juan Manuel Fangio
4CLT/48

18 April
Goodwood, UK
Richmond Trophy
Reg Parnell
4CLT/48

18 April
Goodwood, UK
Chichester Cup
Reg Parnell
4CLT/48

18 April
Goodwood, UK
Easter Handicap
Reg Parnell
4CLT/48

7 May
Perpignan, F
GP du Roussillon
Juan Manuel Fangio
4CLT/48

14 May
Silverstone, UK
R.A.C. Grand Prix
Emmanuel de Graffenried
4CLT/48

22 May
Erlen, CH
GP de la Suisse Orientale
Emmanuel de Graffenried
4CL

29 May
Skarpnäck, S
Stockholm
Summer Swedish Grand Prix
"B Bira"
4CLT/48

29 May Agrigento
Coppa dei Templi
(Porto Empedocle-Agrigento)
Nicola Musmeci
A6GCS

5 June
Palermo-Monte Pellegrino
Nicola Musmeci
A6GCS

19 June
Kanton St. Gallen, CH
Rheineck-Walzenhausen-Lachen
Emmanuel de Graffenried
4CLT/48

3 July
Bolzano-Mendola
Piero Carini
A6GCS

3 July
Petrópolis, BR
Circuito Cidade de Petrópolis
Gino Bianco
8CM

10 July
Albi, F
GP d'Albi
Juan Manuel Fangio
4CLT/48

17 July
Canton Jura, CH
Develier-Les Rangiers
Emmanuel de Graffenried
4CLT/48

24 July
Coppa Galatea
(Pozzillo-Acireale)
Nicola Musmeci
A6GCS

30 July
Silverstone, UK
Midland Motoring Enthusiasts' Club
6th race
Ken McAlpine
8CM

14 August
Belo Horizonte, BR
Pampulha
GP Cidade de Belo Horizonte
"Chico" Landi
4CL

16 August
Messina-Colle San Rizzo
Nicola Musmeci
A6GCS

21 August
Bellevue, F
Louis Gérard
6C-34

21 August
Spa Francorchamps, B
Malchamp
Arthur Legat
6CM

21 August
Enna
Pirato-Enna
Nicola Musmeci
A6GCS

28 August
Enna
Circuito della Cravatta
GP Pergusa
Nicola Musmeci
A6GCS

28 August
Dinant, B
Arthur Legat
6CM

28 August
Lausannne, CH
La Blècherette
GP de Lausanne
Nino Farina
4CLT/48

4 September
Rio de Janeiro, BR
Quinta da Boa Vista
Prêmio Crônica Esportiva Carioca
"Chico" Landi
4CL

17 September
Wat. Glen, NY USA
Seneca Cup
George Weaver
V8Ri

17 September
Goodwood, UK
Daily Graphic Trophy
Reg Parnell
4CLT/48

17 September
Goodwood, UK
Woodcote Cup
Reg Parnell
4CLT/48

17 September
Goodwood, UK
First September Handicap
Ken McAlpine
8CM

25 September
Biella-Oropa
Giovanni Bracco
A6GCS

25 September
Rio de Janeiro, BR
Subida da Gávea
Gino Bianco
8CM

5 November
G.Central Transvaal, ZA
St John Crusader
George S. Cannell
6C-34 aspirato

31 December
São Paulo, BR
Circuito do Pacaembu
Chico Landi
4CL

# 1950

25 February
G.Central Transvaal, ZA
Rand Open Trophy
George S. Cannell
6C-34 aspirato
10 March Siracusa
Coppa d'Oro
Nicola Musmeci
A6GCS

11 March
São Paulo, BR
Interlagos
GP Crônica Esportiva Bandeirante
Francesco Credentino
8CM

26 March
Monza
Coppa Intereuropa GT
Franco Bordoni
A6G

10 April
Goodwood, UK
3rd Easter Handicap
Duncan Hamilton
6CM

10 April
Goodwood, UK
Chichester Cup
"B Bira"
4CLT/48

10 April
Goodwood, UK
Richmond Trophy
Reg Parnell
4CLT/48

10 April
Pau, F
GP de Pau
Juan Manuel Fangio
4CLT/48

7 May
Massawa, Eritrea
Taulud Meeting
Cristoforo Bigi
Maserati Spl

9 May
São Paulo, BR
Interlagos
GP Interlagos
Francesco Credentino
8CM

29 May
Gamston, UK
Formule Libre I
Reg Parnell
4CLT/48

29 May
Gamston, UK
Formule Libre II
Reg Parnell
4CLT/48

10 June
Bridgehampton, NY USA
Formule Libre
George Weaver
V8Ri

11 June
Angoulême, F
Circuit des Remparts
Juan Manuel Fangio
4CLT/48-Engine A6

11 June
Mettet, B
Course de Côte de La Sarthe
Arthur Legat
6CM

11 June
Valangin, CH
Vue des Alpes
Louis Chiron
6CLT/48

9 July
Canton Fribourg, CH
La Sonnaz
Emmanuel de Graffenried
4CLT/48

23 July
Argegno
Argegno-Lanzo d'Intelvi
Giovanni Bracco
A6GCS

7 August
Gamston, UK
Nottingham Trophy
David Hampshire
4CLT/48

27 August
Fasano
Fasano-Selva
Giuseppe Ruggiero
A6GCS

27 August
Thompson, Ct. USA
Thompson Raceway
Formule Libre
George Weaver
V8RI

2 September
Rio de Janeiro, BR
Subida da Canoa
Gino Bianco
8CM

9 September
Curragh, IRL
Wakefield Trophy
Duncan Hamilton
6CM

24 September
Brno, CS
GP Brno
Václav Hovorka
6CM

30 September
Goodwood, UK
2nd September Handicap
Duncan Hamilton
6CM

1 October
Palermo
Favorita
Circuito della Favorita
Nicola Musmeci
A6GCS

7 October
Winfield, UK
Winfield GP
David Murray
4CLT/48

7 October
Gamston, UK
Nottingham SCC Gamston Meeting
Race 2
Roland Dutt
8C-3000

7 October
Gamston, UK
Nottingham SCC Gamston Meeting
Race 4
Roland Dutt
8C-3000

7 October
Gamston, UK
Nottingham SCC Gamston Meeting
Race 8
Roland Dutt
8C-3000

15 October
Rio de Janeiro, BR
Subida da Gávea
Gino Bianco
8CM

17 October
Rio de Janeiro, BR
Subida do Joá
Gino Bianco
8CM

18 December
Rio de Janeiro, BR
Subida da Tijuca
Gino Bianco
8CM

# 1951

19 March
Agrigento
Coppa dei Templi
Giovanni Bracco
A6GCS

26 March
Goodwood, UK
Chichester Cup
Reg Parnell
4CLT/48

22 April
Rio de Janeiro, BR
Boa Vista
Circuito da Quinta de Boa Vista
Gino Bianco
8CM

20 May
Paris, F
Bois de Boulogne
GP de Paris
Nino Farina
4CLT/48

27 May
Sorrento-Sant'Agata
Adolfo Schwelm
A6GCS

2 June
Isle of Man, UK
Castletown Trophy
Reg Parnell
4CLT/48

16 June
Crimond, UK
Aberdeen & District M.C.
Wilkie Wilkinson
4CLT/48

17 June
Palermo-Monte Pellegrino
Nicola Musmeci
A6GCS

7 July
Rio de Janeiro, BR
Subida de Canoas
Gino Bianco
6C-34

21 July
Wicklow, IRL
Leinster Trophy
Bobbie Baird
4CLT/48

21 July
Winfield, UK
Scottish GP
Philip Fotheringham-Parker
4CLT/48

21 July
Thompson, Ct. USA
Thompson Raceway
SCCA National
Formule Libre Handicap
George Weaver
V8RI

21 July
Rio de Janeiro, BR
Gávea
Subida do Joà
Gino Bianco
Maserati 6C-34

12 August
Rio de Janeiro, BR
Subida de Santa Teresa
Gino Bianco
Maserati 6C-34

12 August
Enna
Premio della Montagna
(Pirato-Enna)
Nicola Musmeci
A6GCS

19 August Vermont, Vt. USA
Mount Ascutney Hill Climb
George Weaver
V8Ri

15 September
Wat. Glen, NY USA Seneca Cup
George Weaver
V8Ri

22 October
Rio de Janeiro, BR
Subida de Gavea
Gino Bianco
6C-34

28 October
Vermont, Vt. USA
Mount Equinox Hillclimb
George Weaver
V8Ri

16 November
Vallelunga
Premio Brilli Peri
Inico Bernabei
A6GCS

16 November
Vallelunga
Premio Campari
Inico Bernabei
A6GCS

## 1952

20 April
Thompson, Ct. USA
Thompson Raceway
Formule Libre
George Weaver
V8Ri

24 May
Bridgehampton, NY USA
SCCA National.
Formule Libre
George Weaver
V8Ri

22 May
Modena, Aerautodromo Riunione AC
Modena
Guerino Bertocchi
A6GCM

4 August
São Paulo, BR
Interlagos
Prêmio Crônica Esportiva Paulista
Aristides Bertuol
4CLT/48
27 September
Goodwood, UK
Autumn Race Meeting
First September Handicap
Tony Gaze
8CM

## 1953

15 March
Teresópolis, BR
Subida de Teresópolis
Jorge Poucinhas
8CM

22 March
GP di Siracusa
Emmanuel de Graffenried
A6GCM

22 March
6 April Goodwood, UK
Chichester Cup
Emmanuel de Graffenried
A6GCM

6 April
Goodwood, UK
Lavant Cup
Emmanuel de Graffenried
A6GCM

31 May
Nürburgring, D
Internationales Eifelrennen
Emmanuel de Graffenried
A6GCM

21 June
Circuito di Caserta
Sergio Mantovani
A6GCS/53

28 June
Perugia
Giro dell'Umbria
Luigi Musso/Giuseppe Maria Favero
A6GCS/53

12 July
Circuito di Avellino
Luigi Musso
A6GCS/53

12 July
Valangin, CH
Vue des Alpes
Juan Manuel Fangio
A6GCM

25 July
Wilkes Barre, Pa. USA
Brynfan Tyddyn 1500 & 2000
Fritz Koster
A6GCS

25 July
Wilkes Barre, Pa. USA
rynfan Tyddyn
Sports
Joe Koster
A6GCS

26 July
Rio de Janeiro, BR
Subida da Gávea
Gino Bianco
6C-34

9 August
Freiburg-am-Breisgau, D Freiburg-
Schauinsland
Emmanuel de Graffenried
A6GCM

13 September
Monza
GP d'Italia
Juan Manuel Fangio
A6GCM
(World Constructors' Championship)

20 September
Modena
GP Modena
Juan Manuel Fangio
A6GCM

20 September
Rio de Janeiro, BR
Subida da Tijuca
Gino Bianco
A6GCM

4 October
Genova
Pontedecimo-Giovi
FeliceBonetto
A6GCM

11 October Roma
Criterium di Roma
(Vermicino-Rocca di Papa)
Luigi Musso
A6GCS/53

11 October
Thompson, Ct. USA
Thompson Raceway
SCCA Regional
(Modified 2000)
Fritz Koster
A6GCS

11 October
Thompson, Ct. USA
Thompson Raceway
SCCA Regional
(Formule Libre)
Fritz Koster
A6GCS

11 October Thompson, Ct. USA
Thompson Raceway
SCCA Regional
(Modified 8000)
Fritz Koster
A6GCS

15 November
Modena, Aerautodromo
Campionato Sociale AC Modena
Guerino Bertocchi
A6GCS/53

# 1954

3 January
Rio de Janeiro, BR
Gávea
GP de Rio de Janeiro
Emmanuel de Graffenried
A6GCS/53

10 January
São Paulo, BR
Interlagos
GP de São Paulo
Emmanuel de Graffenried
A6GCS/53

17 January
Buenos Aires, RA
Autodromo 17 de Octubre
GP de la República Argentina
Juan Manuel Fangio
250F
(World Constructors' Championship)

2 February
Orange-Gnoo Blas,
NSW, AUS
South Pacific Trophy
Fred Zambucka
8CM

19 March
Modena, Aerautodromo
Campionati Nazionali Universitari
Cesare Perdisa
A6GCS/53

3 April
Castle Combe, UK
Castle Combe (2500 Sport)
Roy Salvadori
A6GCS/53

3 April
Castle Combe, UK
Castle Combe (Unlimited Sport)
Roy Salvadori
A6GCS/53

15 April
Oulton Park, UK
British Empire Trophy (Sports 2700)
Roy Salvadori
A6GCS/53

30 April
Ibsley, UK
W. Hants & Dorset Formule Libre
Roy Salvadori
A6GCS/53

9 May
Westhampton B., NY USA Suffolk
County SCCA Regional (Modified
8000)
Fritz Koster
A6GCS

9 May
Westhampton Beach, NY Suffolk
County SCCA Regional
(Modified 8000 & Production 5000)
William Eager
A6GCS/53

16 May
Napoli
GP Napoli
Luigi Musso
A6GCS/53

29 May
Aintree, UK
Daily Telegraph Trophy
Stirling Moss
250F

30 May
Thompson, Ct. USA Thompson
Raceway
SCCA New England Regional
(Modified 3000 & Production 2000)
Fred Procter
A6GCS/53

22 May
Modena, Aerautodromo
Riunione dei Primati
Cesare Perdisa
A6GCS/53

22 May
Modena, Aerautodromo
Volante di Legno
Cesare Perdisa
A6GCS/53

5 June
Snetterton, UK
West Essex Car Club Trophy
Roy Salvadori
250F

5 June
Snetterton, UK
Curtis Trophy
Roy Salvadori
250F

6 June
Chimay, B
GP des Frontières
"B Bira"
A6GCM/250F

6 June
Roma
Castelfusano
GP Roma
Onofre Marimón
250F

6 June
Eritrea
Scicchetti-Saladarò
Cristoforo Bigi
4CS Spl

13 June
Eritrea
Nefasit-Asmara
Cristoforo Bigi
4CS Spl

19 June
London, UK
Crystal Palace
National Crystal Palace (2000 Sport)
Roy Salvadori
A6GCS/53

20 June
Spa Francorchamps, B
GP R.A.C. de Belgique
Juan Manuel Fangio
250F
(World Constructors' Championship)

20 June
Caserta
Circuito di Caserta
Luigi Musso
A6GCS/53

27 June
Metz, F
Circuit de Metz
Alfonso de Portago
A6GCS/53

4 July
L'Aquila
Coppa Cidonio
Luigi Bellucci
A6GCS/53

4 July
Rio de Janeiro, BR
Subida do Corcovado
Armando Silva
8CM

11 July
Cortina d'Ampezzo
Coppa d'Oro delle Dolomiti
Sergio Mantovani
A6GCS/53

18 July
Les Sables d'Olonne, F
Circuit des Sables d'Olonnne
Maurice Michy
A6GCS/53

7 August
Oulton Park, UK
Gold Cup
Stirling Moss
250F

7 August
Oulton Park, UK
Oulton Park Formule Libre
Stirling Moss
250F

8 August
Circuito di Senigallia (2000)
Luigi Musso
A6GCS/53

8 August
Genova
Borzonasca-La Squazza
Piero Valenzano
A6GCS/53

15 August
Circuito di Pescara
Luigi Musso
250F

28 August
Castle Combe, UK
National Meeting (Sport, unlimited)
Roy Salvadori
A6GCS/53

5 September
Spoleto-Monteluco
Sergio Ferraguti
A6GCS/53

19 September
Montlhéry, F
Coupes d'Automne
Pierre Monneret
A6GCS/53

25 September
Goodwood, UK
International Sport (2000)
Roy Salvadori
A6GCS/53

25 September
Goodwood, UK
Goodwood Trophy
Stirling Moss
250F

2 October
Aintree, UK
Daily Telegraph Trophy
Stirling Moss
250F

2 October
Aintree, UK
B.A.R.C. Trophy
Stirling Moss
250F

9 October
Snetterton, UK
Formule Libre
Roy Salvadori
250F

10 October
Thompson, Ct. USA
Thompson Raceway
SCCA Regional
(Formule Libre)
George Weaver
V8RI

18 October
Modena, Aerautodromo
Campionato Sociale AC Bologna
Cesare Perdisa
A6GCS/53

11 December
Nassau, BHM
Nassau Trophy (2000)
Al Koster
A6GCS

# 1955

8 January
Ardmore, NZ
New Zealand GP
Prince "Bira"
250F

6 February
Rio de Janeiro, BR
Gávea
GP Rio de Janeiro (Formule Libre)
Armando Silva
8CM

12/13 March
Genova
Coppa del Mare e dei Monti
Piero Valenzano
A6GCS/53

26 March Melbourne, AUS
Albert Park
Argus Trophy
Reg Hunt
A6GCM

26 March
Snetterton, UK
S.M.R.C.
Roy Salvadori
250F

11 April
Goodwood, UK
Glover Trophy
Roy Salvadori
250F

11 April
Pau, F
GP de Pau
Jean Behra
250F

11 April
Bathurst, AUS
Mt. Panorama
Bathurst 100
Reg Hunt
A6GCM

24 April
Thompson, Ct. USA
Thompson Raceway
SCCA New England Regional
(Formule Libre)
Bill Lloyd
300S

24 April
Bordeaux, F
GP de Bordeaux
Jean Behra
250F

30 April
Ibsley, UK
West Hants & Dorset CC
Roy Salvadori
250F

1 May
Thompson, Ct. USA
Thompson Raceway
SCCA Regional
(Unrestricted)
Bill Lloyd
300S

7 May
Silverstone, UK
International Trophy
Peter Collins
250F

7 May
Napoli
Circuito di Posillipo
Luigi Bellucci
A6GCS/53

15 May
Bari
GP Bari (2000)
Cesare Perdisa
A6GCS/53

15 May
Bari
GP Bari
Jean Behra
300S

22 May
Cagliari
Trofeo Internazionale della Sardegna
Gaetano Starrabba
A6GCS/53

28 May
Snetterton, U.K.
S.M.R.C. Formule libre
Roy Salvadori
250F

28 May
Snetterton, U.K.
Curtis Trophy
Roy Salvadori
250F

29 May
Monza
GP SupercorteMayre. 1000 km
Jean Behra/Luigi Musso
300S

29 May
Albi, F
GP d'Albi
André Simon
250F

29 May Thompson, Ct. USA
Thompson Raceway
SCCA New England Regional
(Modified 5000)
Bill Lloyd
300S

29 May Chimay, B
GP des Frontières
Benoît Musy
A6GCS/53

30 May
London, UK
Crystal Palace London Trophy
Peter Collins
250F

19 June
Imola
GP Shell
Cesare Perdisa
A6GCS/53

26 June
Circuito di Caserta
Luigi Bellucci
A6GCS/53

26 June
Porto, P
Boavista
GP do Portugal
Jean Behra
300S

26 June
Trieste-Opicina
Franco Bordoni
300S

17 July
Circuito di Reggio Calabria
Luigi Bellucci
A6GCS/53

30 July London, UK
Crystal Palace
BARC International Trophy Race
Mike Hawthorn
250F

31 July Catanzaro
Giro delle Calabrie
Luigi Bellucci
A6GCS/53

6 August Charterhall, U.K.
Daily Record Trophy
Bob Gerard
250F

28 August Fasano
Fasano-Selva
Attilio Buffa
A6GCS/53

28 August Enna
Circuito della Cravatta
Premio Pergusa
Franco Bordoni
A6GCS/53

28 August Nürburgring, D
A.D.A.C. 500 Km-Rennen
Jean Behra
150S

3 September Aintree, UK
Daily Telegraph Trophy
Roy Salvadori
250F

4 September Thompson, Ct. USA
Thompson Raceway
SCCA National
(Final all Classes)
John Gordon Bennett
300S

4 September Thompson, Ct. USA
Thompson Raceway
SCCA National
(Modified 5000)
Bill Lloyd
300S

4 September Stockholm, S
Skarpnäck
Stockholmsloppet (Production)
André Loens
A6GCS/53

18 September
Catania-Etna
Maria Teresa De Filippis
A6GCS/53

24 September Oulton Park, UK
Gold Cup
Stirling Moss
250F

25 September
Sorrento-Sant'Agata
Luigi Bellucci
A6GCS/53

2 October Padova
Treponti-Castelnuovo
Francesco Giardini
A6GCS/53

23 October Rio de Janeiro, BR
Barra da Tijuca
Subida da Tijuca
Armando Silva
8CM

6 November Caracas, YV
Los Próceres
GP de Venezuela
Juan Manuel Fangio
300S

4 December Palm Springs, Ca. USA
Palm Springs Road Races. Prel. Race
Ken Miles
150S

4 December Palm Springs, Ca. USA
Palm Springs Road Races (1500)
Ken Miles
150S

4 December Palm Springs, Ca. USA
Palm Springs Road Races. Main Race
Masten Gregory
300S

# 1956

7 January Ardmore, NZ
New Zealand GP
Stirling Moss
250F

14 January Levin, NZ
Vic Hudson Trophy
Tom Clark
8CM

15 January San Diego, Ca. USA
Torrey Pines Road Races, 1hr.
(Modified 8000)
MastenGregory
300S

29 January Buenos Aires, RA
1000 km Buenos Aires
Stirling Moss/ Carlos Menditéguy
300S
(Campionato del Mondo Marche)

30 January Orange-Gnoo Blas,
NSW AUS
South Pacific Trophy
Reg Hurit
A6GCM

11 February Fisherman's Bend,
Victoria, AUS
Victorian Trophy
Reg Hunt
A6GCM

3 March Ohakea, NZ
Ohakea Trophy
Tom Clark
8CM
11 March Melbourne, AUS
Albert Park
Melbourne Trophy
Reg Hunt
A6GCM

11 March Roma
Castelfusano
Criterium delle Nazioni
(km da fermo)
Giorgio Scarlatti
A6GCS/53

19 March Monza
Trofeo Vigorelli (T 2.5L/GT 2L)
Franco Ribaldi
A6G/54

19 March Monza
Trofeo Vigorelli (Sport)
Giuseppe Musso
A6GCS/53

2 April Goodwood, UK
Glover Trophy
Stirling Moss
250F

3 April Willow Springs, Ca. USA
Road Racing Register (Sport over
1500)
Jimmy Bryan
300S

21 April Aintree, UK
B.A.R.C. 200
Stirling Moss
250F

29 April Baden, CH
Meeting
Gilberto Cornacchia
200S

29 April Charterhall, UK
National Charterhall (Sport 1500)
Brian Naylor
150S

29 April Charterhall, UK
National Charterhall (Sport 2700)
Brian Naylor
150S
6 May Napoli
Posillipo
GP Napoli (Sport)
Luigi Bellucci
A6GCS/53

12 May Silverstone, UK
National Silverstone (Sport 1500)
Brian Naylor
150S

13 May Monte Carlo, MC
GP de Monaco
Stirling Moss
250F
(Campionato del Mondo Conduttori)

20 May Chimay, B
GP de Frontières
Benoît Musy
300S

20 May Milwaukee, Wi. USA
SCCA Regional Wisconsin GP
Phil Stewart
300S

20 May Cagliari
Trofeo Internazionale della Sardegna
Giorgio Scarlatti
A6GCS/53

21 May London, UK
Crystal Palace
BRSCC London Trophy
Stirling Moss
250F

27 May Nürburgring, D
A.D.A.C. 1000 Km-Rennen
Stirling Moss/Jean Behra/
Harry Schell/Piero Taruffi
300S
(Campionato del Mondo Marche)

30 May Thompson, Ct. USA
Thompson Raceway
SCCA Regional (Open class)
Paul Flichinger
4CL

9 June Oulton Park, U.K.
North Staffs M.C
Bruce Halford
250F

10 June Piacenza
Castell'Arquato-Vernasca
Nando Pagliarini
150S

10 June Montlhéry, F
1000 km de Paris
Jean Behra/Louis Rosier
300S

23 June Aintree, UK
Aintree 100
Horace Gould
250F

24 June Vicenza
Coppa Asiago
(Mosson-Tresché Conca)
Antonio Pozzato
A6GCS/53

29 June Reggio Emilia
Compiano-Vetto d'Enza
Pietro Pagliarini
A6GCS/53

29 giu. 1 lug Buchanan Field, Ca.
USA
San Francisco Region SCCA
(Preliminary race)
Dick Lyons
A6GCS/53

7 July Beverly, Ma. USA
SCCA National (Formule Libre)
George Weaver
4CLT/48 o V8Ti

8 July Napoli
Targa Vesuvio (Pugliano-Stazione)
Mennato Boffa
150S

14 July Silverstone, UK
Daily Express International Trophy
(Sport)
Stirling Moss
300S

15 July Frascati
Trofeo Franco Venturi
(Frascati- Tuscolo)
Roberto Lippi
A6GCS/53

15 July Les Sables d'Olonne, F
GP des Sables d'Olonne
Benoît Musy
300S

22 July Snetterton, U.K.
H.W. Sear Trophy
Roy Salvadori
250F

22 July Snetterton, UK
Vanwall Trophy
Roy Salvadori
250F

22 July Bari
GP di Bari
Stirling Moss
300S

22 July Bari
GP di Bari (2000)
Jean Behra
200S

26 August Caen, F
GP de Caen
Harry Schell
250F

2 September Monza
GP d'Italia
Stirling Moss
250F
(World Constructors' Championship)

15 September Watkins Glen, NY
USA Seneca Cup
George Weaver
4CLT/48

16 September Brescia
Trofeo Lumezzane
(Sarezzo-Lumezzane)
Giancarlo Sala
A6GCS/53

18 September
Sorrento-Sant'Agata
Mennato Boffa
150S

23 September
Catania-Etna
Luigi Bellucci
A6GCS/53

23 September Montlhéry, F
Coupes d'Automne
(GT/T/TS 2000)
Antoine Cicoira
A6G/54

30 September Viterbo
Coppa del Cimino
Giorgio Scarlatti
A6GCS/53

7 October Nuoro
Corsa del Redentore
(Mannasuddas-Nuoro)
Giorgio Scarlatti
A6GCS/53

7 October Montlhéry, F
Coupe du Salon
Francisco Godia Sales
300S

7 October Thompson, Ct. USA
Thompson Raceway
SCCA Regional
(Modified 3000)
Bill Lloyd
300S

14 October Genova
Pontedecimo-Giovi
Giorgio Scarlatti
A6GCS/53

21 October Roma
Castelfusano
GP Roma (corsa 3)
Olinto Morolli
A6G/54

21 October Roma
Castelfusano
GP Roma (corsa 5)
Jean Behra
200S

28 October Torino
Colli Torinesi
(Sassi-Galleria del Pino x 2)
Attilio Buffa
A6GCS/53

28 October Modena, Aerautodromo
Campionati AC Emiliani
Antonio De Berardinis
A6GCS/53

4 November Caracas, YV
Los Próceres
GP de Venezuela
Stirling Moss
300S

25 November Melbourne, AUS
Albert Park
Australian TT
Stirling Moss
300S

2 December Melbourne, AUS
Albert Park,
Australian GP
Stirling Moss
250F

9 December Nassau, BHM
Nassau Trophy
Stirling Moss
300S

Napoli
Agnano-Cappella dei Cangiani
Vincenzo Sorrentino
A6GCS/53

# 1957

1 January Phillip Island, AUS
(race 2)
Stan Jones
250F

13 January Buenos Aires, RA
Autódromo Municipal
GP de la República Argentina
Juan Manuel Fangio
250F
(Campionato del Mondo Conduttori)

27 January Buenos Aires, RA
Autódromo Municipal
GP de la Ciudad de Buenos Aires
Juan Manuel Fangio
250F

24 February La Habana, C
GP de Cuba
Juan Manuel Fangio
300S

19 March Napoli
Agnano-Cappella Cangiani
Giuseppe Ruggiero
A6GCS/53

23 March Sebring Fl., USA
12 hrs Race
Jean Behra/ Juan Manuel Fangio
450S
(World Championship for Marques)

24 March Melbourne, Albert Park
Victoria Trophy
Doug Whiteford
300S

24 March Modena, Aerautodromo
Campionati Nazionali Universitari
Antonio De Berardinis
A6GCS/53

22 April Pau, F
GP de Pau
Jean Behra
250F

27 April Napoli
Circuito di Posillipo
Luigi Bellucci
A6GCS/53

28 April Smartt Field, Mo. USA
SCCA St. Louis Region
(Modified 3000)
Jim Kimberley
200 S

1 May Monza
Trofeo Vigorelli
Luigi Piotti
300S

12 May
Helsinki, SF
Eläintarhanajot (Helsinki GP)
Jo Bonnier
200S

15 May Madrid, E
Barajas
Grand Prix Nacional Sport
Juan Jover
200S

19 May Coffeyville, Ks. USA
Kansas Region SCCA
(Preliminary race)
Dale Duncan
300S

19 May Coffeyville, Ks. USA
Kansas Region SCCA
(Modified 5000)
Dale Duncan
300S

19 May Cumberland, Md. USA Cumberland Sportscar Races
SCCA National (Modified 8000)
Carroll Shelby
300S

19 May Monte Carlo, MC
GP de Monaco
Juan Manuel Fangio
250F
(Campionato del Mondo Conduttori)

26 May Santa Rosa, Ca. USA
Cotati Sports Car Road Races
(Modified 5000)
Carroll Shelby
300S

9 June Lisbon, P
Monsanto
GP do Portugal
Juan Manuel Fangio
300S

9 June Chimay, B
GP des Frontières
Franco Bordoni
200S

9 June Lime Rock, Ct. USA
SCCA National (Modified 5000)
Carroll Shelby
300S

10 June
Sorrento-Sant'Agata
Luigi Bellucci
A6GCS/53

16 June Opatjia (Abbazia), YU
GP Adria
Antonio Pozzato
A6GCS/53

29 June Thompson, Ct. USA
Thompson Raceway
1 hour race
John Fitch
150S

30 June Mont Ventoux, F
Mont Ventoux
Willy Daetwyler
200S
(Campionato Europeo Montagna)

7 July Lime Rock, Ct. USA
SCCA Regional NY Region
(Sports 5000)
John Fitch
150S

7 July Rouen, F
GP de l'ACF
Juan Manuel Fangio
250F
(Campionato del Mondo Conduttori)

28 July Lime Rock, Ct. USA
SCCA New England Regional
Carroll Shelby
450S

4 August Nürburgring, D
GP von Deutschland
Juan Manuel Fangio
250F
(World Constructors' Championship)

4 August Danville, Va. USA
SCCA National (race 5)
Carroll Shelby
450S

4 August Danville, Va. USA
SCCA National (race 10)
Carroll Shelby
450S

11 August Kristianstad, S
GP Sweden
Jean Behra/Stirling Moss
450S
(World Championship for Marques)

11 August Lowood, AUS
Lowood Trophy
Stan Jones
250F

1 September
Aosta-Gran San Bernardo
Willy Daetwyler
200S
(European Mountain Championship)

8 September Cadours, F
GP Cadours
André Loens
200S

8 September Monza
Coppa Intereuropa 2600
Enrico Anselmi
A6G/54

14 September Stillwater, Ok. USA
SCCA Neokla Regional
(Modified unlimited, Preliminary race)
Jim Hall
200SI

14 September Stillwater, Ok. USA
SCCA Neokla Regional
Preliminary race (Modified Unli-
mited)
Dale Duncan
300S

14 September Stillwater, Ok. USA
SCCA Neokla Regional (Main race)
Jack Hinkle
300S

15 September Platamona
Circuito di Sassari
Luigi Bellucci
A6GCS/53

22 September Kanton Bern, CH
Mitholz-Kandersteg
Erwin Sommerhalder
A6GCM/250F

333

22 September Modena
Aerautodromo, GP di Modena
Jean Behra
250F

22 September
Messina-Colle San Rizzo
Luigi Bellucci
A6GCS/53

29 September Genova
Pontedecimo-Giovi
Giorgio Scarlatti
200 SI

29 September Fort Pierce, Fl. USA
SCCA Florida Regionals
Joe Sheppard
200SI

6 October Montlhéry, F
Coupes du Salon
Francisco Godia Sales
200S

6 October Gainesville, Ga. USA
SCCA Atlanta Region
(Modified 5000 & Production 8000)
Joe Sheppard
200SI

6 October
Sorrento-Sant'Agata
Luigi Bellucci
A6GCS/53

6 October
Trieste-Opicina
Adolfo Tedeschi
200S

27 October Casablanca, MA
GP du Maroc
Jean Behra
250F

2 November Palm Springs, Ca. USA
SCCA National (race 5)
Carroll Shelby
450S

3 November Palm Springs, Ca. USA
SCCA National (race 10)
Carroll Shelby
450S

10 November Galveston, Tx. USA
San Jacinto Region SCCA (Prel. race)
J.E."Ebb"Rose
300S

16 November Riverside, Ca. USA
SCCA National (race 10)
Masten Gregory
470S
17 November Riverside, Ca. USA
SCCA National (race 10)
Carroll Shelby
450S

1 December Vallelunga
6 ore Esso (2000 sport)
Odoardo Govoni
A6GCS/53

1 December Nassau, BHM
Nassau TT
Masten Gregory
470S

1 December São Paulo, Interlagos
GP Cidade de São Paulo
Juan Manuel Fangio
300S

7 December Southbridge, NZ
J.F. Tutton Trophy
Frank Shuter
8CM

8 December Rio de Janeiro, BR
Quinta da Boa Vista
GP Cidade de Rio de Janeiro
Juan Manuel Fangio
300S

# 1958

11 January Miami, Fl. USA
Orange Bowl
SCCA National (race 1)
Carroll Shelby
470S

1 February Dunedin, NZ
Dunedin Road Race
Ross Jensen
250F

2 February Buenos Aires, RA
Autódromo Municipal
GP de la Ciudad de Buenos Aires
Juan Manuel Fangio
250F

8 February Teretonga, NZ
Teretonga International
Ross Jensen
250 F

16 Feb. New Smyrna Beach, Fl. USA
SCCA Regional
(Preliminary race)
Joe Sheppard
200 SI

16 Feb. New Smyrna Beach, Fl. USA
SCCA Regional. (Modified 8000)
Joe Sheppard
200 SI

23 February Fisherman's Bend,
Vct. AUS
Victorian Trophy
Stan Jones
250 F

1 March Ardmore, NZ
Ardmore 50
Ross Jensen
250F

9 March Mansfield, Tx. USA
SCCA Regional Red River
(Preliminary race)
Jim Hall
250S

9 March Boca Raton, Fl. USA
(Preliminary race Sports 5000)
Bark Henry
300S

16 March Petrópolis, BR
Prêmio Cidade de Petrópolis
Henrique Casini
300S

30 March Enna,
Autodromo di Pergusa
GP Pergusa
Adolfo Tedeschi
200 SI

7 April Bathurst, AUS
Mount Panorama
Bathurst 100
Doug Whiteford
300S

12 April Palm Springs, Ca. USA
SCCA Pacific Coast
Championship Sprint
Carroll Shelby
450S

20 April Galveston, Tx. USA
Gran Carrera Lafitte (race 4)
Ebb Rose
450S

20 April Galveston, Tx. USA
Gran Carrera Lafitte (race 7)
Ebb Rose
450S

27 April Louisville, Ky. USA
SCCA Regional
(Preliminary race)
Bark Henry
300S

4 May
Bologna-San Luca
Odoardo Govoni
200SI

16 May Chester, SC USA
SCCA Regional (race 3)
Dan Clippenger
450S

1 June Firenze
Coppa della Consuma
Odoardo Govoni
200SI

8 June Piacenza
Castell'Arquato-Vernasca
Nando Pagliarini
200S

8 June Napoli
Targa del Vesuvio
Mennato Boffa
A6GCS

8 June Fort Worth, Tx. USA
Eagle Mountain
SCCA Regional
Jim Hall
250S

22 June Vallelunga
6 ore Esso (2600 GT)
Pietro Bernabei
A6G/54

28 June Rio de Janeiro, BR
Barra da Tijuca
Circuito da Barra da Tijuca
Henrique Casini
300 S

4 July Walterboro, SC USA
SCCA Regional (sprint)
Harry Rollings
450S

6 July Porto Torres,
Marinella
Circuito di Sassari
Adolfo Tedeschi
200SI

6 July Reggio Emilia
Compiano-Vetto d'Enza
Nando Pagliarini
200SI

13 July Vila Real, P
Circuito Vila Real
Stirling Moss
300S

2 August Teretonga, NZ
Ross Jensen
250F

10 August
Trapani-Monte Erice
Mennato Boffa
A6GCS

10 August Karlskoga, S
Kanonloppet
Stirling Moss
300S

31 August Torino
Corsa ai Colli Torinesi
(Sassi-Superga)
Odoardo Govoni
200SI

31 August Courtland, Al. USA
SCCA Regional. (race 3)
Walt Cline
450S

7 September Roma
Criterium di Roma Coppa Gallenga
(Squarciarelli-Rocca di Papa x2)
Adolfo Tedeschi
200SI

14 September
Sorrento-Sant'Agata
Luigi Bellucci
A6GCS/53

14 September Kanton Bern, CH
Mitholz-Kandersteg
Erwin Sommerhalder
A6GCM/250F

20 September Watkins Glen, NY
USA
SCCA National
Phil Cade
V8Ri

28 September Watkins Glen, NY
USA
USAC Watkins Glen International
GP
Jo Bonnier
250F

28 September Genova
Pontedecimo-Giovi
Odoardo Govoni
200 SI

12 October Forth Worth, Tx. USA
Eagle Mountain
SCCA Regional (race 3)
Ebb Rose
450S

13 October Forth Worth, Tx. USA
Eagle Mountain
SCCA Regional (race 6)
Ebb Rose
450S

18 October Lime Rock, Ct. USA
SCCA Regional (1500)
E.F. Spicer
150S

26 October Modena, Aerautodromo
Campionati Emiliani
Odoardo Govoni
200S

2 November Palm Springs, Ca. USA
SCCA Exhibition Race (race 4)
Carroll Shelby
570S

30 November Hammond, La. USA
SCCA Regional Harvest Races
(race 6)
J.E. "Ebb" Rose
450S

5 December Nassau, BHM
Governor's Cup
Ulf Norinder
200S

26 December Phillip Island, AUS
Phillip Island Trophy
Stan Jones
250 F

# 1959

2 March Longford, AUS
Australian Grand Prix
Stan Jones
250 F

7 March Pomona, Ca. USA
USAC Championship (race 6)
Bill Krause
450S

8 March Napoli
Agnano-Cappella dei Cangiani
Mennato Boffa
200 S

30 March Bathurst, AUS
Mt. Panorama
Bathurst 100
Ross Jensen
250 F

12 April Vineland, NJ USA
Vineland Speedway
South Jersey Region SCCA
Main race
Bob Holbert
300S

19 April Stuttgart, Az. USA
SCCA Regional
(Preliminary race)
Bob Aylward
250S

26 April Rio de Janeiro, BR
Barra da Tijuca
Prêmio Crônica Esportiva
Henrique Casini
300S

7 May Palermo
Valdesi-S.Rosalia
Nino Vaccarella
200SI

16 May Vallelunga
6 ore Esso (2600 GT)
Giacomo Moioli "Noris"
A6G/54 Zagato

28 May
Palermo-Monte Pellegrino
Nino Vaccarella
200SI

30 May Bathurst, AUS
Mt. Panorama
Bathurst (race 1)
Ross Jensen
250 F

31 May Enna, Pergusa
Premio Pergusa
Nino Vaccarella
200SI

31 May Coffeyville, Ks. USA
Harris Moore Memorial (race 8)
Jim Hall
450S

7 June
SalsoMayre-S. Antonio
Luigi Dodi
2000

7 June Vineland, NJ USA
Vineland Speedway
South Jersey Region SCCA
(Modified 5000)
Fred Windridge
300S

7 June Vineland, NJ USA
Vineland Speedway
South Jersey Region SCCA
(Modified 8000)
Fred Windridge
300S

14 June Louisville, Ky. USA
SCCA Regional Main race
Fred Windridge
300S

21 June
Circuito di Caserta
Mennato Boffa
200SI

5 July Lake Garnett, Ks. USA
SCCA Regional (Prelimary race)
Jack Hinkle
200S

5 July Lake Garnett, Ks. USA
SCCA Regional (Main race)
Jack Hinkle
200S

12 July Rouen, F
Coupe Delamarre-Deboutteville
Stirling Moss
60

26 July Vineland, NJ USA
Vineland Speedway Philadelphia
Region SCCA (Modified 3000)
Charles Kolb
300S

9 August
Trapani–Monte Erice
Nino Vaccarella
200SI

22 August Vineland, NJ USA
Vineland Speedway South Jersey
Region SCCA (Modified 5000)
Charles Kolb
300S

30 August Torino
Corsa ai Colli Torinesi
(Sassi–Superga)
Nino Vaccarella
200SI

5 September Meadowdale, Il. USA
Meadowdale Raceways
USAC Championship
Formule Libre (race 3)
Lloyd Ruby
450S

5 September Santa Barbara, Ca. USA
CSCC Pacific Coast Campionship
(race 9)
Bill Krause
450S

20 September Lyon, F
Limonest–Mont Verdun
André Testut
250F

20 September Genova
Pontedecimo–Giovi
Odoardo Govoni
60

4 October Belluno
Coppa del Nevegal
"Noris" (Giacomo Moioli)
A6G/54 Zagato

11 October Courtland, Al. USA
SCCA Regional (race 4)
Jim Hall
450S

11 October Zeltweg, A
Flugplatz, Preis Zeltweg
Odoardo Govoni
60

18 October Graz, A
Graz–Thalerhof
Odoardo Govoni
60

18 October Rosario, RA
Copa Acción de San Lorenzo
Roberto W. Bonomi
300S

25 October Dothan, Al. USA
SCCA Regional (race 3)
Jim Hall
450S

25 October Dothan, Al. USA
SCCA Regional (race 6)
E.D. Martin
61

25 October Dothan, Al. USA
SCCA Regional (race 9)
E.D. Martin
61

25 October Kanton Bern, CH
Thun–Heiligschwendi
Erwin Sommerhalder
A6GCM/250F

1 November Vineland, NJ. USA Vineland Speedway South Jersey Region
SCCA Preliminary race (3000)
Ben Diaz
A6GCM/53

8 November Oklahoma City, Ok.
USA
SCCA Regional. "Petit Prix"
Jack Hinkle
200 S

# 1960

24 January Palm Springs, Ca. USA
SCCA Regional (race 14)
Bob Drake
61

13 February Waimate, NZ
Street Circuit
Waimate 50
Johnny Mansel
250F

14 February Willow Spring, Ca. USA
SCCA Regional (Modified 8000)
Bob Drake
61

28 February La Habana, C
GP Libertad
Stirling Moss
61

3 April Riverside, Ca. USA
Examiner GP (USAC)
Carroll Shelby
61

3 April Pensacola, Fl. USA
SCCA National (Modified 8000)
Gaston "Gus" Andrey
61

3 April Lawrenceville, Il. USA
SCCA Regional (race 1)
Dave Causey/Luke Stear
61

3 April Lawrenceville, Il. USA
SCCA Regional (race 2)
Dave Causey/Luke Stear
61

3 April Verona
Stallavena–Boscochiesanuova
Odoardo Govoni
60

10 April Vineland, NJ USA
Vineland Speedway South Jersey
SCCA Regional (race 4)
Ben Diaz
A6GCS/53

17 April San Marcos, Tx. USA
SCCA Regional (race 5)
Jack Hinkle
61

17 April San Marcos, Tx. USA
SCCA Regional (race 8)
Jim Hall
570S

30 April Longview, Tx. USA
SCCA Regional
(Preliminary & Main race)
Jim Hall
61

1 May Vaca Valley, Ca. USA
CSCC (Modified 8000)
Bob Drake
61

7 May Castle Rock, Co. USA
Continental Divide Raceway
(Preliminary race)
Jim Hall
61

8 May Phoenix, Az. USA
SCCA Regional
(Preliminary & Main race)
Bob Drake
61

15 May
Palermo-Monte Pellegrino
Giuseppe Alotta
A6GCS/53

15 May Cumberland, Md. USA
SCCA National (Modified 8000)
Walt Hansgen
61

22 May Thompson, Ct. USA
Thompson Raceway
SCCA Regional (Modified)
Gus Andrey
61

22 May Nürburgring, D
ADAC 1000 Km-Rennen
Stirling Moss/Dan Gurney
61
(Campionato del Mondo Marche)

29 May Santa Barbara, Ca. USA
Goleta CSCC
(Modified 8000)
Bob Drake
61

30 May La Junta, Co. USA
SCCA Regional
Preliminary & Main race
Jack Hinkle
61

30 May Bridgehampton, NY USA
SCCA National (Modified 8000)
Walt Hansgen
61

May Hammond, La. USA
SCCA Regional (Main race)
Jim Hall
570S

12 June
SalsoMayre-S. Antonio
Odoardo Govoni
60

12 June Argegno, (CO)
Trofeo Val d'Intelvi
Giuliano Giovanardi
60

18 June Roosevelt, NY USA
SCCA Regional
Rickenbacker Trophy
Walt Hansgen
61

19 June Oklahoma City, Ok. USA
SCCA Regional
(Preliminary race)
Jack Hinkle
61

19 June Oklahoma City, Ok. USA
SCCA Regional Petit Grand Prix
Jack Hinkle
61

19 June
Circuito di Caserta
Giorgio Scarlatti
60

19 June Roma
Vermicino-Rocca di Papa
Giuliano Giovanardi
60

25 June Castle Rock, Co. USA
Continental Divide
USAC (heat 1)
Bob Schroeder
61

25 June Castle Rock, Co. USA
Continental Divide
USAC (heat 2)
Jim Hall
61

26 June
Varese-Campo dei Fiori
Odoardo Govoni
60

29 June Predappio
Predappio-Rocca delle Caminate
Odoardo Govoni
60

2 July Monopoli
Coppa Monopoli
Umberto Filotico
2000

3 July
Bolzano-Mendola
Nino Vaccarella
200 SI

3 July Galveston, Tx. USA
SCCA Regional (race 3)
Jim Hall
570S

4 July Galveston, Tx. USA
SCCA Regional (race 6)
Jim Hall
570S

4 July Lake Garnett, Ks. USA
SCCA National
Kansas GP
Jack Hinkle
61

10 July
Trento-Monte Bondone
Odoardo Govoni
60

10 July Vaca Valley, Ca. USA
SCCA Regional
(Preliminary & Main race)
Jim Connor
61

10 July Falkenberg, S
Västkustloppet
Bo Ljungfeldt
200S

16 July Castle Rock, Co. USA
Continental Divide Raceways
SCCA National (race 4)
Jim Hall
570S

24 July
Trieste-Opicina
Mennato Boffa
60

31 July Elkhart Lake, Wi. USa
Road America
USAC Road America 200
Jim Jeffords
61

7 August
Trapani-Monte Erice
Nino Vaccarella
200 SI

7 August Montgomery, NY USA
SCCA National
(Modified 8000)
Walt Hansgen
61

3 September Santa Barbara, Ca. USA
SCCA (Preliminary race)
Jim Connor
61

3 September Santa Barbara, Ca. USA
SCCA Ernie MacAfee Memorial
Jim Connor
61

7 September São Paulo, BR
Interlagos
500 km Interlagos
Celso Lara Barberis
300S

11 September Brescia
Trofeo Lumezzane
Coppa Renzo Cantoni
Odoardo Govoni
60

11 September Santa Rosa, Ca. USA
Cotati SCCA Regional
(Preliminary & Main race)
Jim Connor
61

11 September Elkhart Lake, Wi. USA
SCCA Road America 500
Dave Causey/Luke Stear
61

18 September Midland, Tx. USA
SCCA Regional
Jim Hall
61

26 September
Catania-Etna
Mennnato Boffa
60

1 October São Paulo, BR
Interlagos
Torneio Sul-americano
Celso Lara Barberis
300S

2 October Genova
Pontedecimo-Giovi
Odoardo Govoni
60

9 October Thompson, Ct. USA
Thompson Raceway
SCCA Regional (Modified 8000)
Gus Andrey
61

9 October Connelsville, Pa. USA
SCCA Regional
Archie Means
200S

16 October Riverside, Ca. USA
Times GP Consolation (race 2)
Alan Connell
61

16 October Riverside, Ca. USA
USAC Times GP
Bill Krause
61

16 October Modena
Aeroautodromo
Coppa d' Oro ACI
Odoardo Govoni
60

4 November Rio de Janeiro, BR
GP Cidade do Rio de Janeiro
Mario A. Cabral
300S

20 November
Messina-Colle San Rizzo
Nino Vaccarella
200S

11 December Monza
Coppa FISA (gara 6)
Mennato Boffa
60

# 1961

7 January Pomona, Ca. USA
CSCC (Preliminary race)
Bill Krause
61

8 January Pomona, Ca. USA
CSCC (Sports 8000)
Bill Krause
61

11 March Mansfield, La. USA
SCCA Regional
(Main race)
Jim Hall
570S

19 March Napoli
Agnano-Cappella dei Cangiani
Mennato Boffa
60

8 April Hondo, Tx. USA
SCCA Texas Regional
(Preliminary race)
Bob Schroeder
61

9 April Hondo, Tx. USA
SCCA Texas Regional
Carrera del Alamo
Jim Hall
61

9 April Verona
Stallavena-Boscochiesanuova
Mennato Boffa
60

10 April Vineland, NJ USA Speedway
South Jersey Region SCCA
(Main & Preliminary race)
Roger Penske
61

15 April Levin, NZ
Formule Libre race
Brian Prescott
250F

16 April Vienna, A
Aspern
Preis der Wien
Mennato Boffa
60

16 April Stockton, Ca. USA
SCCA Regional
(Preliminary race)
Chuck Sargent
61

16 April Stockton, Ca. USA
SCCA Regional
(Sports 8000)
Chuck Sargent
61

29 April Las Vegas, Nv. USA
Mc Carran Field
SCCA Regional
(Preliminary race)
Jim Hall
61

30-April Las Vegas, Nv. USA
Mc Carran Field
SCCA Regional
Gold Cup
Jim Hall
61

30 April Hammond, La. USA
SCCA Louisiana GP
Bob Schroeder
61

30 April Hammond, La. USA
SCCA Delta Region
(Modified 8000)
Bob Schroeder
61

30 April Danville, Va. USA
SCCA National President Cup
Walt Hansgen
61

6 May Mansfield, La. USA
SCCA Regional
(Preliminary race)
Alan Connell
61

14 May Piacenza
Castell'Arquato-Vernasca
Odoardo Govoni
60

21 May
Palermo-Monte Pellegrino
Emanuele Trapani
2000

28 May La Junta, Co. USA
SCCA Divisional
(Modified 8000)
Jack Hinkle
61

28 May Bridgehampton, NY USA
SCCA National
(Modified 8000)
Walt Hansgen
61

28 May Nürburgring, D
ADAC 1000 Km-Rennen
Masten Gregory/Lucky Casner
61
(Campionato del Mondo Marche)

4 June Firenze
Coppa della Consuma
Odoardo Govoni
60

4 June Rouen
Coupe Delamarre-Deboutteville
Lucky Casner
61

10 June Laguna Seca, Ca. USA
SCCA Regional
(Preliminary race)
Chuck Sargent
61

11 June Laguna Seca, Ca. USA
SCCA Regional (S 8000)
Chuck Sargent
61

11 June Roma
Vermicino-Rocca di Papa
Odoardo Govoni
60

18 June Elkhart Lake, Wi. USA
Road America SCCA National
International June Sprints
Roger Penske
61

18 June Ponca City, Ok. USA
SCCA Regional (race 3)
Jack Hinkle
61

18 June Ponca City, Ok. USA
SCCA Regional (Main race)
Jack Hinkle
61

29 June Reggio Emilia
Compiano-Vetto d'Enza
Mennato Boffa
60

30 June Bloomington, Mn. USA
Met Stadium
SCCA Regional
Don Skogmo
61

1 July Lime Rock, Ct. USA
SCCA National
Roger Penske
61

2 July Courtland, Al. USA
SCCA Regional (Preliminary Race)
Fred Gamble
61

2 July Monopoli
Coppa Monopoli
Umberto Filotico
2000

3 July Courtland, Al. USA
SCCA Regional (Sport unlimited)
Bill Kimberley
61

15 July Santa Rosa, Ca. USA
Cotati SCCA Regional
(Preliminary race)
Chuck Sargent
61

16 July
Aosta-Pila
Odoardo Govoni
60

23 July Meadowdale, Wi. USA
SCCA National. Wisconsin GP
Roger Penske
61

30 July Amalfi
Coppa Primavera
Amalfi-Agerola
Odoardo Govoni
60

30 July Bloomington, Mn. USA
Met Stadium SCCA Regional
Don Skogmo
61

5 August Bridgehampton, NY USA
SCCA National (Modified 5000)
Walt Hansgen
63

6 August Torino
Cesana-Sestrière
Mennato Boffa
60

20 August Vaca Valley, Ca. USA
SCCA Regional (Modified)
Chuck Parsons
61

20 August Indianapolis, In. USA
Raceway Park
SCCA National (Modified 8000)
Walt Hansgen
61

27 August Enna
Autodromo di Pergusa
Premio Pergusa
Mennato Boffa
60

27 August Fasano
Fasano-Selva
Nino Todaro
60

7 September São Paulo, BR
Interlagos
500 km Interlagos
Celso Lara Barberis/
Ruggero Peruzzo/Emilio Zambello
450S

10 September Elkhart Lake, Wi. USA
Road America
500 miles Road America
Walt Hansgen/Augie Pabst
63

24 September
Catania-Etna
Mennato Boffa
60

24 September Reno, Nv. USA
Stead A.F. Base
SCCA San Francisco Regional
(Preliminary race)
Chuck Parsons
61

24 September Reno, Nv. USA
Stead A.F. Base
SCCA San Francisco Regional
(Modified)
Chuck Parsons
61

1 October Norman, Ok. USA
SCCA Regional
Petit Prix
Jack Hinkle
61

8 October Innsbrück, A
Alpenflughafen
Preis von Tirol
Mennato Boffa
60

19 November Hammond, La. USA
SCCA Harvest Race
George Koehne
61

# 1962

14 April Stockton, Ca. USA
SCCA Regional
(Preliminary race)
Chuck Sargent
61

15 April Stockton, Ca. USA
SCCA Regional
(Modified)
Chuck Sargent
61

28 April Alliance, Nv. USA
SCCA Regional
(Preliminary race)
Jack Hinkle
61

20 May São Paulo, BR
Interlagos
Festival Automobilístico do ACEPS
Celso Lara Barberis
300S

26 May Stuttgart, Az. USA
SCCA Regional
(Preliminary race)
Enus Wilson
61

27 May Santa Barbara, Ca. USA
Goleta Ladies' Race
Paula Murphy
?

27 May
Bologna-Raticosa
Odoardo Govoni
60

27 May
Palermo-Monte Pellegrino
Nino Todaro
60

3 June Piacenza
Bobbio-Passo del Penice
Claudio Corini
60

9 June Laguna Seca, Ca. USA
SCCA Regional
(Preliminary race)
Bill Krause
61

10 June Ponca City, Ok. USA
SCCA Regional "Grand Prix"
Jack Hinkle
61

21 June Vallelunga
Premio Campagnano (2000 S)
Odoardo Govoni
60

24 June Palermo
Valdesi-S.Rosalia
Nino Todaro
60

1 July
Bolzano-Mendola
Odoardo Govoni
60

15 July Oakland, Ca. USA
SCCA Regional Grand Prix

Bill Krause
61

15 July Torino
Cesana-Sestrière
Odoardo Govoni
60

22 July Pomona, Ca. USA
USSCC (Preliminary race)
Bill Krause
61

22 July Pomona, Ca. USA
USSCC (Modified 5000)
Bill Krause
61

29 July Minneapaolis, Mn. USA
SCCA Regional (Main race)
Don Skogmo
61

5 August
Trapani-Monte Erice
Nino Todaro
60

19 August Reggio Calabria
Santo Stefano-Gambarie
Nino Todaro
60

19 August Pomona, Ca. USA
USSCC (Modified 5000)
Bill Krause
61

19 August Mankato, Mn. USA
SCCA Regional (Main race)
Don Skogmo
61

2 September
Criterium di Roma
(Squarciarelli -Rocca di Papa x2)
Odoardo Govoni
60

2 September Santa Barbara, Ca. USA
Goleta SCCA Divisional
(Preliminary race)
Bill Krause
61

2 September Santa Barbara, Ca. USA
Goleta SCCA Divisional
(Modified 5000)
Bill Krause
61

9 September
Catania-Etna
Odoardo Govoni
60

23 September Reno, Nv. USA
Stead A.F. Base
SCCA Divisional
San Francisco Region
Bill Krause
61

7 October Città S.Angelo
Coppa Belvedere
Leandro Terra
60

7 October Wichita, Ks. USA
Garden City
SCCA Regional (Main race)
Jack Hinkle
61

4 November
Messina-Colle San Rizzo
Nino Todaro
60

# 1963

21 April Stuttgart, Az. USA
SCCA Regional
(Main race)
Enus Wilson
61

26 May Lawrenceville, Il. USA
SCCA Regional
(Modified)
Otto Klein
250S

2 June
Palermo-Monte Pellegrino
Nino Todaro
60

9 June Rosemount, Mn. USA
SCCA Regional
(Modified & Production unlimited)
Don Skogmo
61

29 June Watkins Glen, NY USA
SCCA Regional
Conrad Kraus
200S

4 August
Trapani-Monte Erice
Nino Todaro
60

4 August Viterbo
Lago-Montefiascone
Franco Bernabei
60

6 October Trapani
Alcamo-Monte Bonifato
Nino Todaro
60

# 1964

6 March São Paulo, BR
Interlagos
GP Rogê Ferreira
Ciro Cayres
450S

30 March Bologna
Coppa Acqua Cerelia
(Vergato-Cereglio)
Odoardo Govoni
60

24 May Firenze
Coppa della Consuma
Odoardo Govoni
60

31 May
Bologna-Raticosa
Odoardo Govoni
60

2 August
Trapani-Monte Erice
Mennato Boffa
60

30 August
Coppa Città di Chieti
Turillo Barbuscia
60

# 1965

20 September Napoli
Targa del Vesuvio
Vincenzo Sorrentino
60

# 1966

12 June São Paulo, BR
Interlagos
Prêmio Aniversário APVC
Ubaldo Lolli
300S

# 1997

31 August Varano de' Melegari
IGT Varano
Alessandro Pifferi
Ghibli

28 September Vallelunga
IGT Vallelunga
Arturo Merzario
Ghibli

# 2004

19 September Orschersleben, D
500 km
Andrea Bertolini/Mika Salo
MC12
(FIA GT World Championship)

14 November Zhuhai, CN
500 km
Andrea Bertolini/Mika Salo
MC12
(FIA GT World Championship)

# 2005

1 May Misano
Campionato Italiano GT
Gabriele Matteuzzi/
Piergiuseppe Perazzini
MC 12

1 May Magny-Cours, F
500 km
Karl Wendlinger/Andrea Bertolini
MC 12GT1

10 July Budapest, H
Hungaroring
Campionato Italiano GT
Gabriele Matteuzzi/
Piergiuseppe Perazzini
MC 12

30-31 July Spa Francorchamps, B
24 Heures de Spa
Timo Scheider/Michael Bartels/
Eric van der Poele
MC 12GT1
(FIA GT World Championship)

28 August Orschersleben, D
500 km
Thomas Biagi/Fabio Babini
MC 12GT1
(FIA GT World Championship)

18 September Istanbul, TN
2 Hours of Istanbul
Timo Scheider/Michael Bartels
MC 12GT1
(FIA GT World Championship)

13 November Vallelunga
6 Ore
Davide Mastracci/Michele Serafini/
Leonardo Maddalena
MC 12

# 2006

26 March Imola
Campionato Italiano GT (gara1)
Gianbattista Giannoccaro/
Toni Vilander
MC 12GT1

7 May Silverstone, UK
Tourist Trophy
Andrea Bertolini/Michael Barthels
MC 12GT1
(FIA GT World Championship)

14 May Misano
Campionato Italiano GT (gara 2)
Luca Cappellari/Miguel Ramos
MC 12

14 May Misano
Campionato Italiano GT (gara 1)
Luca Cappellari/Miguel Ramos
MC 12

28 May Vallelunga
Campionato Italiano GT (gara 1 & 2)
Gianbattista Giannoccaro/
Toni Vilander
MC 12GT1

11 June Magione
Campionato Italiano GT (gara 1)
Luca Cappellari/Miguel Ramos
MC 12

11 June Magione
Campionato Italiano GT (gara 2)
Gianbattista Giannoccaro/
Toni Vilander
MC 12GT1

2 July Orschersleben, D
500 km
Andrea Bertolini/Michael Barthels
MC 12GT1
(FIA GT World Championship)

9 July Monza
Campionato Italiano GT (gara 1)
Gianbattista Giannoccaro/
Toni Vilander
MC 12GT1

9 July Monza
Campionato Italiano GT (gara 2)
Luca Cappellari/
Piergiuseppe Perazzini
MC 12GT

29-30 July Spa Francorchamps, B
24 Heures de Spa
Andrea Bertolini/Michael Barthels/
Eric van der Poele
MC 12GT1
(FIA GT World Championship)

3 September Dijon, F
500 km
Jamie Davies/Thomas Biagi
MC 12GT1
(FIA GT World Championship)

1 October Mugello
Campionato Italiano GT (gara 1 & 2)
Gianbattista Giannoccaro/
Toni Vilander
MC 12

15 October Adria
500 km
Jamie Davies/Thomas Biagi
MC 12GT1

19 November Vallelunga
6 Ore di Vallelunga
Pedro Lamy/Marco Cioci/
Piergiuseppe Perazzini
MC12

## 2007

6 May Silverstone, UK
Tourist Trophy
Thomas Biagi/Mika Salo
MC 12GT1
(FIA GT World Championship)

20 May Bucureşti, RO
2 Hours
Andrea Bertolini/Andrea Piccini
MC 12GT1
(FIA GT World Championship)

8 July Orschersleben, D
500 km
Thomas Biagi/Michael Barthels
MC 12GT1
(FIA GT World Championship)

23 September Brno, CS
2 Hours
Miguel Ramos/Christian Montanari
MC 12GT1
(FIA GT World Championship)

## 2008

2-3 August Spa Francorchamps, B
24 Heures de Spa
Andrea Bertolini/Michael Barthels/
Eric van der Poele/Stéphane Sarrazin
MC 12GT1
(FIA GT World Championship)

5 October Nogaro, F
Circuit Paul Armagnac
2 Heures
Alexander Negrão/Miguel Ramos
MC 12GT1
(FIA GT World Championship)

19 October Zolder, B
2 Heures
Andrea Bertolini/Michael Barthels
MC 12GT1
(FIA GT World Championship)

## 2009

16 May Adria
2 Ore
Andrea Bertolini/Michael Barthels
MC 12GT1
(FIA GT World Championship)

30 August Budapest, H
Hungaroring
2 Hours
Andrea Bertolini/Michael Barthels
MC 12GT1
(FIA GT World Championship)

19 October Zolder, B
2 Heures
Alessandro Pier Guidi/Matteo Bobbi
MC 12GT1
(FIA GT World Championship)

## 2010

4 July Le Castellet, F
Circuit Paul Ricard
FIA GT1
Andrea Bertolini/Michael Barthels
MC 12GT1
(FIA GT World Championship1)

4 July Le Castellet, F
Circuit Paul Ricard
GT4 European Cup (Race 1 & 2)
Alessandro Pier Guidi
Granturismo GT4

19 September Portimão, P
Circuito International do Algarve
FIA GT1
Andrea Bertolini/Michael Barthels
MC 12GT1
(FIA GT World Championship1)

28 November São Paulo, BR
Interlagos
FIA GT1
Enrique Bernoldi/Alexandre Negrão
MC 12GT1
(FIA GT World Championship1)

## 2012

7 October Vallelunga
International GT Sprint Series
(gara 1)
Alessandro Pier Guidi/
Gabriele Gardel
GT3

# Victories with Maserati chassis

## 1950

6 August Freiburg-am-Breisgau, D
Freiburg-Schauinsland
Paul Pietsch
Maserati Milan
Chassis 4CLT48 / Engine Milan

## 1951

26 March Goodwood, UK
Richmond Trophy
Prince "Bira"
So-called Osca
Chassis 4CLT48 /Engine Osca V12

## 1954

30 May Thompson, Ct. USA Thompson Raceway
SCCA New England Regional
Phil Cade
Chassis V8RI/Engine Chrysler

## 1955

19 July Bretton Woods, NH USA
Mt. Washington Hill Climb
Phil Cade
Chassis V8RI/Engine Chrysler

## 1957

20 April Mokul ia, Hi. USA
Dillingham Field
SCCA Hawaii International Novices
Lou Brero jr.
Chassis A6GCS/Engine Chevrolet

## 1960

10 April Vineland, NJ USA
Vineland Speedway SCCA Regional
Race 4
Ben Diaz
Chassis A6GCS/Engine Chevrolet

6 November Rio de Janeiro, BR
Barra da Tijuca
Mecânica Nacional
Ciro Cayres
Chassis 250F/Engine Chevrolet
Corvette

## 1961

15 January São Paulo, BR
Interlagos
Torneio Triangolar Sul-americano
Ciro Cayres
Chassis 250F/Engine Chevrolet
Corvette

4 September Mansfield, La. USA
SCCA Regional
Alan Connell
Chassis 61/Engine Ferrari TR

2 October Green Valley, Tx. USA
SCCA Regional
(Preliminary race)
Alan Connell
Chassis61/Engine Ferrari TR

2 October Green Valley, Tx. USA
SCCA Regional
(Main race)
Alan Connell
Chassis 61/Engine Ferrari TR

29 October Muskogee, Ok. USA
SCCA Oklahoma GP
Alan Connell
Chassis 61/Engine Ferrari TR

## 1962

28 January Daytona Beach, Fl. USA
SCCA National
Alan Connell
Chassis 61/Engine Ferrari TR

18 February Green Valley, Tx. USA
SCCA Regional
(Preliminary race)
Alan Connell
Chassis 61/Engine Ferrari TR

18 February Green Valley, Tx. USA
SCCA Regional
Polar Prix
Alan Connell
Chassis 61/Engine Ferrari TR

7 March Mansfield, La. USA
SCCA Regional
(Preliminary race)
Alan Connell
Chassis 61/Engine Ferrari TR

22 April Lawrenceville, Il. USA
SCCA Regional
Slim Helson
Chassis 200 S/Engine Chevrolet
Corvette

29 July Sebring, Fl. USA
SCCA Divisional
(Main race)
Bob Kingham
Chassis 200S/Engine Chevrolet

12 August Pensacola, Fl. USA
SCCA Divisional
Bob Kingham
Chassis 200S/Engine Chevrolet

7 September São Paulo, BR
Interlagos
500 km Interlagos
Roberto Gallucci
Chassis 250F/Engine Chevrolet
Corvette

# 1963

31 March Lawrenceville, Il. USA
SCCA Regional
(Main race)
Charles Hamill
Chassis 250S/Engine Chevrolet
Corvette

28 July Aspen, Co. USA
SCCA Regional
(Main race)
Yale Thomas
Chassis 200SI/Engine Chevrolet
Corvette

11 August Austin, Tx. USA
SCCAMayor's Trophy
Enus Wilson
Chassis 61/Engine Buick

18 August Rosemount, Mn. USA
SCCA Regional
(Main race)
Scott Beckett
Chassis 61/Engine Ford

25 August Lynndale Farms, Wi. USA
MSSCC
(Main race)
Scott Beckett
Chassis 61/Engine Ford

7 September São Paulo, BR
Interlagos
500 km Interlagos
Roberto Gallucci
Chassis 250F/Engine Chevrolet
Corvette

# 1964

26 April/ São Paulo, BR
Interlagos
Prêmio Constantino Cury
Camillo Christófaro
Chassis 250F/Engine Chevrolet
Corvette

5 July São Paulo, BR
Interlagos
GP Vitória da Democracia
Camillo Christófaro
Chassis 250F/Engine Chevrolet
Corvette

30 August Lynndale Farms, Wi. USA
MSSCC
(Main race)
Scott Beckett
Chassis 61/Engine Ford

27 September São Paulo, BR
Interlagos
250 Milhas de Interlagos
Roberto Gallucci
Chassis 250F/Engine Chevrolet
Corvette

11 October São Paulo, BR
Interlagos
Taça das Américas
Prêmio John Kennedy
Roberto Gallucci
Chassis 250F/Engine Chevrolet
Corvette

# 1965

10 October São Paulo, BR
Interlagos
Festival Interclubes
Camillo Christófaro
Chassis 250F/Engine Chevrolet
Corvette

# 1966

13 February São Paulo, BR
Interlagos
1a Etapa do Campeonato Paulista
Camillo Christófaro
Chassis 250F/Engine Chevrolet
Corvette

# Victories with Maserati engines

## 1932

16 June Torino
Sassi-Superga
Luigi Premoli
BMP
Engine 8C-2800/Chassis Bugatti 35

## 1934

10 June Torino
Corsa ai Colli Torinesi
Luigi Premoli
BMP
Engine 8C-2800/Chassis Bugatti 35

8 July
Varese-Campo dei Fiori
Luigi Premoli
BMP
Engine 8C-2800/Chassis Bugatti 35

15 July Ascoli Piceno
Coppa Ascoli
Luigi Premoli
BMP
Engine 8C-2800/Chassis Bugatti 35

30 September
Lecco-May
Luigi Premoli
BMP
Engine 8C-2800/Chassis Bugatti 35

## 1947

15 May
Corsa ai Colli Torinesi
Sassi-Superga
Giovanni Bracco
Tinarelli Spl
Engine A6/Chassis Fiat 1100

10 August
Aosta-Gran San Bernardo
Giovanni Bracco
Tinarelli Spl
Engine A6/Chassis Fiat 1100

## 1948

11 July Karlsruhe, D
Karlsruher Dreieck-Rennen
Egon Brütsch
EBS
Engine 6C-34/Chassis Westenrieder

15 August Schottenring, D
Rund um Schotten
Egon Brütsch
EBS
Engine 6C-34/Chassis Westenrieder

5 September Baden-Württemberg, D
Eggberg
Egon Brütsch
EBS
Engine 6C-34/Chassis Westenrieder

## 1949

26 June Tübingen, D
Stadtring-Rennen
Egon Brütsch
EBS
Engine 6C-34/Chassis Westenrieder

## 1953

13 June Kirkistown, UK
Ulster
Dick Lovell-Butt
Engine 4CLT48/ChassisBaird Griffin

## 1955

13 August Snetterton, UK
Sports 2750
Roy Salvadori
Cooper Maserati (Gilby)
Engine A6GCS/Chassis Cooper

## 1956

2 June Aintree, UK
BARC 1500
Brian Naylor
Lotus-Maserati
Engine 150S/Chassis Lotus 11

9 June Oulton Park, UK
National Oulton Park (2000 Sport)
Brian Naylor
Lotus-Maserati
Engine 150S/Chassis Lotus 11

16 June Crimond, UK
Aberdeen & District MC (Sport 1500)
Brian Naylor
Lotus-Maserati
Engine 150S/Chassis Lotus 11

16 June Crimond, UK
Aberdeen & District MC (Sport 2750)
Brian Naylor
Lotus-Maserati
Engine 150S/Chassis Lotus 11

30 June Silverstone, UK
Motor Sport Trophy Handicap
Brian Naylor
Lotus-Maserati
Engine 150S/Chassis Lotus 11

30 June Silverstone, UK
National Silverstone
Brian Naylor
Lotus-Maserati
Engine 150S/Chassis Lotus 11

1 July Charterhall, UK
National Charterhall (Sport 1500)
Brian Naylor
Lotus-Maserati
Engine 150S/Chassis Lotus 11

21 July Wicklow, IRL
Leinster Trophy
Brian Naylor
Lotus-Maserati
Engine 150S/Chassis Lotus 11

6 August Mallory Park, UK
NSCC Formule Libre
Brian Naylor
Lotus-Maserati
Engine 150S/Chassis Lotus 11

6 August Brands Hatch, UK
BRSCC Sport
Archie Scott-Brown
Lister-Maserati
Engine A6GCS/Chassis Lister

11 August Crimond , UK
Aberdeen & District MC (Sport 2750)
Brian Naylor
Lotus-Maserati
Engine 150S/Chassis Lotus 11

1 September Silverstone, UK
National Silverstone (Sport 1500)
Brian Naylor
Lotus-Maserati
Engine 150S/Chassis Lotus 11

15 September Silverstone, UK
National Silverstone (Sport 1500)
Brian Naylor
Lotus-Maserati
Engine 150S/Chassis Lotus 11

15 September Silverstone, UK
National Silverstone (Sport 2000)
Brian Naylor
Lotus-Maserati
Engine 150S/Chassis Lotus 11

6 October Silverstone, UK
National Silverstone (Sport 1500)
Brian Naylor
Lotus-Maserati
Engine 150S/Chassis Lotus 11

6 October Silverstone, UK
National Silverstone (Sport 2750)
Brian Naylor
Lotus-Maserati
Engine 150S/Chassis Lotus 11

6 October Silverstone, UK
North Staffs MC. Formule Libre
Brian Naylor
Lotus-Maserati
Engine 150S/Chassis Lotus 11

7 October Snetterton, UK
National Snetterton Handicap
(Sport 2750 esclusi Climax)
Brian Naylor
Lotus-Maserati
Engine 150S/Chassis Lotus 11

7 October Snetterton, UK
National Snetterton (1500 Sports)
Brian Naylor
Lotus-Maserati
Engine 150S/Chassis Lotus 11

## 1957

18 May Silverstone, UK
Maidstone & Mid Kent MC
(Sport 2500, race 1)
Brian Naylor
Lotus-Maserati
Engine 150S/Chassis Lotus 11

18 May Silverstone, UK
Maidstone & Mid Kent MC
(Sports Unlimited)
Brian Naylor
Lotus-Maserati
Engine 150S/Chassis Lotus 11

18 May Silverstone, UK
Maidstone & Mid Kent MC
(Sports)
Brian Naylor
Lotus-Maserati
150S/Chassis Lotus 11

18 May Silverstone, UK
Maidstone & Mid Kent MC
(Sport 2500, race 2)
Brian Naylor
Lotus-Maserati
Engine 150S/Chassis Lotus 11

28 July Snetterton, UK
National Snetterton (Sport 2000)
Brian Naylor
Lotus-Maserati
Engine 150S/Chassis Lotus 11

## 1958

5 May Chimay, B
Grand Prix des Frontières
Brian Naylor
JBW-Maserati
Engine 250S/Chassis JBW

15 June Montlhéry, F
Prix de Paris (Sport 2000)
Brian Naylor
JBW-Maserati
Engine 250S/Chassis JBW

5 October Innsbrück, A
Alpenflughafen
Preis von Tirol
Brian Naylor
JBW-Maserati
Engine 250S/Chassis JBW

## 1959

18 April Aintree, UK
BARC 200
Roy Salvadori
Cooper-Maserati
Engine 250S/ChassisCooper
Monaco T49

2 May Silverstone, UK
International Trophy (Sport)
Roy Salvadori
Cooper-Maserati
Engine 250S/Chassis Cooper
Monaco T49

10 May Napoli
Posillipo
GP di Napoli
Tony Settember
WRE-Naserati
Engine 200S/Chassis WRE

10 May Snetterton, UK
Formule Libre
Brian Naylor
JBW-Maserati
Engine 250S/Chassis JBW

18 May London, UK
Crystal Palace
Norbury Trophy
Roy Salvadori
Cooper-Maserati
Engine 250S/Chassis Cooper
Monaco T49

25 May Mallory Park, UK
Formule Libre
Brian Naylor
JBW-Maserati
Engine 250S/Chassis JBW

26 July Snetterton, UK
Formule Libre
Brian Naylor
JBW-Maserati
Engine 250S/Chassis JBW

2 August Snetterton, UK
Vanwall Trophy
Brian Naylor
JBW-Maserati
Engine 250S/Chassis JBW

8 August Mallory Park, UK
Formule Libre
Brian Naylor
JBW-Maserati
Engine 250S/Chassis JBW

9 August Snetterton, UK
Formule Libre
Brian Naylor
JBW-Maserati
Engine 250S/Chassis JBW

23 August Messina
Laghi Ganzirri
GP Messina
Colin Davis
Cooper-Maserati
Engine 200S/Chassis Cooper
Monaco T49

6 September Snetterton, UK
Scott-Brown Trophy
Brian Naylor
JBW-Maserati
Engine 250S/Chassis JBW

6 September Snetterton, UK
Snetterton Formule Libre
Brian Naylor
JBW-Maserati
Engine 250S/Chassis JBW

20 September Nova Lisbôa, ANG
GP Angola
Curt Lincoln
Cooper-Maserati
Engine 250S/Chassis Cooper
Monaco T49

27 September
Catania-Etna
Nino Vaccarella
Cooper-Maserati
Engine 200S/Chassis Cooper Mona-
co T49

# 1960

27 March Napoli
Agnano-Cappella dei Cangiani
Luigi Bellucci
WRE-Maserati
Engine 200S/Chassis WRE

27 March Snetterton, UK
Formule Libre (race 1)
Keith Greene
Cooper-Maserati (Gilby)
Engine 250S/Chassis Cooper T45

27 March Snetterton, UK
Formule Libre (race 2)
Brian Naylor
JBW-Maserati
Engine 250S/Chassis JBW

18 April Mallory Park, UK
Brian Naylor
Cooper-Maserati
Engine 200S/Chassis Cooper
Monaco T61

18 April Bathurst, AUS
Mount Panorama
Bathurst 100
Alec Mildren
Cooper-Maserati
Engine 250S/Chassis Cooper T51

15 May
GP Napoli
Mennato Boffa
WRE-Maserati
Engine 200S/Chassis WRE

6 June Oulton Park, UK
Brian Naylor
Cooper-Maserati
Engine 250S/Chassis Cooper
Monaco T61

12 June Brisbane, AUS
Lowood
Australian GP
Alec Mildren
Cooper-Maserati
Engine 250S/Chassis Cooper T51

19 June Snetterton, UK
Egerton Trophy
Brian Naylor
JBW-Maserati
Engine 250S/Chassis JBW

21 August Snetterton, UK
National Benzole Trophy
Brian Naylor
JBW-Maserati
Engine 250S/ChassisJ BW

28 August Torino
Colli Torinesi
Sassi-Superga
Gianni Balzarini
WRE-Maserati
Engine 200S/Chassis WRE

31 August Mallory Park, UK
Brian Naylor
JBW-Maserati
Engine 250S/Chassis JBW

4 September Brisbane, Lowood, AUS
Queensland Trophy
Alec Mildren
Cooper-Maserati
Engine 250S/Chassis Cooper T51

18 September Mallory Park, UK
Brian Naylor
JBW-Maserati
Engine 250S Chassis JBW

5 November Caversham, AUS
Western Australia Trophy
Alec Mildren
Cooper-Maserati
Engine 250S/Chassis Cooper T51

# 1961

4 March Johannesburg, ZA
Killlarney
Van Riebeeck Trophy
John Love
Cooper-Maserati
Engine 150S/Chassis Cooper

3 April Mallory Park, UK
Formule Libre
Brian Naylor
JBW-Maserati
Engine 250S/Chassis JBW

23 April Stuttgart, Ar. USA
SCCA Arkansas Regional
(Preliminary race)
Hap Sharp
Cooper-Maserati
Engine 250S/Chassis Cooper T49

23 April Stuttgart, Ar. USA
SCCA Arkansas Region. (Modif.
8000)
Hap Sharp
Cooper-Maserati
Engine 250S/Chassis Cooper T49

7 May Mansfield, Tx. USA
Red River SCCA Regional (Main
race)
Hap Sharp
Cooper-Maserati
Engine 250S/Chassis Cooper T49

3 June Gex, F
La Faucille
Maurice Trintignant
Cooper-Maserati
Engine 150S/Chassis Cooper T45

18 June Piacenza
Bobbio-Passo del Penice
Gianni Brichetti
WRE-Maserati
Engine 200S

2 July
Bolzano-Mendola
Gianni Balzarini
Cooper-Maserati
Engine 200 S

28 August, CH
Klosters-Davos
Gianni Balzarini
Cooper-Maserati
Engine 200S/Chassis Cooper
(European Mountain Championship)

3 December Tucson, Az. USA
SCCA Divisional
(Main race)
Hap Sharp
Cooper-Maserati
Engine 250S/Chassis Cooper T49

# 1962

4 March Mansfield, Tx. USA
SCCA Regional (Main race)
Hap Sharp
Cooper-Maserati
Engine 250S/Chassis Cooper T49

11 March Napoli
Agnano-Cappella dei Cangiani
Vincenzo Sorrentino
WRE-Maserati
Engine 200S/Chassis WRE

1 April Tucson, Az. USA
SCCA Pacific Coast Championship
(5000 Modified)
Hap Sharp
Cooper-Maserati
Engine 250S/Chassis Cooper T49

29 April Alliance, Co. USA
SCCA Divisional
(Main race)
Hap Sharp
Cooper-Maserati
Engine 250S/Chassis Cooper T49

# 1963

7 June Monza
Coppa BP AC Svizzeri
Harry Zweifel
Cooper Maserati
Engine 200S/Chassis Cooper T43

16 June Sierre, CH
Sierre-Montana Crans
George Gachnang
Cegga Maserati
Engine 150S/2000/Chassis Cegga

23 June Vallelunga
Premio Campagnano
Carroll Smith
Cooper-Maserati
Engine 200S/Chassis Cooper Mona-
co T61

# 1964

18 May Goodwood, UK
Whitsun Trophy (Sport & GT)
Roy Salvadori
Cooper-Maserati
Engine 151/Chassis Cooper Monaco
T61

31 May Ardennes, B
Côte d'Herbeumont
Nicolas Koob
ENB-Maserati
Engine 150S/ChassisENB

# 1966

24 April Knutstorp, S
Hastigetstävhy 2000
Picko Troberg
Focus-Maserati
Engine 200S/Chassis Sportscars

21 August Canton Jura, CH
St.Ursanne–Les Rangiers
Jo Siffert
Cooper-Maserati
Engine 300 V12/Chassis Cooper T81

19 September Lyon, F
Jo Siffert
Cooper Maserati
Engine 300 V12/Chassis Cooper T81

23 October Ciudad de México, MEX
Magdalena Mixhuca
Grand Prix de México
John Surtees
Cooper-Maserati
Engine 300 V12/Chassis Cooper T81
(World Drivers' Championship)

# 1967

2 January Kyalami, ZA
South African GP
Pedro Rodríguez
Cooper-Maserati
Engine 300 V12/Chassis Cooper T81
(World Drivers' Championship)

20 May Monza
Coupe Automobile Revue
Jo Bonnier
Cooper-Maserati
Engine 300 V12/Chassis Cooper T81

# 1971

28 April 1 May, MA
Rabat-Marrakech-Casablanca
Rallye du Maroc
Jean Deschazeaux/Jean Plassard
Citroen SM
Engine V6 Citröen-Maserati/
Chassis Citröen

# 1974

1 April Le Mans, F
4 Heures
Guy Chasseuil
Ligier-Maserati JS2
Engine V6 Citröen-Maserati/
Chassis Ligier

13 19 September, F
Tour de France Automobile
Gérard Larrousse/Johnny Rives/Jean-
Pierre Nicolas
Ligier-Maserati JS2
Engine V6 Citröen-Maserati/
Chassis Ligier

Printed by

D'AURIA PRINTING SPA - ASCOLI PICENO

October 2015